▼▼▼▼▼

Dinosaurs
of Utah

▲▲▲▲▲

Dinosaurs of Utah

Frank DeCourten

COLOR ILLUSTRATIONS BY

Carel Brest van Kempen

PHOTOGRAPHS BY

John Telford

Frank DeCourten

▲▲▲▲▲▲▲▲▲▲▲▲▲▲▲▲▲▲▲

The University of Utah Press
Salt Lake City

© 1998 by the University of Utah Press

Color illustrations © 1998 by Carel Brest van Kempen
Line art by Frank DeCourten, unless otherwise noted

Printed on acid-free paper

Permissions on page 272

Book design by Joanne Poon
Printed in Singapore by Tien Wah Press

LIBRARY OF CONGRESS CATALOGING-IN-PUBLICATION DATA

DeCourten, Frank.
   Dinosaurs of Utah / Frank DeCourten ; color illus-
trations by Carel Brest van Kempen ; photographs by
John Telford , Frank DeCourten.
       p. cm.
   Includes bibliographical references and index.
   ISBN 0-87480-556-2 (alk. paper)
   1. Dinosaurs—Utah.   I. Title
QE862.D5D42   1998
567.9'09792—dc21   98-2747

CONTENTS

LIST OF ILLUSTRATIONS

ACKNOWLEDGMENTS

THE SEED FOR THIS book first germinated in the late 1980s while I was teaching a course on dinosaurs at the University of Utah. At that time, it occurred to me that a great deal of what is currently known about dinosaurs has come from the analysis of Utah fossil specimens. And yet, within the vast sea of dinosaur literature, there was no compilation of information on the dinosaurs and Mesozoic environments of Utah. At the same time, I became increasingly disenchanted with dinosaur publications that focused almost exclusively on the animals themselves, with little mention of the habitats and environmental history of the areas they occupied. Thus, in early 1990, I conceived of the present book, which examines Utah dinosaurs in the context of the Mesozoic geologic history of the state. What I envisioned was a comprehensive book that explored the amazing Mesozoic vertebrate fauna of Utah with a strong focus on dinosaurs, written in an informative but casual style. I also wanted the book to be up-to-date, factually accurate, and well illustrated with original photographs, drawings, and paintings. It was only with the involvement of numerous dedicated team members that any of those goals was achieved.

Conceiving a book of this magnitude and writing it are, of course, two different things. While the ideas that are explored in *Dinosaurs of Utah* were still swirling around in my head, new dinosaur discoveries almost continuously were being made in Utah, including a few modest ones of my own. Compiling all the new information, and combining it with more than 100 years' worth of earlier work, was a time-consuming task. Though it was a labor of love, the work still required several years of part-time effort, sandwiched in between collegiate teaching and administrative duties. As the manuscript began to unfold, numerous individuals and institutions expressed an interest in the project. Most of them vanished when the time came to commit real resources to the project. It was not until Jeff Grathwohl of the University of Utah Press stepped forward with a solid commitment and unshakable faith in the book that things began to move forward. With solid project support from the University of Utah Press, the library and museum research for the book was intensified. I am grateful to the staff of the following institutions for their generosity and help during this phase of the work: the University of Utah, Utah Museum of Natural History, University of California Museum of Paleontology, and the research libraries at the University of California, Berkeley and Davis, and the University of Wyoming. I also benefited greatly from correspondence and conversations with many colleagues who were eager to share their insights, including Dan Chure, Sue Ann Bilbey, Frank Brown, David Gillette, Jim Madsen, Jim Kirkland, and Jeff Eaton, among many others. Special mention should be made of the late William L. Stokes of the University of Utah. While Lee did not live to see the book published, he was more influential than he probably ever suspected by virtue of his great enthusiasm for this project.

It was also my privilege to work closely with two very gifted collaborators on *Dinosaurs of Utah*. The original watercolor plates in this book were prepared by Carel Brest van Kempen. It was a sheer delight to work with Carel on these illustrations, learning from his extraordinary insights on the natural world, and marveling at the product of his limitless talent. Many of the photographs were taken by my old friend John Telford, who, as always, created masterpieces with both his camera and dutch oven. This book would have been a much more dreary affair without the contributions of these two people, and I have been personally enriched by working with both of them.

Aside from the professional collaborators, there were many other individuals who contributed to the success of this book by virtue of their friendship, hospitality, and encouragement. My new colleagues at Sierra College, particularly Dick Hilton and Charles Dailey, were always patient with my preoccupation with dinosaurs and paleontology, and listened politely to my dinosaur discourses in the field, in the classroom, and in the taverns. Whenever I returned to Utah to work on the project, I benefited from the generosity of several friends who shared their homes and put up with my frequent intrusions. Tom and Gael Hill never turned me away, worked me hard, and fed me well. Steve D'Eustachio was likewise more gracious than I could expect him to be, so long as I bought the beer. Don Hague, director emeritus of the Utah Museum of Natural History, and his wife, Lorna, hosted me on several occasions and always seemed eager to hear of my latest adventures. Every time I visited the Utah Museum of Natural History, and there were many visits, it seems that I met a smiling face somewhere in the back rooms that banished a few of the old ghosts, at least for a time. Finally, my wife, Cindy, and our daughters, Amy and Bethany, remain remarkably committed to, and patient with, a husband and father who is part cowboy, part writer, part renegade, and a full-time dreamer. My family has survived that onerous combination for decades with love and veneration. I'll never understand why or how.

Frank DeCourten

Photo 1. The Mummy Cliffs near Capitol Reef National Park. John Telford.

Photo 2. Mancos Shale badlands. A mesa near Hanksville exhibits the variety of Mesozoic rock types. Soft gray shale forms the lower slopes and the hard cap is comprised of sandstone. John Telford.

A NYONE FAMILIAR WITH the rugged landforms of Utah sooner or later begins to take cliffs for granted. Vertical walls of rock are abundant in this elevated land of mountains, buttes, mesas, and plateaus. From the edges of the high tablelands, steep slopes commonly cascade down to meet the adjacent lowlands with magnificent abruptness. Like the walls of the rooms in our home, we never lose our awareness of the cliffs around us, but their distinctive aspects and even their spectacular beauty eventually become so familiar that we accept them as just another adornment in an exquisite landscape.

It is easy to understand, then, why so many people traveling east through central Utah tend to overlook a relatively modest red bluff standing north of Utah Highway 24, east of Torrey. These great stone sentinels standing guard over the entrance to Capitol Reef National Park are called the Mummy Cliffs. It's a good name, too, because the castellated red bluffs project countless fluted columns that look, for all the world, like the linen-wrapped remains of ancient Egyptian royalty. The rusty pillars emerge from the cliff with ragged outlines and surfaces streaked by black desert varnish, separated from each other by shadowy clefts. Standing vertically along the highway, they watch the stream of vehicles pass with eerie human-like countenances. Their narrow bases broaden upward into fluted bodies, often capped by a stony "head." Even the most casual of observers will sense that these Utah mummies are relics of the past, objects representing former times and former worlds. Few, however, readily comprehend the immensity of the history these rocks record. That history is unfathomably deep, encompassing hundreds of millions of years, and reducing the actual "ancient" Egyptian mummies to mere youngsters.

The Mummy Cliffs continue east toward Capitol Reef, where they become folded down into the subsurface as younger rock layers are draped over the Waterpocket Fold. Eventually the bold cliffs of sandstone open to the east to reveal a colorful panorama of badlands, ledges, buttes, and plateaus beyond the mouth of the Fremont River. The scenery is astonishing in this area. On any summer morning, the shoulders of Highway 24 are crowded with the cars of tourists photographing the amazing vistas. As visually impressive as it is to most people, this landscape produces a special thrill for the paleontologist. The red ledges, pastel badlands, gray hummocks, and sandstone buttes are the trademark of the Mesozoic Era, the great age of dinosaurs. Just the sight of such landforms brings a flutter to the heart of anyone interested in ancient reptiles. The Mummy Cliffs are the gateway to the Mesozoic wonderland of eastern Utah.

Eastern Utah, from the Four Corners region north to the Uinta Basin, is a natural museum of the Mesozoic Era that has attracted paleontologists to the area for well over 100 years. The rock layers exposed across this bold landscape are mostly of Mesozoic age, from 245 to about 65 million years old. In places, most notably in the deeper canyons of the Colorado River system, older rocks are exposed beneath the overlying red-hued Mesozoic strata. Likewise, on the highest surfaces of eastern Utah's plateaus and mesas, younger rocks overlie the dinosaur-bearing layers. However, over thousands of square miles between the canyon floors and the highest rimrocks, on the broad expanses that seem to sweep from horizon to horizon, the rocky Mesozoic record lays exposed, waiting to be explored. And what a curious world awaits those who investigate the rocks behind the scenery!

Mesozoic Mayhem: Life and Land in Turmoil

The Mesozoic is one of three great eras of geologic time, spanning more than 180 million years between the Paleozoic (570–248 million years ago) and the Cenozoic (65 million years ago to the present) eras. As their names suggest, each era is named for the character of lifeforms, recorded as fossils in the rocks, that dominated the succes-

ONE

The Mesozoic World

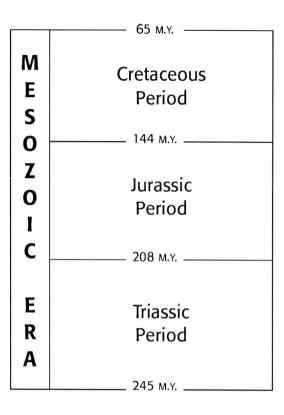

Figure 1-1. The Mesozoic time scale. Because of the uncertainties in the methods of absolute dating, the dates between the various subdivisions can only be approximated to within about 10 percent of the actual age.

MESOZOIC ERA	
	65 M.Y.
	Cretaceous Period
	144 M.Y.
	Jurassic Period
	208 M.Y.
	Triassic Period
	245 M.Y.

Figure 1-2. Some common Paleozoic fossils of Utah. A: *Lithostrotion*, a Mississippian coral; B: *Bathyurellus*, an Ordovician trilobite from the Confusion Mountains; C: *Anthracospirifer*, a Pennsylvanian brachiopod; D: *Faberophyllum*, a solitary coral from the Mississippian Period; E: *Syringopora*, a Silurian coral.

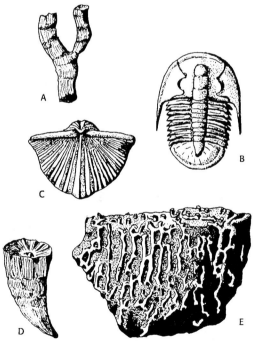

sive phases of our planet's immense history. It was the British geologist John Phillips who in 1840 first suggested the term "Mesozoic" for the era of "middle life." As envisioned by Phillips, the Mesozoic Era encompassed, from oldest to youngest, the Triassic Period, the Jurassic Period, and the Cretaceous Period (Figure 1-1). These periods had been named and classified in other places at other times, but they were all defined on the basis of characteristic and recurring assemblages of fossils. The fossils from the three Mesozoic periods were much different from those of the preceding Paleozoic or the following Cenozoic Era and seemed to constitute a unique stage in the evolution of life. But how was the life of the Mesozoic unique? Let us approach that question first with a brief review of the life of the preceding (Paleozoic) and following (Cenozoic) eras.

The Paleozoic Era is the time period denoting "ancient life." Rocks of this age produce the remains of many primitive organisms such as trilobites, graptolites, crinoids, brachiopods, corals, and armored fish, to name just a few (Figure 1-2). Though some of these groups persist today, the Paleozoic organisms all appear very strange and primitive in comparison with their living descendants. Many of the Paleozoic organisms are now extinct and/or are so bizarre that questions still linger concerning their proper classification and their relationships with modern groups. The Cenozoic ("new life") Era, which follows the Mesozoic, is known as the great Age of Mammals, for it was during the last 65 million years that this class of organisms came to dominate the world's terrestrial ecosystems. In some ways, the "Age of Mammals" designation is unfortunate, because the Cenozoic was also a time of rapid evolution among plants, insects, fish, reptiles, and microscopic organisms of all sorts. Mammals were certainly not the only group to experience explosive evolution during the Cenozoic Era; but since humans belong to this group, I suppose that we have the prerogative (or the arrogance) to call it "our time." Nonetheless, the Cenozoic is definitely the age of "modern life"; few Cenozoic fossils present the same problems of classification and relationship that we see so commonly among the more bizarre Paleozoic forms. The relatively young Cenozoic fossils are, for the most part, similar to living creatures, and can usually be classified with ease (Figure 1-3).

Between the peculiar Paleozoic forms and the much more familiar Cenozoic organisms, then, are the Mesozoic fossils, remains of creatures from the era of "middle life." Many Mesozoic fossils are transitional between the "primitive" and "modern" types, as we might expect; but this is not the case of them all. Among the Mesozoic fauna are scores of animals that are unique, bearing little resemblance to anything that preceded or followed them. This is because the Mesozoic Era was a time of evolutionary experimentation, which followed two notable events in the history of the earth's biosphere: a massive extinction period and the fragmentation of a supercontinent. Both of these events exerted a profound effect on the patterns of evolution and extinction that are recorded by the fossils of Mesozoic age. In the long history of life on our planet, the combination of such circumstances was unique to this era. The animals of the Mesozoic were more than simply "transitional"; collectively, they represent a unique stage in the history of life.

Life of the Mesozoic

At the end of the Paleozoic Era, a great wave of extinction swept the world. The primary victims of this late Paleozoic event were marine invertebrates, such as the trilobites and other primitive organisms mentioned above. It has been estimated that from 70 to 90 percent of the species living in the shallow seas near the end of the Paleozoic Era vanished during the extinction event. On land, the effects of the extinction were less pronounced and the fossil record is not as rich; but it certainly appears that one of the groups hardest hit during the crisis was the amphibians.

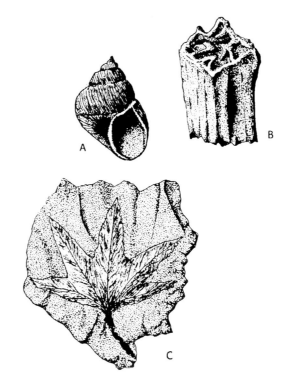

Figure 1-3. Some common Utah Cenozoic fossils. A: *Viviparus*, a Paleocene gastropod (snail); B: a horse tooth from the Pliocene Epoch; C: *Aralia*, an angiosperm leaf from the Eocene.

Amphibians had developed from lobe-finned fish some 100 million years before the extinction, during the Carboniferous Period. They had become remarkably abundant on land as the Paleozoic Era came to a close. There were many giant amphibians during this time, some up to twenty feet long, and among them were fierce alligator-like predators and large browsing plant eaters. Today's small and relatively rare amphibians—the frogs, toads, and salamanders—represent only a small impoverished remnant of the gaudy late Paleozoic assemblage.

As the end of the Paleozoic Era approached, the great amphibians began to die out. Eventually, most of the larger amphibians disappeared altogether, leaving many ecological niches vacant in the swamps and forests of the late Paleozoic Era. The amphibian extinction, in turn, created great evolutionary opportunities for any organisms that could survive the crisis and develop successful adaptations to the rapidly changing environment.

One such group, survivors that weathered the extinction storm to inherit the major ecological niches during the Mesozoic, was, of course, the reptiles. Having developed an externally laid (amniote) egg tens of millions of years prior to the great extinction event, the reptiles could not have been in a better position to replace the amphibians as the dominant vertebrates of the global ecosystem. With a new reproductive system that allowed broad dispersal into dry habitats, the reptiles achieved extremely rapid global distribution during the time that the amphibians were being so drastically affected by extinction. Two biological events, the evolution of the amniote egg and the subsequent extinction of many amphibians, led to one of the most dramatic pulses of evolution ever: the explosive growth and dominance of the reptiles. Though the pattern and timing of the amphibian-to-reptile transition were far from simple, the overall effect was to transform the terrestrial fauna to a reptile-dominated assemblage by the early Mesozoic. We will return to the reptilian takeover in a later chapter; first, let's complete our overview of the Mesozoic world.

No one knows with absolute certainty what caused the great late Paleozoic extinction, which is called the Permo-Triassic Extinction for the two periods of geologic time between which it occurs, the Permian and the Triassic. Many scenarios have been proposed as a cause for this event; they range from shifting continents, to abrupt climate changes, to asteroid impacts. One thing is certain: when the Mesozoic Era began, nearly everywhere in the world the survivors of the extinction were freed from much of the competition their ancestors had faced for millions of years. In response, the land-dwelling reptiles started a collective riot of evolution that was to last for more than 150 million years, until the next biotic calamity. In the process, some of the most peculiar creatures ever to inhabit our planet developed as new body designs were formed, tested, abandoned, and modified through the processes of natural selection.

Mesozoic life was rich and diverse, but it also was a little strange due to the unique pace of evolution and the presence of many "evolutionary experiments." This is why scientists regard the Mesozoic as much more than a simple transition from "primitive" life to "modern" life; it was a time of previously unparalleled evolutionary innovation among the reptiles and, as we shall see, among other groups as well.

On land, in the sea, and in the air, the major ecological niches filled by large animals were dominated by reptiles. Accordingly, the Mesozoic is often referred to as the Age of Reptiles. Dinosaurs represent just the tip of the iceberg of Mesozoic reptilian dominance—the flying and gliding pterosaurs, the marine ichthyosaurs and plesiosaurs, the aquatic and semiaquatic turtles and crocodiles, and the many kinds of snakes and lizards complete the reptilian, or saurian, menagerie that overshadowed other vertebrate groups everywhere in the world. Along with the reptilian congregation were some very peculiar nonreptiles and, muted beneath the ongoing reptilian riot, some very significant evolutionary events also took place in other groups.

For most of the Mesozoic Era, the forests of the world were dominated by relatively primitive plants such as gigantic ferns and the cone-bearing gymnosperms (conifers, cycads, and ginkgoes, among others). The more advanced flowering plants (or angiosperms) arose near the end of the Mesozoic and have now replaced the less specialized gymnosperms as the major component of the modern global flora. In the oceans, the entire marine ecosystem was overturned and reshaped following the Permo-Triassic extinctions. Microscopic plankton such as diatoms, coccolithophores, and other tiny organisms exploded onto the scene during the Mesozoic, replacing the more primitive and less varied Paleozoic forms. The coiled ammonites (Figure 1-4), relatives of the modern pearly nautilus, swarmed in incredible abundance and achieved very large proportions (some species grew as large as wagon wheels). Meanwhile, other types of molluscs, such as clams (bivalves) and snails (gastropods), burrowed through the muddy sediments on the sea floor, where they competed with starfish, sea urchins, and hordes of crustaceans. Some of the gastropods evolved carnivorous traits, feeding on other bottom-living invertebrates and becoming the true "killer snails" of the day. Many of the prey organisms living on the sea floor developed anti-predation adaptations such as thickened shells, swimming abilities, or concealment strategies (burrowing or protective coloration). Overall, the invertebrate fauna populating the Mesozoic sea floor was a well-adapted, mobile, and highly specialized aggregate that replaced the more sessile and generalized Paleozoic assemblage.

Fish prospered during most of the Mesozoic Era, including the peculiar lobe-finned coelacanths thought to be extinct until the accidental discovery of a living species in 1952 in the deep waters offshore from Madagascar. In the Mesozoic oceans, other bony fish specialized in the predation of bottom-living invertebrates. Many of these sturgeon-like fish had shell-crushing teeth and must have been voracious bottom feeders. Later in the Mesozoic, swim bladders developed in fish for the first time, giving rise to swift and agile swimmers well adapted to pursue active prey. There were probably more kinds of sharks, Paleozoic "holdovers," around in the Mesozoic than there are today. Finally, in freshwater environments, lungfish and heavily scaled relatives of the modern gar were particularly abundant in lakes and rivers.

Mammals were few in number and types throughout most of the Mesozoic, but they were present in the undergrowth and in the limbs of the trees, as the dinosaurs and their reptilian kin relegated them to the world's ecological backwaters for more than 140 million years. Sometime during the Mesozoic Era, the small, rat-like mammals nonetheless managed to develop the repro-

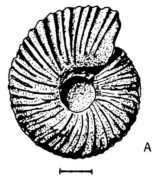
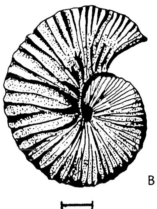
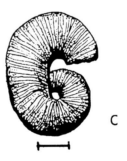

Figure 1-4. Mesozoic ammonites from Utah. A: *Cadoceras*, middle Jurassic; B: *Clioscaphites vermiformis*, late Cretaceous; C: *Scaphites warreni*, late Cretaceous. Bar=1 cm (.04 inches) in all sketches. From Stokes, 1986.

ductive and physiological advantages that serve as the foundation for their dominance in the modern world. Once the dinosaurs as we know them disappeared, the mammals were well equipped to step out from shadows of the Mesozoic world. Birds probably arose from dinosaur ancestors in the early Mesozoic and fluttered, originally with toothed beaks and clawed wings, alongside the

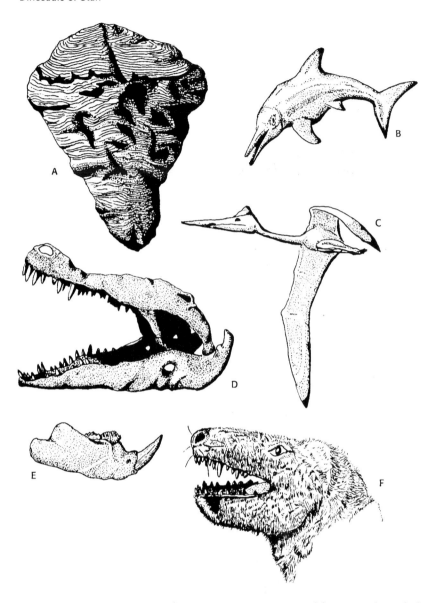

Figure 1-5. Strange creatures of the Mesozoic, excluding dinosaurs. Many of these animals are uniquely bizarre and, though their overall appearance is less primitive than most Paleozoic forms, they are still quite different from anything that exists today. A: A rudist bivalve (clam) that mimics the form of the solitary corals of the Paleozoic Era. The organism inhabiting this shell was, however, much different from any of the corals. B: *Stenopterygius*, a lower Jurassic ichthyosaur; C: *Quetzalcoatlus*, a gigantic pterosaur with a wingspan of up to 50 feet; D: head of *Phobosuchus*, a "fearsome crocodile," exceeding 50 feet in length; E: the lower jaw of *Stygimus*, a small rodent-like Cretaceous mammal; F, *Cynognathus*, a mammal-like reptile from the Triassic Period.

pterosaurs through the skies above the Mesozoic jungles. Add a few enormous marine crocodiles, the manatee-like placodonts, the sea-going plesiosaurs and ichthyosaurs and it can be seen that it was a strange bestiary indeed that ruled the Mesozoic world (Figure 1-5).

Mesozoic Land and Geography

The strangeness of Mesozoic life, particularly in comparison to our own late Cenozoic world, was mirrored in the inanimate Earth as well. If we could revisit a Mesozoic landscape, the conditions around us would seem every bit as exotic as the plants and animals we would observe. The physical processes that operate on and within our dynamic planet to moderate and control the surface conditions seem to have become a bit unusual during the Age of Reptiles. For example, the geography and climate of the time were much different from what we know today. At the beginning of the Mesozoic Era there existed a single, enormous supercontinent known as Pangaea. Assembled from smaller fragments that collided during the Paleozoic Era, Pangaea stretched nearly from pole to pole as an unbroken block of land surrounded by a global ocean. The east-central margin of Pangaea was incised around a large embayment known as the Tethys Sea, creating a narrow "neck" in the supercontinent about where it straddled the equator (Figure 1-6).

The climate at this time was a complex collage of hot and dry conditions in the narrow equatorial regions, temperate conditions farther north and south, and searing interior deserts. Drier environments such as semiarid steppes and true deserts seem to have been more widespread in the early Mesozoic than they are today. In addition, there is no evidence that the planet Earth possessed any appreciable ice caps during this time or during any later portion of the Mesozoic Era. Scientists have inferred from this and other evidence that the overall climate was at least 10°C warmer then than it is today. With all the land on the planet united and connected, there were few barriers to the dispersal and migration of terrestrial organisms during the early Mesozoic, particularly if they were adapted for life in an arid or semiarid setting. This will be an important consideration later in this book where the distribution pattern of dinosaurs and other Mesozoic reptiles is examined.

About 35 million years after the beginning of the Mesozoic Era, Pangaea started to break apart. The rifting was initiated in the Tethys region and penetrated to the west until the great supercontinent had been severed into two large fragments north and south of the equator. The northern portion is known as Laurasia (consisting of the ancient cores of North America, Eurasia, and Greenland); south of the equator was Gondwana (composed of South America, Africa, Antarctica, Australia, and India prior to their individual separation). The two fragments, each much larger than any modern continent, moved slowly apart (Figure 1-6) at a rate of a few centimeters (an inch or so) per year. Eventually, near the end of the Mesozoic, the two fragments of Pangaea themselves broke apart into the smaller continents we are accustomed to in our world. Some of the small fragments later collided with each other, reversing the trend of continental fragmentation that started at the dawn of the Mesozoic. For example, North America bumped into the corner of Asia near the end the Mesozoic Era, while India began its ongoing collision with the southern border of Asia just after Mesozoic time ended.

Thus, the geography of the Mesozoic world was continually changing, following a pattern of generally increasing continental isolation punctuated by occasional rejoining. This unique aspect of the Mesozoic world had a powerful effect on the patterns of dispersal, evolution, and extinction for all life, including the dinosaurs. If Mesozoic life strikes us as strange and peculiar, it is, at least in part, because the patterns of adaptation and natural selection were constantly shifting with each new geographic setting. Mesozoic plants and ani-

Early Triassic: 245 Ma

Early Jurassic: 195 Ma

Late Jurassic: 145 Ma

Middle Cretaceous: 95 Ma

Late Cretaceous: 70 Ma

Figure 1-6. Mesozoic Era continental configurations. Adapted from Sereno, 1991.

mals underwent continuous evolutionary change to keep up with the rapid and profound environmental changes that were taking place.

There is even more strangeness to consider. During the last 50 or 60 million years of the Mesozoic Era, something happened *inside* the earth as well. There is good evidence that the normal circulation of the molten iron deep within the Earth, in the zone known as the outer core, became stagnant or otherwise disrupted late in the Mesozoic Era. Evidence comes from studies of paleomagnetism: the investigation of the magnetic properties of ancient rocks. By examining the paleomagnetic character of rocks of varying ages, geologists have been able to identify literally hundreds of times since the end of the Paleozoic Era when the polarity of the earth's magnetic field reversed itself. The reasons for the periodic reversals of magnetic polarity remain obscure, but since the magnetic field is thought to be produced by the circulation of iron in the outer core coupled with the earth's rotation, geophysicists speculate that the pattern, rate, or direction of interior circulation may shift from time to time, causing the polarity to "flip." We do know that the reversals are a normal part of the earth's interior rhythms. There is no evidence of great extinctions or other natural disasters associated with the magnetic reversals. The reversals seem to occur rapidly (geologically speaking), requiring only a few thousand years to develop. The reversals occur periodically, but in a more or less random pattern, at an average interval of about one-half million years in the relatively recent geologic past. It is interesting to note that we have been in a period of "normal" polarity for nearly 1 million years, so the planet is due for a reversal any time. Humans may understand the process and consequence of the reversals better if we have the opportunity to live through one. There is no need to worry, though, for the geologic record indicates that such reversals are normal and have happened many times in the past without any negative impacts on life.

In the Mesozoic, near the end of the era, this normal and recurrent shifting of the magnetic polarity stopped dead in its tracks. About 118 million years ago, the magnetic field shifted to normal polarity from reversed and stayed that way for at least 35 million years. What happened? Did the currents in the outer core stagnate? Did the inner regions of the earth "overheat" so that rocks below the surface lost their magnetic properties? No one knows. But the long "normal epoch" in the late Mesozoic Era is a unique event in Earth history. Nothing like it has ever been discovered in rocks of any other age. It may be that this period of stability (or stagnation) of the interior earth is related to some of the other peculiar aspects of the Mesozoic world described below. The timing is certainly suspicious, for precisely when the magnetic field stopped reversing its polarity some other very strange things begin to happen on the planet Earth.

During the Cretaceous Period, great volumes of molten rock, or magma, were erupted or emplaced beneath the surface in many places around the globe. In fact, geologists consider the late Mesozoic to be the most intense period of igneous activity since life originated on our planet. It is an undisputed fact that more igneous rock formed, both on the surface (volcanic rocks) and underground (as plutonic rocks, like granite), during the Cretaceous than during any other period of geologic time. For example, in North America the granitic rocks of the Sierra Nevada in California, the Coastal Range of British Columbia, the mountains of central Idaho, and rugged peaks of the Baja California peninsula are entirely of Mesozoic age, mostly from the Cretaceous Period. Elsewhere, in India and Pakistan, lava flooded out onto the earth's surface in unprecedented volume during the late Cretaceous Period, producing over 10,000 cubic kilometers of volcanic rocks known as the Deccan traps. Nearly as impressive quantities of lava were erupted at about the same time in South America and at numerous places on the sea floor.

The Mesozoic Era in general, and the Cretaceous Period in particular, was a time when it could be said that all hell broke loose, all over the world. This great surge of molten rock upward toward the earth's surface during the late Mesozoic Era exerted many secondary effects on the global ecosystem, adding more turmoil to a world already in environmental disarray. Though we do not yet understand exactly how this torrent of rising liquid is linked to the suspected disruption of circulation in the earth's deep outer core, it almost certainly is.

How did this surge of molten material affect the global environment? Let us count the ways! First, there is excellent geochemical evidence that the entire Mesozoic Era, and especially the Cretaceous Period, was a very warm interval in the earth's history. Based on the study of oxygen isotopes in rocks and fossils, it appears that the oceans of the world were about 15°C warmer during the late Mesozoic than they are now. Fossils of warmth-loving plants such as magnolias have been found in the Mesozoic rocks of Greenland, which today is a frigid land supporting few plants. Nowhere in the world is there any evidence of glaciers found in rocks of Mesozoic age. All the available evidence suggests that the Cretaceous Period, and most of the rest of Mesozoic time as well, was very warm. We know that when volcanoes erupt, they liberate enormous quantities of gas along with the lava that flows from them. Steam (water vapor), carbon dioxide (CO_2), sulfurous gases (H_2S, SO_2), and other vapors emanate as towering plumes above the summits of erupting volcanoes. During the Mesozoic, carbon dioxide and other gases from the widespread and intense eruptions must have accumulated in the atmosphere, producing a "super greenhouse" effect, raising the global temperature by at least 10°C. The volcano-induced warmth likely prevented the formation of ice caps and produced a searing climate for at least the last portion of the Mesozoic Era.

Today, the world's ice caps and glaciers contain a little more than 2 percent of the world's water. What would happen if this water were returned to the seas, as it was during most of the Mesozoic, as a consequence of warmer conditions? The sea level would rise. The volume of the Mesozoic seas would also have been greater than that of today's oceans, because water expands as it is heated. Consequently, the lower coastal plains on every continent would be submerged as the bloated oceans rose and crept inland. This is precisely what happened on a global scale during the Cretaceous Period. Starting about 100 million years ago, the borderlands and low interiors of every continent in the world were overrun by the advancing sea. North America was separated into two "island" continents during the Cretaceous Period, as the ancient Gulf of Mexico advanced north through the central plains to meet the water creeping south from the Arctic region. The western margin of the interior seaway ran north and south through central Utah. Similar flooding of continental lowlands occurred simultaneously on all other continents.

At the same time that the continents were being flooded by the rampaging sea, same strange events were occurring on the ocean floor. We know that new oceanic materials are created at the axis of the midoceanic ridges, a great chain of undersea volcanoes which extends more than 65,000 kilometers (40,000 miles) through the center of the ocean basins. This volcanic chain winds around the earth like the stitches on a baseball. From it, enormous slabs of oceanic rock are driven apart by the continuous eruption of lava in the center of the ridge system coupled with the divergent flow of hot, semirigid material beneath them. As the slabs separate, new rocks are formed in the gap between them as lava flows out onto the sea floor to cool and solidify. The "sealed" rift between two slabs is continuously ripped open again as geological forces pull the slabs apart.

Over time, the two oceanic plates diverge from the axis of the midoceanic ridge at an average rate of a few centimeters per year, about as fast as human fingernails grow. This phenomenon is known as sea-floor spreading and it causes the ocean basins to widen through time as the continents on either side are gradually forced farther apart. This movement is similar to that of conveyor belts, positioned end-to-end at the axis of midoceanic ridge, going in opposite directions. In the late Mesozoic Era, the rate of sea-floor spreading increased to as much as 18 centimeters (cm) per year, more than three times the average rate today! The midoceanic ridges were unusually active during the Mesozoic Era, especially during the Cretaceous Period.

Geologists still do not know exactly how molten rock is continuously injected into the axis of the midoceanic ridges, but it almost certainly involves the circulation of material in the earth's mantle, that zone between the crust and the core. As has already been seen, there is evidence that the deeper interior circulation became disrupted during the very same time that the "conveyor belt" on the sea floor was dramatically accelerated. It may be that the normal heat-dissipating currents (whatever their form may be) decayed, and the mantle "overheated" during the late Mesozoic. In response to the extreme heating, pockets of the semisolid material melted and gushed upward as great plumes of molten rock into the axis of the midoceanic ridge system. Elsewhere on the sea floor, huge masses of this fluid pierced the overlying slabs to form great lava plateaus and isolated chains of undersea volcanoes. Many such features are known on the ocean floor and some of the largest are of Mesozoic age. Such mantle plumes may also be responsible for the numerous volcanic eruptions on land. If the rate of sea-floor spreading increased dramatically near the end of Mesozoic time, as an abundance of evidence suggests, then we may assume that the midoceanic ridge itself became larger as the increased heat caused the rocks of the ridge to expand. This thermal "inflation" of the ridge probably reduced the storage capacity of the

world's oceans and exacerbated the simultaneous flooding of the continental lowlands.

These events on the Mesozoic sea floor, coupled with the unusual climatic conditions, produced yet another oddity of the Age of Reptiles. Throughout the world, the mud that accumulated on the sea floor during the late Mesozoic is characteristically rich in carbon. Commonly, there is so much carbon in the fine sediment that the resulting rock exhibits a dark gray or black color. Geologists have coined the term "black shale" to describe such rocks. Black shales are particularly widespread from the Cretaceous Period, but they are also common from the Jurassic, especially in Europe.

In Utah, the black shale episode is recorded by the late Cretaceous Mancos Shale, which forms the striking barren badlands at Factory Butte and around the Hanksville Basin, east of Capitol Reef National Park. Most of the carbon in these deposits originated as the organic residue from planktonic organisms floating near the surface of the sea. When these organisms died, their remains descended toward the sea floor as a more or less constant rain of organic matter rich in carbon. On today's sea floor, most of this organic material is consumed by mud-feeding organisms or decomposed by bacteria and other microbes. Modern sea floor mud contains some carbon, but in most places it is not rich enough in organic material to develop a black color.

The prevalence of black shale in the Mesozoic suggests that either the population of decomposing organisms on the sea floor was small or the rate of organic production in the planktonic realm was unusually high. It is likely that both factors contributed to the abnormally widespread black shale of the Mesozoic Era. The warmth of Mesozoic times, probably enhanced by the volcano-generated greenhouse effect near the end of the era, would have produced a "bloom" of plankton in the seas. Also, the warm global climate produced the marine equivalent of a year-round growing season for millions of years. The increased amount of carbon dioxide in the late Mesozoic atmosphere might have acted much like plant fertilizer, leading to a great proliferation of photosynthetic phytoplankton. Whatever organisms lived on the ocean floor at that time no doubt experienced a deluge, rather than a gentle rain, of organic matter from above.

At the same time, the global warmth would have slowed down or perhaps even sporadically eliminated the circulation of water in the deeper ocean basins. This is likely because, in today's oceans, the cold, dense seawater from the frigid polar regions sinks to continuously displace the less dense, warmer bottom water of the abyssal plains. This sinking cold water drives the entire cycle of top-to-bottom oceanic circulation. In the warm Mesozoic, without the cold polar conditions, the bottom waters may have become stagnant and depleted in the oxygen and nutrients necessary to sustain large populations of scavengers and decomposing microbes. This scenario is certainly a plausible interpretation of the ubiquitous Mesozoic black shales. Thus, even the deepest sea floor environments seem to have been affected by the disarray of the Mesozoic world.

The final element of ecological chaos in the Mesozoic comes at the very end, about 65 million years ago at the close of the Cretaceous Period. There is now very good evidence that some type of extraordinarily explosive event, or events, occurred. On a scale that appears to be almost global, sediment deposited at this time has produced concentrations of elements such as iridium that are extremely rare on the earth's surface. In addition, in these same deposits geologists have discovered unusually "shocked" mineral grains, peculiar microscopic globs of carbon that appear to be the "soot" of global wildfires, and tiny spheres of glassy material. The debate over the origin of these oddities continues; interpretations include the impact between the earth and a large asteroid, a shower of smaller objects from space,

or a series of violent volcanic eruptions. It is impossible to adequately review the issue here, but nearly all geologists agree that the Mesozoic Era went out with a bang—a fitting end to a convulsive phase in the history of our planet. We will further examine the events and the conditions that accompanied the end of the Mesozoic in Chapter 9.

In summary, the dinosaurs were not the only extraordinary aspect of nature in the Mesozoic Era. In contrast to the familiar patterns and natural rhythms of today, the entire era was a time of the peculiar, the bizarre, and the extreme. Whenever we contemplate the dinosaurs from the perspective of life in our own Cenozoic Era, we should remember that they inhabited a world that was very different from our own.

The Nature of the Mesozoic Rock Record of Utah

Rocks formed during the Mesozoic Era are widespread in Utah, particularly in the Colorado Plateau geographic province of the eastern and southern portions of the state. Statewide, Mesozoic rocks are exposed over more than 25,000 square miles, including the majestic landscapes of red-rock canyons, pastel-colored badlands, and imposing cliffs in southeastern Utah. These rocks are predominantly sedimentary, consisting of mineral grains of various sizes that accumulated in the lakes, riverbeds, dunes, and floodplains of ancient Utah. Over the millions of years since their deposition, the grains have become compacted and cemented into layers of solid stone. Sandy grains (.06 mm–2.0 mm in size) have become sandstone, while accumulations of finer particles are represented by siltstones and mudstones. Cobbles and pebbles laid down by swift rivers during the Mesozoic are now recognized as conglomerates, which appear somewhat similar to concrete. These layers, or strata, represent the pages of nature's autobiography, for in them are recorded the conditions and the life of ancient Utah.

Since sedimentary rocks form at the surface of the earth, under conditions that we can directly observe, it is often possible to determine the environment at the time of their deposition with some degree of certainty. For example, by studying the size, shape, and arrangement of grains in a sandstone, we might be able to ascertain whether the sand accumulated in a dune, as a sand bar in a river, or along the beach of some ancient lake or sea. In a similar manner, features of conglomerates such as the orientation of the pebbles, their style of layering, and their size and composition can allow geologists to determine the size and type of river that deposited them, the direction of flow, and the likely source of the rock particles.

As researchers examine the characteristics of many sedimentary rock layers that formed at the same time over a broad area, it becomes feasible to reconstruct the major features of the landscape at the time the grains were deposited. Such reconstructions of ancient environments are important in the study of any group of organisms, including dinosaurs, whose remains might be incorporated into the rock as fossils. This is because the complete understanding of any prehistoric animal requires some knowledge of the environment in which it lived. Fortunately, the sedimentary rocks that produce Utah's dinosaurs often contain a wealth of clues about the local environment as well.

Paleontologists are thus much like detectives, trying to assemble the clues from the rock record to formulate some idea of which dinosaurs lived in which environments. Whenever dinosaur bones are discovered by paleontologists, the fossils are carefully excavated and information on the nature of the enclosing rock and associated fossils is meticulously recorded. Without all the associated data, fossils can only tell us part of the story. Scientists are left, in that case, with many frustrating questions that cannot be answered. This is one reason why dinosaur excavations often

take years to complete; it is a slow, meticulous process that requires patience and persistence.

If sedimentary rock layers can be thought of as the pages in a natural history book, then sequences of layers might be regarded as chapters. By convention, geologists have described successive layers of sedimentary rock that record a particular chapter in geologic history as a formation. A formation is a sequence of rock layers that have similar characteristics such as grain size, composition, bedding thickness, etc. The combination of such features serves to distinguish the rocks in the particular formation from other layered sequences above and below it. Since the rocks that comprise a formation are more or less uniform in their characteristics, they represent sediment that accumulated under similar conditions in similar environments.

The boundaries between successive formations are placed where the characteristics of the rocks change—for example, where a coarse sandstone is overlain by a fine mudstone. Such shifts represent changes in the nature of sediment accumulation, which, in turn, suggest changes in the environment of deposition. Formations, then, represent chapters or phases of more or less constant conditions in the overall continuum of environmental change recorded by successive formations. Formations are generally named for localities where the rock unit is particularly well exposed or was first studied and defined. Cedar Mountain, for example, is the highest point in the San Rafael Swell of central Utah. The Cedar Mountain Formation consists of sedimentary rocks that are best exposed in that location, even though the layers extend beyond the mountain itself and have been identified in many other regions. On occasion, when a particular type of rock comprises nearly all of a formation, the word "formation" is replaced with a name reflective of that dominant lithology, or rock type. Such is the case in formations like the Entrada Sandstone and the Tropic Shale. As an illustration of the abundance and diversity of Mesozoic rocks in Utah,

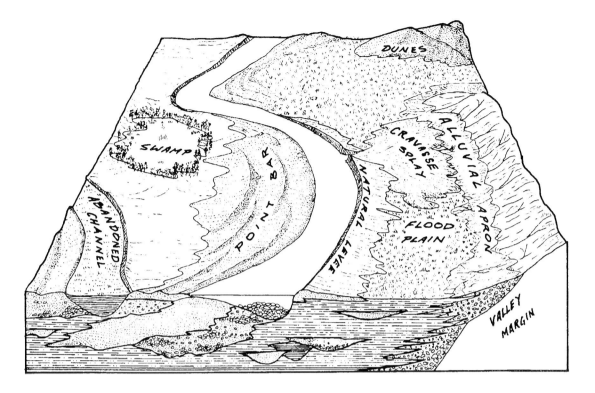

Figure 1-7. Sedimentary deposits associated with river systems. Note the complex intermingling of various types of sediment and the rapid lateral change from one type of deposit to another. The layers and lenses of sand, gravel, silt, and clay record both the lateral movement of the shifting rivers and the accumulation of sediment through time.

over 200 different formations from this era are recognized in the state.

When the rocks of a sedimentary formation were originally deposited, layers of sediment spread out over a broad area as horizontal sheets of sand, mud, or silt. The sheets were as continuous laterally as were the specific conditions of their deposition. Some formations may extend over hundreds of thousands of square miles if the sedimentary basin was that large and the conditions within it did not vary. On the deep sea floor, for example, sediment of uniform characteristics accumulates over enormously broad areas. However, the Mesozoic rocks of Utah that produce dinosaur fossils consist mostly of sediment that was deposited on land, not on the broad ocean floor. On land, the agents such as rivers, wind, gravity, or ice, which transport and deposit sediment, usually drop grains in smaller and more restricted sites, such as lake basins, river floodplains or dune fields. Consequently, few Mesozoic formations in Utah have a wide lateral extent and, with a few exceptions, most are restricted to a rel-

atively small area. This is one reason why so many different formations have been identified in the Mesozoic sequence of Utah.

The Mesozoic rock record of Utah is heterogeneous, changing in character as one moves from place to place. For example, the late Cretaceous strata in Utah include conglomerate in Echo Canyon, sandstone near Ferron, coal in Carbon County and elsewhere, shale in the Hanksville Basin, and mudstone almost everywhere else. Such variety is a general characteristic of any sequence of sedimentary rocks deposited on land, and the dinosaur-bearing rocks of Utah are certainly no exception. Figure 1-7 illustrates the different types of sediment that can be deposited in a terrestrial setting.

Another factor that limits the extent of any rock formation is erosion. It has been at least 65 million years since the Mesozoic formations of Utah were deposited; for some of them, more than 200 million years have elapsed. The blanket of sediment that originally accumulated may have been partially removed by subsequent erosion so that the rock layers now cover only a fraction of the area they once occupied. Geologists can trace some formations across the erosional gaps from one isolated locality to another by a practice known as correlation. Recall, however, that land-deposited sedimentary rocks typically exhibit pronounced lateral variations. Consequently, we may observe coarse sandstone in one locality and by the time we have traced (or correlated) it to a distant exposure, the particular sandstone interval may be represented by conglomerate, or limestone, or shale. In such instances, we might be tempted to assign the rocks of the two separated localities to different formations since they are composed of different materials, even though they accumulated or were deposited at the same time. The practice of distinguishing these related rocks has further contributed to the proliferation of formation names for the Mesozoic rocks of Utah.

In many cases, it is possible to subdivide a formation into smaller sequences or portions that represent a variation of the overall geological characteristics. Such subdivisions of formations are called members. The Morrison Formation, a famous dinosaur-producing formation in the Rocky Mountain region, has been split into at least three members in most places in Utah where it is exposed: the Brushy Basin Member, the Salt Wash Member, and the Tidwell Member. In some exposures of the Morrison Formation, additional members may be present. The Morrison Formation consists of a heterogeneous, or varied, mixture of sedimentary rocks deposited in a large interior basin during the late Jurassic Period. The portion of it in central Utah that consists of river-deposited sandstone and conglomerate is known as the Salt Wash Member, while the other members of the Morrison consist of other types of sediment that accumulated in slightly different environments.

In a similar manner, it is sometimes feasible to group several formations into larger entities known as groups. A group is a set of rock forma-

tions that have some overall similarity even though they differ individually. For example, the Glen Canyon Group in southern Utah consists of, in ascending order (oldest to youngest), the Wingate Sandstone, the Kayenta Formation, and the Navajo Sandstone. These early Jurassic formations are dominated by sandstone in all three cases, but the details of their textures, compositions, sedimentary structures, and other features are individually distinctive. Thus, although all three formations consist principally of sandstone, different kinds of sand were deposited under different conditions in the three components of the Glen Canyon Group. As in the case of formations, geologic groups and members are also named in reference to geographic localities where the constituent strata are well exposed.

During the long span of the Mesozoic Era, a variety of sediments accumulated in central and southern Utah. At times, great rivers ran through the region, depositing varying kinds of sediments in their channels and on the adjacent floodplains (Figure 1-7). At other times, dry winds blew great volumes of sand into the region to form extensive dune fields. Occasionally, oceans penetrated into Utah, and the rock record of these intervals is dominated by sediments that accumulated on the shallow sea floor or along the beaches and coastal plains bordering the seas. Because the environments were constantly changing and never uniform across the entire region, the sedimentary record of these Mesozoic events is a rather complex mixture of sandstone, mudstone, conglomerate, shale, coal, limestone, and other types of rocks. These are sediments that contain the fossils of Utah's dinosaurs.

We will explore the various formations in much more detail in the chapters that follow. This overview of the Mesozoic rock record of Utah would be incomplete, however, if another type of deposit found within this mixed assemblage of sedimentary rocks was not pointed out, one that is very important in the study of Utah dinosaurs. During most of the Mesozoic Era, volcanic activity was taking place near, or in, Utah. In particular, scientists know that central Arizona, eastern Nevada, and southern Idaho were the sites of numerous Mesozoic eruptions. Eastern Utah was thus surrounded by volcanically active regions. From time to time, great clouds of volcanic ash that were discharged from the erupting volcanoes drifted over the Utah region to settle out as relatively thin sheets across the floodplains, dunes, or beaches. Some of the volcanic ash was reworked by wind or water to become mixed with the silt and mud that was being deposited at the time. As this mixture weathered, the ash produced clay minerals that form the rock known as bentonite. Many of the dinosaur-producing mudstone sequences in Utah and adjacent regions are "bentonitic," meaning that they are rich in this weathered form of volcanic ash. Sometimes the ash layers, usually only a few inches thick, were quickly buried under additional layers of sediment and underwent little weathering or disruption. Such layers of ash are often found sandwiched between sandstone, siltstone, or mudstone in Utah's Mesozoic formations.

Though they represent only a small fraction of the Mesozoic rock record, the thin volcanic ash layers are extremely important. This is because the ash (and, less frequently, the bentonite) contains minerals that can be dated with various techniques that rely on the gradual decay of radioactive elements. While it is beyond the scope of this book to review the process in detail, these techniques, collectively known as radiometric dating, can provide reasonably precise dates for the formation of the ash layers. Because the sedimentary rocks that contain the ash layers consist of mineral grains derived from a variety of source rocks, there is no way to directly date them radiometrically. If scientists attempted to do so, they would probably get such a variety of results that the data would be virtually meaningless. In any case, the radiometric measurements would be the age of the mineral grain, not necessarily the time when it was deposited in Utah. Only the volcanic

sediments can provide meaningful radiometric dates, since they often contain datable minerals that formed at essentially the same time the ash accumulated. Not all ash layers can be reliably dated, however. To be datable, the ash must not have weathered excessively prior to its burial and must contain certain mineral crystals, such as the mica biotite or the feldspar sanidine, that have enough radioactive elements (potassium, in this case) to be accurately measured.

There are, however, many datable ash layers scattered though the Mesozoic rock sequences in Utah. By providing temporal reference points in the sedimentary record, their presence in dinosaur-bearing sequences allows us to estimate the times when various types of dinosaurs lived in Utah. For example, at the Cleveland-Lloyd Dinosaur Quarry, the bone-producing horizon, or section, in the Morrison Formation is situated between two layers of slightly altered volcanic ash that still contain datable minerals (Figure 1-8). The layer above the quarry yields a radiometric date of about 147 million years; the layer below is about 152 million years old (Bilbey, 1992, cited in Chapter 6). Paleontologists can estimate, therefore, that the dinosaurs preserved at this site lived in Utah between 152 and 147 million years ago. Without the datable minerals derived from the volcanic ash, all scientists could say is that the Cleveland-Lloyd dinosaurs were "late Jurassic" in age, a time span encompassing more than 20 million years, from 163–144 million years ago. The ashy materials in the Morrison Formation at this locality allow scientists to estimate the absolute ages of dinosaurs with much greater precision than would otherwise be possible. (See Chapter 6 for details on the relationship between the volcanic ash layers and the bone bed at the Cleveland-Lloyd Quarry.)

The Dinosaur Fossil Record

As we explore the dinosaurs of Utah, it is best to be mindful of the limitations of the evidence

Photo 3. Dinosaur footprints, such as these near Moab, record information about the movement, speed, size, posture, and foot anatomy of the animals that made them. Frank DeCourten.

Photo 5. Rounded and highly polished stones such as these from Cretaceous strata in the San Rafael Swell may represent gastroliths, or "stomach stones," of dinosaurs. John Telford.

Photo 4. Impressions of dinosaur skin, such as this one from the Neslen Formation of central Utah, are important trace fossils. Photograph courtesy of Mary Droser, University of California, Riverside.

upon which paleontologists base their reconstructions of these extinct animals and the vanished world they inhabited. Even though paleontologists have been studying dinosaurs for more than 150 years, there are still many lingering questions and nagging uncertainties about the animals. Many of these mysteries are attributable to the imperfections of our primary data of dinosaurs, the fossils recovered from Mesozoic strata.

Dinosaur fossils are more varied than most people suspect. When people think of dinosaur fossils, most immediately envision a preserved skull or perhaps a skeleton entombed in rock. And many such fossils have been discovered, although they still remain exceedingly rare. Much more commonly, however, researchers find single isolated bones, or even fragments of bone, preserved in varying degrees of perfection. Besides bones and teeth, though, paleontologists can gain additional information from other kinds of di-

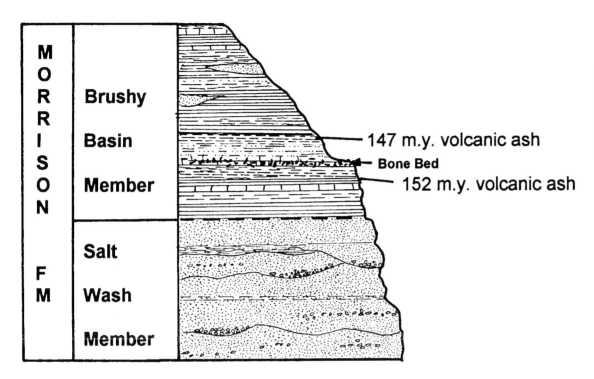

Figure 1-8. The Morrison Formation at the Cleveland-Lloyd Dinosaur Quarry in Emery County, Utah. Data from Bilbey, 1992, cited in Chapter 6.

nosaur fossils. The footprints and trackways of dinosaurs and other terrestrial creatures have been found in many places in Utah, sometimes in spectacular abundance. Footprints are known as trace fossils, because they do not represent preserved remains of organic tissues. Nonetheless, they can provide a surprising amount of information on such aspects of dinosaurs as their foot morphology (or structure), style and rate of locomotion, migratory behavior, and even their community structure or group behavior. The study of dinosaur tracks and trace fossils has become an exciting subdiscipline of paleontology in the past twenty years and researchers have gained many new profound insights about dinosaurs through the analysis of their trace fossils.

Another type of trace fossil important in the study of Utah's dinosaurs is skin impressions. Skin impressions were formed when soft sediment accumulated over and around a dinosaur carcass. After the remains were buried, the soft

tissues decomposed, leaving the surface features of the skin preserved as a replica in the surrounding sedimentary rock. Like footprints, skin impressions do not represent the preservation of the actual body tissues; but they can still provide a great deal of information on the structure and appearance of the integument, or body covering, of dinosaurs. Such features as scales and scale clusters, nodes of some bones, skin folds, and wrinkles can be faithfully recorded as skin impressions.

In recent years, there have been many discoveries of dinosaur eggs, eggshells, and nesting sites. From these, scientists have learned much about the nesting habits, patterns of embryonic development, and reproductive behavior of some types of dinosaurs. While completely preserved dinosaur nests or eggs have not yet been found in Utah, fragmentary eggshells are common in some of the Mesozoic rock units. Gastroliths, or "stomach stones," are very common in several different dinosaur-producing rock formations in Utah. These smooth, rounded, and highly polished stones are interpreted to be gizzard stones and suggest that at least some dinosaurs had such an organ to supplement their dentition, or teeth, in the processing of food. In this regard, some of the herbivorous dinosaurs might have been similar to modern birds.

On rare occasions, researchers sometimes find fossilized dinosaur droppings, known as coprolites, or even the stomach contents, preserved after the soft tissues of the dinosaur have decayed. Such objects can provide information about the diets of dinosaurs, the structure of their digestive tracts, and the ways in which their food was processed. Combined with the preserved bones and teeth, all of these accessory fossils provide scientists with a wealth of information about Utah dinosaurs. But how good is the fossil record of dinosaurs? How complete and accurate a picture of dinosaurs can researchers reconstruct on the basis of this tangible evidence of the distant past?

There are really two questions that scientists must ask about the adequacy of the fossil record of dinosaurs. First, is fossilization common enough to give them a reasonably complete sampling of the dinosaur populations that inhabited Utah during the Mesozoic Era? Second, are the data that we have biased in any way that might affect the researchers' perceptions of the relative abundance and the anatomy of the various dinosaurs? There is almost universal agreement among paleontologists that the answer to the first question is "no" and the answer the second question is "yes." The fossil record of the dinosaurs is undoubtedly a numerically poor sample and it also is highly biased. Let's explore the reasons why.

Numerical Quality of the Fossil Record

If we look around at the modern world, we soon become familiar with the normal sequence of events that follows the death of any organism that lives on land. Consider, for example, the ultimate fate of a sheep that dies from natural causes during the summer on a tract of Utah rangeland. After death, the normal immunological defenses the sheep enjoys during life no longer operate. Decomposition begins on the microbial scale as bacteria and other organisms begin to flourish in the sheep's remains. The by-products of microbial decomposition include toxins and gases that cause the carcass to bloat and results in the characteristic odor of rotting flesh. Scavenging animals soon are attracted to the remains. Ravens, coyotes, and other creatures arrive at the scene to consume portions of the carcass. Perhaps the scavengers remove a leg, or a portion of the back, or a shoulder. In this way, parts of the carcass eventually disappear. Insects attack the remaining carcass, often laying eggs in the rotting flesh, which serves as food for the larvae that soon hatch. When all the soft tissues have been consumed by microbes, scavengers, or insects, the remaining bones become scattered about as the connective tissues (ligaments, tendons, and cartilage) no longer hold the bones together. The isolated and scattered bones lie under the sun and eventually become bleached and cracked as they dry out. Rodents gnaw on the bones. Inevitably, even the most durable tissues such as teeth and hooves are reduced to splinters and powder under the combined attack of physical decay and biological decomposition. Within a few months, or perhaps a year or so, no trace of the sheep carcass remains. The existence of the sheep has not been recorded in the fossil record of the future.

With a few variations on this scenario, the same sequence of events must have been the rule for any land-living creature during the Mesozoic Era. Fossilization is only possible if the normal process of post-mortem decay and decomposition is interrupted before all the remains disintegrate completely; for example, one way fossilization is possible is when the carcass of the animal is buried soon after its death, before microbes, scavengers, and the elements can get to it. If, by chance, an animal dies while it is crossing a river, or standing along the edge of a lake, or climbing through sand dunes, preservation of its remains is much more likely. Even in these cases, however, fossilization is not guaranteed. A carcass floating in a river can still be completely decomposed. For any of its tissues to be preserved, the animal must die in a spot along the river where sediment is actively being deposited. If death occurs while the creature is walking along a sand bar, for instance, the sand and silt may pile up and cover the carcass before decomposition advances very far. Yet, how often are carcasses buried in this manner? Certainly it is a rare event. The process of fossilization begins only when such rare and fortunate (for the paleontologist, at least) conditions are met. In many cases, only a portion of the carcass may be buried prior to complete decomposition, allowing a partial skeleton, perhaps only a single bone, to escape decay. The vast majority of dinosaurs, or any animal for that matter, that ever lived on the earth's surface disappeared without a trace, as their remains underwent the normal process of complete decomposition.

Even after the burial of a body, fossilization is still not ensured. In the geological environment, organic materials are not always stable. Microbial decay can still occur. Fluids moving through the sediment, either before or after it hardens into stone, can dissolve some of the skeletal tissues or obliterate them beyond recognition. Sometimes, though, buried organic remains can be altered in such a way as to increase their stability in the geological environment. For example, the open spaces in porous tissues such as bone or wood can become filled with minerals such as silica (SiO_2) or calcium carbonate ($CaCO_3$). This process is known as permineralization, and it is a very common mode of preservation in dinosaur fossils. Other methods of stabilizing biological remains in the geologic environment include the complete replacement of the organic tissues by mineral substances and the formation of natural replicas of the remains, known as molds and casts, among many others. Many dinosaur fossils are preserved

through a combination of these processes. The dinosaur bones from Dinosaur National Monument, for example, have been partly permineralized by silica and iron oxide, while some of the original tissues have been replaced with calcium compounds (Hubert and others, 1996). If some form of stabilization does not affect the original organic material, it is unlikely that any portion of the buried carcass will survive millions of years of exposure to the high temperatures, enormous pressures, and reactive chemicals present in the hostile geologic environment. So, even if we consider only the minuscule fraction of animals that become buried immediately after death, only a small number of them will ever become fossilized.

Finally, remember that for a fossil to be useful to scientists, someone has to discover it. This, of course, requires that the buried and preserved remains have to somehow find their way back to the earth's surface. This usually requires geologic uplift of the region, which initiates erosion that, in turn, wears away rock layers as they are elevated to expose the formerly buried strata. Fossils emerge only when the rock layers that contain them crumble and decay at the earth's surface. Unless someone appears at just the right time, the fossils will also succumb to the agents of weathering and erosion. Thus, finding a fossil requires good timing: if paleontologists arrive at the scene too early, erosion will not have exposed the fossils to view; if they are too late, erosion will have obliterated the fossil. In either case, researchers will not gain the information the fossils convey. In light of these considerations, we must acknowledge that only a small fraction of all the dinosaur fossils that exist has been discovered and studied.

In summary, the fossil record of any group of prehistoric animals represents only a tiny representation of the original population. The fossil record is a numerically poor sampling. How poor? Paleontologists universally agree that only a small percentage of all the creatures (estimates vary from a fraction of 1 percent to 3 percent) that have ever lived on the earth are known from the fossil record. For dinosaurs, the percentage may be a little higher due to the frenzied collecting that began in the late 1800s and continues today. Russell (1995) has estimated that about 8 percent of all dinosaur types that ever existed have been identified by paleontologists. In any case, the number of known dinosaurs is relatively small, and this means students of the animals are basing their perceptions on fragmentary material representing an extremely restricted view of the Mesozoic biosphere.

Being aware of this limitation of the fossil record of dinosaurs should not make us any less enchanted by the creatures. There are thousands of dinosaur bones in museums all over the world, and many more dinosaur fossils await discovery in Utah and elsewhere. If we accept the notion that fossilization is an extremely rare event, then every dinosaur bone represents literally millions of creatures that did not leave any evidence of their existence. To be preserved in the fossil record at all, any group of organisms most likely had to be abundant, diverse, and persistent during its time. Collectively, the dinosaur fossil record is nowhere near a representative sampling of the original populations; but by understanding the limitations of the data, scientists can come to understand that this captivating group of ancient reptiles was one of the most successful groups of animals to ever inhabit the earth. For all its numerical deficiencies, the fossil record of dinosaurs is all we have; there is no alternate source of information to consult. The fossils, along with the skill in interpreting them, still allow rsearchers to formulate some valid perceptions of these fascinating creatures.

Biases in the Dinosaur Fossil Record

A moment's reflection about the process of fossilization leads us inevitably to another conclusion about the dinosaur fossil record—it must also be highly biased in a number of ways. Con-

sider, for example, the likelihood of a habitat bias. This is to suggest that some dinosaurs, those living in habitats where sediment accumulates in great quantities, will probably have been more often preserved as fossils than will have been other dinosaurs living elsewhere. Consequently, dinosaurs adapted to swampy or riparian (adjacent to rivers) habitats might be expected to leave more abundant fossils behind because in those locations sediment is continuously deposited. But what about the upland dwellers? Were there montane dinosaurs in the Mesozoic, living in habitats now occupied by animals such as mountain goats and bighorn sheep? Almost certainly there were; but since mountains and uplands are characterized by vigorous erosion, not deposition of sediment, the alpine dinosaurs would be much less likely to be preserved as fossils. Nearly all of what we know about dinosaurs comes from the study of the lowland dwellers that dominate the fossil record.

Paleontologists universally acknowledge another kind of bias in the fossil record, the anatomical bias, which means that certain tissues and parts of dinosaurs are preserved more often than others. Clearly, the hard tissues such as bones and teeth will more commonly survive the processes of decomposition, weathering, burial, and post-burial degradation to become fossils than will the less durable portions of the anatomy. For this reason, researchers know next to nothing about the details of dinosaur eyes, hearts, and kidneys. Occasionally, researchers get insights concerning the soft tissues of dinosaurs from such things as trace fossils, gastroliths, and skin impressions; however, unless the soft organs of dinosaurs left some scar or feature on bone, scientists can usually study them only through inference, speculation, and comparison with living animals.

In some cases, it is possible to acquire information about soft tissues from the bones that enclosed them. For example, we do know something about the overall morphology of dinosaur brains because many brain cavities have been identified in well-preserved skulls. From these cavities scientists can produce casts, usually of latex or plaster, that allow them to determine the size and shape of the brain, the location and arrangement of lobes within it, and the branching pattern of major nerves. But we know nothing of the brain tissues themselves. In a similar manner, researchers can estimate the size and shape of such organs as lungs and intestines by observing the configuration of the rib cage or the pelvis of various dinosaur skeletons, but no one has any precise understanding of the anatomy of these organs.

Even among the harder tissues of dinosaur bodies, there is a bias: small and delicate bones are much less common as fossils than are the more massive elements such as limb bones and armor plates. Thus, the fossil record of dinosaurs is highly biased toward teeth (many species of dinosaurs have been named solely on the basis of teeth or even a single tooth fragment), the larger and more robust bones, spikes, and claws. This situation reflects the anatomical bias of fossilization.

In addition, scholars anticipate that the fossil record of dinosaurs is also biased toward some kinds of dinosaurs. We might call this the systematic, or taxonomic, bias. For example, some of the smaller and more birdlike dinosaurs had very delicate, partially hollow bones. Their remains are not nearly as common in the fossil record as are the massive bones of the lumbering sauropods such as *Apatosaurus* (commonly known formerly as "Brontosaurus"). Even though they might have been living in the same area and in equal numbers, sauropods left behind many more fossils than the smaller, more lightly built creatures. Because paleontologists find very few fossils of them, we may, if we are not careful, conclude that the little dinosaurs were very uncommon. In fact, however, they may have been extremely abundant, but their small and delicate bones were only infrequently preserved as fossils.

Finally, it is important to note that there has been a historical preference among paleontolo-gists for large dinosaur fossils. This has led to another type of bias in the dinosaur fossil record, the collecting bias. Ever since dinosaurs were first discovered, people have been awestruck by their gigantic dimensions. As museums began to exhibit skeletons of dinosaurs, the clear emphasis was on size—the bigger the dinosaur, the better. Furthermore, large fossil bones are hard to miss in the field. The six-foot-long femur of an *Apatosaurus* weathering out of a hillside would not go unnoticed for long. One has to look harder to find the bones of small dinosaurs. Many small fossil bones doubtless were left behind in favor of larger, more obvious bones by collectors of the late 1800s and early 1900s. Only during the past fifty years or so have paleontologists been carefully looking for small bones and collecting them from dinosaur quarries. For these reasons, the collections of dinosaur fossils that now exist in museums all over the world are strongly biased toward the larger types of dinosaurs.

We know that many dinosaurs were relatively small creatures, even when fully grown. *Compsognathus*, a small theropod, was not much larger than a modern rooster, and the ornithopod *Hypsilophodon* was generally about the same size as a large domestic turkey (Callison and Quimby, 1984). A recent analysis of body-size estimates for dinosaurs has shown that some 26 percent of all known dinosaurs weighed less than 100 kg (about 220 pounds), the approximate weight of a large human (Peczkis, 1994). This same study revealed that, even though only 14 percent of the known dinosaurs were truly gigantic animals (10–100 metric tons; 1 metric ton = 2,200 pounds), during the early "bone rush" period from 1870 to 1900, dinosaurs in this size range accounted for 36 percent of the collected material. This clearly illustrates the historical collecting bias in favor of the fossils of the larger dinosaurs. Even though the dinosaurs included some of the largest terrestrial animals ever to exist on the earth, they certainly were not all behemoths of colossal proportions.

In summary, the fossil record of dinosaurs is

a numerically poor sampling of the original Mesozoic population of the animals and it is strongly biased in terms of habitat preferences, anatomy, and types of creatures it reveals. In any study of dinosaurs, these limitations of our basic data should be kept in mind. Also, one should not expect full answers to many of the questions that remain about dinosaurs. Today, after more than 150 years of fossil collecting and analysis, there are still many lingering mysteries concerning the dinosaurs and other aspects of the Mesozoic world they inhabited. Only persistent study and the discovery of more fossils can lead researchers to a greater understanding of dinosaurs and toward solutions to some of the mysteries. Given the nature of the fossil record, there will probably never be answers to some questions. However, mysteries and uncertainties motivate us as intelligent and inquisitive creatures. Human beings have been driven to expand our knowledge in a similar way to *Tyrannosaurus* being driven to attack prey. This insatiable hunger for learning is the hallmark of our species; it is why we have books, schools, libraries, computers, universities, and museums. For those interested in dinosaurs, it is also a reason to love Utah.

D INOSAURS ARE unquestionably the most familiar of all prehistoric creatures. For nearly a century, representations of these animals have been a notable element in our popular culture, appearing in movies, books, posters, as toys, on children's lunch pails, and in myriad other forms. Consequently, most people became aware of the general appearance of dinosaurs at an early age, and many children soon learned to pronounce the names and identify a few of the basic types of dinosaurs. A likeness of a *Tyrannosaurus* is, for most, as identifiable as a photograph of the family dog.

However, if a person were asked to define precisely the group of reptiles known as dinosaurs, he or she might hesitate a bit. One might immediately respond that dinosaurs were large reptiles that lived long ago and are now extinct. That definition might suffice for a few of the best-known and most popular types of dinosaurs such as *Tyrannosaurus*, *Stegosaurus*, *Apatosaurus*, and *Triceratops*; however, glance through any book on dinosaurs and you will soon discover that these reptiles were amazingly varied in terms of size, shape, behavior, anatomy, and general appearance. Dinosaurs are so diverse that paleontologists have named as many as 800 different types (though not all of these are currently considered valid). When we ponder the incredible variety of dinosaurs, we might wonder what set of characteristics they all shared. What is it about dinosaurs that allows people to place them together in a group that is distinct from other reptiles?

The term "dinosaur" was first used in 1842 by Richard Owen, an illustrious British anatomist, to embrace a small number of large prehistoric reptiles that were then known only from a handful of fossils. To Owen, the fossils were clearly of reptilian character, though there was at the time some controversy concerning the type of animals they represented. Owen invented his new term from Greek roots that mean literally, "terrible lizards" or "terrible reptiles." Owen probably considered these reptiles "terrible" because they were unbe-

lievably large in comparison to today's reptiles. Imagining what these animals would have been like while alive, Owen must have developed a fearsome perception of them.

Since Owen's time, thousands of dinosaur fossils have been collected from localities all over the world, including such remote places as Antarctica. Every time a new "terrible lizard" was discovered, it was placed into Owen's group if it was large, reptilian, and extinct. However, it wasn't long before paleontologists began to wonder about the basic biological characteristics of all the varied types of dinosaurs that were being discovered. Some soon sought to define the term "dinosaur" more precisely. In addition, by the late 1800s it was becoming increasingly obvious that, with so many different types of dinosaurs, a classification scheme should be developed that would allow researchers to place similar animals together in smaller groups of closely related types.

On these matters—the definition of the dinosaurs and their classification—there were considerable differences of opinion among paleontologists. Even today, there has not been established an exact definition of the dinosaurs that satisfies every scientist. Moreover, there continues to be disagreements among paleontologists on how to precisely subdivide these reptiles in smaller groups of similar and related animals. There is no universally accepted scheme for the detailed classification of dinosaurs into groups such as species, genera, families, etc. The discussion that follows will present a common view among contemporary dinosaur paleontologists. The modern definition of the dinosaurs and the system scientists use to classify them have both been evolving since Owen first coined the term. In the future, as more fossils are discovered and knowledge of dinosaurs becomes more complete, the current classification will probably be modified to accommodate both the new discoveries and our changing perceptions of the relationships between various groups. Such is the nature of classification schemes; they are never static, be-

TWO

What Is a Dinosaur?

cause human knowledge of any aspect of nature is always expanding.

Dinosaurs Defined

Modern paleontologists are in general agreement that all dinosaurs, regardless of their individual specializations and characteristics, possess a collective set of characteristics that sets them apart from other groups of reptiles. Dinosaurs had at least seventeen unique skeletal characteristics that can be used to formally define them (Novas, 1996). It is important to remember, however, that no single characteristic defines an animal as a dinosaur. Instead, it is the combination of many traits that characterizes the group as a natural subdivision of the reptiles. It is beyond the scope of this book to list all the detailed skeletal features that distinguish the dinosaurs as a group; however, what follows will help the reader become familiar with a few of the dinosaurs' most important attributes.

First, all dinosaurs were inhabitants of the land, with specializations that enabled them to move efficiently across the varied terrain. Many dinosaurs were well adapted to live in coastal plains, along river courses, or in swampy regions where the land and water met; however, none of the animals we call dinosaurs were specifically adapted to live exclusively *in* water. The long-necked plesiosaurs and the dolphin-like ichthyosaurs were well adapted for life in the Mesozoic seas, but neither of these groups of reptiles is considered to be dinosaurs. Likewise, dinosaurs did not fly or glide through the air. The Mesozoic skies were full of aerial reptiles (known as pterosaurs), but none of them are true dinosaurs. Some dinosaurs may have been able to climb trees or perhaps dig burrows in the ground, but such habits were merely variations on the general theme of terrestrial adaptation.

Although reflecting their adaptations to differing terrestrial environments, the skeletons of all dinosaurs still exhibit some common architec-

tural patterns (Figure 2-1). All dinosaurs possessed at least three vertebrae in the sacrum, that portion of the backbone that was connected to the blade-like hip bones (ilium). Some dinosaurs had as many as six or seven vertebrae in the sacral portion of the backbone, fused into a solid mass of bone. This relatively rigid bracing allowed dinosaurs to effectively transmit the thrust of their hind legs to their bodies. In addition, the dinosaurs had an erect posture, with the limbs positioned vertically beneath the body. This stance allowed the dinosaurs to move over land much more efficiently than other reptiles (for example, crocodiles and lizards) that have a more sprawling pose, with the limbs extended outward from the body.

The erect positioning of the limbs of dinosaurs is reflected in the shape and configuration of their thigh bones (femora), hip socket (acetabulum), ankles, and feet. The femur is the largest bone in the hind limb and, in dinosaurs, typically has an offset head connected to the main shaft by a narrowed neck of bone (Figure 2-1A). The angled head of the femur inserted into a hip socket that was at least partly open, and the upper hip bone (ilium) had a strong bony crest that buttressed the offset end of the femur (Figure 2-1B). The main shaft of the femur could thus be positioned vertically under the dinosaur while the head inserted into the pelvis at an angle. The open arrangement of bones around the hip socket allowed a deeper insertion of the femur and a more rigid bracing of that bone to the pelvis.

The structure of dinosaur ankles and feet reveals additional specializations for the animals' terrestrial locomotion. The ankles of dinosaurs were uniquely designed to allow great flexibility in the fore/aft direction with a minimum of inward/outward movement (Figure 2-1C). The simple hinge-like arrangement of the dinosaur ankle is known as the mesotarsal condition; it allowed the dinosaurs to propel themselves forward with speed, efficiency, and stability. In addition, most dinosaurs stood only on their toes (digitigrade

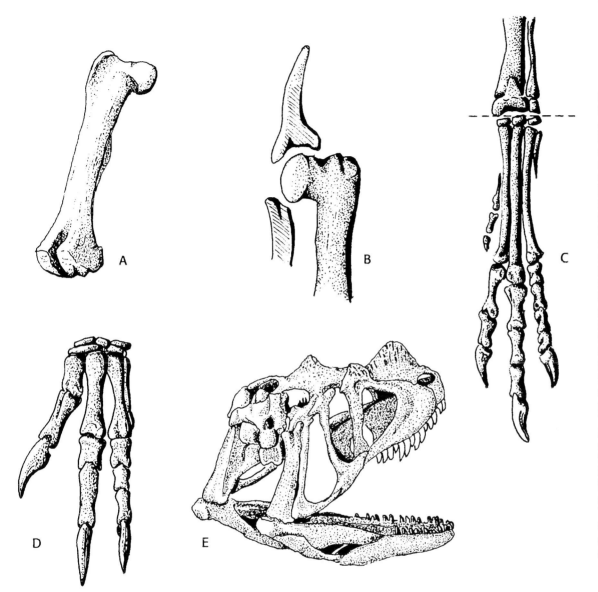

Figure 2-1. Unique skeletal features of dinosaurs. A: Femur with offset head joined to main shaft via a narrowed neck. B: The pelvis has an opening (acetabulum) where the end of the femur inserts. Note the thickened ridge of bone on the ilium, immediately above the femur; this ridge helped buttress the head of the femur. C: The simple hinge-like mesotarsal ankle of dinosaurs. Note that the foot has only three well-developed toes instead of the usual five seen in modern reptiles. D: A dinosaur hand with a somewhat opposable first digit, or "thumb." E: A typical dinosaur skull. On either side of the skull behind the orbit are two openings: the lower temporal fenestra and the upper supratemporal fenestra. The presence of two such openings identify dinosaurs as members of the subclass Diapsida.

condition), with the ankle elevated high above the ground by the elongated foot bones known as metatarsals in the hind feet or metacarpals in the forefeet. Of the five toes in a typical reptile foot, one or two are either greatly reduced or absent in the feet of dinosaurs. The effect of this foot and leg structure was to increase the overall length of the leg, extend the stride, and minimize the frictional contact with the ground. These are all specializations for efficient running and walking on land. The modern horse has evolved some of

these same basic adaptations, superimposed on a mammalian, rather than a reptilian, body plan.

The hands of dinosaurs were also modified in ways that are, among reptiles, unique. The outermost two fingers (digits 4 and 5, the "pinky" and the "ring finger") were greatly reduced or missing altogether. In addition, digit 1 (the "thumb") was usually twisted somewhat so that it was at least partially opposable to the other two fingers (Figure 2-1D). This specialization permitted bipedal dinosaurs (those that moved on two legs) to use their hands for grasping and manipulating objects in ways that modern reptiles cannot. In many quadrupedal dinosaurs, the hands were modified much like the feet to provide support and efficiency of movement. In the latter case, the bones of the hand were relatively robust and the tips of the fingers bore small hoof-like structures. The hands of quadrupedal dinosaurs looked more like feet, as they were modified to support the body rather than to manipulate objects.

The skulls of dinosaurs were constructed from dozens of bones and were highly varied in response to the specializations of diet, sensory organs, behavior, and other factors. However, an examination of the skull of any dinosaur reveals that there were more openings and cavities between the various bones than are present in most modern reptiles. The specific pattern of the openings is different in various types of dinosaurs, but all had two perforations on either side of the skull behind the orbit (eye socket). These two openings are known as the temporal fenestrae, and the paired holes identify the dinosaurs as diapsid reptiles (Figure 2-1E). Among modern reptiles, only crocodiles and the primitive sphenodontid lizards retain the two complete temporal fenestrae. Turtles have no temporal openings at all, and the other modern reptiles, snakes and lizards, have a modified diapsid pattern of temporal openings. The other perforations in the skulls of dinosaurs are related to the distribution of stresses in the skull, the attachments of certain muscles in the head and jaws, or the housing of special organs and glands. Most dinosaurs had a very flexible skull with moveable joints between many of the individual skull bones. In contrast, the skulls of most mammals (including humans) are formed of only a few rigidly fused, plate-like bones that have little flexibility. The dinosaur brain was housed inside a bony capsule (brain case) that was located within the perforated shell formed by the bones of the skull. In short, the skulls of dinosaurs were more open and more loosely assembled than are the skulls of most mammals. This is one reason why it is so rare to find a completely preserved dinosaur skull with all the bones connected and intact.

In defining the term "dinosaur," paleontologists are in general agreement about one last element: the dinosaurs all lived during the Mesozoic Era. As we will see, the earliest dinosaur fossils are found in rocks that were deposited some 20 million years after the Triassic Period began. The youngest strata that produce dinosaur bones are from the late Cretaceous Period. Although many reptiles of the late Paleozoic Era may have looked like dinosaurs, none of them had the unique set of characteristics outlined above and thus are classified in other categories. One such reptile, the sailbacked *Dimetrodon* of the Permian Period (late Paleozoic Era) is often mistaken for a dinosaur but actually belongs to the group of reptiles known as the pelycosaurs, which in fact are not closely related to the dinosaurs. Likewise, in Cenozoic rocks we find the fossils of animals that were perhaps large and dinosaur-like in their general appearance (mammoths and the titanotheres, for example), but they are all mammals, not reptiles.

There is currently some controversy about whether or not a few of the dinosaurs might have survived into the earliest part of the Cenozoic Era. In eastern Montana, dinosaur teeth and reptilian bone fragments have been found in rocks deposited just after the end of the Mesozoic Era, but it is not clear that these fossils were from animals that lived during that time. The fossils in question may have been redeposited from Cretaceous-age sediments that were being eroded by early Cenozoic rivers in Montana. In any case, if any dinosaurs did persist into the Cenozoic Era, it was only a couple of different types and they did not last long. Excluding the birds, which some scientists refer to as "avian dinosaurs," most paleontologists consider dinosaurs to be exclusively Mesozoic reptiles.

Classification of Dinosaurs

All fossils are assigned to various groups under the same system of classification used by biologists for living creatures. In this system, there are seven main hierarchical levels of classification, as follows, using humans as an example:

KINGDOM: *Animalia* (all animals)
PHYLUM: *Chordata* (all chordates)
CLASS: *Mammalia* (all mammals)
ORDER: *Primates* (humans, apes, lemurs, monkeys)
FAMILY: *Hominidae* (human-like primates)
GENUS: *Homo* (modern or nearly modern humans)
SPECIES: *sapiens*

Even though there are sometimes difficulties in applying this system of classification to ancient life, it does allow us to arrange organisms in groups of more or less related and similar types. Note that as we proceed from the highest level (Kingdom) to the lowest level of classification (Species), the categories become increasingly exclusive and contain both fewer and more similar groups of organisms. The kingdom Animalia encompasses all animals, while the species *sapiens* contains just one. In addition to these seven main levels of classification, scientists sometimes recognize intermediate levels. For example, a suborder is a level of classification below the order but above the family. Thus a suborder is a group of organisms more restrictive than an order but more inclusive than a family. A superfamily would, in a similar way, be a group of several families, but it is more restrictive and less inclusive than an order. Sometimes a subcategory can be further divided into even smaller assemblages. An infraorder, for example, is a subset or smaller division of a suborder, but it is still a larger array of organisms than is a family or a superfamily.

Let us begin our review of dinosaur classification at the class level. As we have seen, all dinosaurs are members of the class Reptilia. This class includes all other reptiles, both living and extinct, of which there are hundreds. The classification of reptiles, even if we consider only the living types, is not very straightforward. This is because the reptiles are extremely varied and, as a class, include many different types. If we include the extinct reptiles in our classification as well, then things become even more confusing, because many of the ancient reptiles, like the dinosaurs, are not comparable to any modern group and thus can't be easily placed in any category of living reptiles.

The reptiles have traditionally been subdivided into subclasses based on the pattern of temporal fenestrae. Dinosaurs belong to the subclass Diapsida because, as has been noted, they all had two temporal openings in the skull. The Diapsida, however, include more than just dinosaurs. Scientists also place the sphenodontid reptiles, crocodiles, snakes, and lizards into this group, even though the latter two groups have a modified diapsid pattern of temporal openings. Consequently, the Diapsida is still a large subgroup of reptiles that begs for further subdivision. Snakes and lizards, because they have both modified the original diapsid pattern by reducing the lower of the two fenestra to only a partial opening, are placed together in the infraclass Lepidosauria. The lepidosaurs are thus the "modified diapsids"; all other diapsid reptiles retain two complete temporal fenestrae. These non-snake and non-lizard diapsid reptiles all belong to infraclass Archosauria.

The Archosauria include the dinosaurs, the crocodiles, the extinct pterosaurs, and the living sphenodontids, along with many other less familiar extinct groups. These subgroups of archosaurs are usually separated into formal orders: the crocodiles into the order Crocodilia, the pterosaurs into the order Pterosauria, and so on. The dinosaurs, however, have been placed into one or

Figure 2-2. Pelvic structure of dinosaurs. A: Pelvis of *Ceratosaurus*, a saurischian dinosaur; B: pelvis of *Scelidosaurus*, an ornithischian dinosaur. Note that in the order Saurischia the pubis extends forward and down from the center of the pelvis to form a tri-radiate pattern. In the Ornithischia, the pubis is positioned nearly parallel to the ischium, which points down and back from the center of the pelvis.

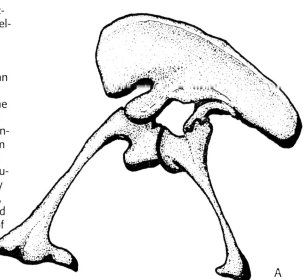

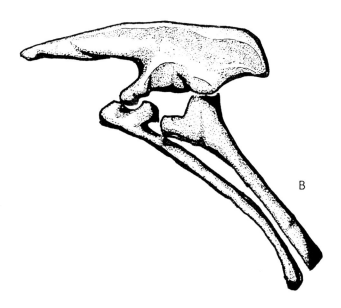

the other of two orders: the Ornithischia and the Saurischia. This is an important and unique point in the classification of the animals we call "dinosaurs"—this group actually consists of two orders of organisms. It should be remembered in contemplating the relationships among dinosaurs that they consist of two separate orders and include animals that were not necessarily closely related.

To use a more familiar illustration, recall that the mammals are a class (Mammalia), just as are the reptiles. There are about two dozen different orders of living and extinct mammals. Humans belong to the order Primates; elephants belong to the order Proboscidea. People and elephants are greatly different creatures and generally would not be considered closely related. However, humans are as similar to elephants as the various ornithischian and saurischian dinosaurs were to each other. We tend to think of the dinosaurs as a unified group of ancient reptiles that were closely related, very similar to one another, and shared a common evolutionary history. The classification of dinosaurs in two separate orders suggests, however, that they were extremely varied as a group, shared only a few basic characteristics, and had many different and unique ancestries. It wouldn't make much sense to place humans and elephants together as a group of closely related organisms, but that is precisely what has been done in the case of dinosaurs.

This classification is significant in that for many of the fundamental questions about dinosaurs there are no simple answers that are universally true of all types. Were dinosaurs warm-blooded? Were dinosaurs capable of bearing live offspring? Were dinosaurs the ancestors of birds? Were dinosaurs intelligent? Because of the dinosaurs' great variation, reflected in their two-order classification, the answers to such broad questions about dinosaurs are almost always: some were, some were not.

The two orders of dinosaurs are established on the basis of the arrangement of bones in the

A DINOSAUR FAMILY TREE

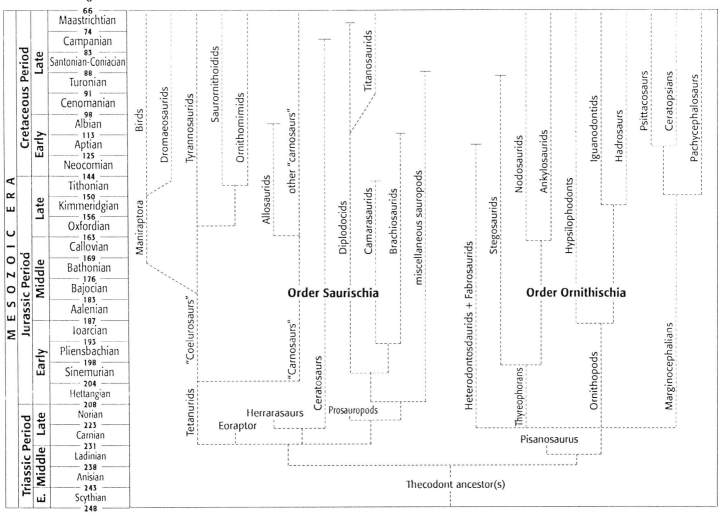

Figure 2-3. The relationships and time range of the groups of Utah dinosaurs. This family tree is not complete, for it emphasizes those dinosaurs that existed, or are likely to have existed, in Utah. A complete phylogeny, or family tree which represents all known dinosaurs, would require much more space.

pelvis. In the reptilian pelvis, there are three large bones: the blade-like ilium, the down-and-backward-projecting ischium, and the pubis, positioned in front of the ischium and below the ilium (Figure 2-2). In one order of dinosaurs, the Saurischia, these three bones diverge from each other in a triradiate form, with the pubis extending down and forward from the center of the pelvis. In the Ornithischia, the pubis is positioned more or less parallel to the ischium and thus projects backward and down from the hip socket. In many ornithischian dinosaurs, the pubis has a forward-projecting prong that protrudes beneath the anterior (front) portion of the ilium.

These two orders of dinosaurs were named and defined in 1888 by H.G. Seeley because the construction of the pelvis of various dinosaurs is similar to either the modern lizards (saurischians) or to the living birds (ornithischians). We suspect now that some dinosaurs are very closely related to birds; in fact, the ancestors of the birds probably were early dinosaurs. Confusingly, though, these bird ancestors were members of the order Saurischia, not the Ornithischia, as we might expect from the names alone. It appears that the avian (bird) style of pelvic design evolved at least twice—once in the ornithischian dinosaurs and again among the true birds as they developed from their saurischian dinosaur ancestors. The dinosaur-bird connection will be examined in a little more detail later in this chapter.

Both the Saurischia and the Ornithischia are diverse orders. Each of these two great dinosaur groups consists of scores of different types. The orders are so varied that paleontologists have subdivided each into a number of suborders. The suborders have, in turn, been divided into infraorders, superfamilies, and families. At these lower levels of classification, there is still no universal agreement on how best to define the various subgroupings and rank the taxonomic categories. The following summary represents a consensus view among most paleontologists and emphasizes those groups of dinosaurs that are important in Utah. Other classification schemes have been proposed and might be favored by some scientists. Classifications are not static and unchanging; they evolve continuously as more is learned about the diversity of dinosaurs and as scientific knowledge of their anatomy increases. Classification schemes, especially those for prehistoric creatures, are always somewhat subjective and never completely adequate. This should not be surprising given the imperfections and limitations of our basic data, the fossils themselves. For reference, the major groups of dinosaurs discussed below, along with their approximate range in time, are summarized in Figure 2-3.

Saurischian Dinosaurs

Among the Saurischia, two suborders have been established: the Theropoda and the Sauropodomorpha. The Theropoda, or theropods, were all bipedal carnivores such as *Tyrannosaurus* and *Allosaurus*, the state fossil of Utah. However, not all theropods were as large and fearsome as these giants. The twenty-pound *Compsognathus*, one of the smallest dinosaurs known, also belongs to this group. On the basis of the details of the skull, teeth, vertebral column, limbs, and feet, the theropods in turn have been subdivided in two

groups: the Ceratosauria and the Tetanurae. The Ceratosauria include the earliest and most primitive of the theropods and are typified by such dinosaurs as *Dilophosaurus* (of *Jurassic Park* fame), *Coelophysis*, one of the earliest dinosaurs from North America, and Utah's own *Ceratosaurus*, the namesake for the group.

The Tetanurae are the later, more highly specialized theropods and include a great variety of bipedal carnivores. Several families have been established among the tetanurine theropods; they include the Allosauridae (*Allosaurus* and close relatives), the Tryrannosauridae (*Tyrannosaurus, Albertosaurus*, and others), the Dromaeosauridae (small and swift predators with large slicing claws on the hind feet), the Ornithomimidae (medium-sized, mostly toothless, birdlike carnivores), and several others less common in Utah.

The Sauropodomorpha, or sauropods, were large quadrupedal, herbivorous saurischians. Perhaps the most familiar of the great sauropods is *Apatosaurus*, commonly (though inaccurately) known as *Brontosaurus*. Weighing in at over 50 tons for the largest types, the sauropods included the largest land animals to ever live on the earth. Most of the sauropods had a very small head supported on a long neck, a massive body, and a long tail. To support the immense weight of the animal, the limbs of sauropod dinosaurs were designed to function like massive columns positioned vertically beneath the body. The bones of the feet were thick and robust, splayed out to support a nearly circular pad of shock-absorbing cartilage, much like the foot of an elephant. With so much mass to sustain, paleontologists have long marveled over the small heads and relatively simple dentition (teeth) of the sauropods, which seem to be inadequate for processing the large amounts of plant food they would have required. As will be seen, however, the sauropods probably had accessory masticating organs or elaborate digestive pathways that enabled them to consume and process great amounts of plant food.

The suborder Sauropodomorpha is subdivided into at least five families. Among Utah's sauropods, the three most important families are the Brachiosauridae (brachiosaurids), the Camarasauridae (camarasaurids), and the Diplodocidae (diplodocids). A fourth group, the Titanosauridae, is also present in the late Cretaceous Period, but this family is much less common in Utah than are the other three.

The brachiosaurids are typified by *Brachiosaurus*, the namesake for the group, which had longer forelimbs than hindlimbs. The humerus (upper forelimb bone) was as long as (or sometimes longer than) the femur (thigh bone) in brachiosaurids, raising the animal's shoulders above its hips. This unique characteristic gave the brachiosaurids a giraffe-like posture. The tails of brachiosaurids were relatively short and thick compared to those of other groups of sauropods. The brachiosaurids were the largest of all dinosaurs; included in this group was the enormous *Ultrasaurus*, which may have weighed up to 60 tons.

The camarasaurids were modest-sized sauropods, with overall body length ranging from 40–60 feet. The most distinctive characteristic of the camarsaurids was their blunt, bulldog-like snout, with the nostrils placed high on the forehead, above the eyes. The teeth of the camarasaurids were thick, broad, and gently curved into a spoon-like shape. Camarasaurids had relatively short and muscular necks, compared to other sauropod dinosaurs. The forelimbs of the camarsaurids were slightly shorter than the hindlimbs.

The diplodocid sauropods had distinctive long and slender skulls, with simple peg-like teeth. The nostrils of diplodocids were positioned on top of the head, just a little forward of the eyes. The diplodocids were lightly built and slender sauropods, with extremely long necks and tails. The neck of the largest *Diplodocus* individuals, for example, was nearly 35 feet long and was constructed from fifteen individual vertebrae. The tails of the diplodocids were extremely long, con-

sisting of as many as eighty vertebrae, and gradually tapered to a slender, whip-like tip. The diplodocids were the longest of all the great sauropods; but, because of their slender physique, they were not the heaviest. There were many different kinds of diplodocid sauropods, including *Diplodocus*, *Apatosaurus*, *Barosaurus*, *Mammenchisaurus* (from China), *Seismosaurus*, and *Dystylosaurus*.

The Titanosauridae, represented in Utah by *Alamosaurus* from the late Cretaceous Period, is a poorly known family consisting of only three genera that are reasonably well represented in the fossil record. The titanosaurids were medium- to large-sized sauropods, ranging in length from about 35–65 feet. One of the most distinctive aspects of the titanosaurids is their body armor, composed of small circular nodes of bone in the skin. The armored skin is only known in *Saltosaurus*, but it may have been present in other genera of this family. The titanosaurids also had very distinctive tail vertebrae, featuring a hollow cavity on the front end and a convex "ball" on the rear surface.

The earliest dinosaurs known from the fossil record were saurischians. They were relatively small, but otherwise they were similar to the theropods in that they had a bipedal stance and were carnivores. As the theropods evolved steadily throughout the Mesozoic Era, the ceratosaurs and various tetanurines emerged through the development or evolution of numerous specialized adaptations that were superimposed on the basic body structure of their ancestors.

The sauropods represent a radical departure from this basic design. The herbivorous diet and quadrupedal posture of the sauropods occurred in response to their exploitation of a new ecological opportunity: that of a large terrestrial browser. Taking full advantage of the abundant plant food available in the lush Mesozoic forests required some important changes of the basic saurischian anatomy. A larger and more complex digestive system was required to process plant fodder, because it contains durable organic compounds such as cellulose and lignin—compounds so tough as to be nearly indigestible. In comparison to meat and other animal tissues, vegetation is also a lower-quality food, yielding less energy per pound. This also requires modifications of the teeth, body, and digestive system to allow for the adequate processing of a great quantity of plant food. In spite of the radical design changes that were necessary, any dinosaur that could develop adaptations to become a plant eater, or herbivore, would have enjoyed a great advantage in the early Mesozoic Era—there was, at that time, little competition for the plant food in the early Mesozoic forests. Thus, processes of natural selection that facilitated plant eating gradually produced the sauropod modification of the original dinosaur body plan.

There is one primitive group of dinosaurs, restricted to the early Mesozoic, that seems to represent the transition from the swift carnivorous theropods to the lumbering herbivorous sauropods. This group is known as the prosauropods, regarded by most paleontologists as the basal group (or infraorder) of the suborder Sauropodomorpha. The earliest prosauropods were small and bipedal; however, as new forms developed during the late Triassic and early Jurassic periods, they become more fully quadrupedal. The overall build of most prosauropods is similar to the sauropods, but they were much smaller and less bulky. Two of largest prosauropods, *Riojasaurus* and *Plateosaurus*, were only 34 feet and 25 feet long, respectively. Other prosauropods were only about 10 to 15 feet long. The teeth of prosauropods are generally spatulate in form and have serrated edges that would have been well suited for shredding plant food.

It is certainly tempting to view the prosauropods as the ancestor to the later sauropods, but this would probably be incorrect. The prosauropods have only four functional toes in their hind feet; the fifth digit is greatly reduced and nonfunctional. True sauropods retain all five toes in their hind feet. It is unlikely that the fifth toes on the hind feet would have "reemerged" in the sauropods after it was reduced in their ancestors. Thus, the prosauropods are probably not the evolutionary progenitors of the later sauropods; instead, these two groups are more likely descended from a common, albeit unknown, theropod-like ancestor. In any case, the prosauropods do represent the transition from bipedal, carnivorous saurischians to quadrupedal herbivores of the same order.

Ornithischian Dinosaurs

The ornithischian dinosaurs (order Ornithischia) consist of an amazingly varied assemblage of exclusively herbivorous types. The ornithischians came in all sizes, including armored and unadorned varieties, quadrupeds and bipeds, swift runners and cumbersome plodders. In fact, if a random sample of live ornithischian dinosaurs could be viewed, one would behold an array so heterogeneous that it might be questioned why paleontologists assign all of them to a single order. It is the structure of the pelvis that primarily unites all the ornithischians. In all of these dinosaurs, the pubis does not project forward and down as it does in the saurischians; instead, it lies parallel to the ischium, so that it extends from the region of the acetabulum (hip socket) down and to the rear. In some of the later ornithischians, most notably the horned ceratopsians (for example, *Triceratops*) and the armored ankylosaurs, the pubis is shortened and develops a forward-projecting prong, but the basic ornithischian pattern is still discernible.

This arrangement of bones in the ornithischian pelvis is similar to the pattern of modern birds, although most birds possess a highly modified pelvis due to their adaptations for flight. It should be remembered, however, that the ornithischian dinosaurs are not closely related to birds, in spite of the name given to the order. The similarities in pelvic design between the modern birds and the ornithischian dinosaurs appear to have arisen from two independent evolutionary events. The name Ornithischia has fostered a common misconception that these dinosaurs are the progenitors of the birds. It bears repeating, then, that the ancestors of the birds probably developed with the earliest saurischian theropods and not with any of the ornithischians.

Aside from the distinctive structure of the pelvis, the entire group of ornithischians share a few other general characteristics that seem to be related to their herbivorous diets. The rows of teeth in the jaws of all ornithischian dinosaurs are inset, to one degree or another, toward the center of the mouth. This inward orientation of the tooth rows gives the ornithischian a pronounced recess, or "pocket," in the cheek region. The cheek pocket probably served as a food pouch and was used to hold masses of vegetation while it was being chewed. It is possible to imagine what a typical ornithischian dinosaur such as one of the "duckbill" types might have looked like when feeding—leaves stuffed into the bulging cheek pouches, the snout wrinkling with each stroke of the jaws, the sounds of leaves being crushed or sheared.

Many ornithischians also possessed a wicker-like network of bony rods (ossified tendons) laced along the backbone and the tail. These rods helped to stiffen the tail and brace the backbone. Most ornithischian dinosaurs thus had stiff tails that helped to counterbalance and/or stabilize them while they were running, walking, or feeding.

As a further adaptation for plant eating, the ornithischian dinosaurs all possessed a unique bone at the tip of the lower jaw, the predentary. The predentary supported a toothless bill, which looked in many forms like an upside-down hoof, that was used to chop or pluck vegetation. Furthermore, the joints between the tooth-bearing bones of the upper jaw were usually rather loose in ornithischians, allowing their jaws to pivot inward and outward as they chewed. This move-

ment permitted the lateral movement of the upper and lower tooth surfaces past each other. Such movement would have been extremely efficient in grinding, shredding, and pulverizing plant matter. Even the restructuring of the ornithischian pelvis can be regarded as an adaptation to herbivory. With the forward-pointing pubis folded back against the ischium, more space was available to house the larger digestive mass required for processing plant food. Thus, most of the features that distinguish the Ornithischia from the Saurischia are related to the strictly plant-eating habits of the former.

The Ornithischia is a much more diverse order than the Saurischia; the subdivision of this group of dinosaurs therefore has been the subject of lengthy debate among paleontologists. Though some controversy still persists, four or five major groups within the Ornithischia are now regarded as suborders or infraorders. The Thyreophora ("shield bearers"), for example, is a subdivision of the ornithischian dinosaurs that includes the quadrupedal armored types. The Thyreophora is, in turn, composed of two groups possessing different types of armor: 1) the Stegosauria, with large plates positioned vertically along the back and spikes located mostly on the tail; and 2) the Ankylosauria, with heavy, flat-lying plates of bone covering much of the body surface. Some of the ankylosaurs were so thoroughly armored that even their eyelids were protected by solid bone.

The Ornithopoda ("bird foot") is a large subdivision of the Ornithischia that includes most of the bipedal varieties. The most familiar of the ornithopods are the "duckbill" dinosaurs, with their characteristically broadened snouts. There are many kinds of ornithopods, including some with elaborate bony crests on the head (for example, the "snorkel-crested" *Parasaurolophus*), relatively primitive types such as Utah's *Camptosaurus* and *Tenontosaurus*, and even some small varieties such as *Dryosaurus*, which is also known from Utah localities. While the ornithopods are most often described as bipedal dinosaurs, the fingers of many of them bore small hoof-like claws, suggesting that at least occasionally they supported themselves in a quadrupedal posture.

In the Cretaceous Period, the Ceratopsia ("horn-face") became one of the most abundant and diverse groups of ornithischian dinosaurs ever. The ceratopsians are typified by their most familiar representative, *Triceratops*, which had three prominent horns and an enormous bony frill extending backward from the posterior edge of the skull. The ceratopsians also had a well-developed "beak" used to chop and cut tough, low-growing vegetation. Ceratopsian dinosaurs have left mostly fragmentary remains in the late Cretaceous strata of Utah, but their fossils are extremely abundant in rocks of this age in Montana, Canada, and Asia. Ceratopsian bone beds in those places provide good evidence that these dinosaurs traveled across the ancient landscape in gigantic herds.

The Pachycephalosauria ("thick-headed reptiles") is a rather bizarre group of ornithischian dinosaurs characterized by dome-like heads, the result of the great thickening of the bones forming the roof of the skull. Pachycephalosaurs also had blunt nodes or spikes around the edges of the their skulls, creating an even more peculiar appearance. Pachycephalosaurs are not common in Utah, but they have been identified in abundance from Montana, Wyoming, Canada, and elsewhere. Because they shared an expanded and decorated margin of the skull with the ceratopsians, the pachycephalosaurs are sometimes united with the horned dinosaurs in a group known as the Marginocephalia.

Dinosaur Genera and Species

Like all other organisms, living and extinct, the dinosaurs are placed into species and genera at the lower levels of classification. Paleontologists generally refer to various dinosaurs by identifying only these two categories, even though an ani-

mal's complete pedigree would include all the levels of classification. Thus, *Stegosaurus stenops* is a ornithischian dinosaur (of the group Thyreophora) that belongs to the genus *Stegosaurus* and the species *stenops*. By convention, the genus name is always listed first and capitalized, while the species name follows in lower case. Both genus and species names are usually italicized or underlined to emphasize that they are formal categories of classification with specific definitions. In discussing dinosaurs, terms such as "tyrannosaurs" or "brachiosaurids" are often used to describe a general type or group of dinosaurs that may represent a specific taxonomic category (such as a family) or might designate a certain group of similar dinosaurs, without reference to a formal category of classification. In instances of such informal use of names, the terms are not capitalized or italicized.

At the species level, in both paleontology and biology, scientists group together organisms that are so similar that reproduction between any two individuals of opposite sexes would be possible. Different species of the same genus cannot interbreed, even though they may look quite similar to us. Confirming reproductive viability, and therefore species validity, is a relatively easy task for a biologist studying modern animals. We know, for example, that mountain lions (*Felis concolor*) cannot successfully mate with house cats (*Felis domesticus*); so the two felines are placed in separate species, although they belong to the same genus because they are otherwise very similar to each other. For dinosaurs, recognizing valid species is a bit more conjectural. There is no way to be absolutely certain that *Stegosaurus stenops* (abbreviated *S. stenops*) could not have interbred with *S. armatus*. In addition, the limitations of the fossil evidence prevent us from knowing to what degree the soft tissues of *S. stenops* and *S. armatus* were similar or different. Therefore, species in paleontology are established on the basis of much less complete information than the biologist uses to recognize groups of very closely related organisms in the modern world. Dinosaur species are established on the basis of the similarity of skeletal features represented by preserved bones and teeth, and, as has been noted, this aspect of dinosaurs is rarely known in its entirety.

The discussions that follow will concentrate on the various genera of dinosaurs. Some genera include several species, while others only have one. Because of the fragmentary nature of the fossil record, paleontologists must often attempt to identify dinosaur species and genera on the basis of very little and/or poorly preserved material. Consequently, it is not surprising that some dinosaur species are controversial and that debates persist about which dinosaur species are valid and which are not. Sometimes new discoveries cause scientists to reassign a species to a new genus, abandon some species that prove to be invalid, or otherwise restructure an animal's classification to accommodate new information. This aspect of dinosaur classification will always exist, and there will always be some uncertainty about the lower levels of taxonomy.

It may be that many of our named dinosaur species, presently numbering over 800, are invalid because they actually represent, for example, males and females or different growth stages (juveniles or adults) of the same species. In addition, some species of dinosaurs are based on meager fossil information (a single tooth fragment, for example) and these may be invalidated at a later time by the discovery of more complete skeletons. Another factor that contributes to our confusion is that without the entire population available for study, we can never be absolutely certain what the range in variation *within a species* was. Without this information, determining the degree of similarity required for different fossils to be assigned to a single species is always a matter of individual judgment and interpretation. Though paleontologists are currently making great progress in recognizing the range of variation within some

dinosaur species (see Carpenter and Currie, 1990), the limitations, or scrappiness, of the fossil record will never allow scientists to know it all.

These uncertainties generally become less severe as we ascend the hierarchy of classification from the species level to the genus, to the family, and so on. This is another reason for concentrating on the genus level in this study of Utah dinosaurs. In so doing, at least some of the confusion and uncertainty that will always exist at the species level can be avoided. Currently, approximately 270 genera of dinosaurs have been established by paleontologists. This number is subject to change in the future, as some genera will be combined or abandoned while new genera are established to accommodate new discoveries.

Biology of the Dinosaurs: A Brief Review

A brief comparison between books on dinosaurs published today and twenty-five years ago reveals some radical differences in our perceptions of these ancient reptiles. This highly publicized "dinosaur revolution" reflects not just new dinosaur discoveries made over the past two or three decades but also a shift in the way paleontologists view dinosaurs and in the methods they use to analyze dinosaur relationships and study the original fossils. Today, researchers can study the chemistry and structure of dinosaur bones in ways that paleontologists one hundred years ago could never have imagined. They can now apply certain aspects of medical technology such as CT (Computed Tomography) imaging to explore structures in dinosaur fossils that were never revealed to earlier generations of scientists. Soon, researchers may be able to sequence some of the genetic code of dinosaurs from the DNA that might be preserved in their fossils, although they cannot at present decipher the code as was done in the *Jurassic Park* motion picture. In addition, the modern construction of dinosaur family trees employs a method known as cladistic analysis, which involves less guesswork and results in more testable patterns of proposed relationships than early methods based on gross anatomical similarities alone. While it is beyond the scope of this book to fully explore each of these new techniques and discoveries, they have provided the impetus for the current paradigm or model of dinosaur biology.

The new view of dinosaurs completely reverses the dated perceptions of them as sluggish and stupid, biologically inefficient, and evolutionary dead ends. We now have good evidence that dinosaurs were mostly very active and agile creatures, that at least some forms were gregarious and social, and that many were probably warm-blooded (endothermic), with some form of insulation (feathers, or hair-like modified scales). Some dinosaurs appear to have been relatively intelligent as well. When thinking of dinosaur biology, it is important to remember that the animals we call "dinosaurs" represent an incredibly diverse array, classified into two different orders. Accordingly, there are very few simple statements that would be entirely true or untrue of *all* dinosaurs. With this in mind, let's briefly examine a few such questions.

Were dinosaurs warm-blooded like mammals and birds?

This is an important question because biologists recognize a fundamental metabolic dichotomy among modern animals: the cold-blooded "lower" vertebrates (fish, amphibians, and reptiles) and the warm-blooded "higher" vertebrates (birds and mammals). Note that the groups of animals in these two categories are *classes*; class Aves and class Mammalia constitute the higher vertebrates, while the classes Osteichthyes (bony fish), Chondrichthyes (cartilaginous fish), Amphibia, and Reptilia make up the lower vertebrates. Therefore, the question is really: Were dinosaurs higher or lower vertebrates?

Traditionally, because dinosaurs were classified as reptiles, they were placed with the lower vertebrates and assumed to have been cold-blooded, or ectothermic. This, in turn, implied that dinosaurs were relatively slow and inefficient in terms of locomotion. It also suggested that dinosaurs were less active than birds or mammals and that they were restricted to warm habitats due to their inability to maintain a relatively high and constant body temperature.

On the contrary, there are presently many pieces of evidence that suggest that at least some dinosaurs had metabolic rates comparable to birds and mammals and were probably just as efficient in locomotion, feeding, and reproduction as are any of the higher vertebrates. The overall architecture of dinosaur skeletons, particularly of the theropods and small ornithopods, features a design built for speed and agility. This is seen in the bracing of the tail, the structure of limbs and feet, and in the muscle attachment scars on the bones of the hind limbs and pelvis. The microstructure (histology) of fossil bones belonging to these groups of dinosaurs is more similar to modern endothermic animals than to cold-blooded reptiles. Some small dinosaurs appear to have had feathers or feather-like scales that were probably used for insulation, because the animals' skeletal structure suggests that they could not fly. Why should such dinosaurs have insulation if they did not possess an endothermic metabolism? Furthermore, recent discoveries of dinosaur fossils in Alaska and Antarctica suggest that dinosaurs had a pole-to-pole distribution during the Mesozoic Era. Such global distribution, even when corrected for the climate and geography of the Mesozoic Era, demonstrates that dinosaurs could thrive under conditions that would greatly restrict the distribution and abundance of ectothermic animals.

The latest stir in the dinosaur ectothermy-endothermy debate is the controversy over turbinate bones. Turbinate bones are paper-thin scrolls of bone that are packed into the nasal cavity of all terrestrial vertebrate animals. The function and structure of the intricately folded mass of turbinate bones is twofold. First, the posterior bones usually support thin layers of tissue laced with nerves that respond to aromatic molecules carried in the air; they serve to enhance the sense of smelling and are called olfactory turbinates. Nearly all land-living animals have olfactory turbinates; in those with a keen sense of smell, such as dogs, the turbinates are remarkably well developed. In addition, other turbinate bones (usually those forward of, or anterior to, the olfactory turbinates) support moist tissue that alternately warms and cools the air passing into and out of the lungs. This warming and cooling helps control the moisture loss associated with high breathing rates. These bones are known as the respiratory turbinates.

While most creatures have olfactory turbinates, it is a simple empirical observation that only the modern endotherms have respiratory turbinate bones in the nasal cavity. In modern birds and mammals (except for those that live in water), the respiratory turbinates are essential, because without them the animals' high rates of breathing would lead to an excessive, even lethal, loss of moisture. Therefore, the presence or absence of turbinate bones in dinosaurs would seem to be a good way to determine whether they were endothermic. If dinosaurs have such bones, they were probably warm-blooded with high rates of respiration; if not, the dinosaurs were probably not endothermic, at least not to the same degree that modern birds and mammals are.

Although many well-preserved dinosaur skulls have been examined (Ruben and others, 1995), no respiratory turbinates have ever been observed in the nasal cavity. However, does this mean that dinosaurs were ectothermic, or cold-blooded? Not exactly, because the thin and delicate turbinates are rarely preserved, even in the skulls of extinct mammals. The scrolls of turbinate bones are so fragile that they are easily destroyed or damaged beyond recognition during the process of fossilization.

Dinosaurs may have had turbinate bones, but paleontologists haven't yet found a skull well enough preserved to reveal them. Using CT-scan technology on a well-preserved skull of a "duck-bill" dinosaur, one researcher (Horner, 1995) found evidence of the attachment of olfactory and respiratory turbinate bones to the walls of the nasal chamber but did not find the turbinate bones themselves. Thus, the issue of turbinate bones in dinosaurs is still unsettled; more well-preserved dinosaur skulls must be carefully examined before scientists can prove or disprove their existence. In summary, there is no single piece of evidence that conclusively proves that dinosaurs were warm-blooded; but, taken as a whole, the considerations outlined above suggest strongly that some dinosaurs may have had an endothermic metabolism.

However, it appears that the larger dinosaurs such as the sauropods would have had great difficulty preventing lethal overheating during periods of activity if they were, in fact, endothermic. It has recently been proposed that some larger dinosaurs may have had a sort of dual-mode metabolism; they may have been able to switch between endothermy when at rest (when internal heat would be needed) and ectothermy during periods of strenuous activity (when internal heat was not needed). We should also acknowledge the possibility of dinosaurs possessing a unique sort of metabolism somewhere between the endothermy of today's mammals and the ectothermy of lizards and snakes. Consider, for example, the plates of *Stegosaurus*. If these plates functioned, as has been suggested, as heat-dissipating and heat-absorbing devices, then *Stegosaurus* may have been able to maintain a relatively high and constant body temperature without necessarily being dependant on its internal metabolism to do so. Even though birds and mammals maintain their body temperatures with high metabolic rates, there may have been other ways for dinosaurs to achieve endothermy. There was perhaps more than one way to heat (and cool) a dinosaur.

In summary, a good case can be made that at least some dinosaurs were probably endothermic. These would include the smaller theropods, the ornithopods, the ceratopsians, and perhaps others. The larger dinosaurs, such as sauropods, may not have been truly endothermic, while other groups such as stegosaurs and ankylosaurs may have been homeothermic, maintaining a constant body temperature but without high metabolic rates. Therefore, to the question, "are dinosaurs 'higher' vertebrates with an active metabolism like birds and mammals?" our only answer for such a varied group of organisms as dinosaurs can be that some were, some were not. What is true about dinosaur metabolism is that there is no evidence that dinosaurs were uniformly ectothermic, as are all living members of the class Reptilia. The long-standing assumption of ectothermy in dinosaurs probably simply followed their original placement in the class Reptilia, the reasoning being: All living reptiles are ectothermic,…dinosaurs are reptiles,…thus, dinosaurs must have been cold-blooded. The growing acceptance of the notion of endothermy for at least some dinosaurs leads to another, more intriguing, question: were dinosaurs, then, really reptiles? The key to answering this question comes in the form of the next element of the new view of dinosaurs.

Were dinosaurs evolutionary dead-ends?

It has long been assumed that the dinosaurs died out about 65 million years ago, at the end of the Cretaceous Period, the last of the Mesozoic periods. No indisputable trace of dinosaur fossils has ever been recovered from rocks younger than latest Cretaceous. Their abrupt extinction, coupled with their dissimilarity to any living organism, led to the traditional view of dinosaurs as obsolete and antiquated relics of an ancient

world. In fact, the very term "dinosaur" is often used to describe anything old and outdated, such as the computer I am using to write these words.

The lack of any living representatives of the orders Ornithischia and Saurischia seems to suggest that the dinosaurs were indeed biological novelties and evolutionary dead-ends, creatures that developed prior to the emergence of modern animals with "superior" biology such as birds and mammals. We assume that the mammalian and avian dominance in the modern world is a reflection of their greater success in adaptation, feeding, and reproduction. Over the past three decades, however, new information from the fossil record suggests that this view is false.

The ancestry of mammals can be traced all the way back to the Paleozoic Era, particularly the Permian Period, when "mammal-like" reptiles were among the most widespread of all terrestrial vertebrates. Typified by their most familiar representative *Dimetrodon* (which is often misrepresented as a dinosaur in toys and children's books), this large group of reptiles belongs to the subclass Synapsida. The term "mammal-like reptiles" describes the combination of mammalian and reptilian skeletal features observed in the skulls of the synapsids. For example, the skull of *Dimetrodon* has only a single temporal opening and the teeth are varied in size and shape. Both of these traits are typical of mammals. And yet this same animal possessed a basically reptilian pattern of skull bones and limb construction. The synapsids therefore represent a group of animals transitional between the true reptiles and the true mammals. The synapsids emerged from more primitive ancestors during the great reptilian explosion that occurred near the end of the Paleozoic Era.

The synapsids gave rise to a more advanced and even more mammal-like group of reptiles in the early Triassic Period: the therapsids. The therapsids became extremely diverse and abundant as Triassic time proceeded, eventually begetting such descendants as the theriodonts and ictidosaurians, which seem to be more reptile-like mammals

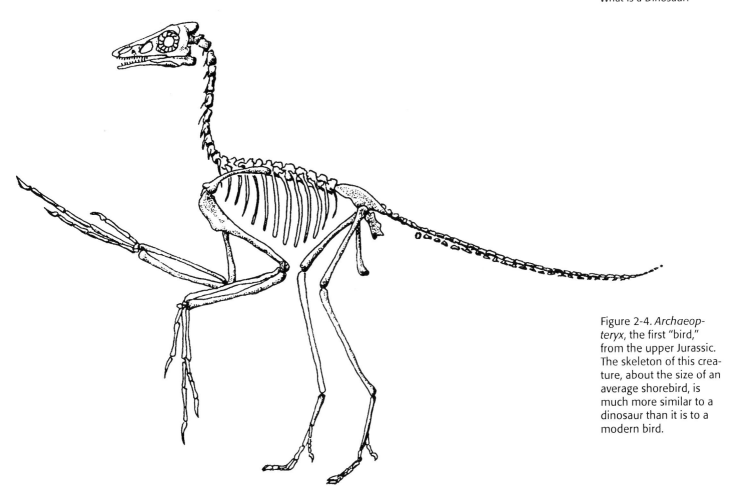

Figure 2-4. *Archaeopteryx*, the first "bird," from the upper Jurassic. The skeleton of this creature, about the size of an average shorebird, is much more similar to a dinosaur than it is to a modern bird.

than mammal-like reptiles. By the end of the Triassic Period or very early in the Jurassic at least five different orders of animals existed that are clearly mammalian in their overall characteristics (Figure 1-5F). While these early mammals were all small and rather primitive by today's standards, looking for the most part like rodents, they were nonetheless mammals and undoubtedly possessed the biological refinements that prompt us to consider mammals "higher" vertebrates. The earliest true mammals were probably endothermic, reproduced via internal fertilization and gestation, had advanced sensory organs, and were relatively "intelligent," with large brains.

While it is beyond the purpose of this book to review the finer details of the evolution of mammals, it is interesting to point out that dinosaurs developed and evolved not in the absence of mammals but in conjunction with them, outcompeting them in the ecological niches they came to dominate. If dinosaurs really were "lower" vertebrates, it is difficult indeed to understand why they restricted a group of "superior" organisms to the ecological backwaters of the world for more than 140 million years. Only when the dinosaurs vanished did the mammals manage to exploit the habitats and niches the great reptiles occupied for most of the Mesozoic Era. Perhaps, as has previously been suggested, the dinosaurs were not so primitive and not as biologically antiquated as has traditionally been thought.

However, what about the other group of higher, endothermic vertebrates, the birds? For over a century, we have known very little about the early history of the class Aves. Bird bones are usually very delicate and are very unlikely to experience fossilization. Consequently, paleontologists interested in reconstructing the evolutionary history of birds have historically had little to go on. However, new information from the fossil record, acquired during the past thirty years or so, is beginning to clarify the ancestry of the class Aves.

In 1861, the first fossils of the earliest bird were discovered in southern Germany. This fossil, named *Archaeopteryx* ("ancient wing"), was preserved in exquisite detail, including the fine imprints of feathers along the forelimbs and tail. The designation of *Archaeopteryx* as the "first bird" was based primarily on the presence of feathers and a few other birdlike characteristics of its skeleton. As additional specimens of *Archaeopteryx* came to light, it became more obvious that this animal was much more reptilian than it was avian. With its long bony tail, sharp teeth, diminutive breastbone, clawed fingers, and legs designed for running, *Archaeopteryx* (Figure 2-4) resembled what was basically a small, feathered dinosaur. This early "bird" is, in fact, a "dino-bird" and suggests that it is among Mesozoic reptiles that the ancestors of the birds originated.

As a result of more recent excavations, the list of dino-birds has grown considerably since the discovery of *Archaeopteryx*. From the late Jurassic on through the Cretaceous Period, we now know of many other birdlike creatures including *Mononykus*, a large ostrich-like dino-bird, the swimming predator *Hesperornis* ("yesterday's bird"), and the rooster-like *Patagopteryx* from South America. The case for feathered dinosaurs received additional support in late 1996 when scientists attending a gathering of paleontologists in New York revealed photographs of what appears to be a mane of downy feathers preserved on a small early Cretaceous dinosaur from China. After it is studied in detail, this specimen may shed additional light on the history of birds. More recently, in the spring of 1997, a remarkably birdlike

theropod was reported from the late Cretaceous strata of South America (Novas and Puerta, 1997). This small dinosaur, named *Unenlagia comahuensis,* was similar to *Archaeopteryx* in the hind limbs and pelvis but folded its forelimbs against its body in a fashion almost identical to that of modern birds. *Unenlagia* also had a unique shoulder joint that allowed the forceful lifting of the arms in a manner similar to the way birds flap their wings during flight. Although the evolutionary chain leading from *Archaeopteryx* to modern birds is still incomplete, enough of its individual links have been discovered to strongly suggest that the origin of the birds and the early history of the dinosaurs are very closely intertwined.

The dinosaur-bird nexus is evident within the reptilian realm as well. Some of the smaller theropod dinosaurs, particularly those that emerged in the late Cretaceous Period, are remarkably birdlike in their overall appearance and anatomical structure. The family Ornithomimidae includes, along with its namesake genus *Ornithomimus* ("bird mimicker"), such forms as *Struthiomimus* ("ostrich mimicker"), *Gallimimus* (the famous flocking "chicken mimickers" of *Jurassic Park*), and *Avimimus* ("bird mimicker"). The lightly built skeletons and the hind limb and foot structure of the ornithomimids is amazingly similar to that of the modern ground birds. Birdlike aspects are even noted among other theropods classified outside the family Ornithomimidae. Examples include *Saurornithoides* ("birdlike reptile") and *Ornitholestes* ("bird thief").

Thus, as we trace the evolution of birds backward in time, they exhibit a general trend toward a more reptilian or dinosaurian form with increasing age. And at least some dinosaurs, most notably the small theropods, became more birdlike as the Mesozoic Era drew to a close. The big question then becomes: "What, exactly, is the relationship between birds and dinosaurs?" Unfortunately, the precise answer must await the discovery of more fossils of both groups, because there are still many gaps in our current understanding of the ancestries of the two lineages. However, it seems highly probable that there is a very close connection between the emergence of the birds and the proliferation of the dinosaurs. We know that the ornithomimids cannot be the ancestors of the birds because *Archaeopteryx*, along with its more birdlike descendants, appears in the fossil record tens of millions of years *before* the bird-mimicking dinosaurs. However, it is plausible that dinosaurs and birds evolved from a common ancestor earlier in the Mesozoic Era.

Natural selection evidently so strongly favored the development of avian features (endothermy, agility, flight, intelligence) that two separate but closely related lineages of reptiles followed that evolutionary path. One became the modern birds, the other produced the ornithomimid dinosaurs. Recall that another group of reptiles, the order Pterosauria, also adapted aerial abilities in the Mesozoic; however, these reptiles are not similar to either birds or dinosaurs in the details of their anatomy. The pterosaurs may have responded to the same evolutionary pressures that directed the development of birds and birdlike dinosaurs, but they are less closely related to either group than birds and dinosaurs are to each other.

Most paleontologists agree that when the earliest ancestor of the birds is discovered, it may well turn out to be very closely related to the early saurischian dinosaurs. In other words, birds and dinosaurs may have originated from the same common ancestor. Both groups have modified the ancestral skeletal architecture in their own ways but retain many overall similarities inherited from their common progenitor. The birdlike dinosaurs and true birds evolved alongside one another during most of the Mesozoic, sharing a more or less parallel evolutionary history. One should be careful to avoid misinterpreting that statement to envision some close relationship between, for example, the sauropods or the ceratop-

sians and today's robins. Remember, dinosaurs were a extraordinarily diverse assemblage of reptiles. The birds are probably closely related to some, but not to all, of the dinosaurs. The best candidates for recognition as "dino-birds" would be the small, advanced theropods. It is interesting in that regard to observe the term "raptor," formerly reserved for hawks, eagles, and other birds of prey, becoming more commonly applied to the dromaeosaurids (small, swift theropods) as well. It is fitting in more ways than one.

If we accept that there is a strong historical link between birds and dinosaurs, then should we reassess our notions of "higher" vertebrates? Do the dinosaurs really belong in the class Reptilia, which was created for quite unbirdlike creatures such as snakes, lizards, and turtles? Are dinosaurs really reptiles? Should they not, in view of the new interpretations of their biology and evolutionary relationships, be more closely allied to the "higher" vertebrates such as birds and mammals? Such questions have provoked some paleontologists to suggest that dinosaurs deserve their own class, separate from the reptiles of today's world. The class Dinosauria has not been formally established, but many scientists are already using the term to acknowledge the unique nature of dinosaurs with respect to other reptiles. There is general agreement now that the closest living relative of the dinosaurs is not any of the modern reptiles but instead is found among the birds.

Someday it is likely that scientists will embrace a new formal class Dinosauria, which would consist of the two orders of dinosaurs along with a third order or subclass, the Aves. Such a classification would recognize the close kinship between birds and dinosaurs, would acknowledge the true biological nature of dinosaurs, and would forever separate them conceptually from turtles, snakes, and lizards. At present, all we can do is to understand that dinosaurs technically belong to the class Reptilia, but know that they were very special reptiles.

Therefore, while it is true that there are no

living dinosaurs, it might not be completely accurate to view them as evolutionary dead-ends. The dinosaurian imprimatur remains firmly stamped in today's fauna within the class Aves—the birds. The next time you see a pheasant run across a field, or watch a rhea strut around at the local zoo, or marvel at the speed of a roadrunner along the edge of a desert highway, you might think of them as latter-day dinosaurs. In a very real sense, that's probably just what they are.

THE TRIASSIC PERIOD, the earliest portion of the Mesozoic Era, began about 248 million years ago. It was one of the most interesting phases in the history of the planet, a time of great change in land, life, and climate. At the beginning of the Triassic, the supercontinent Pangaea had become fully assembled via the joining of smaller land masses during the preceding Paleozoic Era. This gigantic continent was short-lived; by the end of the Triassic it began to show signs of its eventual fragmentation. The core of modern North America began to separate from the rest of Pangaea along an enormous rift that passed between Greenland and Norway, extended south along the modern Atlantic coast (the Newark Rift), and curved west into the Gulf of Mexico region. The rift zone was a depressed region of active faulting and intense volcanic activity, much like the modern East African Rift that separates Kenya and Tanzania from the rest of Africa. It would take the remainder of the Mesozoic Era for North America to become fully detached from Pangaea as the modern Atlantic and Gulf of Mexico ocean basins developed. But the initial rumblings of this great supercontinental fragmentation began in the Triassic.

As the global geography began to change during the Triassic, the climate became modified as well. Early in the Triassic, Pangaea was dominated by a monsoonal climate, with wet intervals alternating with droughts (Dubiel and others, 1991). Later in the Triassic, the climate appears to have become drier throughout much of world. Thick layers of salt, formed through the evaporation of large bodies of seawater, and extensive dune deposits are both common indicators of increasing Triassic aridity in many parts of Pangaea. In addition, sedimentary rocks of this age are so commonly stained red by iron oxides that the Triassic is known as the "great age of red beds." The climatic significance of the red beds continues to be debated by geologists, but most believe that they indicate a warm, and probably dry, climate.

These changes in the geography and climate of the world stimulated some fascinating patterns of evolution among global flora and fauna during the Triassic Period. As noted in Chapter 1, the Triassic was the beginning of the great reptilian takeover on land and in the sea. The numerous Permo-Triassic extinctions had cleared many of the major ecologic niches in both the terrestrial and marine realms of their primary late Paleozoic occupants. On land, the reptiles were the principal beneficiaries of the evolutionary opportunities created by the extinctions. So many different groups of reptiles developed during the transition from Paleozoic to Mesozoic time that the Triassic assemblage of animals is a confusing and complex array. To complicate matters even more, some of the Triassic reptiles, such as the mammal-like therapsids, represent "holdovers" from the earlier late Paleozoic fauna. Included somewhere in that complex horde of reptiles were the ancestors of the dinosaurs, accompanied by many other specialized reptiles representing separate lineages. While it is impossible to fully review all the different groups of Triassic reptiles here, it is still useful to illustrate the reptilian diversity of time by briefly examining those forms represented by fossils found in western North America.

Phytosaur remains (Figure 3-5B) are one of the most common types of reptile fossils found in the Triassic rocks of the Southwest. These semiaquatic reptiles were predators that looked much like a modern crocodile and seem to have lived in or near rivers. With long pointed snouts and jaws lined with sharp conical teeth, the phytosaurs were probably voracious predators of fish and smaller reptiles living in the rivers they inhabited. The largest phytosaurs were nearly 20 feet long.

Aetosaurs (Figure 3-5C) were also crocodile-like in their general body plan, but these animals were herbivorous and possessed heavy plates of bony armor (scutes) along with prominent defensive spikes in the shoulder region and along the flanks. Some of the aetosaurs had blunt snouts, evidently for rooting through plant litter and soil, along with leaf-shaped teeth for shearing vegeta-

THREE

Dawn of the Utah Mesozoic

tion. These features suggest that they ate roots, low-growing shrubs, or aquatic plants growing in or along the banks of Triassic rivers.

The Rauisuchians include several types of carnivorous reptiles that were quadrupedal with more or less erect limbs; thus, they were better adapted for terrestrial locomotion than were the phytosaurs and aetosaurs. The largest rauisuchian in North America was *Postosuchus*, a 12-foot-long predator that probably weighed in at some 400 pounds (Figure 3-5G). The rauisuchians looked a bit like massive, long-legged alligators.

Dicynodonts (Figure 3-5D) were large plant-eating mammal-like reptiles (therapsids) that typically had paired tusks for rooting. The dicynodonts were squat and thick-bodied, with large heads tipped with a beak-like apparatus. Canadian paleontologist Dale Russell refers to the dicynodonts as "cowturtles" (Russell, 1989), and the name fittingly describes their general appearance and is also suggestive of their combination of reptilian and mammalian skeletal features. The therapsids also included some carnivorous forms, known as cynodonts, that had an overall dog-like appearance.

Rhynchosaurs are squat, rather pig-like herbivorous reptiles represented by *Paradapedon* (Figure 3-5E), one of the most common North American members of the group. The bones forming the snout of most rhynchosaurs curved over the lower jaw to form a prominent "overbite." This feature, coupled with small, peg-like teeth probably allowed the rhynchosaurs to root through soil and plant litter to find their food.

In addition to these extinct groups of reptiles, the earliest representatives of more familiar forms also emerged during the Triassic. Primitive members of the turtle, true crocodile, and lizard clans can all be found in rocks of Triassic age. The landscapes of the world were definitely filled with reptiles during the Triassic.

None of the groups of reptiles identified above are closely related to the dinosaurs. Sometime in the early Triassic, among the ongoing reptilian riot, a group of slender-legged, mostly quadrupedal carnivores emerged. This set of reptiles has traditionally been assigned to the group known as the "thecodonts." Paleontologists are becoming increasingly reluctant about using the term thecodont, however, because that category is not well defined and there is lingering uncertainty about its taxonomic validity. Whatever they represent (an order? a subclass? an unnatural array of unrelated types?), the animals we call thecodonts all seem to be better adapted for terrestrial locomotion than their contemporaries from the Triassic Period. With limbs positioned directly beneath the body and ankles and feet designed for swift walking or running, the thecodonts became extremely successful and varied, eventually developing carnivorous members that were, at least partially, bipedal. *Euparkeria*, for example, possessed reduced forelimbs that suggest that it was beginning to use its hind limbs as the main method of propulsion. This predator looked, for the most part, like a small carnivorous dinosaur. The thecodonts, at least those similar to *Euparkeria*, were probably close to the ancestors of the first dinosaurs.

No one knows for sure where or exactly when the first dinosaurs originated. There seems to be many candidates from South America for the "first dinosaur" award. *Staurikosaurus*, a 6-foot-long, bipedal predator from Brazil, seems to be on the threshold of the Dinosauria, because its pelvis has a small opening for the end of the femur and its hind limbs were evidently positioned vertically beneath the body. Its bones were recovered from rocks that are not precisely dated but seem to be between 235 and 225 million years old (middle Triassic age). However, *Staurikosaurus* is so primitive in other aspects of its skeleton that it cannot be confidently assigned to either the Ornithischia or the Saurischia. Other, perhaps slightly younger, South American reptiles are similarly dinosaur-like but are comparatively primitive. *Herrerasaurus* and *Eoraptor*, for example, are both extremely "dinosaurian" bipedal carnivores from the late Triassic Period of northwestern Argentina. Of the two, *Eoraptor* is more primitive and lacks some key features of the Dinosauria. *Herrerasaurus* is more typical of later theropods, but it is still primitive in comparison to the true theropod dinosaurs. To make matters even more intriguing, a contemporary from the same area, *Pisanosaurus*, is clearly related to the ornithischian dinosaurs. *Pisanosaurus* was unquestionably a plant eater, as evidenced by its well-worn simple teeth, but it did not have the fully developed dinosaurian type of ankle. Scientists continue to debate whether or not *Pisanosaurus* represents the oldest ornithischian dinosaur or something close to the ancestor of that group. The absolute age of these specimens is somewhat uncertain; most evidence suggests that they are around 228 million years old (Rogers and others, 1993). We can conclude that the age of dinosaurs was on the threshold of opening some 17 million years after the Triassic began. By that time, at least three groups of dinosaur-like creatures existed in South America. Thus, the first ancestral dinosaur must have originated from unknown thecodont ancestors even earlier in the Triassic.

In North America, the earliest dinosaurs appear at almost the same time that the *Pisanosaurus-Herrerasaurus-Eoraptor* assemblage emerged in Argentina. The Chinle Formation of the Colorado Plateau region, the Dockum Formation (or Group) of Texas, and the Newark Supergroup (Cumnock, Pekin, and New Oxford formations) of New Jersey have all produced dinosaur bones. These strata are all about the same age as, or perhaps slightly younger than, the dinosaur-bearing rocks of South America. In addition, dinosaur fossils have been discovered in roughly contemporaneous strata in North Africa (Morocco), Nova Scotia, South Africa, Scotland, and India. Even though the fossil record of the first dinosaurs is very sketchy, it appears that they achieved a worldwide distribution almost immediately after their origin, wherever that event may have initially occurred. Such rapid dispersal is

reasonable given the great mobility of dinosaurs and the unified nature of the earth's land masses during the later part of the Triassic. With bodies designed for swift and efficient movement over land, and with few oceanic barriers to their migration, the world's first dinosaurs spread to every corner of Pangaea with remarkable swiftness.

Utah in the Early Triassic

Reflecting the great environmental and geographic changes that took place on a global scale, the Triassic Period was also an important transitional phase in the geologic history of Utah. The changes that occurred in Utah during the Triassic

Photo 6. The Moenkopi Formation near Goblin Valley. Red mudstone and tan sandstone in the foreground represent the early Triassic Moenkopi Formation. Several formations comprising the Glen Canyon Group are exposed in the cliffs beyond. John Telford.

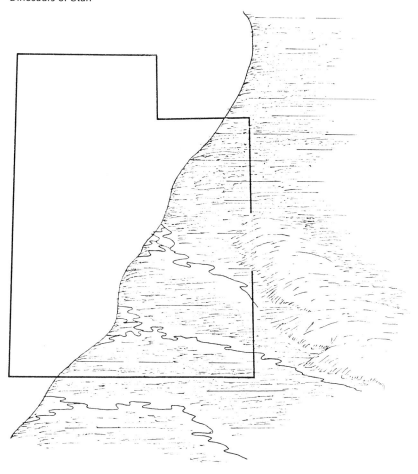

Figure 3-1. Early Triassic paleogeography of Utah. The Moenkopi Formation represent sediments that accumulated on the mud flats and floodplains of the low coastal plain. To the west, layers of marine mud accumulated on the floor of the early Triassic sea. The shoreline that separated land from sea in the early Triassic shifted back and forth across central Utah several times, producing the complex interfingering of marine and nonmarine deposits observed in the Moenkopi Formation.

set the stage for events and landscapes that would follow in later portions of the Mesozoic Era. These geological changes occurred during the middle part of the Triassic Period. Thus, Utah landscapes and environments in early Triassic time are much different than those that existed in the late Triassic. It is important to review these profound events carefully, because they had, for those of us interested in dinosaurs, an extremely important consequence: collectively, the geologic events of the middle Triassic created enormous tracts of dinosaur habitat. Utah would never have become populated by such a wondrous array of dinosaurs had the stage not been set by the mid-Triassic upheaval.

When the Triassic Period began 248 million years ago, nearly all of western Utah was covered by a broad, shallow sea. The shoreline of this sea

slashed diagonally through Utah from roughly the southwest corner to the eastern end of the modern Uinta Mountains, which were not yet elevated. Offshore from the coastline, mud and sand were washed from the exposed land to the east, settling on the ocean bottom to form layers of shale, siltstone, and sandstone. Elsewhere on the sea floor, where calcium carbonate was precipitated from ocean water, layers of silty limestone accumulated. Today, these marine sediments of western Utah are represented by such rock units as the Thaynes, Dinwoody, and Woodside formations. Fossils of marine invertebrate animals such as sea urchins, clams, brachiopods, and cephalopods clearly indicate the oceanic nature of these deposits. Sedimentary rocks of this general type and age extend to the west across western Utah and Nevada, suggesting that the open ocean stretched a considerable distance in that direction. In central Nevada, at the Berlin-Ichthyosaur State Park in northern Nye County, muddy limestones of early Triassic age have produced spectacular fossils of these gigantic marine reptiles. So far, no Triassic marine reptiles have been found in western Utah, but they almost certainly existed in the shallow water that covered that part of the state some 240 million years ago.

Along the early Triassic coastline was a low, featureless plain that gradually ascended to the east. Rivers draining more distant elevated areas flowed sluggishly to the west and northwest (Figure 3-1) across the nearly flat coastal plain. As the rivers approached the sea, they slowed, dropping much of their load of suspended silt and mud and building up broad mud flats in the process. The mud flats, and the river floodplains leading to them, extended southeast from the coastline across all of eastern Utah and even covered portions of modern-day Colorado, Arizona, New Mexico, and Wyoming. As much as 1,500 feet of fine-grained silt, locally mixed with sand and clay, accumulated on these expansive mud flats and floodplains. These sediments are now known as the Moenkopi Formation in southern Utah and the Four Corners area, the Ankareh Formation in the Wasatch Mountain region, and the Popo Agie Formation of Wyoming and Idaho. Emulating Triassic rocks elsewhere in the world, the Moenkopi and contemporaneous rocks are thoroughly stained red by the oxidation ("rusting") of iron-bearing mineral grains. The Triassic "age of red beds" begins with the deposition of the Moenkopi Formation and its equivalent units west of the early Triassic shoreline.

The low relief of the central Utah coastline, coupled with strong climatic shifts that induced temporary changes in the level of the sea, caused the early Triassic shoreline to migrate east and west several times. Each time the sea penetrated into eastern Utah, it submerged the mud flats and floodplains, covering them with thin layers of limestone or other marine sediments. When the marine advance, known as a transgression, was over, the sea withdrew to the west. The withdrawal (regression) of the ocean from eastern Utah allowed river-deposited mud to bury the thin limestone deposited earlier. This cycle of coastal oscillation occurred several times, giving rise to a zone of complex interfingering between marine and non-marine sediments in the early Triassic rock record of central Utah. Around Kanab, for example, the Moenkopi Formation consists mostly of mud-flat and floodplain deposits but also contains three portions deposited either under ocean water or close to the edge of the sea. These marine or marginal marine portions of the Moenkopi in this area are known as the Timpoweap, Virgin Limestone, and Shnabkaib members.

In western Utah, the early Triassic marine strata have produced abundant fossils of invertebrate organisms that lived in the shallow oceanic setting. The rich fossil fauna from such units as the Thaynes Formation is dominated by cephalopod molluscs but also includes bivalves, crinoids, and brachiopods. In contrast, fossils are not particularly common in the non-marine early Triassic rocks of eastern Utah. From the few fossils that are preserved in the Moenkopi Formation, we know that the mud flats and swampy floodplains were populated by a variety of terrestrial and semiaquatic vertebrates. Not surprisingly, given the abundance of water in these habitats, amphibians dominate the scanty Moenkopi vertebrate fauna. Several different types of amphibians have been identified, some of them fairly large. Fragmentary remains of terrestrial reptiles also have been discovered in the Moenkopi, but their abundance pales in comparison with the much more common amphibians.

Fortunately, there is another source of information on the nature of terrestrial life in Utah during the early Triassic. Footprints and trackways of land animals are very common in the mudstones and siltstones of the Moenkopi Formation. Evidently, the sticky mud that was deposited along the low coastal plain served as a perfect medium for the preservation of footprints made by animals moving across the landscape. Some spectacular early Triassic trackway sites have been discovered in the Colorado Plateau region, and the footprints have been intensively studied by paleontologists in recent years. While some of the footprints are clearly reptilian in form, none of them can be confidently attributed to dinosaurs. The Moenkopi-age tracks in the Colorado Plateau seem to have been made by a variety of non-dinosaurian reptiles such as rauisuchids, ornithosuchids, lizards, and therapsids.

From the footprints and body fossils, it thus appears that although a diverse reptile fauna existed in the Utah region during the early Triassic the scene was still dominated by amphibians. This may be because the swampy environment favored the amphibians or, perhaps, because the reptilian "takeover" had not yet progressed to the point that reptiles were the dominant element in the terrestrial fauna of western North America. Whatever the reason, the non-marine vertebrate fossils and tracks from the Moenkopi Formation offer good evidence that the age of dinosaurs had

Photo 7. Ripple marks in the Moenkopi Formation near Capitol Reef National Park were formed by tidal currents oscillating across a coastal mud flat. John Telford.

not begun in Utah in early Triassic time. No solid evidence of dinosaurs has ever been discovered in rocks of this age.

The Late Triassic: A Time of Change

During the middle portion of the Triassic Period, the geological setting of Utah began to change in ways that were extremely important in creating the Mesozoic wonderland in the eastern part of the state. North America began to separate from the rest of Pangaea as rifting and volcanic activity commenced along what is now the northern Atlantic seaboard. As the supercontinent was stretched and its crust thermally weakened, the North American portion of it was forced to the northwest by a rift valley that would eventually develop into the modern Atlantic Ocean basin. Although the western part of the embryonic North American continent was not directly affected by the rifting, it did begin to yield to the compressive forces that were generated as that portion of Pangaea began to move against, and over, the sea floor to the west.

The geological serenity that prevailed in western North America during the late stages of Pangaea was replaced by compressional forces that caused uplift of the earth's crust throughout the Great Basin and Rocky Mountain regions. No major mountain ranges were elevated during the Triassic Period, but there were many areas that began to rise as immense compressional forces began to warp the earth's crust upward. One such uplift was a gentle arching of the earth that emerged in eastern Nevada and western Utah, referred to by Stokes (1986) as the Mesocordilleran High. The lifting of the Mesocordilleran High raised the ancient sea floor of western Utah and caused the withdrawal of the early Triassic seas from most of the Great Basin, including western Utah. As the early Triassic sea floor emerged in the Great Basin region, the west coast of North America advanced to the west and hundreds of miles of new land appeared where there had for-

mally been ocean. With the Mesocordilleran High serving as a barrier between Utah and the proto-Pacific Ocean, the geographic setting of Utah changed from a coastal scene to one of an interior basin. As will be seen in chapters to come, the seas did return briefly to Utah in later times, but they came from the north or south. Once the Mesocordilleran High developed, it forever prevented the seas to the west from submerging any part of Utah.

The compression that lifted the Mesocordilleran High was the result of tectonic plates moving in opposite directions: the North America Plate, a west-moving fragment of Pangaea, was sliding over one or more oceanic plates that were moving eastward. The oceanic plates sliding beneath western North America were bent and forced downward under the overriding continent in a process known as subduction. This action eventually results in the partial melting of the subducted slab of rock as it encounters higher temperatures with increasing depth in the earth's interior. The molten rock that forms from this melting eventually may rise through the crust above to be erupted as lava or to be emplaced as masses of rock similar to granite if it cools before it reaches the surface. In western North America, Triassic volcanic and granitic rocks are fairly common, whereas they are very rare in earlier periods. In later phases of the Mesozoic Era, the igneous activity, the crustal uplift, and the mountain-building that began in the Triassic intensified throughout the West. The geological convulsions of the mid-Triassic are just the beginning of processes that dominated the Mesozoic history of Utah and adjacent regions.

As these great changes were under way, the deposition of mud and sand in central Utah apparently was suspended for a time. Responding to the rising land in western Utah, the rivers that deposited the Moenkopi sediments either shifted their courses or began to erode some of the sediment they had previously spread out across the Colorado Plateau. Everywhere in the Colorado

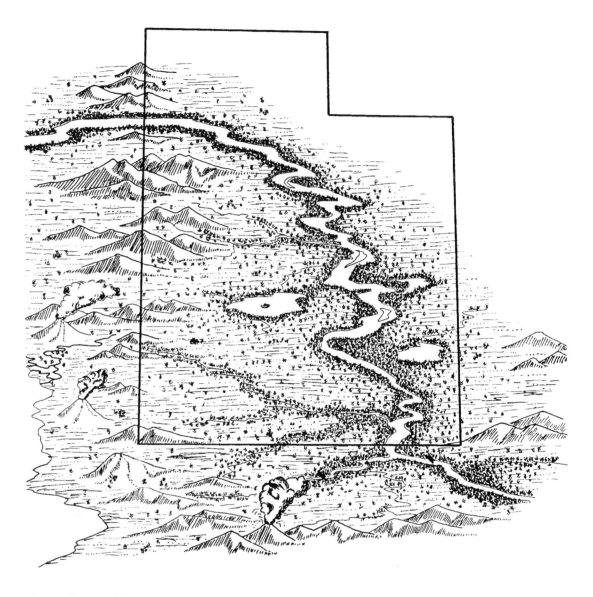

Figure 3-2. Late Triassic landscape of Utah. The former coastal plain was transformed into an interior basin surrounded on its sides by elevated terrain such as the Mesocordilleran High. The Chinle Formation, or Group, was deposited in streams, lakes, and river floodplains within this partially enclosed basin. The floor of the basin was heavily forested and the rivers ran in a general northwesterly direction.

Plateau the top of the Moenkopi Formation is marked by an irregular surface that was produced during this period of erosion and/or nondeposition. Such a surface is known as an unconformity, a break in the geological record. All unconformities represent a gap in our chronological record of land and life. It is difficult to tell exactly how much time is represented by the unconformity at the top of the Moenkopi Formation. A good guess is approximately 15 million years. When the deposition of sediment resumed in the later Triassic, the local environment had changed considerably

and, much to the delight of dinosaur lovers, so had the creatures it sustained.

The Chinle Formation: The Age of Dinosaurs Begins

With the emergence of the Mesocordilleran High in western Utah and eastern Nevada in middle Triassic time, the landscapes of east-central Utah were dramatically changed. The low coastal plain that existed during the time that the Moenkopi Formation was being deposited was transformed into an interior basin surrounded by higher terrain on at least three sides (Figure 3-2). To the southwest of this basin rose the slopes of the Mesocordilleran High, while highlands of presumed volcanic origin in central Arizona formed the southern margin of the basin. In addition, judging from the patterns of sediment dispersal during late Triassic time, it appears that a hilly terrain existed in central Colorado, representing the eroded roots of the Ancestral Rocky Mountains, which had been uplifted during the late Paleozoic Era. This interior basin seems to have been open to the north and northwest.

The high lands surrounding the basin on the east, south, and west served as watersheds, capturing moisture from the passing storms. As the water from the marginal highlands descended toward the center of the basin, it collected into larger streams that eventually flowed northwest out of the basin toward the sea in western Nevada. This river system originated in the area of the modern Texas Panhandle and ran northwest until in met the sea in central Nevada. Geologists have named this large river the Chinle Trunk River (Riggs and others, 1996). This river, along with numerous tributaries that flowed into it, deposited gravel, sand, and mud across the broad floor of the interior basin of south-central Utah (Figure 3-2). The surface of the basin was nearly flat, and some of the sluggish rivers emptied into lakes that dotted the floodplains. The volcanic activity in adjacent regions periodically produced clouds of ash that drifted over the basin to settle out in layers across the low plain. The assemblage of sediment that documents the existence of this interior basin is thus a complex mixture of conglomerate, sandstone, mudstone, and volcanic ash. Named for a small outpost on the Navajo Reservation of northern Arizona, this sequence of rocks has traditionally been known as the Chinle Formation.

All of the sediments in the Chinle Formation were deposited in non-marine settings such as lakes, stream channels, river floodplains, and swamps. It is a heterogeneous assemblage of conglomerate, sandstone, mudstone, and shale representing a variety of specific sedimentary environments. Thin layers of volcanic ash are scattered throughout this sequence of sedimentary rocks. The ash is sometimes altered into a clay mineral known as bentonite and reworked into the fine silt deposited in ponds or floodplains to produce bentonitic mudstones. When the soft ash or bentonite is exposed at the surface, oxidation of metals in the volcanic materials produces shades of purple, brown, yellow, and lavender. The poorly lithified sediment is rapidly eroded by water and wind to produce a gullied landscape, the classic "badlands" of western lore. Some of the most scenic landscapes in the world develop from the weathering and erosion of the Chinle Formation. The soft pastel-banded hills and colorful badlands of the Painted Desert of northern Arizona are named for the distinctive colors of the Chinle rocks exposed in that area. Similar exposures of the Chinle Formation can be found in many places in southern and southeastern Utah.

Geologists have developed several different ways of subdividing the complex and regionally variable stratigraphy of the Chinle Formation, and several different members have been established within this rock unit. In Utah, the most important subdivisions are the Shinarump, Petrified Forest, Mossback, Owl Rock, and Church Rock members (Figure 3-3). In adjacent portions of the Colorado Plateau—Arizona and New Mexico—other members have been recognized. Recently, it has been suggested by Spencer Lucas (1991a, 1991b) that the Chinle should be elevated to the rank of a group consisting of several newly named formations, with some of the older members being raised to formation status. Consequently, the nomenclature applied to the Chinle Formation (or Group) is a somewhat confusing tangle of names that vary from place to place. This is not surprising, though, because the sedimentary rocks of this unit were deposited in exclusively non-marine environments that had

Photo 8. Outcrop of the Chinle Formation along the east side of the San Rafael Swell. The prominent light-colored cliff is Wingate Sandstone. The Chinle Formation forms the varicolored slope from the base of the Wingate cliff to the bottom of the gulch. John Telford.

limited geographical range and shifted continuously through late Triassic time. The stratigraphic nomenclature of the Chinle Formation is complex because of the extreme variability of the sediments it contains. A similarly complex pattern is found in other Mesozoic rock units of the Colorado Plateau, as will be seen in later chapters. Recall from Chapter 1 that this pattern of lateral variability is a normal feature of sedimentary rocks deposited by river systems. This review of the Chinle rocks and fossils will use the traditional subdivisions (members) of the Chinle Formation, though some scientists are now starting to use the stratigraphic units proposed by Lucas.

Resting above the unconformity marking the top of the Moenkopi Formation throughout most of southeastern Utah is a layer of conglomerate and coarse sandstone up to several hundred feet thick. This gravelly material at the base of Chinle is known as the Shinarump Conglomerate. It is considered by most geologists to be the first subdivision of the Chinle Formation. The Shinarump Conglomerate was deposited by swift rivers flowing toward the northeast across southern Utah. As the rivers periodically shifted their courses back and forth across the lowlands of southern and eastern Utah, a broad sheet of coarse deposits was formed. The sand and gravel of the Shinarump is usually well cemented and commonly forms a hard "cap" that protects the softer sediment of the underlying Moenkopi Formation from the ravages of erosion. Many of the mesas and benches of southern Utah have lower slopes of soft, red rock that ascend to a horizontal caprock of Shin-

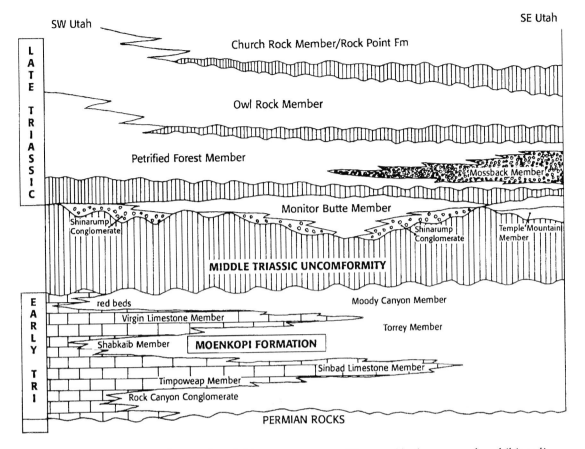

SW Utah

SE Utah

Church Rock Member/Rock Point Fm

Owl Rock Member

Petrified Forest Member

Mossback Member

Monitor Butte Member

Shinarump Conglomerate

Shinarump Conglomerate

Temple Mountain Member

MIDDLE TRIASSIC UNCOMFORMITY

red beds

Moody Canyon Member

Virgin Limestone Member

Torrey Member

Shabkaib Member

MOENKOPI FORMATION

Sinbad Limestone Member

Timpoweap Member

Rock Canyon Conglomerate

PERMIAN ROCKS

LATE TRIASSIC

EARLY TRI

Figure 3-3. The Triassic rocks of southeast to east-central Utah. Vertical ruling represents gaps, or unconformities, in the sequence.

arump Conglomerate. Good examples of this are Hurricane Mesa, near Zion National Park, and the Mummy Cliffs near Torrey.

Above the Shinarump Conglomerate are other units that record different conditions of sediment deposition. The Petrified Forest Member, for example, consists of variegated red, green, and purple siltstone and mudstone that contains abundant bentonite. Most of this fine-grained material accumulated in swamps and lakes that developed on the low and poorly drained floor of the interior basin in Utah and adjacent states. The fine grains of silt were primarily derived from the south, but the volcanic ash represented by the bentonite probably drifted in from the west, where there is good evidence for volcanic activity during the late Triassic. Some units within the Chinle Formation consist of reddish-brown to purple siltstone and fine sandstone that lacks bentonite and contains small grains of mica and

quartz. These red beds commonly exhibit sedimentary rock features produced by flowing water, such as ripple marks and cross-bedding. Most of the Chinle red beds represent sediment that accumulated on the floodplains adjacent to the larger stream courses. Units deposited primarily on floodplains include the Church Rock Member (or Rock Point Formation of the Chinle Group). Other units with the Chinle sequence consist of a mixture of lakebed clays, river-channel sands and gravel, and floodplain silt. The Monitor Butte Member and Owl Rock Member are examples of such heterogeneous units. Finally, there are other subdivisions of the Chinle, such as the Mossback and Cameron members (or formations) that represent relatively coarse-grained sands and gravel that accumulated in the channel of the larger rivers, much like the Shinarump Member. The Chinle Formation is thus a complex assemblage of sediments deposited in a variety of specific settings across the lower interior basin of late Triassic time.

Non-dinosaur Fossils of the Chinle Formation: A Rich Ecosystem Revealed

In contrast to the sparse assemblage of fossils preserved in the underlying Moenkopi Formation, fossils occur in amazing abundance in the Chinle sediments. The list of fossils from the Chinle beds is a long one indeed; it includes plants, invertebrates, footprints, and vertebrate material. The various depositional environments in which Chinle sediments accumulated all had relatively high potential for preserving fossils of the organisms harbored there.

In places, the fossil plants from the Chinle Formation are so spectacularly abundant that in 1962 Petrified Forest National Park was established in northeastern Arizona to protect the great number of enormous fossil logs weathering out of the soft pastel mudstones. Elsewhere in the Colorado Plateau, fossil plant material is commonly found in exposures of the Chinle Formation, although nowhere else does the abundance rival that of the national park. In Utah, fossil plants from Chinle sediments occur in notable abundance in areas around the Circle Cliffs (near Capitol Reef National Park) and in the San Rafael Swell. More than fifty different kinds of plants have been identified from the Chinle Formation including fungi, lycopods (relatives of the club mosses), ferns, conifers, ginkgoes, and cycads. The large trees preserved at Petrified Forest National Park and elsewhere are mostly the remains of *Araucarioxylon*, a large conifer. Preserved logs of *Araucarioxylon* have been found that are up to 7 feet in diameter and over 120 feet long. Even such large fossil specimens are incomplete; the living tree must have been even larger.

The giant conifers might have been the most impressive element of late Triassic flora in the Colorado Plateau, but there were many other plants of lesser stature growing in their shadows.

Ferns and horsetails carpeted the forest floor, while cycads similar to the modern "sego palms" and ginkgoes stood a bit higher as shrubs. One major group of modern plants that is not represented in the Chinle flora is the flowering plants, or angiosperms. These plants, with their flowers and seed-bearing fruit, dominate the modern global flora but did not appear until the late Cretaceous Period. Thus, the forests of the basin in Chinle time were lush and dense, but they consisted of an aggregation of relatively primitive types of plants. From the character of the flora and other factors, researchers have concluded that the climate nurturing these forests was warm and humid, at least during the early part of the time represented by the Chinle Formation. A stroll through the forest in late Triassic Utah might have been similar to hiking through today's rain forests in the Amazon Basin, although you wouldn't see any flowers or fruit in the prehistoric forest. Near the end of the Triassic Period, during the time represented by the upper Petrified Forest Member, the Chinle forests appeared to have became a bit more open as a general trend toward a drier and more seasonal climate seems to have somewhat limited the density of the plant growth.

For most of the late Triassic, the lowland basin of southeastern Utah was without doubt a well-watered terrain. The basin was laced by rivers and dotted with lakes and ponds. Not surprisingly, the Chinle Formation produces a diverse fossil fauna dominated by aquatic forms. The fossils of freshwater bivalves and the burrows of crustaceans (crayfish) are fairly common in some portions of the Chinle Formation. In addition, many kinds of fossil fish have been discovered in the Chinle Formation from localities throughout the Colorado Plateau. Around Zion National Park and in the Lisbon Valley area of San Juan County, the Chinle sediments have produced specimens of *Cionichthys*, *Hemicalypterus*, *Ceratodus*, and several other species of fish (Figure 3-4). Among the fish, *Ceratodus* is particularly interesting because it belongs to the order Dipnoi, which includes the living Australian lungfish, its close relative. Lungfish are specifically adapted to life in ephemeral streams that periodically dry up. During droughts, the lungfish burrow into the drying mud, seal the cavity with mucus, and wait for the waters to flow again. The presence of lungfish in the Chinle Formation suggests that the climate alternated between humid and dry conditions, perhaps on a seasonal basis. The late Triassic fish fed on plants, molluscs, and other fish populating the sluggish rivers of the Chinle basin area.

In addition to the fossil fish, a diverse array of semiaquatic vertebrates has also been recovered from the Chinle Formation in the Colorado Plateau region. Several different amphibians are known from the Chinle strata; the most common and best known of them is *Metoposaurus*. This amphibian had an almost comical appearance, with a huge flattened spade-like head and laughably small legs on a body some 6 feet long (Figure 3-5A). Lining the jaws of *Metoposaurus* were many sharp pointed teeth, clearly indicating the predatory habits of this amphibian. Most likely, *Metoposaurus* and other similar amphibians spent most of their lives in the rivers, lakes, and ponds of the Chinle basin lying in wait on the bottom for any unwary prey that ventured within reach of their "fish-trap" jaws. *Metoposaurus* and its kin (the metoposaurids) would have been extremely clumsy on dry land and probably never traveled far from the water's edge. Other, less common, amphibians from the Chinle include *Buettneria* and *Apachesaurus*.

In addition to the fish and amphibians, there were other vertebrates swimming the Chinle streams and lakes. In many localities where fossils have been found in the Chinle beds, phytosaurs are the most common of all vertebrates. The phytosaurs (Figure 3-5B) looked much like a modern crocodile, but the resemblance was only superficial. Phytosaurs are placed in a different category (usually the family Phytosauria or the "Parasuchidae" of the order Thecodontia) from modern crocodiles and alligators (the order Crocodilia)

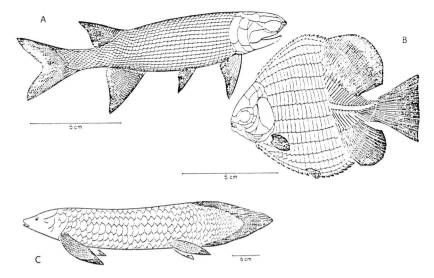

Figure 3-4. Fossil fish from the Chinle Formation of Utah. A: *Cionichthys*, a bottom-feeding fish known from San Juan County; B: *Hemicalypterus*, a deep-bodied browser that probably consumed aquatic plants; C: *Ceratodus*, an omnivorous lungfish than lived in the streams and rivers of late Triassic Utah. After Colbert, 1972.

because they are distinguished from them by some unique anatomical features. Most notably, the phytosaurs had their external nostrils positioned on a small mound between, and slightly forward of, the eyes. Crocodiles have nostrils located at the tip of the snout, also on a slightly raised bony platform. Because their nostrils are on the snout, crocodiles have a bony palate on the roof of the mouth that separates the airway from the normally water-filled mouth cavity. This nasal architecture allows crocodiles to breathe while they swim and float mostly submerged, with just their nostrils and eyes above water. The phytosaurs could likewise remain mostly submerged, breathing through the nostrils located on the top of the head. In phytosaurs, air flowed directly from the nostrils downward into the throat without traveling the length of the snout. Hence, phytosaurs did not possess the secondary bony palate that crocodiles have. To enhance their swimming abilities, the bodies of both phytosaurs and crocodiles are long and streamlined, with broad flexible tails designed to swing laterally in a serpentine fashion.

The bodies of phytosaurs were up to 20 feet or more in length and armored with somewhat rectangular plates of bone (scutes) imbedded in the skin, much like a modern crocodile. With

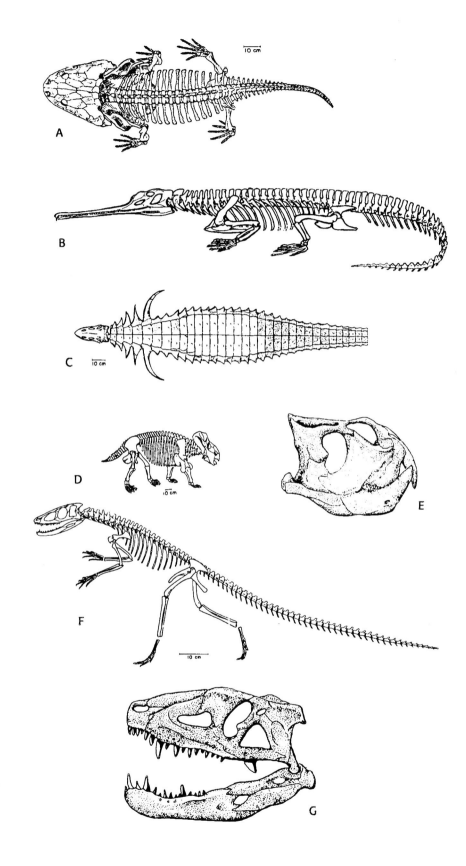

Figure 3-5. Late Triassic non-dinosaur vertebrates from the Chinle Formation and correlative units of western North America. A: *Metoposaurus*, a carnivorous labryinthodont amphibian; B: *Rutiodon*, one of the most common of several different kinds of phytosaurs known from the Chinle sequence; C: *Desmatosuchus*, a herbivorous semiaquatic reptile of the "upland" fauna of the Chinle; D: *Placerias*, a dicynodont therapsid ("mammal-like reptile"); E: *Parapedon*, a rhyncosaur with an approximately 15-cm (6 inch)-long skull; F: *Hesperosuchus*, a small lizard-like "pseudosuchian" that, despite its overall appearance, was not a dinosaur; G: skull of the large rauisuchian *Postosuchus*, about two feet long. A–D, and F, after Colbert, 1972; E, from Carroll, 1988, cited in Chapter 1; G, after Chatterjee, 1985.

their short and stubby legs, it appears that phytosaurs spent most of their time in the water, where they must have been a top predator. The teeth of phytosaurs are of several types, varying from sharply pointed and conical to blade-like in form, clearly designed to capture a mobile prey animal. Phytosaurs probably consumed anything they could catch or find, just as modern crocodiles do. Fish, amphibians, and other unwary reptiles constituted the main portion of a phytosaur's diet.

Several genera of phytosaurs are known from late Triassic strata in the Colorado Plateau region, among which the best known are *Rutiodon* and the classic *Phytosaurus*. Although the phytosaurs were crocodile-like in their ecological habits and general appearance, it is important to bear in mind that they are not closely related to the modern crocodiles. The earliest true crocodiles did appear in the late Triassic Period, but these creatures were rather small, lizard-like animals. The similarity between the phytosaurs and the modern crocodiles is a good example of convergent evolution, the development of similar characteristics by two unrelated groups of animals through their adaptation to similar habitats and ecological niches. For some reason, phytosaurs are relatively rare in Utah outcrops of the Chinle Formation. Elsewhere in western North America—in Texas, Arizona, New Mexico, and Wyoming—phytosaurs are among the most common vertebrate fossils in rocks of Chinle age. Only recently have phytosaurs been identified in the Chinle strata of the San Rafael Swell region of central Utah (Lucas and others, 1993).

In addition to the aquatic and semiaquatic vertebrates, the Chinle and equivalent late Triassic strata have produced the remains of a great variety of reptiles that were better adapted to dry land, or "upland," habitats. Among this group are the aetosaurs and the dicynodonts. The aetosaurs (suborder Aetosauria, family Stagnonlepididae) were herbivorous reptiles that looked somewhat like a plant-eating crocodile (Figure 3-5C). The most distinctive feature of the aetosaurs was their heavy armor—an impenetrable pavement of bony plates that covered the back, tail, and flanks of these reptiles. In addition, the aetosaurs had large spikes extending from the shoulder and neck region, tapering toward the back to blunt nodes along the flanks. The heads of aetosaurs were relatively small and their jaws were lined with diminutive, weak teeth. The aetosaurs seem to have been only slightly better suited for crawling on dry land than were the phytosaurs. They probably lived mostly along riverbanks and lake shores where soft vegetation on low-growing shrubs was available in abundance. Of the several genera of aetosaurs known from the Chinle Formation, the most common are *Desmatosuchus* and *Typothorax*.

The dicynodonts are mammal-like reptiles (order Therapsida) that resembled a reptilian version of a pig. For example, *Placerias*, the most common Chinle dicynodont, was 3–5 feet long and rather bulky, with short legs and a large head (Figure 3-5D). *Placerias* had two large tusks that projected down and outward from the upper jaw. There were no other teeth in the jaws of this strange dicynodont; instead, the snout was tipped by a curved beak with sharp edges of bone along the jaws, similar to the rostrum of a turtle. *Placerias* probably ate tough, low-growing vegetation. The prominent tusks of these dicynodonts were probably used for a variety of tasks, including rooting and digging for food, defending against predators, and sparring with members of its own species for mates. *Placerias* was a fully terrestrial animal and probably foraged through the lush late Triassic forests a considerable distance from water.

In addition to the animals already described, the "upland" fauna of the Chinle Formation included other reptiles that are less common or are known only from very fragmentary material. *Hesperosuchus* (Figure 3-5F) was a 4-foot-long, bipedal "thecodont" that was a very agile and active predator, consuming insects and small lizards. In New Mexico, Arizona, and Wyoming, fossils of several different rauisuchians (quadrupedal and probably carnivorous reptiles) and lizard-like rhyncosaurs have also been discovered in Chinle-equivalent rock units. None of these miscellaneous reptiles have yet been discovered from the late Triassic rocks of Utah; but, since they are known from surrounding areas, it is likely that they lived everywhere on the floor of the Chinle basin. Certainly, these and many other types of reptiles await discovery from the Utah exposures of the Chinle Formation.

The vertebrates that we have thus far reviewed make up a rich and diverse assemblage consisting of aquatic and terrestrial forms. The low, forested basin of Chinle time in Utah was literally crawling with dozens of different types of reptiles and amphibians, each adapted for a specific habitat and ecologic niche. The scene had changed dramatically from the relatively barren coastal plain of Moenkopi time, and, by the late Triassic, the overall conditions in the interior basin of central Utah seem to have been optimal for reptiles. A warm, humid climate supported a lush tropical forest that, in turn, provided excellent habitat for a varied reptilian fauna. In fact, we have yet to explore what some consider to be the most fascinating element of the late Triassic reptilian fauna. The adaptive radiation of reptiles in the Triassic also produced a group of bipedal carnivores that were to dominate the terrestrial ecosystem in the coming geologic periods. The colorful Chinle strata provide us with our first glimpse of these creatures, almost lost among the complicated mosaic of metoposaurs, phytosaurs, aetosaurs, and dicynodonts. In the Colorado Plateau, the age of dinosaurs begins in the late Triassic. It is among the Chinle fauna that we find the first hint of dinosaurs in the Southwest.

Traces of Dinosaurs of the Chinle Formation

The evidence for the earliest dinosaurs in the Utah region comes from the study of reptile footprints and trackways preserved in the strata of the Chinle Formation. Currently, no fossil bones that indisputably belong to late Triassic dinosaurs have been collected from exposures of the Chinle in Utah. As we shall see, several different dinosaurs are known from the Chinle in nearby areas, but it is the footprints in this formation that first announce the emergence of dinosaurs in Utah. It is probably only a matter of time and further exploration before scientists find the fossil remains of the track makers, but for now all we have are the footprints. However, a footprint or track preserved in rock can tell us much about Utah's first dinosaurs.

Footprints and trackways of terrestrial animals are fairly common in upper portions of the Chinle sequence such as the Church Rock Member or Rock Point Formation (Lockley and Hunt, 1995). In the past decade or so, the study of dinosaur tracks has produced many new and important insights on Mesozoic reptiles worldwide. With respect to dinosaur tracks, one of the most intensely studied regions in the world is the Colorado Plateau–Rocky Mountain region. Spearheaded by Martin Lockley, teams of researchers have discovered, documented, mapped, and analyzed literally hundreds of track-bearing rock sequences in Colorado, New Mexico, Arizona, Utah, and other western states. In the Chinle sediments of Utah, Lockley and his colleagues have discovered footprints in numerous places; but three localities stand out as especially revealing for our purposes: the area around Dinosaur National Monument, Shay Canyon north of Monticello, and along the northern shore of Lake Powell. For full descriptions of these sites, see Lockley and Hunt (1995) and the many reference citations therein.

Paleontologists have traditionally assigned latinized names to footprints in a manner similar to that used for the naming of body fossils. The names are useful because the overall morphology of each distinctive track (its size, length and number of digits, shape of the toes, etc.) thus can be summarized with a single term, known as an ichnogenus and/or ichnospecies. Each ichnogenus refers to a certain type of footprint, while the ichnospecies represents variations on the general morphological pattern that defines the ichnogenus. It is important to bear in mind that it is usually impossible to relate with absolute certainty any ichnogenus or ichnospecies with a specific track-making animal; paleontologists can only make inferences on the identity of the track maker by comparing the foot anatomy of known prehistoric creatures with the pattern that characterizes the various ichnogenera and ichnospecies. In many cases, a single type of track (that is, a specific ichnogenus) may have been made by several different animals. Similarly, a single animal species may leave several different types of tracks depending on the various individuals' size, age, speed of locomotion, and type of substrate walked upon. Nonetheless, tracks preserved in rock can provide valuable information on the overall composition and nature of the terrestrial vertebrate fauna. This is particularly true in rock sequences such as the Chinle in Utah, where body fossils are relatively rare.

In the vicinity of Dinosaur National Monument, late Triassic footprints and trackways have been discovered at over thirty-five sites (Lockley and Hunt, 1995). Among these tracks is the ichnogenus *Grallator*, a three-toed track up to several inches in length that almost certainly was made by a bipedal dinosaur (Figure 3-6A). With the sharp claw marks that terminate each of the three toe marks, *Grallator* most likely represents a small theropod dinosaur. In addition, researchers have recorded the tracks of a large quadrupedal animal that had smaller forelimbs than hind limbs (Figure 3-6B). These rounded tracks, about 20–25 cm (8–10 inches) in diameter, appear to be similar to sauropod tracks from the Jurassic and Cretaceous periods, but they are smaller and have somewhat less distinct toe impressions. These tracks may belong to the ichnogenus *Tetrasauropus* (Figure 3-6D), considered to be the footprints of a

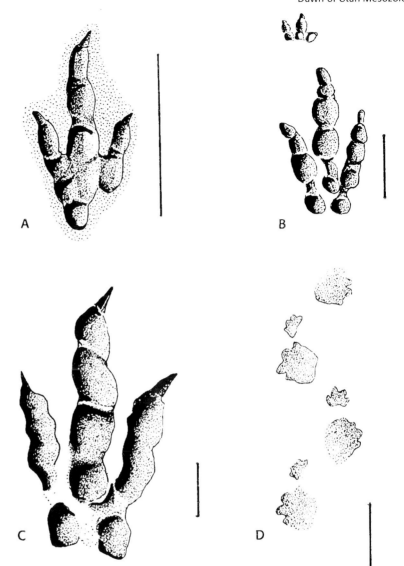

Figure 3-6. Late Triassic dinosaur tracks from the Chinle Formation of Utah. A: *Grallator* track, attributed to a theropod dinosaur; B: *Atreipus* track from the Chinle sequence near Lake Powell. Note the small imprint of the forefoot, or manus, and the blunt claw marks on the larger hind foot impression. These tracks may have been made by an ornithischian dinosaur. C: A large *Atreipus*-like track from the Shay Canyon locality. This track has sharp claw impressions and was probably made by a large theropod dinosaur. D: *Tetrasauropus*-like track from the Dinosaur National Monument area. Tracks of this type may have been made by a prosauropod dinosaur. Scale bar=5 cm (2 inches) in all sketches. After Lockley and Hunt, 1995.

prosauropod dinosaur. Associated with the theropod and possible prosauropod tracks in the Dinosaur National Monument area are other
ichnogenera most likely made by primitive
sphenodontid lizards (*Rhynosaurpoides*),
aetosaurs (*Brachychirotherium*), and mammal-
like reptiles.

To the south, in Shay Canyon and around
Lake Powell, horizons in the upper portion of the
Chinle Formation have produced tracks preserved in sandstone and mudstone of the Church
Rock Member (or Rock Point sequence). Once
again, tracks made by non-dinosaur reptiles are
common at these localities, including ichnogenera *Brachychirotherium* and *Pentasauropus*, the
latter most likely made by a dicynodont reptile
similar to *Placerias*. Some of the tracks, however,
appear very likely to have been made by dinosaurs. Three-toed tracks, similar to the ichnogenus *Atreipus*, have been observed at both
localities (Lockley and Hunt, 1995). The *Atreipus*-
like tracks are more or less similar to the
Grallator-type tracks described earlier, but at Shay
Canyon they are very large, reaching lengths of
about 20 cm (8 inches) (Figure 3-6C). What
could be considered the "heels" of *Grallator* and
Atreipus actually represent the "ball" of the foot of
the digitigrade track makers and exhibit slightly
different patterns. In addition, the impressions of
the pads on the underside of the toes are different
in the two ichnogenera. These considerations suggest that *Grallator* and *Atreipus* tracks were made
by different dinosaurs; both were probably early
bipedal theropods. Along the shores of Lake Powell, tracks resembling *Atreipus* also have been discovered in the upper Chinle Formation, but they
vary slightly from the classic form of this ichnogenus in that they commonly lack the sharp claw
marks on the tips of the toe impressions. In addition, many of the large *Atreipus*-like tracks from
Lake Powell are associated with much smaller
footprints that may represent the forefoot (or
manus) of a quadrupedal, rather than bipedal,
reptile (Figure 3-6B). Moreover, the Lake Powell

tracks are smaller than the Shay Canyon tracks,
reaching lengths of only about 12 cm (5 inches)
(Lockley and Hunt, 1995). Scientists are still not
sure what dinosaur might have made the
Atreipus-like tracks at the Lake Powell site. It may
have been an early ornithopod dinosaur or, alternately, it could have been left by an unknown
quadrupedal theropod. In any case, these odd
tracks provide evidence of more than a single
type of dinosaur inhabiting the interior basin
during late Chinle time.

The footprint record of the Chinle strata in
Utah attests to a diverse population of reptiles
during the late Triassic Period. The three-toed
tracks are most probably the traces of dinosaurs
because, as was pointed out in Chapter 2, the reduction of digits in the hands and feet (from the
primitive pattern of five) are hallmarks of the Dinosauria and not a common trait in other reptile
groups. While many footprints are also known
from the underlying Moenkopi Formation of
early Triassic age, none of these prints show the
advanced foot morphology that characterizes the
dinosaurs. Thus, the "Age of Dinosaurs" begins in
Utah during the time represented by the Chinle
Formation.

Most scientists estimate that the Chinle Formation (or Group) encompasses the interval
from about 225–210 million years ago. It is clear
from the footprint evidence that by this time
there were several different kinds of dinosaurs
ambling around the interior basin of central Utah
where the Chinle sediments were being deposited.
These first dinosaurs shared their lush habitat
with a great variety of reptiles, fish, and amphibians. Dinosaurs were present in the Chinle landscape, but they were not yet the dominant
terrestrial vertebrates. They were, in fact, relatively rare in comparison to the abundant non-
dinosaur reptiles and amphibians. Unfortunately,
the Chinle deposits of Utah have not yet produced any fossils of the dinosaurs that may have
left the tracks preserved in the Chinle Formation;
however, good guesses can be made about their

Plate 1.
A late Triassic landscape of central Utah. *Coelophysis*, a small theropod dinosaur, and *Rutiodon*, an aquatic phytosaur, lived along the stream banks and floodplains adjacent to rivers flowing across Utah.

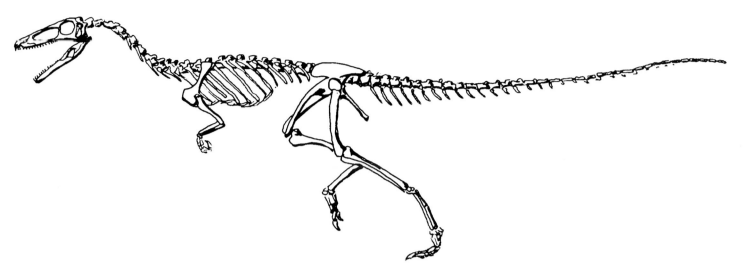

Figure 3-7. *Coelophysis* from the Chinle Formation of New Mexico and Arizona. Based on reconstruction of Lucas, 1994, cited in Chapter 1.

identity by looking just beyond the borders of Utah into New Mexico and Arizona.

The Track Makers: Chinle Dinosaurs of New Mexico and Arizona

The late Triassic Chinle interior basin extended well beyond Utah into the surrounding portions of the Colorado Plateau in northwest New Mexico and northern Arizona. Fluvial (river-deposited) and lacustrine (lake-deposited) sediments accumulated in these areas during the same that the Chinle sediments were being laid down in Utah. The general environments in Arizona and New Mexico were similar to those already described for Utah in the late Triassic, but the specific pattern of sediment deposition varied somewhat, leading geologists to recognize different subdivisions (members or formations) of the Chinle sequence deposited near the margins of the basin.

The most famous Chinle vertebrate fossil locality is the Ghost Ranch Quarry, located in Rio Arriba County, New Mexico, near the town of Abiquiu. Excavations at this site, conducted primarily during 1947 and 1948 by Edwin H. Colbert of the American Museum of Natural History, have produced dozens of skeletons of a small theropod dinosaur traditionally known as *Coelo-*

physis along with fossils of phytosaurs and other reptiles. To this day, *Coelophysis* remains the best-known dinosaur from the late Triassic, although other types have been discovered in more recent years. *Coelophysis* was a small (7–8 feet long), delicate animal with long and slender forelimbs ending in strongly clawed hands (Figure 3-7). The skull, positioned at the end of a highly flexible neck, is low and lightly built, with many small piercing teeth positioned along the jaws. The hind limbs of *Coelophysis* are rather birdlike, with three functional toes on each foot. A fourth digit (actually the "first," or the big toe) is present in the feet of *Coelophysis*, but it is so reduced in size that it did not reach the ground. *Coelophysis* probably subsisted on a diet of insects, small amphibians, and lizards. There is evidence from Ghost Ranch that this animal may have been cannibalistic in times of stress, consuming small individuals of its own species. This dinosaur belongs to the Ceratosauria, those "primitive" theropods that lack many of the refinements developed by later and more advanced members (the Tetanurae) of the suborder Theropoda. Judging from the structure and size of its foot, *Coelophysis* is an excellent candidate for being considered the creator of at least some of the tracks preserved in Utah exposures of the Chinle Formation. The size and morphology of the foot of *Coelophysis* seems to be a pretty good match for the general pattern of *Grallator* and *Atreipus* tracks. *Coelophysis* has also been identified in the Chinle Formation of northern Arizona, so we know that this primitive theropod was widespread. It almost certainly lived in Utah, though researchers have not yet discovered any fossil evidence for its presence there.

In addition to *Coelophysis*, paleontologists have recently discovered evidence for other small theropod dinosaurs in the Chinle Formation (see, for example, Heckert and others, 1994). The newly discovered theropods are all smaller than *Coelophysis*, about 3–5 feet long, but they appear to be a similar type of ceratosaur, although there are hints of more "advanced" characteristics in at least one of the new forms. *Coelophysis* was certainly not the only theropod inhabiting the Chinle landscape, but more study and more fossils will be required to identify the others with certainty. The validity of the name *Coelophysis* for the most common Chinle dinosaur has recently been challenged by some paleontologists for reasons that have to do with the naming of organisms (Heckert and others, 1994). An alternate name, *Rioarribasaurus*, has been proposed for this dinosaur, but most paleontologists at this time have elected to use the traditional name *Coelophysis*. *Rioarribasaurus* is mentioned here to avoid confusion for readers who might encounter that name in other publications; *Rioarribasaurus* and *Coelophysis* are the same animal.

In northern Arizona, the Petrified Forest Member has produced abundant vertebrate fossils at Petrified Forest National Park. The vertebrate fauna preserved at this locality is dominated by phytosaurs, aetosaurs, metoposaurid amphibians, and other non-dinosaurian reptiles. *Coelophysis* is known to occur in this assemblage, though its remains are relatively rare. In addition, the teeth of several different ornithischian dinosaurs have recently been discovered from exposures of the Chinle Formation in the Petrified Forest area (Pa-

dian, 1990; Hunt and Lucas, 1994). Several genera of mostly small ornithischian dinosaurs have been established on the basis of these isolated teeth. *Revueltosaurus* is the most common and largest of these new genera.

The teeth of *Revueltosaurus*, about 17 mm (.75 inch) long when complete, have flattened triangular crowns with small denticles along the edges (Figure 3-8A). These teeth are clearly not those of a theropod dinosaur such as *Coelophysis*, which had blade-like teeth with sharp, serrated edges. The teeth of *Revueltosaurus* were designed to shred vegetation, and they exhibit wear along the points of contact with opposing teeth. Unfortunately, scientists know nothing about the post-cranial skeleton of *Revueltosaurus*, so it is impossible to determine what type of ornithischian dinosaur it represents.

Revueltosaurus was evidently widespread during the late Triassic, because its teeth have been found in New Mexico as well as in Arizona. It almost certainly lived in Utah as well. Just above the top of the Shinarump Conglomerate in the Petrified Forest area, another ornithischian, known as *Tecovasaurus*, has been identified, once again on the basis of very small (2–3 mm) isolated teeth (Figure 3-8B). This genus also occurs in the late Triassic rocks of Texas. Finally, in New Mexico, a third late Triassic ornithischian has been discovered near the top of the Chinle-equivalent strata known as the Bull Canyon Formation. Also based on isolated teeth, this genus has been named *Lucianosaurus* (Hunt and Lucas, 1994; Figure 3-8C).

Thus, it appears that ornithischian dinosaurs ranged throughout the entire span of time represented by the Chinle Formation in areas near Utah. The teeth of these dinosaurs provide tantalizing hints of an apparently diverse community of herbivores that accompanied *Coelophysis* as the earliest dinosaurs in the American Southwest. Perhaps the ornithischians, known only from isolated teeth in adjacent regions, produced some of the tracks that have been discovered in the

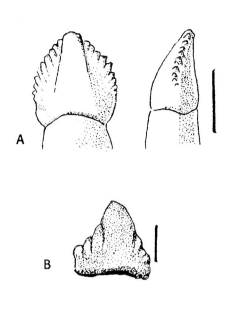

Figure 3-8. The teeth of Ornithischian dinosaurs of the Chinle Formation, New Mexico and Arizona. A: *Revueltosaurus*; note the relatively large size of this tooth; bar=5 mm (.2 inch). B: *Tecovasaurus*, known from Texas and Arizona; bar=2 mm. C: *Lucianosaurus*, from New Mexico; bar=1 mm. Figures redrawn from Padian, 1990 and from Hunt and Lucas, 1994.

Chinle sediments of Utah. As has been seen, the *Atreipus*-like tracks of the Lake Powell region may have been made by an ornithischian dinosaur. All of the late Triassic dinosaurs known from New Mexico and Arizona most likely lived in Utah as well, and it can be expected that their remains may be discovered in Utah exposures of the Chinle Formation someday.

The Mid-Triassic Unconformity: A Frustrating Gap

The new discoveries of dinosaur fossils in the Chinle and age-equivalent strata clearly demonstrate that several different types of dinosaurs had become established in the Colorado Plateau region in the late Triassic Period. They were perhaps not the most dominant element of the terrestrial vertebrate fauna, but the dinosaurs were certainly here between 225 and 210 million years ago. Re-

call that no trace of dinosaurs is found in the underlying Moenkopi Formation, which represents deposits that formed along the early Triassic coastal plain between about 248–240 million years ago. Where did the Chinle dinosaurs come from? Did they originate in western North America or were they immigrants from South America or elsewhere? What were the ancestors of *Coelophysis*, *Revueltosaurus*, and other Chinle dinosaurs? Unfortunately, paleontologists have no answers to these questions, and it is likely that the mysteries are going to persist for some time. For this, the widespread mid-Triassic unconformity is to blame.

As has been mentioned, following the deposition of the Moenkopi Formation sediments, geological events began to transform the low coastal plain of central Utah into the interior basin of late Triassic (Chinle) time. Evidently, however, no sediments were deposited in Utah during the roughly 15 million years that the geological transition was taking place. This fact has produced an extensive regional unconformity in the Triassic rock record that separates the two formations throughout the Colorado Plateau region (Figure 3-3). This mid-Triassic unconformity separates more than just two rock formations, however; it also divides Utah's Triassic history into the early Age of Dinosaurs (Chinle) and the pre-dinosaur time period (Moenkopi). In between, scientists have no information at all. There is only a scoured surface of erosion between rock layers to record the time when the dinosaurs first entered, or evolved in, Utah. All researchers can be sure of is that sometime between about 240 and 225 million years ago dinosaurs joined the reptilian menagerie in the Colorado Plateau region.

By the end of the Triassic Period, there were several different types of dinosaurs present in the American Southwest. They were evidently evolving rapidly in comparison to other groups of reptiles, becoming more dominant and larger as Triassic time drew to a close. This late Triassic dinosaur fauna was a prosperous assemblage, living in what might almost be considered a reptilian Garden of Eden. Then, about 210 million years ago, just before the beginning of Jurassic time, a combination of geological and biological events punctuated the evolutionary rhythm of these early dinosaurs to set the stage for the next phase of Mesozoic madness—the early Jurassic.

FOUR

The Early and Middle Jurassic

A Time of Transition

NEAR THE CLOSE of the Triassic Period, some important changes began to affect the land and life of Utah. Even as the last layers of the Chinle Formation were being deposited, geological events were in the process of ushering in a new landscape and inducing profound changes in the climate of the interior basin of the Colorado Plateau region. The supercontinent Pangaea was beginning to show more obvious signs of its fragmentation at the end of the Triassic Period than it had earlier. The great Triassic rift valleys forming along the eastern edge of North America deepened and began to divide that continent from the Eurasian land mass. The modern North Atlantic Ocean basin was about to be initiated in latest Triassic time. The entire supercontinent was slowly sliding north as it broke apart. The portion of it that was to become North America led the way, accelerated by the extra push toward the pole that resulted from the rifting occurring along its eastern (by today's geography) edge.

As North America moved north, it eventually left the warm, moist tropics and entered the subtropical zone of dry climate that prevails at a latitude of about 25 degrees north of the equator. As a consequence, the climate of Utah became more arid at the end of Triassic time than it had been during earlier portions of that period. Similar climatic changes were taking place elsewhere in the world as the progressive rifting of Pangaea caused profound changes in global geography and climate.

The Late Triassic Extinctions

Paleontologists have long recognized that the transition from Triassic to Jurassic time was marked by some significant changes in the character of life on a global scale. These changes were the result of the extinction of many existing groups of organisms, followed by the adaptive radiation (a sort of evolutionary expansion) of the survivors and the emergence of new groups of organisms near the end of the Triassic Period. During the past two decades, intensive research on the Triassic-Jurassic event has resulted in some new perceptions of the timing and pattern of this biotic turnover (Hallam, 1991; Benton, 1991). These events, in turn, have important consequences relating to our understanding of the history of dinosaurs in western North America and elsewhere.

The effects of the extinctions that occurred near the end of the Triassic Period are evident in many different groups of organisms that occupied a variety of habitats. In the seas, the groups most strongly impacted by extinction at this time included some types of ammonites (the ceratites), many reef-building organisms (sponges, bryozoans, and calcareous algae), echinoderms (such as sea urchins and their kin), and brachiopods. The bivalve molluscs (clams) were also affected, exhibiting a 90 percent reduction in the numbers of species during the transition. Among marine and freshwater fish, a 33 percent decline has been documented near the end of the Triassic Period (Benton, 1989). The effects of the extinction event on terrestrial plants seem to have been more subtle, but there was a gradual decline in ferns and an increase in the diversity of cycads and conifers from late Triassic through mid-Jurassic time.

The pattern of the Triassic-Jurassic turnover among the terrestrial vertebrates is, of course, our main concern, because dinosaurs were present both before and after the event. About half of the families of Triassic terrestrial reptiles had become extinct by the beginning of Jurassic time. The main victims of late Triassic extinction in the terrestrial realm were several groups of non-dinosaurian reptiles including the rhyncosaurs, rauisuchians, ornithosuchians, phytosaurs, and mammal-like dicynodonts. Not all of these groups died out at exactly the same time, but their numbers were sharply reduced in the late Triassic. By the beginning of the succeeding Jurassic Period, they had all disappeared from the fossil record. Taking the place of these groups that vanished during the Triassic-Jurassic transition were the survivors of the extinction event and some newly evolved forms. The crocodiles, turtles, pterosaurs, and some sphenodontid reptiles were among the newcomers, and they all experienced dramatic adaptive radiation in the Jurassic Period. In addition, the mammal-like reptiles became even more like mammals after the end of the Triassic Period, as the cynodonts and dicynodonts (such as *Placerias*) were replaced by a variety of creatures that seem to be much more advanced toward "mammalness." In the Jurassic, there is a great proliferation of such mammalian groups as the morganucodonts, docodonts, and triconodonts (among many others). These creatures so closely resemble primitive mammals that they can confidently be considered the earliest members of that class. Scientists no longer need to refer to these Jurassic beasts as "mammal-like" reptiles, for they are clearly members of the early mammal lineage.

What about the dinosaurs? How did they change across the Triassic-Jurassic boundary? Recall that dinosaurs were a minor component of the Chinle fauna and consisted of several ceratosaurian theropods (*Coelophysis* and others) and, evidently, several primitive ornithischians (*Revueltosaurus*, *Tecovasaurus* and others). Although the early Jurassic record of dinosaurs is a bit sketchy in western North America, scientists do know that the quadrupedal prosauropods were much more common in the early Jurassic than they were at any time in the Triassic Period, even though the footprint evidence suggests that they may have been present near the end of the latter period. In addition, within the theropod lineage there emerges in the early Jurassic larger and more specialized ceratosaurs, such as the double-crested *Dilophosaurus*. Reasonably complete specimens of ornithischian dinosaurs are also known from the early Jurassic strata of western North America, and these include the armored *Scutellosaurus*

along with other primitive types. The tracks preserved in early Jurassic rocks of the Colorado Plateau indicate not only a general increase in the size of dinosaurs but also an increase in the diversity of the dinosaur communities (Lockley and Hunt, 1995). Even though knowledge of the dinosaur fauna of the early Jurassic Period in Utah is limited by the scarcity of fossils, paleontologists can nonetheless discern an obvious change as we cross the Triassic-Jurassic boundary. What could have caused the great faunal turnover at the end of the Triassic Period?

The causes and timing of the Triassic-Jurassic extinction and the subsequent faunal turnover have been controversial issues for many years among paleontologists. It now seems that there were probably two pulses of extinction: one that occurred about 223 million years ago, at the end of the Carnian Age of the late Triassic, followed by a second, less severe, wave of extinction at the very end of the Triassic (the Norian/Rhaetian Age) about 210 million years ago (Benton, 1991). If this is true, then it becomes very difficult to relate the late Triassic extinctions to any single sudden cause. Some scientists have suggested that the forty-five-mile-wide Manicougan Crater in northern Quebec, Canada, is the scar of an asteroid impact that may have caused the late Triassic extinctions. The crater seems to be approximately the right age, but a twofold nature of the extinctions is difficult to reconcile with a single agent of sudden biotic upheaval such as an asteroid impact.

Other scientists have proposed that the regression of shallow seas at the end of the Triassic may have altered climates and geography to the point that many groups of organisms could not keep pace with the environmental changes. This explanation has some merit (remember that the "Moenkopi seaway" of western Utah did withdraw to the west in late Triassic time); however, in this case, we might expect to see a continuous and gradual transition rather than a one-two punch of

Photo 9. The Glen Canyon Group near Goblin Valley. The nearest cliff is comprised of Wingate Sandstone. The ledgy beds at the top of this cliff represent the Kayenta Formation. Navajo Sandstone is exposed in the most distant light-colored cliffs. John Telford.

extinction. As shall be seen, the early Jurassic rock record of Utah (and elsewhere) indicates that there was a pronounced shift toward drier and more strongly seasonal climatic conditions near the end of Triassic time.

It may be that the Triassic-Jurassic transformation of the global biota was caused by a combination of all these factors, and perhaps others that we have yet to discover. If it was such an interplay of several different events that produced the environmental changes leading to the extinctions, then scientists would expect the patterns of biotic change to vary at different locations, at different times, and in terms of which groups of organisms were affected. And, in fact, such a complex pattern of biotic turnover is precisely what the fossil record is beginning to suggest for the end-Triassic

event. To settle this question once and for all, much more information will be needed on both the late Triassic and early Jurassic faunas than is currently available. In any case, though its ultimate causes are still a mystery, the faunal change that accompanied the beginning of the Jurassic Period brought with it a whole new assemblage of dinosaurs to Utah and adjacent regions.

The Early Jurassic Rock Sequence of Utah

Almost everywhere in central and eastern Utah, the Chinle Formation is overlain by several formations of early Jurassic age that consist primarily of sandstone. These formations comprise the Glen Canyon Group and include, in ascending order, the Wingate Sandstone (and its lateral equivalent in southwest Utah, the Moenave Formation), the Kayenta Formation, and the Navajo Sandstone (Figure 4-1). This threefold package of rock formations is usually easy to recognize in the canyon country of eastern Utah on the basis of the unique weathering profile of the three main components. The massive Wingate Sandstone typically erodes into magnificent sheer cliffs, up to 400 feet high and often stained with black streaks of desert varnish, that extend for miles as an unbroken wall. Comb Ridge, south of Monticello, is an impressive exposure of Wingate Sandstone (and other early Jurassic strata) that traverses more than sixty miles as a nearly continuous facade of solid stone. The Kayenta Formation, resting above the Wingate Sandstone, is a heterogeneous sequence of reddish-brown sandstone, siltstone, and mudstone of varying hardness. The Kayenta normally weathers into uneven slopes broken by many small ledges and benches. The ledges mark the exposure of one of the harder layers of rock, while the smooth slopes between them are eroded from the softer units. Above the Kayenta slope, an enormous wall of white to reddish sandstone towers to heights of well over 1,000 feet. This cliff consists of the Navajo Sandstone, one of the most impressive cliff-forming rock sequences in the world. Navajo Sandstone cliffs are particularly impressive in the Zion National Park region, where they tower to heights exceeding 1,500 feet, but they are prominent features of the landscape wherever the formation is exposed.

The sandstones that dominate the Glen Canyon Group, the Wingate and Navajo formations, are mostly composed of sand grains smaller than about 0.5 mm in size. The sand grains commonly have abraded or "frosted" surfaces. Outcrops of these sandstones commonly exhibit spectacular large-scale cross-bedding that produces the sweeping etching on cliffs and bald knobs (known as "slickrock") throughout the canyon country of southeastern Utah. These features provide evidence that the vast amounts of

Photo 10. Large-scale tangential cross-bedding reflects the eolian (wind-deposited) origin of the Navajo Sandstone in the San Rafael Swell. John Telford.

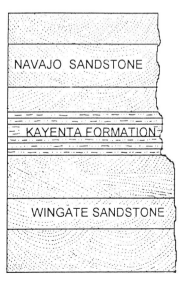

NAVAJO SANDSTONE

KAYENTA FORMATION

WINGATE SANDSTONE

Figure 4-1. The Great Sand Pile: The Glen Canyon Group of eastern and southern Utah.

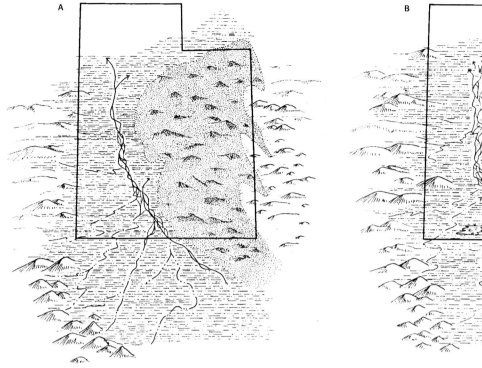

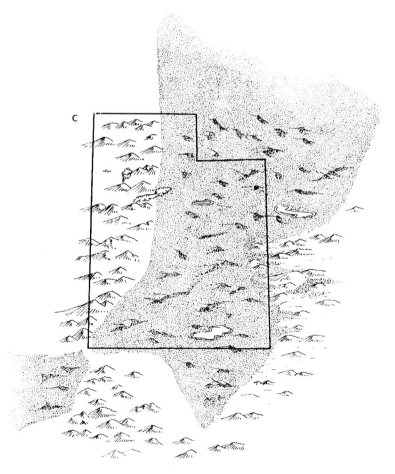

Figure 4-2. Paleogeography of Utah during early Jurassic time. A: The Wingate Sandstone erg was the first of two large dune fields to develop in the early Jurassic. To the southwest of the erg, fluvial sediments of the Moenave Formation were deposited at the same time. B: The braidplain on which fluvial sediments of the Kayenta Formation were deposited. C: The immense Navajo sand sea covered at least 400,000 square kilometers (150,000 square miles) of western North America.

sand in the Wingate and Navajo formations represent windblown particles that accumulated in an immense dune field. Such large dune fields, like the "sand sea" of the modern Sahara Desert of north Africa, are known as ergs. Sandstones that represent wind-transported accumulations are referred to as eolian deposits. The ergs represented by the Wingate and Navajo sandstones were of impressive extent, at times approaching Saharan proportions during the early Jurassic. This is especially true of the Navajo Sandstone, which can be traced northward from southern Utah well into Wyoming, where it is known as the Nugget Sandstone. To the southwest, the Navajo erg extended into the Mojave Desert region of southeastern California, where the sand deposits are referred to as the Aztec Sandstone (Figure 4-2C). Thus the Navajo-Nugget-Aztec erg covered much of the southwestern portion of North America, just as modern north Africa is mostly covered by Saharan sand. The Navajo Sandstone erg covered at least 160,000 square miles, based on the current extent of the Navajo and correlative formations. Because the modern distribution of the Navajo-Nugget-Aztec sand deposits has been reduced by post-Jurassic erosion, the original erg might have been as much as twice that size. The early Jurassic sand sea of western North America was larger than the modern Sahara erg and is comparable to the spacious dune fields of the Empty Quarter in modern Saudi Arabia. During Wingate Sandstone time, the erg was somewhat smaller and only covered the eastern half of Utah plus a small portion of adjacent areas (Figure 4-2A).

The orientation of the cross-beds in such sand deposits can provide information on the direction of sand transport. For the Navajo Sandstone, the sand grains were derived mainly from the north and northwest, blown into the interior basin from that direction in successive "waves" of sand, some up to fifty feet high (Young, 1987). The sand accumulated across the floor of the central Utah interior basin, which was still sur-

rounded by highlands to the west, south, and east. In western Utah and eastern Nevada, the Mesocordilleran High, which began to develop in late Triassic time, became even more prominent in the Jurassic as igneous activity and compressional forces became active in the region (Hintze, 1988; Miller and others, 1987; Miller and Hoisch, 1995). To the south, the ergs were limited by chains of volcanic mountains in south-central Arizona, from which a broad slope descended to the north into Utah's interior basin (Riggs and Blakey, 1993). East and southeast of the sand seas, in Colorado and southeast of the Four Corners region, low hills and benches served as barriers to the dune fields. To the north, beyond the open end of the interior basin, the great sand sheets extended to the shoreline of the early Jurassic seas, located in what is now Wyoming, Montana, and Idaho. The sandy beaches of this coastline must have been the source for much of the sand deposited in the early Jurassic ergs. Thus, the eolian deposits that dominate the Glen Canyon Group signify the burial of the old Chinle basin under sheets and dunes of wind-driven sand derived from the north and northwest. The movement of such massive amounts of sand requires a dry and windy climate. The relatively verdant, well-watered basin of the late Triassic became a searing desert in the early Jurassic. In the context of such an acute shift in the regional environment, the Triassic-Jurassic biotic transition, or change of life forms, certainly comes as no surprise.

Though the Glen Canyon Group is dominated by eolian sandstone, which documents an enormous and persistent desert, it also contains other types of deposits that are extremely important as sources of information about the animals that inhabited the erg. In all large ergs there are interdune areas where the infrequent rainfall may become ponded in ephemeral, or playa, lakes. Such lakes are short-lived, usually disappearing in a matter of days in the blistering climate of the desert. In addition, groundwater occasionally rises to the surface in places like the modern Sahara to form spring-fed oases, which represent the only semipermanent bodies of water in the otherwise barren sandy landscape. As large dunes migrate in the downwind direction, the dry sand is blown along over and past the more cohesive and moist sediment below, resulting in the lowering of the land surface as the dunes pass. The process of lowering the surface by blowing away the dry sand and silt is known as deflation. Deflation basins between the crests of advancing dunes can temporarily capture rainwater or allow groundwater to seep to the surface from a moist substrate. The momentary abundance of water in these deflation basins may allow plants to germinate, giving rise to a small pocket of productivity in the midst of a biological wasteland.

The deflation basins, ephemeral lakes, and oases of sandy deserts act like biotic magnets, attracting great numbers of animals to drink, to feed on whatever plants might be growing at the water's edge, or to lie in wait for prey to approach. In the early Jurassic sandstones of Utah, such interdune deposits are represented by thin and laterally discontinuous lenses of mudstone and limestone that are interbedded with the much thicker and more extensive eolian sandstones. The deflation surfaces appear as prominent horizontal planes, known as "first-order bounding surfaces," among the complex pattern of sweeping cross-beds that typify eolian sandstones. Many deflation surfaces and lenses of interdune deposits occur in the Navajo Sandstone and some are known from the Wingate. It is in these zones that both fossils and footprints principally occur in these two eolian formations (Winkler and others, 1991). In addition, the early Jurassic ergs were laced by dry washes that channeled runoff into the temporary lake basins following the rare cloudbursts. Sand would periodically drift into the washes, only to be scoured away during a subsequent desert flash flood. Some of the sandstone layers in the Navajo and Wingate represent reworked eolian sand

spread out across the floor of the dry washes during flood events.

In the case of the Wingate Sandstone, the relatively small erg covered only the eastern half of Utah (Figure 4-2A). On its southwestern margin, a complex river system separated the erg from the foothills of the Mesocordilleran High to the west. This river system transported water and sediment to the northwest, toward the sandy beach beyond the open end of the interior basin. The wind would then blow the sand back into the erg. Some of the sand and silt carried by the river system was deposited along its course and over the adjacent floodplain. These river-deposited sediments flanking the eolian sandstones of the Wingate comprise the major portion of the Moenave Formation. The Moenave Formation is restricted to southwestern Utah and northwestern Arizona and is equivalent to at least the upper part of the Wingate Sandstone, into which the fluvial sediments pass as they are traced east. The Moenave fluvial system drained the slope descending from the volcanic highlands of south-central Arizona and carried water around the Wingate erg. The river plain habitat with its more plentiful water probably supported a richer biota than the sand sea to the northeast during Wingate-Moenave time.

The development of ergs in the early Jurassic occurred, as has been suggested, in two phases: a relatively small Wingate erg and the much larger, and later, Navajo erg. Between these two episodes of sandy deserts, a large river system similar to the Moenave fluvial complex evidently covered the entire portion of eastern Utah. Thus, the Kayenta Formation that separates the Navajo and Wingate sandstones consists almost entirely of river-deposited sand, silt, and mud. For some reason, the amount of sand blowing into the interior basin diminished during Kayenta time. The rivers draining to the northwest began to penetrate into the older Wingate erg, picking up great amounts of loose sand. The rivers developed braided patterns as huge sandbars choked the channels and forced the streams to fork and split as the water they carried passed around the sandy obstructions. As the braided pattern developed, a broad plain laced by numerous criss-crossing watercourses evolved on top of the buried Wingate erg. Such a broad surface of sediment transported by a braided stream system is known as a braid plain. The Kayenta Formation represents a braid plain interlude between two episodes of erg development. The climate in Kayenta time was probably still desert-like, but dune fields were only a restricted element of the scene during that brief phase of a river-dominated arid landscape (Figure 4-2B). In the northeast corner of Utah, around Dinosaur National Monument, the Glen Canyon Group consists of about 700 feet of eolian sandstone without the fluvial Kayenta component. Evidently the braidplain made by the Kayenta fluvial system did not extend into this corner of Utah, where the dune fields persisted throughout the entire early Jurassic.

Paleontology of the Glen Canyon Group: A New Array of Dinosaurs

Our knowledge of the life that existed in and around the great ergs and braidplains of the early Jurassic is meager. It is based on a few rare fossils preserved in the Glen Canyon Group and, to a greater degree, on the somewhat more abundant footprint evidence. The scarcity of fossils probably results from at least three factors. First and foremost, deserts are generally regions of minimal biological productivity. The lack of water would have restricted the growth of plants, which, in turn, meant limited food resources for herbivores and few prey animals for carnivores. Modern deserts are known for their stark and lifeless appearance, a consequence of the minimal life in such hostile environments. The desert landscapes of the early Jurassic throughout the Colorado Plateau region were certainly more barren than

Photo 11. This dinosaur track in the Dinosaur Canyon Member of the Moenave Formation in southwestern Utah were probably made by prosauropods.
Frank DeCourten.

were the landscapes in the preceding late Triassic Period (Chinle time). Second, the constant shifting of sand as large dunes migrated across the erg would have resulted in the alternate burial and re-exposure of the organic remains. Such events do not favor the preservation of fossils. Finally, the cliff-forming nature of the eolian sandstones that dominate in the Glen Canyon Group makes it difficult for scientists to find the few fossils that are preserved in these rocks. The vertical walls of rock are, for the most part, impossible to survey in any detailed manner for fossils. Most of the fossils that have been found in these formations were located either in blocks that have fallen from the cliffs or in the few areas where the strata are exposed along the level ground surface.

Nevertheless, researchers do have some fossils and a number of footprints from the Glen Canyon Group, enough to demonstrate that dinosaurs and other creatures did live among the dunes and along the watercourses of early Jurassic Utah. Moreover, the dinosaurs and other terrestrial vertebrates known from these rocks indicate a much different community from that represented in the underlying Chinle Formation. The Triassic-Jurassic transition is clearly evident when the two fossil assemblages are compared.

Dinosaur Footprints from the Glen Canyon Group

The footprints of dinosaurs and other vertebrates are fairly common in many horizons in the Wingate, Kayenta, and Navajo formations. Footprints tend to be more common in the finer-grained mud and silt deposited by rivers that ran through or beside the erg and in the silty limestone and mud that accumulated in oasis-like interdune ponds. The water at such sites would have attracted great numbers of animals, and the soft, tacky mud at the water's edge would have served as a good medium for the preservation of footprints and trackways, recording the comings and goings of life drawn in from the surrounding desert. Some footprints have been discovered in the dune sands as well, and many of them appear to have been made when the sand was moistened by dew or rain and therefore more cohesive than it was normally. During the explosion of interest in the study of dinosaur footprints in the past two decades, considerable attention has been directed toward the tracks of the Glen Canyon Group (see, for example, Lockley and Hunt, 1995; Baird, 1980; Lockley, 1991a; Stokes, 1978; Stokes and Madsen, 1979; among many other studies). The following information is based on these recent studies.

The dinosaur footprints preserved in the Wingate Sandstone are dominated by large three-toed tracks, 15–20 cm (6–8 inches) long. These tracks are generally about twice the size of similar tracks known from the Chinle Formation. The tracks usually have sharp claw impressions, indicating a theropod dinosaur some 3–4 feet high at the hip. Such a theropod would have been significantly larger than *Coelophysis* or any other bipedal dinosaur known from the late Triassic. Such tracks are known as *Eubrontes*, and they can be thought of as an overgrown *Grallator*-type track made by a larger animal. In southwestern Utah, the fluvial Moenave Formation (equivalent to the upper Wingate) also has produced *Eubrontes* tracks (Figure 4-3B) along with other smaller theropod footprints (*Grallator* type; Figure 4-3A). Elsewhere in Utah, *Batrachopus*, a type of footprint thought to have been made by a primitive crocodilian reptile, occurs in the Moenave Formation.

The Kayenta Formation also produces relatively abundant footprints, including the *Eubrontes* type similar to those of the Wingate. Also known from the Kayenta are some very interesting three-toed tracks that sometimes have smaller four-digit impressions associated with them. These tracks, known as *Anomoepus*, suggest a dinosaur that was capable of shifting its stance from bipedal to quadrupedal while it walked, the smaller four-digit track representing the forefoot, or "hand," impression. Finally, the Kayenta Formation has also produced some very small (a little less than 2.5 cm, 1 inch, long) three-toed tracks that have very slender toe impressions. These tracks may have been made by baby theropods or, perhaps, they represent footprints left by early birds. Recall that the first bird probably originated from its dinosaur-like ancestor sometime prior to the late Jurassic. The birdlike tracks of the Kayenta might actually represent the earliest evidence of avian creatures.

In summary, the footprints from the Wingate Sandstone and the Kayenta Formation suggest a dinosaur-dominated community of terrestrial vertebrates living in the ergs and braidplains in Utah in the early Jurassic. There is little evidence from the footprint record of the other, non-dinosaur, reptiles (rauisuchians, phytosaurs, etc.) that were so common in the Chinle Formation. Evidently, those reptiles had become victims of the Triassic-Jurassic extinctions. By early Jurassic time, the dinosaurs were beginning to take over.

It is in the Navajo Formation that the dinosaur footprint record explodes, revealing the presence of many new varieties of dinosaurs, other reptiles, and (probably) primitive mammals. Vertebrate tracks are known from the Navajo Sandstone at numerous localities in Utah and range from tiny, birdlike footprints barely an

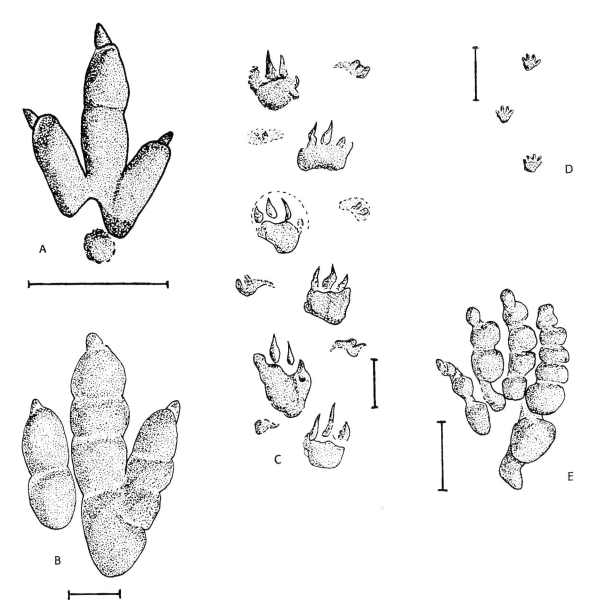

Figure 4-3. Early Jurassic tracks of the Glen Canyon Group of eastern and southern Utah. A: Small *Grallator* tracks; and B: much larger *Eubrontes* tracks from the Moenave Formation of southwestern Utah; both made by theropod dinosaurs. C: *Navahopus* from the Navajo Sandstone, a possible prosauropod trackway; D: *Brasilichnium* from the Navajo Sandstone; E: *Otozoum*, possible prosauropod tracks from the Navajo Sandstone near Moab. Bar in all sketches=10 cm (4 inches). A and B from Miller and others, 1989; C–E from Lockley and Hunt, 1995.

inch long to much larger tridactyl (three-toed) prints more than 1 foot in length. These forms are generally similar to the *Grallator-Eubrontes* family of footprints and were probably made by small and large theropod dinosaurs, respectively, or perhaps even by birds (for the smallest tracks). In addition to these footprints, the track assemblage in the Navajo Sandstone includes many other interesting forms. *Brasilichnium*, for example, is a small, oval track ranging from about 2.5–7.5 cm (1–3 inches) wide and having four

or five stubby toe impressions (Figure 4-3D). *Brasilichnium* tracks look much like the footprint of a dog and have at least two characteristics suggesting mammal origin: wide feet (broader than they are long) and short toes (Lockley and Hunt, 1995). Some very mammal-like reptiles known as tritylodonts (more about them later) are known from the fossils of the Glen Canyon Group. *Brasilichnium* is thought by most paleontologists to represent tracks made by tritylodonts or other animals similar to them. Lizard tracks, given the

Photo 12. A large three-toed dinosaur footprint in the Navajo Sandstone in Buckhorn Wash, San Rafael Swell. John Telford.

inward, suggesting a robust "thumb" on the front feet of the creator of the print. Thus, these two types of tracks could have been made by a group of large dinosaurs that had four well-developed toes on their hind feet, were capable of both quadrupedal and bipedal posture, and had forefeet (or "hands") with a long first digit. The best candidates for being the originator of *Otozoum* and *Navahopus* from the Navajo Sandstone are the prosauropods, which have all the characteristics suggested by the tracks. Since skeletal remains of prosauropods are known from the Navajo Sandstone, it is reasonable to associate *Otozoum* and *Navahopus* with two different types, or sizes, of prosauropods walking among the dunes of the Navajo erg. Overall, the abundant and varied dinosaur tracks assemblage preserved in the Navajo Sandstone suggests that the trend toward greater dinosaur size, dominance, and diversity continued throughout the time represented by the Glen Canyon Group.

Dinosaur and Related Fossils from the Glen Canyon Group

name *Lacertipus*, are often associated with mammal-like tracks in the Navajo Sandstone.

With respect to dinosaurs, perhaps the most significant tracks to occur in the Navajo Sandstone are the large four-toed tracks known as *Otozoum* and similar, but smaller, footprints referred to as *Navahopus*. *Otozoum* tracks are a foot or more in length and about 8 inches wide (Figure 4-3E). In trackways with several *Otozoum* prints aligned in sequence, there are no smaller forefoot impressions, suggesting that the track maker was a large biped. In *Navahopus*, the smaller (12–15 cm, or 5–6 inches, long) four-toed hind-foot prints are associated with 5-cm (2-inch)-wide forefoot prints, implying a quadrupedal track maker with larger hind limbs than forefeet (Figure 4-3C). The front foot impressions in *Navahopus* bear a pronounced claw mark directed

Until the early 1980s, researchers knew very little about the animals that inhabited the early Jurassic ergs of Utah and adjacent regions. There were some sporadic reports of vertebrate fossils from the region as early as the 1930s (for example, Brown, 1933; Camp, 1936), and by the late 1950s a few more discoveries had been made (Lewis, 1958; Welles, 1954). In the late 1970s and early 1980s intensive collecting from the Kayenta Formation of northern Arizona by the Museum of Northern Arizona, the Museum of Comparative Zoology at Harvard University, and the University of California Museum of Paleontology produced abundant fossil material and stimulated great interest in the fauna of the Glen Canyon Group. As a result, scientists can now recognize a distinctive early Jurassic dinosaur fauna, accompanied by a variety of non-dinosaurian vertebrates, from the Colorado

Plateau region. Knowledge of this fauna is still incomplete, however, and it is based primarily on specimens discovered in northern Arizona. Since the ergs and erg-margin environments of the early Jurassic extended over the entire Colorado Plateau region, it is likely that the Arizona forms also existed in Utah. As scientists continue to search for fossils from the Glen Canyon Group in Utah, it is likely that they will confirm the presence of these forms (and perhaps even discover new types) from the southeastern part of the state.

With one fascinating exception, the oldest fossils known from the Glen Canyon Group are found in the Moenave Formation, the lateral equivalent of the Wingate Sandstone. Only one identifiable fossil, other than the footprints already described, has been found in Utah exposures of the mostly eolian sandstones of the Wingate. Morales and Ash (1993) reported phytosaur remains in the lowermost part of the Wingate Sandstone in the vicinity of Big Indian Rock, north of Monticello. How the remains of aquatic creatures like phytosaurs came to be preserved in these eolian sandstones is an interesting mystery. Since the fossil phytosaur material came from the lower Wingate Sandstone, just above its contact with the underlying Chinle beds, the bones may have weathered out of the Chinle sediments prior to the deposition of the Wingate sands. However, the fossils appear to be uneroded, so they might represent the remains of phytosaurs that somehow managed to live in Utah as the dunes advanced inland. However they may have come to reside where they were found, these remains probably represent the last of the phytosaurs; no trace of them is found in rock layers younger than the Wingate Sandstone.

Recall that the Moenave Formation represents sediment deposited in a river system that skirted the Wingate erg on the southwest. The Moenave river plain must have been a much more fertile realm than the scorched and gusty Wingate

desert. It is not surprising that most of the fossils from the earliest part of the Jurassic Period come from the Moenave Formation, not the Wingate Sandstone. The most common vertebrate from the Moenave Formation is the early crocodile *Protosuchus* (Brown, 1933; Colbert and Mook, 1951). This reptile probably lived in the rivers that deposited the Moenave sediments, but it seems to have possessed a more erect stance, and therefore was somewhat better adapted for terrestrial locomotion, than modern crocodiles. Perhaps the streams flowing along the southwest margin of the Wingate erg were shallow and/or ephemeral. *Protosuchus* appears to have been well adapted for such a river system.

There are some scrappy, or fragmentary, indications of dinosaurs in the Moenave Formation, but the bones collected thus far are too few and fragmentary to identify with precision. However, dinosaur footprints in the Moenave Formation in Warner Valley southeast of St. George (Miller, Britt, and Stadtman, 1989) indicate the presence of at least three different types of dinosaurs living along the floodplains of the Moenave river system. A large bipedal theropod, a smaller *Coelophysis*-like carnivore, and possibly a prosauropod dinosaur all tramped through the fine sand and mud deposited at this site during the early Jurassic. As shall soon be seen, this set of footprints is perfectly compatible with the types of dinosaurs known from Glen Canyon strata in other locations. Thus, paleontologists know that at least several different types of dinosaurs were prowling the edge of the Wingate erg.

The Kayenta Fauna

The Kayenta Formation, because of its fluvial origin, has produced the vast majority of fossils known from the Glen Canyon Group. The Kayenta vertebrate fauna is a rich one, indeed. *Protosuchus* was still present in Kayenta time, but was joined by several other types of crocodilians

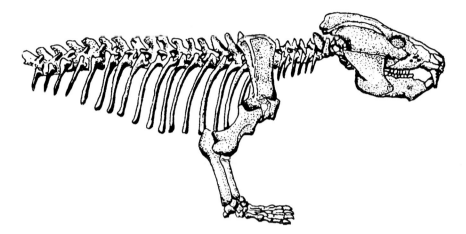

Figure 4-4. *Kayentatherium,* an early Jurassic tritylodont. Skull is about 25 cm (10 inches) long. Adapted from Carroll, 1983.

such as *Eopneumatosuchus* (Crompton and Smith, 1980). Fossils of turtles and frogs, both aquatic animals, also have been found in the Kayenta Formation. The advanced herbivorous mammal-like reptiles known as tritylodonts were especially abundant and diverse during Kayenta time. *Kayentatherium* (Figure 4-4) is the most common of this group and may be close to the ancestor of later Mesozoic mammals. Some early members of those advanced mammal groups are known from the Kayenta Formation. *Morganucodon* and *Dinnetherium,* for example, both have been recovered from Arizona localities and are so far along the evolutionary path to becoming mammals that most paleontologists place them into the class without question.

What were the tritylodonts and other herbivores eating? Plant fossils are not abundant in the Kayenta Formation, but occasional fragments of fossil wood suggest that plants existed across the floodplains and along the river channels. There may have been genuine forests growing on the higher slopes of the Kayenta watershed. Two different pterosaurs also have been identified from Kayenta sediments, including *Rhamphinion,* named on the basis of fragmentary fossils found in northern Arizona (Padian, 1984). *Rhampinion* was about the size of a large hawk, with a wingspan of about four feet. These pterosaurs represent the oldest-known flying reptiles in

North America. It is clear from this partial list of Kayenta fossils that the river systems of Kayenta time were populated by many different kinds of aquatic, terrestrial, and aerial vertebrates, a situation that contrasts sharply with the barren sandy desert of Wingate time.

Dinosaurs are also known from Arizona exposures of the Kayenta Formation and almost certainly lived in Utah as well. Relatively complete and well-preserved fossils of two different crested theropods have been found in these strata. The first Kayenta theropod was discovered in 1942; it was first referred to as *Megalosaurus wetherilli,* and was later renamed *Dilophosaurus wetherilli* (Welles, 1954; Welles, 1970). Additional specimens of *Dilophosaurus* recovered from Arizona localities in the 1960s have greatly improved our knowledge of *Dilophosaurus,* the "doubled crested reptile" (Welles, 1984). This dinosaur was a fearsome beast, with sharp, dagger-like teeth lining the jaws of a skull that sported two large crests of bone flaring upward from the head (Figure 4-5). It was approximately 18 feet long when full grown, weighed some 600–700 pounds, and held its ornate head 6–7 feet off the ground.

The function of crests on the skull of *Dilophosaurus* is still conjectural, but they certainly contributed to a more threatening countenance. Perhaps the crests were used to attract mates or to discourage competitors. The bone in the crests was very thin, so it is unlikely that the crests were used in head butting or defense. This theropod was fully bipedal and, although the legs were not as long as those of more advanced theropods, it was probably a speedy animal. Because *Dilophosaurus* has several relatively primitive features, such as four fingers on its reduced forelimbs, it belongs to the unadvanced group of theropods known as ceratosaurs. Primitive though it may have been, *Dilophosaurus* was probably the largest of the dinosaur predators inhabiting the Kayenta landscape. Welles (1984) noted that the bone at the tip of the snout (the premaxilla) was weakly

Figure 4-5. *Dilophosaurus*, a theropod from the Kayenta Formation.

attached to the rest of the skull, suggesting that *Dilophosaurus* could not have generated a very powerful bite. This provides some evidence that *Dilophosaurus* may have pecked at its prey in a manner similar to the way a vulture dismembers and consumes the carcass of a dead animal. If *Dilophosaurus* was a scavenging theropod, its primary killing weapons may have been the sharp claws that tipped three of the four fingers on its hand. In addition to consuming the remains of animals that had already died, it is likely that *Dilophosaurus* occasionally used its speed to catch smaller and slower animals, ripping them with the talons of the forelimbs. There is no solid evidence that *Dilophosaurus* could spit poison, as the down-sized individuals of this species were depicted doing in the popular movie *Jurassic Park*—that behavior is sheer Hollywood hype. Besides, with all its other weapons—speed, agility, claws, and dental daggers—why would it need poison, particularly if the primary food of *Dilophosaurus* consisted of already dead creatures?

Syntarsus kayentakatae is another ceratosaurid theropod that, as the species name suggests, is also known from the Kayenta Formation of Arizona. *Syntarsus* was a small theropod, about the same size as *Coelophysis* of the late Triassic and only about half as large as *Dilophosaurus*. It also had a crest running along the top of its skull, but its crest appears to have been much less pronounced than the double crest of *Dilophosaurus*. The approximately 9-inch-long skull of this theropod was equipped with dozens of sharp, curved teeth, all smaller than about one inch in length (Figure 4-6). *Syntarsus*, while it is still considered to be a ceratosaur, is the most advanced member of that group. Several of the ankle bones of *Syntarsus* were fused to form a strong joint with motion restricted to the fore-and-aft plane. The foot is extremely birdlike, suggesting that *Syntarsus* was quick and agile. Evidently, *Syntarsus* preyed on smaller and more elusive creatures than did *Dilophosaurus*, such as lizards and mammal-like reptiles. The two known Kayenta theropods, or other predators similar to them, may likely be the originators of the three-toed footprints in the Kayenta sediments at Warner Valley and other sites in Utah. It may be more

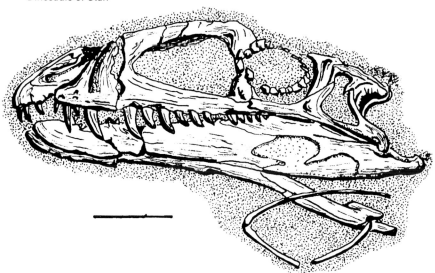

Figure 4-6. Skull of *Syntarsus* as it was discovered in the Kayenta Formation of northern Arizona. The ring of small bones in the orbit, the sclerotic ring, surrounded the eye. The slender bones in the lower right are the hyoid bones. Bar=5 cm (2 inches). After Rowe, 1989.

than a coincidence that the theropod tracks in the Kayenta Formation and the theropod fossils it has thus far produced seem to come in two size ranges: small (*Grallator* and *Syntarsus*) and large (*Eubrontes* and *Dilophosaurus*).

In addition to these dinosaur predators, the remains of herbivorous dinosaurs have also been discovered in the Kayenta Formation. The prosauropod *Massospondylus* is known from the Kayenta on the basis of a single nearly complete, but distorted, skull (Attridge and others, 1985; Figure 4-7A). Prosauropods were one of the first groups of dinosaurs to evolve during the great Triassic radiation of reptiles. By early in the Jurassic, the prosauropods had spread across North and South America and into Europe, Asia, and Africa. In their general appearance, the prosauropods were similar to the great sauropods that would follow them in the later Jurassic, with a long neck and tail; but they were much smaller and had a less bulky build. The teeth of prosauropods were simple and flattened in shape like a spatula, with numerous bumps (or serrations) along the edges (Figure 4-7B). The forelimbs of prosauropods were smaller than the hind limbs, but not by much. This primitive group of saurischian dinosaurs probably walked in a quadrupedal fashion most of the time (Figure 4-7C), but they were no doubt capable of rising

up on their hind limbs in a bipedal posture when it was advantageous to do so.

Prosauropods were almost certainly herbivorous; one famous specimen of *Massospondylus* was discovered in Africa with a mass of gastroliths preserved within the rib cage, suggesting the presence of a gizzard-like organ to help grind plant fodder. The *Massospondylus* from the Kayenta Formation is almost identical to specimens of this genus from southern Africa. Interestingly, the southern Africa specimens come from rocks that were also deposited in an arid or semiarid environment, much like the Kayenta Formation of the Colorado Plateau. Apparently, *Massospondylus* was specialized for plant eating in such dry habitats. There are, however, some unique features that were observed for the first time in the skull of the Kayenta specimen. The Arizona specimen evidently had dozens of small (about 1 mm, .04 inch, long) conical teeth on its palate. The function of these tiny teeth is uncertain, but palatal teeth have never been observed in any other dinosaur. The skull of the Arizona *Massospondylus* also has a pronounced "overbite," as three of the teeth in the front of the upper jaw hung out over the lower jaw (Figure 4-7A).

With the discovery of *Massospondylus* in the Kayenta Formation, the existence of prosauropods in the Colorado Plateau during the early Jurassic is firmly established. Scientists may also have discovered the group of creatures that left the larger tracks such as *Otozoum*, *Tetrapodichnus*, *Navahopus*, and *Anomoepus* in the late Triassic and early Jurassic rocks of Utah. Since trackways of probable prosauropod origin are also known from the late Triassic Chinle Formation, this group of dinosaurs was probably present in the Colorado Plateau for millions of years before the animals' oldest known remains were preserved in the sediments of the Kayenta Formation.

Massospondylus was not the only herbivorous dinosaur inhabiting the Kayenta river system. Fossils of the earliest North American ornithis-

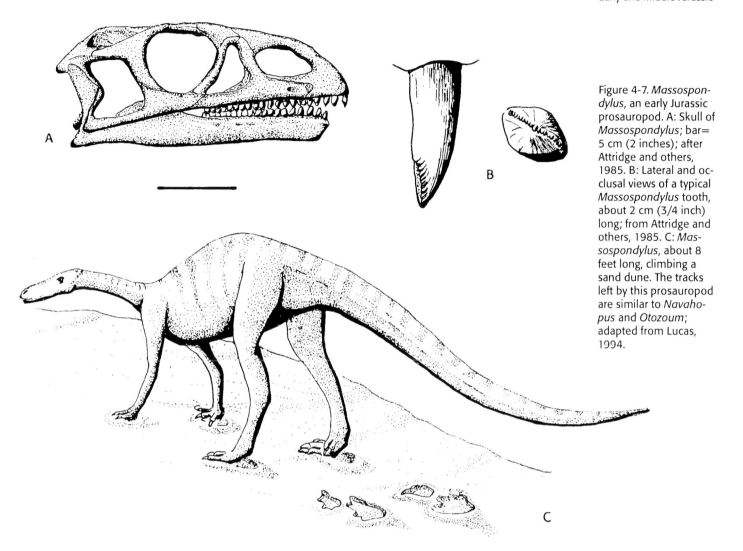

Figure 4-7. *Massospondylus*, an early Jurassic prosauropod. A: Skull of *Massospondylus*; bar= 5 cm (2 inches); after Attridge and others, 1985. B: Lateral and occlusal views of a typical *Massospondylus* tooth, about 2 cm (3/4 inch) long; from Attridge and others, 1985. C: *Massospondylus*, about 8 feet long, climbing a sand dune. The tracks left by this prosauropod are similar to *Navahopus* and *Otozoum*; adapted from Lucas, 1994.

chian dinosaurs also have been discovered in the Kayenta Formation, again from northern Arizona localities. Two different Kayenta ornithischians are known, both of relatively primitive character. *Scutellosaurus* (Figure 4-8) is the better known of the two, represented by at least one nearly complete skeleton and additional fragmentary fossils (Colbert, 1981). *Scutellosaurus* belongs to a primitive group of ornithischians known as the fabrosaurs. The fabrosaurs (family Fabrosauridae) are known primarily from the early Jurassic in southern Africa, but they now have been found elsewhere in strata ranging from the late Triassic to the Cretaceous. The group is considered to be primitive because, among other features, their teeth are relatively simple and leaf-shaped compared with the more complex grinding teeth of later ornithischians. In addition, the pubis is parallel to the ischium in the fabrosaurs (as it is in all ornithischians), but it lacks the well-developed forward extension, the prepubic process, that characterizes the more advanced members of this order. Currently, only a few types of fabrosaurs are known, including the namesake genus *Fabrosaurus* (also known as *Lesothosaurus*), *Gongobusaurus* from eastern Asia, and possibly *Technosaurus* from the late Triassic of Texas. Most paleontologists regard the fabrosaurs as a short-

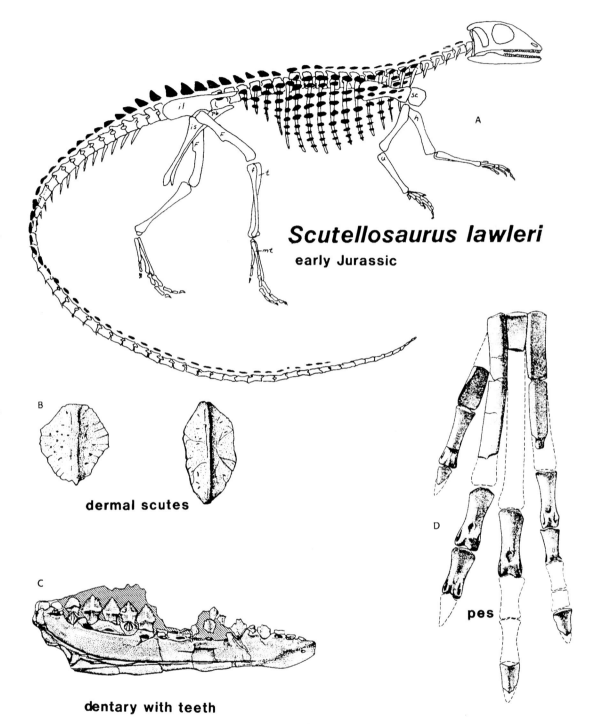

Figure 4-8. *Scutellosaurus*, an ornithischian dinosaur from the Kayenta Formation. A: Reconstruction of the skeleton of *Scutellosaurus*. Note the extremely long tail and numerous scutes covering the body. This small dinosaur stood about 15 inches tall at the hips and was a little over 4 feet long. B: Typical scutes from *Scutellosaurus*, the largest about 2 cm (3/4 inch) long. C: A fragment of the dentary bone from the lower jaw, with several teeth; total length approximately 5.8 cm (2.3 inches). D: Left pes, dorsal view; total length, 10.7 cm (4.2 inches). All figures from Colbert, 1981.

Scutellosaurus lawleri

early Jurassic

dermal scutes

dentary with teeth

pes

lived group of primitive ornithischians that were replaced in mid-Jurassic time by the more advanced ornithopods.

Scutellosaurus from the Kayenta Formation was not a large dinosaur. It was only about 4 feet in length, about two-thirds of which was accounted for by its very long tail (Figure 4-8A). The exaggerated tail would have made it difficult for *Scutellosaurus* to move in a bipedal fashion, unless its body forward of its hips was heavier than the light and delicate bones seem to suggest. It appears that this was precisely the case, however, because *Scutellosaurus*, as the name suggests, was covered by an extensive jacket of bony armor plates, or scutes. There were several hundred scutes imbedded in the skin of *Scutellosaurus*, forming a knobby shield over most of its body. The armor scutes exhibit a variety of shapes; those in Figure 4-8B exhibit the typical form of scutes covering the back of *Scutellosaurus*. The weight of all these scutes may have been the reason for the unusually long tail—it was necessary to counterbalance the heavily armored trunk of this small dinosaur. The well-developed armor of *Scutellosaurus* is unique among the fabrosaurs and, for this reason, some paleontologists consider this dinosaur to be a primitive member of either the ankylosaur or stegosaur families. However, aside from the scutes, there are few similarities between the skeleton of *Scutellosaurus* and the ankylosaurs or stegosaurs, and it is probably best categorized as a modified fabrosaur. In any case, the armor scutes of *Scutellosaurus* clearly related in some way to the thyreophoran dinosaurs ("shield bearers") that appear later in the Mesozoic Era.

The teeth of *Scutellosaurus* were small and leaf-like, similar to the teeth of most other fabrosaurs (Figure 4-8C). They are clearly the teeth of a herbivore, designed to shred and strip vegetation, but they were probably not very effective in grinding or pulverizing plant material. The foot of *Scutellosaurus* has four toes, but only three of them contacted the ground to support the body (Figure 4-8D). The fourth toe (digit 1, equivalent to a human's big toe) was reduced to a stubby prong. With the reduced first toe held above the ground surface, *Scutellosaurus* would presumably have left a small tridactyl hind-foot track similar to those preserved in the Kayenta Formation at Warner Valley and elsewhere. The four-toed foot of *Scutellosaurus* is also a relatively primitive feature observed commonly in the fabrosaurid group of ornithischians.

Scelidosaurus is another armored ornithischian known from the Kayenta Formation, but its identification is more tentative, based solely on isolated scutes (Padian, 1987). Isolated scutes are not uncommon in the Kayenta Formation; after all, these thick and solid plates of bone are among the most durable portions of a dinosaur skeleton. For many years, the isolated scutes of the Kayenta Formation were thought to have been the remains of aetosaurs, the armored herbivorous thecodonts of the late Triassic. In fact, the assignment of the Kayenta Formation to the Jurassic Period was delayed until recent years because it was thought to contain the scutes of late Triassic reptiles. Recently (Padian, 1987), however, these scutes were identified as belonging to the ornithischian dinosaur *Scelidosaurus* on the basis of their unique curved and partially hollowed conical form (Figure 4-9). The scutes of aetosaurs are more elongated, less conical, and have a different pattern of sculpturing. Thus, there were no aetosaurs living on the Kayenta floodplains; the scutes actually belong to another primitive ornithischian dinosaur.

Scelidosaurus was one of the first dinosaurs discovered in Europe, where it is represented by nearly complete fossil skeletons. Even though this dinosaur is known in the Kayenta Formation only from isolated scutes, it appears to have been very similar to the better-known European specimens. *Scelidosaurus* was larger than *Scutellosaurus*, with a body length of about 13 feet. Unlike *Scutellosaurus*, however, it was evidently more quadrupedal in stance, with relatively robust forelimbs (Figure 4-10). The teeth of *Scelidosaurus*

Figure 4-9. A scute of *Scelidosaurus* in lateral, dorsal, and ventral views. Note the concave underside of the scute, a feature unique to this ornithischian dinosaur. Bar=1 cm. From Padian, 1989.

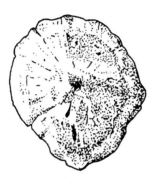

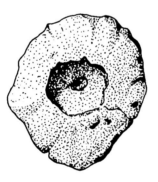

were still small and simple, much like the teeth of fabrosaurs. *Scelidosaurus* was probably less mobile and agile than the smaller *Scutellosaurus* and likely spent most of its life slowly browsing through the undergrowth of the sparse forests of the early Jurassic.

It is interesting to note that the first two ornithischian dinosaurs to appear in the Colorado Plateau region, *Scutellosaurus* and *Scelidosaurus*, were both well armored. The scutes imbedded in the skin of both of these dinosaurs probably helped them repel the attacks of predators. *Scutellosaurus*, in particular, because of its small size, might have been the target of constant assaults from *Dilophosaurus*, *Syntarsus*, and other crocodilian predators. The large size of *Scelidosaurus* might have deterred some of the smaller carnivores, but additional protection would have been valuable when it confronted the ferocious dilophosaurs. There must have been many dramatic struggles between dinosaur predator and prey along the Kayenta riverbanks and floodplains.

Fossils from the Navajo Sandstone: Life in the Sand Sea

After the deposition of the last fluvial sediments in the Kayenta Formation, sand once again crept into the low basin of eastern Utah from the north and northwest. Eventually, windblown sand accumulated to build a complex of dunes and interdune areas similar to the erg of Wingate time but of much greater magnitude. The Navajo Sandstone, along with its equivalent units (the Nugget Sandstone to the north, the Aztec Sandstone to the southwest), represents this second early Jurassic sand sea. The Navajo erg dwarfed the earlier Wingate desert, extending from at least southeastern California well into Wyoming and covering nearly all of Utah (Figure 4-2C). Scientists infer that the climate must have become more arid after the Kayenta fluvial interlude, allowing the reestablishment of a sandy desert environment.

Plate 2.
An early Jurassic oasis. *Dilophosaurus* stalks prey among the sand dunes of the Four Corners region while pterosaurs watch from their perches.

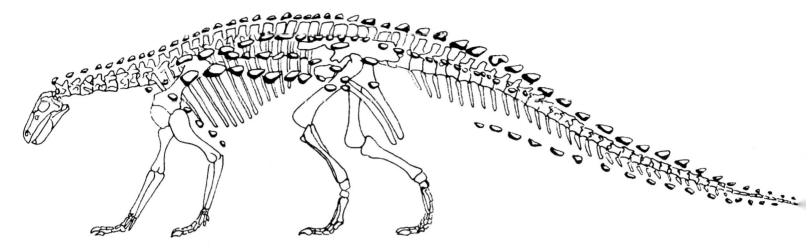

Figure 4-10. Skeleton of *Scelidosaurus*. Based on Czerkas and Czerkas, 1991, cited in Chapter 1.

The desolation of the Navajo sand sea must have rivaled the barrenness of the modern Saudi Arabian deserts. Such an austere setting would have sustained minimal biological productivity compared to the relatively fecund habitats of Kayenta time. It is therefore no surprise to learn that, like the Wingate Sandstone, the Navajo Sandstone contains few fossils. It does, however, furnish some intriguing clues about the nature of the terrestrial fauna in Utah about 190 million years ago, as the early portion of the Jurassic Period drew to a close.

Footprints of terrestrial vertebrates are not uncommon in the Navajo Sandstone in Utah, Arizona, Colorado, and Wyoming. As we have already seen, the footprints are most often preserved in the thin, lenticular sequences of playa or oasis sediments that were deposited between massive sand dunes. The track assemblage, or "ichnofauna," of the Navajo Sandstone is a diverse assortment of markings probably left by a variety of animals moving through the great erg. This ichnofauna is also highly controversial. The various tracks preserved in the Navajo Sandstone have sparked considerable debate on the identity of the track makers. The Navajo footprints have been attributed by various scientists to the activity of early mammals, prosauropod dinosaurs, theropod dinosaurs, crocodiles, and lizards (see Lockley and Hunt, 1995, for a good summary).

Creating perhaps the most contention among all the footprints in the Navajo Sandstone are those originally ascribed to pterosaurs (Stokes and Madsen, 1979), named *Pteraichnus*. The *Pteraichnus* tracks from the Navajo Formation were first found around Moab but have since been discovered elsewhere in the western states in rocks of Jurassic age (Figures 4-11, 4-15). *Pteraichnus* tracks are extremely controversial trace fossils. Some scientists consider them to be the footprints of crocodiles (Padian and Olsen, 1984) rather than of pterosaurs. Other theories abound for the origin of these small tracks, and there is still no universal agreement on their origin. It should be pointed out that the earliest-known North American pterosaur fossils (*Rhamphinion*) are found in the Kayenta Formation, so the interpretation of the Navajo *Pteraichnus* markings as pterosaur traces is not completely unreasonable. The Navajo tracks were found in association with eolian sandstones deposited along the edge of a body of water. The footprints were evidently impressed in the moistened sand at the edge of the water. This, coupled with the fact that isolated pieces of fossil wood are sometimes found in the Navajo Sandstone, creates an interesting image of what parts of the great erg might have looked like. Between the crests of gigantic sand dunes, hundreds of feet high, there were probably many low basins where water would collect, at least temporarily. The moisture would support the growth of large (tree-sized?) plants. The water would attract dinosaurs and other animals, while the pterosaurs would perch on the limbs above, waiting for smaller prey, like lizards and mammals, to emerge from the surrounding sand sea. On occasion, animals would perish close to the water's edge. The pterosaurs undoubtedly would swoop down to scavenge at least a portion of the carcass as food. Such bodies of water in the Navajo erg were not permanent or widespread, but they would have been good places to catch a glimpse of life in the surrounding dune fields.

Fossil bone is found in the Navajo Sandstone, though rarely. The prosauropod *Ammosaurus* has been identified in the Navajo Sandstone of northeastern Arizona (Galton, 1971). The *Ammosaurus* remains from the Navajo were not complete, but they did include some well-preserved bones of the vertebral column, pes (feet), manus (hands), and limbs. *Ammosaurus* appears to have been a rather small, broad-footed quadrupedal animal, a little over 3.5 feet long, of the same overall body shape and form as *Massospondylus*. The manus (hand) of *Ammosaurus* was about 10 cm (4 inches) wide and possessed a large claw that projected inward. There were three well-developed digits on the manus, plus two others that were significantly reduced in size. The pes (foot) was larger, about 25 cm (10 inches) long, with four relatively large toes and a tiny vestigial fifth digit. The structure of the manus and pes of *Ammosaurus* is typical of the prosauropods, and it is likely that *Massospondylus* had similar appendages. Either of the two prosauropods would have made tracks like *Navahopus* (Figure 4-3C) when walking quadrupedally and would have left footprints similar to *Otozoum* or *Anomoepus* while walking on the hind limbs alone. The skull of *Ammosaurus* is unknown and this makes it difficult to compare this prosauropod directly to *Massospondylus*, for which most of the postcranial skeleton remains a mystery. It may be that *Massospondylus* and *Ammosaurus* represent

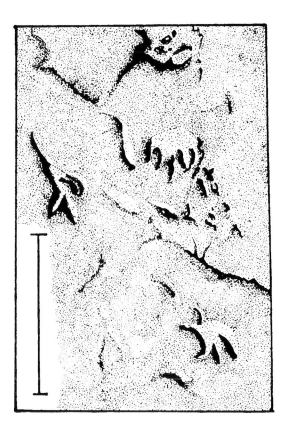

Figure 4-11. *Pteraichnus* tracks from the Navajo Formation near Moab, Utah. These tracks were originally attributed to pterosaurs in 1979, an interpretation that has been vigorously debated ever since. From data in Stokes and Madsen, 1979.

different parts of the same animal. For now, and until more complete fossils of both genera are found, the two are considered to be separate but similar genera.

The only other documented occurrence of dinosaur fossils in the Navajo Sandstone is from a site in Segi (or Tsegi) Canyon in northern Arizona, where a poorly preserved partial skeleton of a small theropod dinosaur was discovered in the 1930s. This dinosaur was named *Segisaurus* after the canyon in which it was found (Camp, 1936; Brady, 1936). *Segisaurus* appears to have been similar to *Coelophysis* in general appearance. It was a small, gracile predator and almost certainly belongs with *Coelophysis*, *Syntarsus*, and *Dilophosaurus* in the relatively unspecialized ceratosaurian subdivision of the Theropoda. The recovered skeleton of *Segisaurus* is too poorly preserved and incomplete to say much more about it with certainty.

In summary, the meager dinosaur fauna of

the Navajo Sandstone includes prosauropods and theropods that appear to be more or less similar to those present in the older Kayenta Formation. In addition, the remains of tritylodont mammals that are nearly identical to *Kayentatherium* have recently been discovered in the Navajo Sandstone (Winkler and others, 1991). From this, we can conclude that during the time of the great Navajo erg, the sand sea was populated by a few hardy relics or survivors of the more luxuriant landscapes of the Kayenta river basin. The vertebrate fauna of the Navajo Sandstone, to the extent that it is known, seems to be a depleted relict of the richer Kayenta assemblage.

Middle Jurassic Marine Invasion

Although eolian sandstone continued to accumulate in various areas of eastern Utah after the early Jurassic, the Navajo Sandstone marks the last time that a truly immense erg existed in the Colorado Plateau region. About 185 million years ago, during the middle Jurassic, the scene began to change again and the community of terrestrial vertebrates that inhabited eastern Utah was confronted with another profound environmental transformation. Seas returned to east-central Utah during the middle Jurassic, penetrating into the state from the north. Broad areas of Idaho, Montana, and Wyoming were submerged as the marine waters crept over the Nugget-Navajo dune fields. As the sea transgressed to the south, it eventually covered much of southern Utah, submerging the sandy habitat of the prosauropods and ceratosaurs. At its maximum extent, the middle Jurassic seaway of Utah reached as far south as the Zion National Park area. The middle Jurassic seaway of central Utah was a relatively narrow arm of the ocean that was bounded on the west by the Mesocordilleran High and to the east and south by the highlands that circled the older erg basin (Figure 4-12). Elsewhere in western North America, in areas of lesser relief, the middle Jurassic seas flooded enormous tracts of low-lying land. With

respect to dinosaurs, the main effect of this marine incursion was a drastic reduction of the habitat available to terrestrial animals. Dinosaurs persisted in Utah in the middle Jurassic Period, but they were restricted to the low coastal plains that surrounded the middle Jurassic seaway. Consequently, the fossil record of middle Jurassic dinosaurs in Utah and other western states is extremely sparse. The middle Jurassic, from about 185–160 million years ago, remains one of the most mysterious chapters in the story of North American dinosaurs. However, researchers do have enough clues from rocks formed during this "missing link" interval to know that dinosaurs still populated the habitats of east-central Utah and to recognize a few of the basic types.

Rocks of the San Rafael Group

Above the Navajo Sandstone in most areas of eastern and southern Utah are several formations consisting of sediment deposited either within the middle Jurassic seaway or around its edges. Collectively, this set of formations is known as the San Rafael Group, named for the San Rafael Swell region of Emery County where it is well exposed (Thompson and Stokes, 1970; Peterson, 1988). In this region, the San Rafael Group consists of the Page Sandstone, the Carmel Formation, the Entrada Sandstone or Formation, the Curtis Formation, and the Summerville Formation (Figure 4-13). This group of formations is dominated by red and brown mudstones and siltstones, alternating with lighter-colored sandstones, beds of gypsum, and occasional thin limestone layers. These sediments, a mosaic of marine and terrestrial deposits, accumulated near the eastern margin of the narrow middle Jurassic seaway. To the west, strata correlative with the San Rafael Group, such as the Arapien Shale and Twin Creek Limestone, are entirely marine in character. East of the San Rafael Swell region, in the Canyonlands National Park and Moab area, the San Rafael Group is composed mostly of nonmarine sediments de-

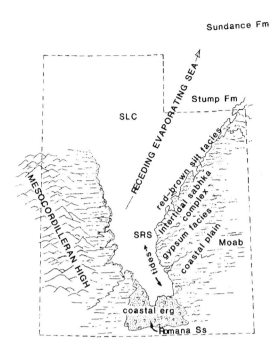

Figure 4-12. The Middle Jurassic Seaway in Utah.

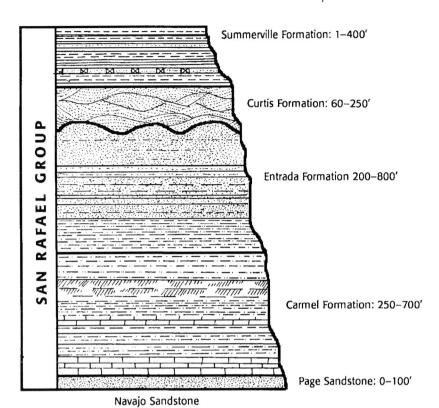

Navajo Sandstone

Figure 4-13. The San Rafael Group of east-central Utah. These formations grade into marine deposits to the west and into non-marine sediments to the east. Thicknesses are approximate and vary from place to place in eastern Utah.

posited in coastal dune complexes, river floodplains, lagoons, and other marginal marine environments.

The seaway that extended south into Utah during the middle Jurassic time evidently did not penetrate very far into western Utah. In this area, the Mesocordilleran High had developed into a conspicuous mountain terrain as the result of numerous bodies of magma raising the earth's surface, represented today by the intrusive igneous rocks of the House Range of Millard County, the Deep Creek Range of western Tooele County, and the Snake Range in eastern Nevada. These granitic rocks all yield radiometric dates clustering in the middle to late Jurassic Period. It is likely that the intensified igneous activity in this region in the middle Jurassic produced numerous volcanic eruptions, but the rocks formed during such events have long since been removed by erosion. To the south, the presumed volcanic arc of south-central Arizona still served as a topo-graphic barrier, although the middle Jurassic seaway never came very close to these peaks. However, the Carmel Formation near Kanab, Utah, contains large boulders of volcanic rocks carried more than 180 miles, probably during catastrophic floods, from sources to the southwest (Chapman, 1993). The south-central Arizona volcanic chain was the probable source of these boulders. The volcanic activity that was under way along the southern margin of the Colorado Plateau seems to have flared up significantly around 170 million years ago, as the sediments of the Carmel Formation were being washed into southern Utah (Blakey and Parnell, 1995). To the east, in Colorado, the land surface rose gently in a series of undulating hills of low stature. The eastern boundary of the interior basin was not as sharply defined as were the western or southern margins.

By the beginning of middle Jurassic time, the continued rifting and northward movement of

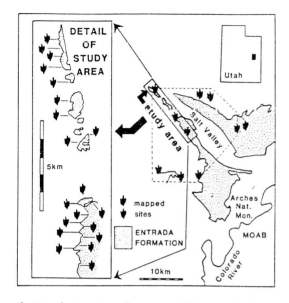

Figure 4-14. The Moab megatracksite in eastern Utah. Millions of tracks have been discovered in the uppermost layers of the Entrada Formation. From Lockley and Hunt, 1995.

the North American fragment of Pangaea had carried Utah to a latitude of about 25 degrees north of the equator. The climate was still warm and relatively dry. Evaporation rates were very high and, from time to time, so much water was removed from the narrow sea that layers of salt and gypsum (evaporite deposits) formed in and around the submerged basin. These evaporite deposits are especially prominent in the Arapien Shale and the Carmel Formation. On the eastern side of the seaway, a broad and low coastal plain developed on which various sediments were deposited. In places, coastal dunes formed as wind-driven sand and silt were piled along the edge of the seaway. Such middle Jurassic eolian deposits are found in the Slickrock Member of the Entrada Formation around Moab. Elsewhere on the eastern margin of the seaway, broad mud flats and coastal plains were buried by layers of fine-grained silt and mud deposited by sluggish rivers draining the low country to the east. The Summerville Formation consists mostly of such sediments, and parts of the Entrada Formation (the Dewey Bridge and more "earthy" facies) contain similar materials. The Curtis Formation consists of pale greenish sandstone, which represents offshore sandbars produced by tidal surges in the ancient seaway. The tidal currents piled sediment

up in great submerged hummocks and constantly reworked the sandy material across the shallow ocean floor. It is in sediments originally deposited on the muddy and sandy eastern margin of the middle Jurassic seaway that most of our information on dinosaurs is found.

Fossils and Footprints of the Middle Jurassic

Only one significant occurrence of vertebrate fossils is known from the San Rafael Group of central Utah. The remains of a small (about 22 cm, or 9 inches, long) and primitive crocodile known as *Entradasuchus* have been discovered in the Moab Member of the Entrada Formation (Lockley and Hunt, 1995). In view of the mostly muddy and swampy conditions that prevailed on the east side of the middle Jurassic seaway, it is not surprising that crocodile fossils occur in these rocks. There must have been other vertebrates accompanying *Entradasuchus* on the low coastal plain, but no body fossils of such creatures have yet been discovered.

Footprints from various horizons in the San Rafael Group tell a much different story. The ichnofauna from these strata is rich and profuse and it affirms the activity of great numbers of terrestrial animals on the eastern margin of the seaway. Particularly impressive is the "megatracksite" at the boundary between the Entrada and Summerville formations in the Moab and Arches National Park area (Lockley and Hunt, 1995; Lockley, 1991a,b). This locality, known as the Moab megatracksite, contains literally millions (perhaps billions) of tracks and covers an area exceeding 120 square miles (Figure 4-14). The track-bearing horizon, the surface separating the Entrada Formation from the overlying Summerville Formation, was heavily trampled by thousands of dinosaurs traveling along the early Jurassic coastal plain in eastern Utah.

The extreme numbers of tracks preserved at the Moab megatracksite might be a little misleading, however. In part, it reflects the minor uncon-

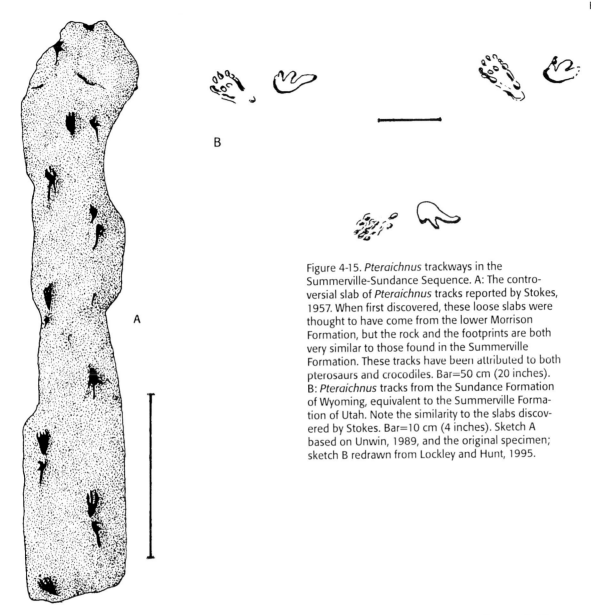

Figure 4-15. *Pteraichnus* trackways in the Summerville-Sundance Sequence. A: The controversial slab of *Pteraichnus* tracks reported by Stokes, 1957. When first discovered, these loose slabs were thought to have come from the lower Morrison Formation, but the rock and the footprints are both very similar to those found in the Summerville Formation. These tracks have been attributed to both pterosaurs and crocodiles. Bar=50 cm (20 inches). B: *Pteraichnus* tracks from the Sundance Formation of Wyoming, equivalent to the Summerville Formation of Utah. Note the similarity to the slabs discovered by Stokes. Bar=10 cm (4 inches). Sketch A based on Unwin, 1989, and the original specimen; sketch B redrawn from Lockley and Hunt, 1995.

formity (indicating a gap in time) between the two formations in this part of Utah. After the deposition of the uppermost layers of sediment in the Entrada Formation, there evidently was a break in the deposition of sediment for an unknown interval of time. The uppermost layers of the Entrada Formation were exposed during this hiatus, and groups of dinosaurs moving along the coastal plain could have left many tracks over a long period of time. Eventually, the sediments of the lower Summerville Formation were deposited

across the top of the trampled surface, probably as the result of a slight rise in the level of the middle Jurassic seaway. Thus, the millions of tracks in the Moab megatracksite may signify not just the abundance of dinosaurs but also a lengthy interval of exposure of the upper Entrada beds to track-making activities.

Most of the individual tracks in the Moab megatracksite were made by large three-toed dinosaurs, with feet 12–18 inches long. Many of these tridactyl tracks have sharp claw impres-

Photo 13. Several members of the Carmel Formation resting on the Navajo Sandstone (massive tan material in lower left), exposed in a roadcut along I-70 in Emery County. The bright white unit is a thick layer of gypsum that was deposited along the edge of the middle Jurassic seaway in central Utah. The gypsum is sandwiched between red mudstone and yellow-gray limestone. Frank DeCourten.

Photo 14. Sandstone of the Entrada Formation near Hanksville. John Telford

Photo 15: Dinosaur tracks in the Entrada Formation near Moab. Frank DeCourten.

sions, but others do not. This suggests that both theropod and ornithopod dinosaurs were responsible for the tracks.

Other formations belonging to the San Rafael Group have also produced dinosaur tracks, although not in the stunning abundance seen at the Moab megatracksite. Near Redfleet Reservoir north of Vernal, for example, the Carmel Formation has produced dozens of three-toed tracks made by small theropod dinosaurs (Lockley and Hunt, 1995). The Carmel tracks are about 7.5 cm (3 inches) or less in length. Some of the Carmel footprints have very slender toe impressions and might be attributable to birds. Quadrupedal dinosaurs do not appear to have been very common along the eastern shore of the middle Jurassic seaway. The plentiful dinosaur tracks observed at numerous localities in the Entrada and Carmel formations provide incontrovertible evidence that, despite the rarity of their fossil bones, great

numbers of dinosaurs did populate the eastern margin of the middle Jurassic seaway.

Within the main body of the Summerville Formation other very interesting tracks have been found that shed additional light on the nature of the terrestrial vertebrate community of middle Jurassic Utah. *Pteraichnus*, the tracks arguably made by pterosaurs, are known from several localities in the Summerville Formation in Utah and its northern equivalent in Wyoming, the Sundance Formation (Figure 4-15). Unlike the *Pteraichnus* tracks from the Navajo Sandstone, the Summerville-Sundance tracks are better preserved, more complete, and more accurately conform to what is known about pterosaur feet, hands, and locomotion (Lockley and Hunt, 1995). Although none of their fossil bones have yet been found in the Summerville sequence, we can be confident, on the basis of the *Pteraichnus* tracks, that pterosaurs sailed through the skies of eastern

Utah during the middle Jurassic. Most paleontologists believe the pterosaurs to have been well adapted to coastal environments, where they fed on fish living in the shallow seas and lagoons. They could be considered the large shorebirds of the Jurassic, and it is reasonable to assume that the periphery of Utah's seaway would have been a suitable habitat for them.

The middle Jurassic seaway of central Utah was the result of a temporary incursion of the seas from the north. By about 160 million years ago this sea was withdrawing to the north, into Wyoming and Montana. The low basin in east-central Utah was once again exposed as habitat for terrestrial vertebrates. Rivers flowing from the adjacent highlands once again began to wash sediment into the basin, while plants began to carpet the surface of the basin. As the end of the Jurassic Period drew near and the seaway vanished, there was a great expansion of dinosaur habitat in Utah. The stage was set for a dramatic proliferation of dinosaurs and the creation of Utah's own "Jurassic Park."

U TAH STATE HIGHWAY 24 is one of the most scenic byways in the world. Immediately south of its junction with Interstate 70, nine miles west of Green River, the ribbon of asphalt meanders south through stunning badlands gouged from layers of soft rock of incandescent colors. The bald hummocks and barren mounds almost shine with pastel bands of lavender, brown, vermilion, and ocher, streaked with layers of ashen gray. Rising and falling with the undulating land, the highway crosses the San Rafael River bottom about five miles south of I-70. At this point, the badlands begin to diminish as the road continues south across the vast San Rafael desert country, sprinting for the Henry Mountains looming on the distant horizon. Few travelers along this segment of Highway 24 can resist the temptation to stroll through the variegated wonderland along the highway, exploring the countless gullies and nooks cut into the soft rocks. An excursion out into these badlands almost always results in some interesting treasures—a rusty Prince Albert tobacco can with crumpled and yellowed claim papers from the uranium-mining days, a rouge-colored rattlesnake slithering along a gully bottom until it disappears under a rock, or perhaps the disintegrating carcass of a 1948 pickup truck. Those who possess eyes tuned to things geological, and who have the patience to look carefully, will also find small fragments of fossil bone almost anywhere in these badlands. The fossil bone betrays the age and identity of the rock strata exposed in the etched hills. These picturesque knolls are the icons of the late Jurassic Morrison Formation: the dinosaur graveyard of the West.

The Morrison Formation

Following the withdrawal of the middle Jurassic seaway in central Utah about 165 million years ago, the interior basin was once again exposed as land for the remainder of the Jurassic Period. Rivers flowing from the bordering ramparts col-lected within the basin again, as they had during late Triassic (Chinle) time. This time, however, the principal watersheds appear to have been the highlands to the west and, to a lesser degree, those in central Arizona and southern Nevada to the southwest. The Mesocordilleran High of earlier Jurassic time became much more prominent in the late Jurassic as widespread igneous activity elevated and enlarged the ancient mountain system of western Utah and eastern Nevada. Many bodies of magma were emplaced, primarily between about 170 and 140 million years ago, across the eastern Great Basin (Armstrong and Suppe, 1973; Hintze, 1988). Bodies of granite in the House and Deep Creek mountain ranges of western Utah, the Snake Range of eastern Nevada, and dozens of other nearby localities record the surge of molten rock from below. The Mesocordilleran High was almost certainly further elevated by the explosive eruption of some of this magma, forming a series of volcanic peaks that have long since been obliterated by erosion. In addition, in the Newfoundland Mountains of northwestern Utah, there is good evidence of late Jurassic uplift produced by folding and crumpling of the earth's crust under enormous compressive forces (Allmendinger and Jordan 1984; Allmendinger and others, 1984).

The upward rush of magma bodies, the eruption of volcanoes, and the compression of the eastern Great Basin all served to hoist the Mesocordilleran High to unprecedented elevation. As the mountains rose, they became more effective in capturing moisture from the late Jurassic clouds. Flowing from enhanced watersheds and racing down steeper slopes, the rivers draining the east flank of the Mesocordilleran High became the primary source of both the water and sediment that was transported into the lowlands of east-central Utah during late Jurassic time. As the rivers carried sediment from the highlands to the west, a vast alluvial plain was constructed from the sediment grains they deposited across the floor of the east-central Utah lowland. Layers of gravel, sand, and mud were spread out over

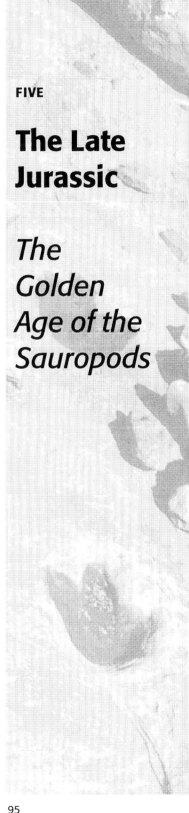

FIVE

The Late Jurassic

The Golden Age of the Sauropods

Photo 16. Colorful outcrops of the Morrison Formation along Utah Highway 24, west of Green River.
John Telford.

Photo 17. The Morrison Formation at Buckhorn Flat, San Rafael Swell. The line separating the lower red beds from overlying tan units is the contact between the Summerville and Morrison formations. Above this line, the Tidwell (soft slope), Salt Wash (sandstone ledges), and Brushy Basin (soft pale purple beds) members are exposed in the cliff. The lower conglomerate of the Cedar Mountain Formation caps the hill.
John Telford.

700,000 square miles of what is now Wyoming, Utah, Colorado, New Mexico, and Arizona (Figure 5-1). These are the sediments of the Morrison Formation.

The Morrison Formation was named in the late 1800s for the small town of Morrison, Colorado, about twenty miles southwest of Denver. This formation was traced by geologists over hundreds of miles into adjacent states throughout the Rocky Mountain region. The Morrison Formation is one of the most widely distributed rock sequences in the world, and it is also one of the most intensely studied. In the 1950s, rich uranium ores were discovered in the Morrison and Chinle formations of the Colorado Plateau, triggering the great "uranium boom," a notable chapter in the human history of eastern Utah and western Colorado. The search for uranium also brought a small army of geologists to the region to determine the origin of the ore bodies and to investigate the controls on their distribution. Even today, after several decades of intensive mining, the Morrison Formation is estimated to contain about half of the uranium reserves of the United States (Peterson and Turner-Peterson, 1987). As geological studies of the Morrison Formation progressed over the past quarter-century, as many as eight different members have been established for the formation in the Colorado Plateau region. The numerous subdivisions reflect the extreme heterogeneity of the Morrison sediments, a product of the largely fluvial (river) and lacustrine (lake) processes of deposition. In the dinosaur country of eastern and central Utah, three of these members are usually present: the Tidwell Member, the Salt Wash Member, and the Brushy Basin Member, in ascending order (Figure 5-2). Elsewhere in the Colorado Plateau, particularly in the Four Corners region and in northern Arizona, other members have been identified that are less important to the story of Utah dinosaurs.

One reason, of course, why the Morrison Formation has been so well studied is because it has produced literally tens of thousands of di-

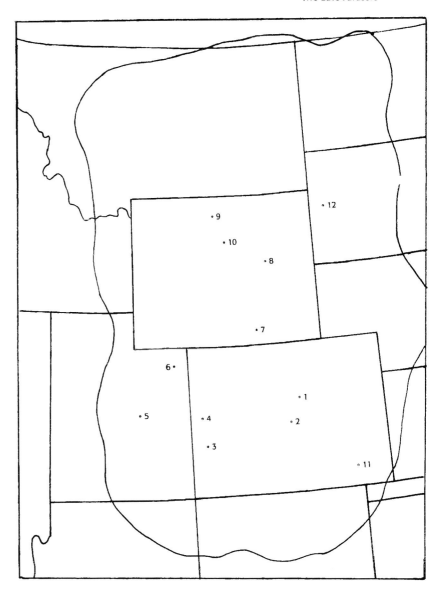

Figure 5-1. Distribution of the late Jurassic Morrison Formation in western North America and principal dinosaur quarries and localities. The major quarries are mostly located within the Brushy Basin Member. 1: Morrison, Colorado; 2: Garden Park area, Colorado; 3: Dry Mesa-Potter Creek area, Colorado; 4: Grand Junction area, Colorado; 5: Cleveland-Lloyd Quarry, Utah; 6: Dinosaur National Monument, Utah; 7: Como Bluff area, Wyoming; 8: Southern Bighorn Basin, Wyoming; 9: "Big Al" *Allosaurus* Quarry, Wyoming; 10: Howe Quarry, Central Big Horn Basin, Wyoming; 11: Purgatorie River tracksite, Colorado; 12: Piedmont Quarry, Black Hills Area, South Dakota. Map adapted from Dodson and others, 1980.

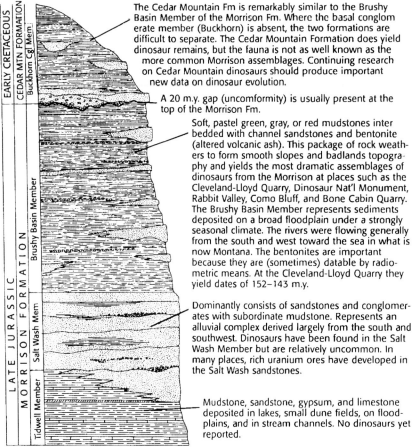

The Cedar Mountain Fm is remarkably similar to the Brushy Basin Member of the Morrison Fm. Where thc basal conglomerate member (Buckhorn) is absent, the two formations are difficult to separate. The Cedar Mountain Formation does yield dinosaur remains, but the fauna is not as well known as the more common Morrison assemblages. Continuing research on Cedar Mountain dinosaurs should produce important new data on dinosaur evolution.

A 20 m.y. gap (uncomformity) is usually present at the top of the Morrison Fm.

Soft, pastel green, gray, or red mudstones interbedded with channel sandstones and bentonite (altered volcanic ash). This package of rock weathers to form smooth slopes and badlands topography and yields the most dramatic assemblages of dinosaurs from the Morrison at places such as the Cleveland-Lloyd Quarry, Dinosaur Nat'l Monument, Rabbit Valley, Como Bluff, and Bone Cabin Quarry. The Brushy Basin Member represents sediments deposited on a broad floodplain under a strongly seasonal climate. The rivers were flowing generally from the south and west toward the sea in what is now Montana. The bentonites are important because they are (sometimes) datable by radiometric means. At the Cleveland-Lloyd Quarry they yield dates of 152–143 m.y.

Dominantly consists of sandstones and conglomerates with subordinate mudstone. Represents an alluvial complex derived largely from the south and southwest. Dinosaurs have been found in the Salt Wash Member but are relatively uncommon. In many places, rich uranium ores have developed in the Salt Wash sandstones.

Mudstone, sandstone, gypsum, and limestone deposited in lakes, small dune fields, on floodplains, and in stream channels. No dinosaurs yet reported.

Summerville, Wanakah, or Romana Formations underlie the Morrison

Figure 5-2. The Morrison Formation of east-central Utah. Three subdivisions are usually recognized in the dinosaur country of Utah: the Tidwell Member, the Salt Wash Member, and the Brushy Basin Member. Elsewhere in Utah, particularly around the Four Corners region, other members may be present.

nosaur bones from dozens of sites throughout the West. The Morrison Formation is one of the most prolific sources of dinosaur fossils in the world. Unlike the earlier periods of dinosaur history in Utah, known only from isolated and sparse fossil material and from footprint evidence, the late Jurassic record explodes into dazzling abundance. However, before reviewing the rich dinosaur fauna from the Morrison Formation, let's explore late Jurassic landscapes of Utah by examining the sediments in which the fossils are preserved.

The Tidwell Member is the oldest of the three main members of the Morrison Formation recognized in most localities in east-central Utah (Figure 5-2). This sequence of rock layers is usually

between 25 and 75 feet thick in eastern Utah, but it includes as much as 300 feet of sediments in adjacent areas. The Tidwell Member is a soft, slope-forming unit consisting of a varied assemblage of sedimentary rocks, including pale brown sandstone, red-gray mudstone, gypsum, and limestone (Peterson, 1988). The mudstones of the Tidwell Member sometimes contain hard nodules of reddish-orange chert, a microcrystalline form of silica (SiO_2). These chert nodules are so brilliantly colored that they have become a favorite of rockhounds, who commonly refer to them as "sunset agate."

The sediments of the Tidwell Member seem to have been deposited on the poorly drained surface of a lowland basin. The limestone of the Tidwell Member commonly contains fossils of ostracods (small aquatic crustaceans), charophtyes (a green algae common in bodies of fresh water), and gastropods that indicate deposition primarily in lakes and ponds. The mudstones in the Tidwell probably represent fine silt and clay that accumulated along the edges of the lakes, on mud flats, or in swampy areas (Peterson and Turner-Peterson, 1987). Most of the sandstones appear to have been deposited by relatively small steams or, in places, as small patches of dune sand transported by wind. No evidence of large, vigorous river systems has been observed in any of the Tidwell sediments. The base of the Tidwell Member is marked by a prominent and widespread unconformity, below which the beds of various formations of the underlying San Rafael Group were beveled prior to the deposition of Tidwell sediments. This unconformity signifies an extensive period of erosion following the retreat of the middle Jurassic seaway from central Utah. The erosion probably occurred around 160 million years ago and may have persisted for several million years. The Tidwell Member has produced only a few dinosaur bones, but the first dinosaur fossils ever discovered in Utah came from this member (Gillette, 1993). It appears that either the terrestrial habitats of central Utah during Tidwell time were not particularly well suited for large terrestrial animals, or that the conditions did not favor the frequent preservation of their remains, or both.

Above the Tidwell Member throughout east-central Utah is a ridge- and bench-forming sequence dominated by coarse, cross-bedded sandstone and conglomerate known as the Salt Wash Member of the Morrison Formation. The coarse-grained sediments of the Salt Wash Members are relatively hard and more resistant to weathering than are the softer rocks above and below them. The cross-bedding of sandstones and orientation of pebbles in the conglomerates of the Salt Wash Member indicate deposition by swift rivers flowing mainly from the highlands to the west and southwest (Peterson and Turner-Peterson, 1987). The Salt Wash Member varies in thickness from 150 feet to 300 feet in central Utah, but it thickens as it is traced to the west, providing further evidence of sediment transportation from that direction. The sandstone and conglomerate in the Salt Wash Member were probably deposited by a complex braided river system that spread sand and gravel eastward from the foothills of the Mesocordilleran High as a broad alluvial apron, sloping down from the western highlands to the lower terrain in central Utah. As the many small braided streams descended from the western mountains, they eventually collected into fewer but larger meandering streams flowing across the more level ground in eastern Utah.

Many of the individual layers of sandstone in the Salt Wash Member are broadly lenticular, tapering laterally to thin edges and eventually disappearing over distances ranging from several yards to several miles. Between the lenticular sheets of sand and gravel, or adjacent to their edges, greenish-gray mudstone and clay-rich limestones are common in the Salt Wash Member, particularly in easternmost Utah. These fine-grained components of the Salt Wash Member represent sediments deposited during floods on the nearly flat surfaces separating the many river

channels. Scattered throughout the Salt Wash Member and sometimes mixed into the sandstone, conglomerate, and mudstone are thin layers of bentonite, the clay-rich rock derived from volcanic ash. The bentonite of the Salt Wash Member was no doubt derived from the volcanically active highlands to the west, which would have periodically discharged great clouds of ash that drifted downwind over the low basin to the east.

Dinosaur fossils have been found in the Salt Wash Member at dozens of localities in Utah and Colorado, but they are usually fragmentary skeletons or isolated bones. This probably reflects the vigorous energy of the rivers that transported and deposited most of sediments observed in the Salt Wash Member. Skeletal remains would most commonly have been broken apart and scattered by the swift water or flood surges in such a setting. Only occasionally would relatively complete carcasses of dinosaurs be buried intact and preserved as fossils.

The youngest member of the Morrison Formation in the northern and central Colorado Plateau is the Brushy Basin Member. It consists mostly of soft, slope-forming mudstone and shale interbedded with less common limestone, coarse sandstone, and conglomerate. Typically, the dominant mudstones of the Brushy Basin Member are beautifully variegated, exhibiting pastel bands of purple and maroon, red and gray, ocher and rose. These distinctive colors arise from the oxidation of metals such as iron and manganese in the sediments. Layers of volcanic ash, usually altered to bentonite, are fairly common in the Brushy Basin Member. Some of the volcanic ash layers and bentonitic claystones contain mineral crystals that can be dated by radiometric techniques. These dates provide important information on the absolute age of some dinosaur-producing horizons.

The mudstones were deposited in a variety of rather tranquil sedimentary environments, including the channels and muddy banks of sluggish rivers, swamps and bogs, and shallow

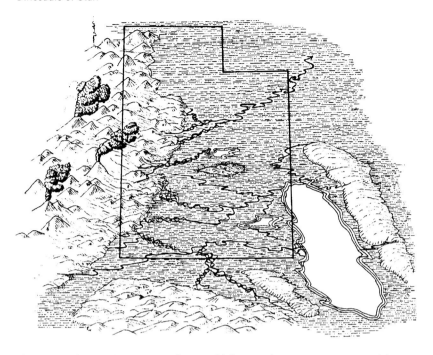

Figure 5-3. The Morrison landscape of Utah. In the late Jurassic Period, east-central Utah was a broad, undulating lowland circled on three sides by mountainous terrain. West of the interior basin, the old Meso-cordilleran High was uplifted by volcanic activity and the deformation related to the early stages of the Sevier Orogeny. The rivers carrying water and sediment into the basin ran mainly in a west-to-east direction across the lowland. Numerous lakes, some of them highly alkaline, dotted the landscape, and vegetation was concentrated along watercourses and lakeshores.

ephemeral lakes. In the eastern portion of the Colorado Plateau, some of the mudstones of the Brushy Basin Member contain minerals such as analcime and clinoptilolite that are thought to have formed as volcanic ash reacted with the alkaline water of a large temporary lake (Peterson and Turner-Peterson, 1987). Such lakes are known as playas and are particularly common in arid regions. The water in playa lakes gathers for a short time following a period of heavy rain, but it soon evaporates under the influence of a dry, desert-like climate. As the lake diminishes through evaporation, its water becomes more saline and alkaline. Eventually the water disappears altogether, leaving a blinding white lakebed behind, blanketed by a crust of minerals precipitated from the vanished water. Around the edges of the playa, the drying mud commonly shrinks to form an intricate network of cracks that can be preserved when the deposition of sediment is resumed following the next cloudburst. Mudcracks are not uncommon in some of the fine-grained deposits of the Morrison Formation. From the distribution of the minerals produced in such a playa basin in southwest Colorado, Turner and others

(1991) postulated that an enormous alkaline lake existed in southwestern Colorado during Brushy Basin time (Figure 5-3). This lake was some 300 miles long, comparable in size to modern Lake Michigan. There were probably many other, much smaller, playa lakes dotting the low interior basin during the time that the Brushy Basin sediments were deposited.

The coarsely granular sediments in the Brushy Basin Member are commonly arranged in lenticular bodies representing the filled channels of rivers, or as broad but thin sheets of sand signifying floodwaters surging from swollen rivers across the adjacent floodplains. These coarse-grained deposits were deposited mostly by rivers that flowed from the west in braided or winding courses. Many of the rivers eventually drained into low lake basins or valleys in the eastern portion of the Colorado Plateau.

The Brushy Basin Member is one of the most richly fossiliferous non-marine sedimentary rock sequences in the world; that is, simply put, it contains numerous and varied fossils. Dozens of dinosaur bone quarries have been established in exposures of the Brushy Basin Member in Utah, Wyoming, Colorado, and South Dakota. (Most of the major dinosaur quarries shown in Figure 5-1 are situated in the strata of the Brushy Basin Member.) From these sites, tens of thousands of bones have been excavated and many more remain locked within the Brushy Basin sediments. In Utah, the Brushy Basin Member produces truly spectacular concentrations of dinosaur bone at the Cleveland-Lloyd Quarry in Emery County and at Dinosaur National Monument, northeast of Vernal. Elsewhere, scores of less impressive accumulations of fossils have been found in the Brushy Basin Member throughout east-central Utah. Virtually anywhere these soft mudstones are exposed, there is a good chance of finding dinosaur bones or teeth.

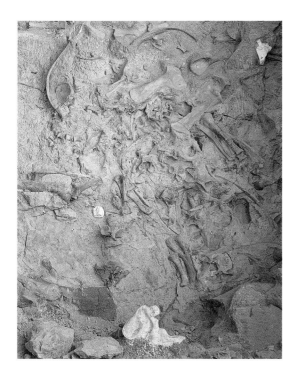

Photo 19. A large petrified log weathering out of the Morrison Formation near Escalante. Frank DeCourten.

Photo 18. Most of the bones seen in this view of the bone bed at Dinosaur National Monument belong to sauropod dinosaurs. John Telford.

The Morrison Landscape: A Land Alive

The Morrison Formation probably encompasses some 10 million years of the late Jurassic Period, from approximately 150 million years ago to about 140 million years ago. During this span of time, the landscapes of east-central Utah evolved steadily in response to geologic events that occurred both within the region and around the periphery of the modern Colorado Plateau. From the distribution of the various members of the Morrison Formation, and from the variations in their thickness and composition, it appears that the earth's crust in Utah and Colorado experienced modest movements related to compressional forces that were transmitted inland from the western edge of North America. This compression caused some areas of the Colorado Plateau to rise, forming uplifts that affected the patterns of streamflow of the late Jurassic rivers. Between the elevated Mesocordilleran High on the west and the ancient Uncompahgre Highland to the east, the Zuni Uplift rose along the Arizona–New Mexico boundary, the Monument Uplift of southern Utah and northern Arizona was activated, and the Emery Uplift emerged in central Utah (Peterson and Tyler, 1985; Peterson and Turner-Peterson, 1987). None of these disturbances of the earth's crust resulted in prominent mountain systems, but they were sufficiently high to direct the drainages of the regions toward lower areas adjacent to them.

While these structures were rising, other areas of the Colorado Plateau were subsiding to form basins in which unusually thick sequences of sediment accumulated as the streams converged toward the lowest points. In southwestern Colorado, the previously described playa-lake complex recognized in the Brushy Basin Member developed in such a low basin. Elsewhere in the late Jurassic interior basin, smaller areas, such as the Henry Basin of central Utah, also were formed or developed. The pattern of uplifts and basins shifted constantly through the time that the sediments of the Morrison Formation were being deposited. The rivers draining the Morrison plain continually shifted their locations and directions as small basins became filled with sediment and new areas began to subside. The uplifted regions were soon (in geologic time) reduced by erosion, but many of them may have experienced later pulses of reactivation. The Morrison Formation was thus deposited on an active landscape that was continually rising in some places while sagging in others. All this geological ruckus was but a hint of even more drastic events taking place beyond the Colorado Plateau region.

The late Jurassic was the time of the great Nevadan Orogeny in western North America. This period of intense mountain building was related to the convergence of great underground slabs of rock, known as lithospheric plates, along the western edge of the continent. As North America smashed into the leading edge of an oceanic plate moving to the east, rocks were crushed, splintered, and forced upward to form the famous Franciscan complex of the California Coast Range. Inland from the coast, the Sierra Nevada region was ablaze with volcanic activity and constantly shaken by earthquakes generated as the rocks fractured. Even in Nevada, western Utah, and Idaho, far inland from the zone of plate convergence, the compressional forces were sufficient to drive great slabs of rock eastward along low-angle fractures appropriately known as thrust faults. As the slabs were thrust to the east, they piled up like shingles on a roof to create an extensive mountain belt in the eastern Great Basin. This ancient mountain system is known as the Sevier Orogenic Belt, a feature that was to become even more prominent in the Cretaceous Period. The late Jurassic deformation was merely the first rumblings in the Sevier Orogenic Belt. Nonetheless, powerful forces began to elevate the Mesocordilleran High, already swollen from the volcanic activity that began millions of years earlier. The geological disturbances linked to the Nevadan Orogeny thus resulted in widespread ge-

ological havoc throughout western North America. The relatively subtle basins and uplifts that formed in central Utah during the late Jurassic are just a whisper of the chaos and change that were taking place elsewhere. The West was genuinely wild in the late Jurassic. What an exciting world the dinosaurs lived in!

The climate of Utah in the late Jurassic seems to have been almost as riotous as the geologic environment. The gypsum, playa-lake sediments, and scattered patches of eolian sandstone in the various members of the Morrison Formation all seem to suggest generally arid conditions throughout the time represented by this formation (Peterson and Turner-Peterson, 1987). On the other hand, the Morrison Formation has produced at least thirty-four genera of fossil plants (Tidwell, 1990). This floral assemblage is dominated by conifers but includes many ferns, seed-ferns, cycads, and ginkgoes—all of which require abundant moisture. In places such as Escalante Petrified Forest State Park, the striking abundance of plant fossils in the Morrison Formation indicates there were fairly dense clusters of vegetation, composed of large conifer trees with an undergrowth of smaller shrub-like plants. In addition, the great numbers of herbivorous dinosaurs preserved in the Morrison seem to suggest a large population of herbivores, many of gigantic size, that would have required a prodigious food supply. The overall character of the Morrison flora is most similar to that of the verdant forests that grow in the humid subtropics of today's world, not that of a dry desert environment (Tidwell, 1990). A mysterious paradox of the Morrison Formation is the apparent contradiction between environmental interpretations based on the rocks (dry climate) and those inferred from the fossil plant evidence (humid climate).

There is at least one plausible explanation for this intriguing conundrum. If the climate of the Morrison basin was strongly seasonal in the late Jurassic, then periods of drought would have alternated with periods of abundant moisture. There would have been times during the rainy season when the low basin received copious runoff from the surrounding highlands. During such times, the rivers flowing across the uneven land would have been flushed and swollen. Many temporary lakes, large and small, would have formed in low areas from impounded flood waters. For a few weeks or months following the floods, the landscape would have become carpeted with vegetation. In places, such as along the shores of lakes and rivers, water may have been so plentiful that small patches of forests might have been established. Eventually, however, the land dried out as the rainy season ended and the climatic cycle passed into the drought stage. The Morrison plain then lost its green blush as plants withered and died from the lack of moisture. The surviving herbage became concentrated along the banks of permanent streams and around the larger temporary lakes where water supplies were still adequate. Eventually, many of the lakes disappeared completely, leaving parched lake bottoms mantled with a pallid crust of minerals such as gypsum. The dry lakebeds would have been encircled by a ring of scrawny stubs of dead plants. At the height of the drought cycle, many of the riverbeds became dry, while the wind kicked up dust devils everywhere across the thirsty landscape. Animals perished in great numbers from the lack of food and water during the droughts. Eventually, the rains returned, and with them came the rebirth of life as the cycle was renewed. Such a seasonal climate would have allowed for the profuse growth of vegetation during times of abundant moisture, but it would also have resulted in dry intervals recorded by the gypsum, eolian sandstones, and mud-cracked playa-lake sediments observed in parts of the Morrison Formation. Such a scenario is not a certainty, but it is a possible explanation for the problem.

We know that in the modern world such strongly seasonal climates can support large and diverse populations of terrestrial vertebrates. The most obvious example would be the savannahs of east Africa, which experience profound climatic oscillations between rainy intervals and scorching droughts. The mammals of east Africa survive the droughts by migrating to less affected areas, by storing food energy in the form of fat produced when food is abundant, and by a remarkable array of behaviors designed to conserve water and energy. But there is one very important difference between modern Africa and Jurassic Utah: in Africa, the primary food for most herbivores is the grass that grows across the vast plains. These grasses are well adapted to the cyclic climate—they can persist in dormancy during the droughts but sprout quickly and grow rapidly when moisture is available. The vigorous regeneration of the African grasses following droughts can provide a great amount of food for herbivorous mammals in a relatively short time. Thus, the African grasslands recover swiftly from the dry season. But grasses are angiosperms and did not develop until the end of the Mesozoic Era; there were no grasses in Utah during the late Jurassic. Many of the plants identified to date in the Morrison flora do not appear to be very well adapted to dry, cyclic climates. Furthermore, the Morrison flora consists mostly of trees or shrub-sized plants that do not seem capable of carpeting the land with vegetation the way modern grasses do.

What then was the primary food source for the dinosaurs and other herbivores? What type of plant was the ecologic equivalent of the modern grasses during the late Jurassic? We have no certain answers for these questions. Perhaps the ferns or cycads of the Morrison flora possessed reproductive mechanisms or growth rates different from those of the living representatives of those groups. Maybe the landscape was blanketed by a "fern prairie" unlike anything that exists in the modern world. There might have been other plants, unknown from the fossil record, that provided a significant portion of the food base for the Morrison ecosystem. What is certain, given the stupendous number of their fossils preserved in the Morrison Formation, is that the herbivorous dinosaurs in late Jurassic Utah found food…and in great abundance.

If the low undulating plain of central Utah was seasonally arid and occasionally wet during the late Jurassic, then the animals that populated the basin would probably have migrated in rhythm with the seasons, just as the mammals of modern east Africa do. During wet cycles, plants would have been abundant and the herbivorous animals would be dispersed widely across the verdant countryside. Predators would roam throughout the region, feeding on the feeble, the young, or the isolated herbivores. The rivers would have been brimming with water, and crocodiles, turtles, and fish would have flourished during these times. Such aquatic vertebrates are known from the Morrison Formation in Utah, but their fossils are mostly confined to specific strata and are not found distributed randomly throughout the various rock layers.

As the dry season approached, the rivers would dwindle to trickles of water before vanishing completely to leave dry streambeds behind. The aquatic vertebrates would perish in great numbers, their remains providing food for scavengers. On occasion, a few of the bones of crocodiles, turtles, or fish might have become buried, producing the scant remains that are known to occur in parts of the Morrison Formation. The lakes and ponds would shrivel, becoming more alkaline as they lost water through evaporation while retaining all the dissolved minerals. Eventually only the parched crust of minerals would remain to mark the former existence of the lakes and ponds. Once in a while, the cracked and curled mud in the lake basins might have contained the fragmentary skeleton of a fish, a victim of the drought. As the landscape browned, the plant-eating dinosaurs, larger and more mobile than other reptiles, would have been forced to migrate as their search for water and food became

desperate. Contrary to the older views of most scientists about dinosaurs, paleontologists are now in general agreement that even the massive sauropods were capable of extensive overland travel (Chure, 1983). As herds of sauropods, groups of camptosaurs (an ornithopod), and individual stegosaurs moved across the land, many of them no doubt would succumb to the blistering drought. The rotting carcasses of the weaker animals dotted the endless plain as the wind blew veils of dust across the barren land. Along the larger stream courses, a little muddy water might still have been available. This water would have attracted the migrant dinosaurs in great numbers. Dinosaur fossils sometimes occur in great concentrations in the Morrison Formation, and the gathering of many animals around water sources during the dry season may be a part of the explanation for this pattern (more will be examined about Utah localities of this type later). Predators also would have been concentrated in areas where the migrating herds of herbivores were gathered. It is easy to imagine the Morrison theropods lurking behind a rise or watching the migrating sauropods and ornithopods from some overlook, waiting for an opportunity to strike.

Recall that the Morrison Formation covers an area exceeding 700,000 square miles, stretching from Arizona and New Mexico northward to the Canadian border. This north-south distance, some 900 miles, corresponds to more than thirteen degrees of latitude. It is likely that the dry season occurred in late summer and early fall and that it would have begun earlier in the southern portion of the basin than farther north. Thus, northward migrations during the droughts would eventually have led the dinosaurs to more abundant water and vegetation. As the dry conditions spread north during late Jurassic summers, one might envision waves of dinosaurs moving in that direction, too. Conversely, during the late winter and spring, warm and moist conditions would develop first in the south. The northward migration of the dry season might have been reversed at

Plate 3.
A Morrison landscape.
Distant volcanoes
vented ash clouds that
settled across the low-
land basin of central
Utah.

that time of year. Scientists don't know for sure what the breeding patterns of the Morrison Formation dinosaurs might have been, but it is certainly plausible to imagine a breeding season that would have coincided with the time when resources were most abundant. In such a scenario, reproduction would have been optimized by establishing breeding grounds in the places, and during the times, that food and other resources were easily found. Though it is impossible to verify the notion of two annual migrations for the dinosaurs from their fossil record in the Morrison Formation, there are some indications that such events really happened in the Utah region.

Dinosaur bone fragments can be found virtually anywhere in the Morrison Formation. Well-preserved skeletons and mass accumulations of fossils are less common, but scraps of fossil bone are found virtually everywhere in the Morrison strata, particularly in the Brushy Basin Member. If the late Jurassic dinosaur populations migrated twice a year (or perhaps even more often) across the alluvial basin, then individual dinosaurs could have died just about anywhere during a typical year. The unusually broad distribution of preserved dinosaur bone is consistent with the suggestion of migratory behavior. In addition, paleontologists have documented a number a dinosaur trackways in the sediments of the Morrison Formation in Utah, Colorado, and adjacent states (Lockley and Hunt, 1995), including one of the world's largest footprint assemblages, which is along the Purgatorie River in Colorado (Lockley and others, 1986).

At the Purgatorie River site, over 100 trackways have been documented from a single horizon in the upper part of the Morrison Formation. Most of these tracks were made by dinosaurs moving to the northwest along the shore of a large lake (Lockley and others, 1986). The trackways were made primarily by sauropod and ornithopod dinosaurs, both of which appear to have been moving through the area in groups or herds.

These herbivorous dinosaur footprints are mostly arranged in groups of parallel and closely spaced trackways, apparently made at the same time. The trackways of theropods are rare at the Purgatorie River site, suggesting a predator-prey ratio of about one to thirty. The relatively small number of predators suggested by this trackway evidence is also characteristic of the mammal communities of modern east Africa. In comparison with the vast herds of migrating antelope, zebras, and wildebeest in that area, there are comparatively few lions, cheetahs, and hyenas. Similar proportions between dinosaur predators and prey seem to have existed in western North America during the late Jurassic. Scientists have no way of knowing exactly why the dinosaurs were traveling along the edge of the lake in southeastern Colorado during Morrison time. Perhaps it was just part of their daily routine; on the other hand, the herds might have been wandering northwest during an annual migration. At the very least, the Purgatorie River tracksite demonstrates that sauropod and ornithopod dinosaurs did travel in herds and that these groups were moving in a specific direction. The dinosaurs that made the trackways along the Purgatorie River definitely were going somewhere, for some reason.

Combining all the known geological and paleontological evidence, it is possible to reconstruct the overall character of the Morrison alluvial plain in east-central Utah. It was a low region, hilly in places, that was laced by small rivers flowing from the west across the terrain in either sinuous or braided patterns (Figure 5-3). At a latitude at the time of 20–30° north of the equator, the late Jurassic climate was warm and semiarid, subject to strong seasonal variations. Many temporary lakes developed during the wet season. The larger lakes may have been semipermanent features of the landscape, holding water that was highly mineralized by the great rates of evaporation. Vegetation was generally sparse; but along the stream banks and lake margins, and during the moist climatic cycles, it might have been rela-

Table 1: Dinosaurs of the Morrison Formation

ORDER SAURISCHIA

Suborder Sauropodomorpha

FAMILY DIPLODOCIDAE

Diplodocus*
Barosaurus*
Apatosaurus*
?Dystrophaeus*
Supersaurus
?Amphicoelias
Seismosaurus

FAMILY BRACHIOSAURIDAE

Brachiosaurus
Ultrasaurus
?Dystylosaurus

FAMILY CAMARASAURIDAE

Camarasaurus*
(Cathetosaurus?)

FAMILY CETIOSAURIDAE

?Haplocanthosaurus*

Suborder Theropoda

Ceratosauria

Ceratosaurus*

Tetanurae

FAMILY ALLOSAURIDAE

Allosaurus*
Saurophaganax?

FAMILY TYRANNOSAURIDAE

Stokesosaurus*

FAMILY MEGALOSAURIDAE

Torvosaurus

FAMILY DROMAEODAURIDAE?

Marshosaurus*

FAMILY TROODONTIDAE

Koparion*

FAMILY ORNITHOMIMIDAE

?Elaphrosaurus

FAMILY UNCERTAIN

Coelurus*
Ornitholestes*

ORDER ORNITHISCHIA

Suborder Ornithopoda

FAMILY HYPSILOPHODONTIDAE

Dryosaurus*
?Othnielia*

FAMILY FABROSAURIDAE

Nanosaurus (or *Othniella?*)*

FAMILY IGUANODONTIDAE

Camptosaurus*
Iguanodon

Suborder Stegosauria

FAMILY STEGOSAURIDA

Stegosaurus*

Suborder Ankylosauridae

FAMILY NODOSAURIDAE (?)

Mymoorapelta

Taxa known from Utah localities appear with an asterisk (*). Queries (?) indicate tentative identifications based on fragmentary material or indicate those taxa for which family membership is uncertain.

tively dense. Volcanic eruptions in nearby regions periodically produced clouds of ash that descended over the landscape. Powerful earthquakes in the surrounding mountains repeatedly shook the region. The ground vibrated for other reasons as well: great herds of dinosaurs were constantly on the move across this basin in search of food, water, or mates.

Dinosaurs of the Morrison Formation: A Magnificent Menagerie

The dinosaur fauna of the Morrison Formation is one of the richest and most diverse fossil assemblages in the world. It includes at least twenty-seven genera, some of which include several different species (see Table 1). The number of dinosaurs known from the Morrison Formation in-

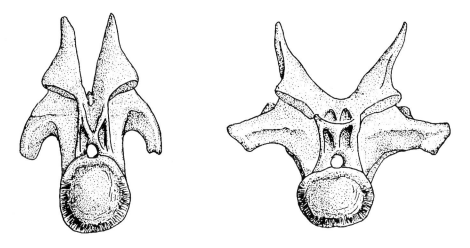

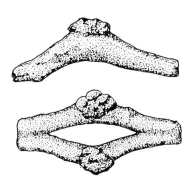

Figure 5-4. The divided neural spines of *Diplodocus*, top left, and *Apatosaurus*, top right, are characteristic of the family Diplodocidae. The chevron bones of the tail are also uniquely split into a double keel-shaped rod, such as these from *Diplodocus*, seen in top and side views (lower center).

creases steadily, as new specimens are regularly being discovered throughout western North America. The first dinosaur remains ever discovered in Utah were found in the Morrison Formation in San Juan County in 1859 (Gillette, 1993), and new material has been turning up ever since. The Morrison dinosaur fauna has thus been studied by a small army of paleontologists for more than 135 years. A great deal of what scientists know about dinosaurs in general is based on the examination of fossils collected from the Morrison Formation in Utah; yet researchers still have much to learn and many mysteries to solve concerning the nature and history of Utah's late Jurassic dinosaurs. However substantial the knowledge of Morrison dinosaurs appears to be, there will always be some uncertainties that await resolution. Understanding the late Jurassic di-

nosaurs of Utah and the world in which they lived is a task that will never be completed, because every new discovery prompts new questions. In the discussion that follows, the Morrison dinosaur fauna will be examined on the basis of the best available data, the existing fossils, and the current consensus among paleontologists as to how that data should be interpreted. As is the case with any issue in paleontology, controversies abound concerning the Morrison dinosaurs, and it would require many more pages than this book contains to adequately review them all.

Sauropod Dinosaurs of the Morrison

The late Jurassic is commonly referred to by scientists as the "Golden Age of the Sauropods" because this group of saurischian dinosaurs is remarkably abundant and diverse on a global scale in faunas of this age. In Utah and adjacent regions, this sauropod dominance is clearly reflected by the fossils excavated from the Morrison Formation (see Table 1). In major museums throughout the world, Morrison Formation fossils (or replicas of them) have been used to construct skeletal mounts that illustrate the general characteristics of this suborder. The sauropods known from the Morrison Formation belong to at least four different families: the Diplodocidae, the Brachiosauridae, the Camarasauridae, and the Cetiosauridae.

⚶   Family Diplodocidae

The diplodocid sauropods are named after *Diplodocus*, a well-known member of the family. All diplodocids share some basic skeletal characteristics that are used to define the group and distinguish them from other sauropod dinosaurs. The skulls of diplodocids are lightly built and relatively long and slender, much like a horse's skull. The teeth were of simple peg-like form and were confined to the front of the mouth; the diplodocids did not possess "molars," or cheek teeth.

Plate 4.
A *Diplodocus* herd
marching across
the Morrison inte-
rior basin.

CP.Bresvan Kempen '96

Figure 5-5. The sacral (hip) vertebrae of the diplodocid sauropods have very tall neural spines, such as these from *Apatosaurus*, seen in lateral and posterior views (right and left, respectively).

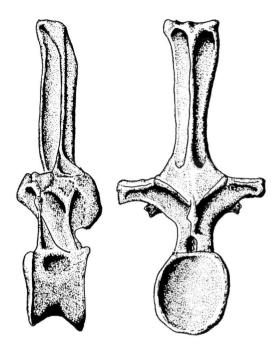

The nasal opening in all diplodocids is positioned high on the skull above, and a bit forward of, the eyes (Figure 5-7). The elongated necks of the diplodocids had at least fifteen vertebrae (called cervical vertebrae), compared to the ten to twelve vertebrae comprising the back (known as dorsal vertebrae). The vertebrae at the base of the neck and through the shoulder region have a deep V-shaped cleft in the diplodocids (Figure 5-4A,B), presumably for the attachment of a large ligament that helped to maneuver the neck. In the hip region, the bones of the back had tall neural spines projecting upward from the main body (or centrum) of the vertebrae (Figure 5-5). These tall spines served to anchor the large muscles and ligaments in the hips and rump of diplodocids. The long tails were constructed of as many as eighty individual bones (the caudal vertebrae). The last thirty or forty caudal vertebrae were slender and highly elongated, indicating that the tails of all diplodocids tapered to a whip-like tip. Below the caudal vertebrae in the middle part of the tail, the small bones known as chevrons were uniquely forked into a double keel-like form in the diplodocids (Figure 5-4C), unlike the simple Y-shaped blades typical of other sauropods. These atypical chevrons in *Diplodocus* inspired the genus name, which means "double beam."

✿ DIPLODOCUS

Diplodocus was a large but relatively slender and lightly constructed sauropod. Though full-grown adults may have attained lengths of 70–85 feet and stood about 13 feet high at the hip, they only weighed between 13 and 17 tons. Like other diplodocids, the skull was narrow and long, with small pencil-like teeth projecting forward from the front of the mouth (Figure 5-7). In most fossil specimens of this dinosaur, the teeth show little wear and were apparently not used for chewing plant fodder. The nostrils opened high on the head of *Diplodocus*, well above the eyes. The shoulders were lower than the hips and, as in all diplodocids, the neural spines of the vertebrae in the shoulder region were divided by a deep V-shaped cleft. Three species of *Diplodocus* are recognized by most paleontologists: *D. longus*, *D. carnegii*, and *D. hayi* (McIntosh, 1990). A fourth species, *D. lacustris*, was based solely on a few teeth and is probably a dubious categorization. In Utah, *D. longus* was evidently the most common species, but *D. carnegii* has also been reported from the state. The differences between the various species of *Diplodocus* are not dramatic and it would probably have taken close examination to tell them apart in Utah during the late Jurassic.

Diplodocus appears to have been a gregarious sauropod. In several Morrison localities, the remains of many individuals are found clustered together. At the Howe Quarry in northern Wyoming, for example, at least nineteen individuals of *Diplodocus* are represented by thousands of bones preserved in that location. It is likely many individuals of *Diplodocus* roamed the Morrison plain in herds that were composed of both adults and juveniles. Researchers can only speculate about the social behavior that might have ex-

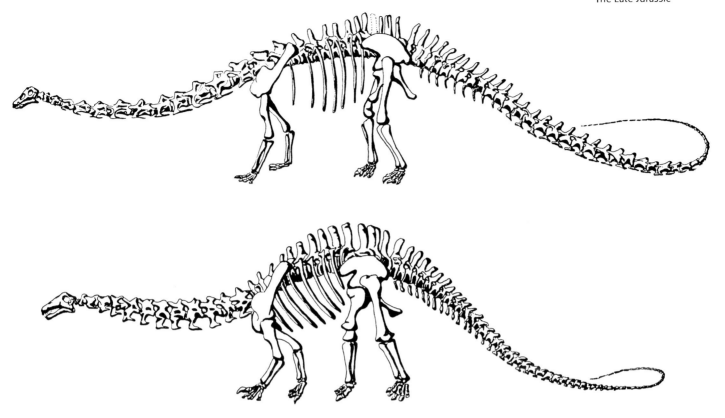

Figure 5-6. Reconstructed skeletons of *Diplodocus* (top) and *Apatosaurus* (bottom). Though these two diplodocid sauropods were of comparable length, *Diplodocus* was much more slender and lightly built than *Apatosaurus*.

isted in such *Diplodocus* herds. Was there a dominant "bull"? Were the young placed in the center of the herd for protection? How did individuals in the herd communicate? For herding behavior to be an effective survival strategy, some degree of social structuring seems necessary. In the modern world, such social organization is commonly observed in herds of large mammals such as elephants, bison, and caribou. In fact, it appears that these herds would collapse into chaos without such instinctive or "intelligent" group behavior. The evidence for herding behavior in *Diplodocus* and other sauropods is strengthened by trackways such as those preserved at the Purgatorie River site and by the broad distribution of sauropod remains in the Morrison Formation. Though scientists cannot prove the notion, it certainly seems likely that the late Jurassic dinosaur migrations in Utah involved the movement of many groups of giant sauropods across the spacious Morrison basin.

Diplodocus, and many other sauropod dinosaurs, have long been considered to have been high browsers, feeding on the foliage of large tree-sized plants. Conifers were probably the largest plants in the Morrison flora, but ginkgoes, cycads, and tree ferns also grew to considerable heights. Recently, some paleontologists have begun to question the idea that the sauropods fed exclusively on the leaves of tall trees (Alexander, 1985). Studies of the mechanics of sauropod necks (see, for example, Parrish and Stevens, 1995) indicate that the vertical flexing of the neck was actually limited by the way the cervical vertebrae are positioned and interlock with one another. To illustrate this, make a fist with one of your hands and raise your arm so that the back of your hand is level. Keeping your fist level, extend your index finger and try to lift it, as if you were attempting to point toward the ceiling. Note the angle made between your level fist and your extended index finger; this angle roughly corresponds to the max-

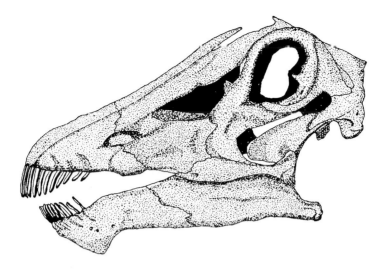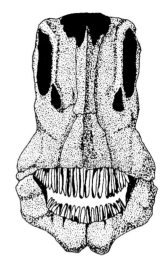

Figure 5-7. Skull of *Diplodocus*, in side and front views. Like those of all diplodocid sauropods, the skull is relatively long, narrow, and light. Note that the simple teeth project slightly forward and do not extend to the rear of the jaw. The nostrils were located high on the head, well above and slightly forward of the eyes.

imum angle possible between the body and neck of most sauropods. The diplodocid dinosaurs could not elevate their necks to a vertical position. The tall neural spines in the hip region of the diplodocids suggest, however, that they could probably rear up on their hind limbs to gain a little more vertical reach. Many specimens of sauropods exhibit some fusion of the caudal vertebrae about where the tail would have contacted the ground in such a tripodial stance (Figure 5-12). Thus, sauropods like *Diplodocus* could feed on high vegetation, but that was probably not the main function of their long neck. Instead, the neck appears to have been more flexible in a horizontal plane and could be swung from side to side in a wide arc. This motion would have allowed a diplodocid to reach low-growing plants covering a large area without having to continuously reposition its body. We might envision *Diplodocus* feeding: moving slowly and infrequently, and sweeping its head from side to side while nipping the leaves of low-growing shrubs. Once in a while, it would raise its head to reach a particularly succulent leaf, to scan the horizon for predators, or to check the position of the herd. The elevated posture might also have been used to gain access to higher food during droughts or when traveling through "overgrazed" areas.

The small teeth of *Diplodocus* are shaped like simple pegs and generally show little sign of wear. From this, scientists conclude that they were not used to chew food. Instead, it appears that the teeth were used primarily to rake vegetation into the mouth or to strip leaves from branches. Since the efficient digestion of plant material requires that it be pulverized somehow, we might wonder how *Diplodocus* and its kin "chewed." It is highly probable that sauropods with such weak dentition possessed some kind of accessory organ like a gizzard that was used to masticate food after it was swallowed. In modern birds (and some reptiles as well), the gizzard is a muscular organ that contains small stones swallowed by the animal. As the gizzard muscles contract, the ingested food is ground into a pulp by the stones. Modern birds, particularly those that eat grain or seeds (such as chickens), require such an accessory organ because they don't have teeth. The diplodocids did have teeth, but they were few and puny. Paleontologists often find relatively large, smooth, rounded, and highly polished stones in exposures of the fine-grained mudstones of the Morrison Formation in Utah. Because they are much larger than the silt and clay particles composing the mudstones, these stones were probably not deposited by the same low-energy streams that laid down the finer sediment surrounding them. These stones are often called gastroliths ("stom-

Photo 20. A portion of the "cliff" at Dinosaur National Monument. The thigh bones (femora) of an *Apatosaurus* (robust) and a *Diplodocus* (more slender) lie parallel to each other near the left side of the photograph. John Telford.

ach stones"), suggesting that they might represent the gizzard stones of sauropod (or other) dinosaurs. David Gillette has found gastroliths that are clearly associated with skeletal remains of the giant diplodocid sauropod *Seismosaurus* in the Morrison Formation of New Mexico. The clustering and alignment of the gastroliths at the New Mexico locality suggest that *Seismosaurus* may have had two gizzard-like organs as part of its digestive tract (Gillette and others, 1990). In the case of *Seismosaurus*, the evidence for sauropod gastroliths is fairly convincing, but often such stones are found scattered throughout the Morrison Formation without an association with any skeletal remains. Identifying isolated stones in the Morrison Formation as dinosaur gastroliths is somewhat speculative, and there is currently no

test that can be applied to the isolated "gastroliths" that would prove they were once carried along in the gastric mill of a dinosaur; but it is likely that at least some of the stones were regurgitated by passing sauropods or were left after the complete decomposition of a sauropod carcass.

🐾 *APATOSAURUS*

Apatosaurus, a relative of *Diplodocus* within the family Diplodocidae, is known from several different localities in Utah, Wyoming, and Colorado. It is also one of the most familiar sauropods to many people because of the popularization of the old name "*Brontosaurus*" for this genus in the mass media over the past seventy years or so. Even today, many adults remain confused by the tangled taxonomy, although children generally seem able to resolve the conflicting nomenclature with greater ease. The story behind the confusion is a bit complicated, but it is worth repeating since it reveals some of the difficulties faced by paleontologists studying the incomplete remains of dinosaurs.

It all started in 1877 when the illustrious Yale paleontologist O.C. Marsh first coined the name *Apatosaurus* for a partial skeleton of a juvenile sauropod excavated from the Morrison Formation near Garden Park, Colorado. Two years later, in 1879, Marsh described the fragmentary remains of a much larger sauropod found at Como Bluff, Wyoming, as *Brontosaurus*. Neither specimen had an attached skull, although fragmentary sauropod skulls were found in nearby quarries. In 1883, Marsh attempted to reconstruct the skeleton of the gigantic *Brontosaurus* and, because many portions of it were missing, he had to make some guesses about the unknown parts. For the most part, Marsh made good guesses; however, from the various sauropod skulls that had been found in the Morrison Formation, he picked one that was very similar to *Camarasaurus* (discussed later in this chapter). When Marsh's reconstruction was complete, *Brontosaurus* possessed a stubby, compact head unlike the slender elongated skulls typical of all diplodocids. The error went uncorrected for many decades and popular images of the blunt-faced *Brontosaurus* were disseminated all over the world. Later studies revealed that the original fossils of *Apatosaurus* and *Brontosaurus* actually represented small and large individuals, respectively, of the same genus. The rule in paleontology is that the first name applied to a genus is retained while subsequent names are regarded as synonyms and abandoned. The public, however, had never heard of *Apatosaurus*, and the rejected name *Brontosaurus* persisted in popular culture for years.

Even after the taxonomic error had been corrected, though, there was still the problem of the wrong skull. It wasn't until the 1970s that this mistake was finally discovered. By carefully reviewing the original field notes and quarry maps and by reexamining an isolated sauropod skull found at Dinosaur National Monument in Utah, David Berman and John McIntosh finally identified the correct skull for *Apatosaurus* (Berman and McIntosh, 1978). To this day, the *Apatosaurus* skull found at Dinosaur National Monument is the only one known for this genus that is reasonably complete.

The correct skull for *Apatosaurus* is clearly of the diplodocid type and indicates a close relationship between *Diplodocus* and *Apatosaurus*. *Camarasaurus*, the true owner of the head originally placed on "*Brontosaurus*," is a much different type of sauropod and is not placed into the family Diplodocidae. It is interesting to note that "*Brontosaurus*" is only one of the inaccurate names that have been applied to *Apatosaurus*; others include "*Atlantosaurus*" and "*Elosaurus*," both of which were assigned to fragmentary remains that probably represent *Apatosaurus*. The Greek language roots for *Apatosaurus* mean "deceptive reptile"— a most appropriate name!

Apatosaurus was about the same length as *Diplodocus*, approaching 75 feet in adults, but was much heavier, weighing in at some 35–45 tons (Figure 5-6). This bulky sauropod had forelimbs that were a little shorter than the hind limbs, giving the massive body a slight forward tilt. The long neck was constructed of fifteen cervical vertebrae; those near the base of the neck had divided neural spines similar to the posterior cervical vertebrae of *Diplodocus* (Figure 5-4A). The neural spines on the vertebrae in the hip region were undivided, very tall, and massive (Figure 5-5). Like all diplodocids, the tail was long, consisting of up to eighty vertebrae, and ended in a slender whip-like tip. *Apatosaurus* had a large claw on the "thumbs" (digit 1) of its forefeet. These claws probably helped provide leverage to swing the front of the body from side to side while *Apatosaurus* fed on low-growing vegetation by sweeping its neck back and forth close to the ground.

The skull of *Apatosaurus* is very similar to that of *Diplodocus*, with an elongated muzzle, tiny peg-shaped teeth at the front of the jaws, and nostrils placed high on the top of the head. The placement of the nostrils on the top of the skull of *Apatosaurus* and other diplodocids earlier led to the now-discarded speculation that these sauropods were aquatic animals and used their high nostrils in conjunction with their long necks to breathe while the body remained submerged in lakes or ponds. The "snorkeling sauropod" myth has now been laid to rest by numerous studies (for example, Coombs, 1975) that have revealed problems with this perception. Among the many reasons scientists have abandoned the aquatic image for *Apatosaurus* and its kin are: 1) their necks could not be raised vertically; instead, they were designed to be held horizontally or inclined upward at a low angle; 2) abundant footprint evidence suggests that the sauropods were capable of efficient movement over dry land; 3) if sauropods were submerged to a depth equal to the length of their necks, the water pressure would have prevented them from expanding their lungs enough to force air down the long trachea; 4) the legs of *Apatosaurus* and other sauropods were extremely heavy and pillar-like and had thick pads of shock-absorbing cartilage where they joined. The foot bones were broadly splayed and the feet had circular pads on the soles much like the feet of elephants. It is unlikely that the limbs and feet of sauropods would be like this if they were not used to support the massive bodies of these dinosaurs on land.

Even though the evidence for sauropods being fully terrestrial is unequivocal, the placement of the nostrils on top of the head of *Apatosaurus* (and *Diplodocus* as well) is an intriguing puzzle. Why didn't the nose simply open at the tip of the snout as it does in many other dinosaurs? Some paleontologists (Bakker, 1988) have suggested that perhaps the diplodocids possessed a proboscis of some sort like an elephant or a tapir. In both of these mammals the nostrils open relatively high on the skull and the fleshy "trunk" is elongated and lined with powerful muscles. Elephants and tapirs use their trunks to manipulate food objects, to strip vegetation, to transfer water into the mouth, and to perform a variety of other tasks that require a prehensile appendage. No one is sure whether or not the diplodocid sauropods had trunks, and paleontologists will probably never know for certain. If they did have trunks, it would be hard to imagine a more bizarre face garnishing the ends of their long necks.

Both *Apatosaurus* and *Diplodocus* possessed extremely long tails. In both dinosaurs, the tail tapered to a slender whip-like tip. The last dozen or so tail bones were very slender and shaped like simple rods. Since the tail tapers like an old-fashioned bullwhip, it is tempting to think of it being used in that manner as a defensive organ. Could the tail of *Apatosaurus* deter an attacking theropod by snapping back and forth along the ground? Could this whiplash have toppled predators by slapping their legs out from under them or delivering a painful snap to the body? Perhaps, but this was almost certainly not the primary means of defense for *Apatosaurus* and other diplodocids. Whenever predators attacked, the giant sauropods probably needed little else than their great bulk for adequate defense. Modern elephants do not appear to have any highly specialized defensive organs, and yet they have little to fear from lions and other predators in their habitat. The very size of a healthy adult elephant is usually all that is required to discourage a lion or pack of hyenas from assaulting such large animals. In addition, the herding behavior of elephants extends the protection of large adult size to the smaller and weaker individuals within the herd. The late Jurassic theropods probably did not launch a full-scale attack on an *Apatosaurus* or

Plate 5. *Apatosaurus* feeding. The long necks of these sauropods may have allowed them to reach a considerable amount of plant food without having to move their massive bodies.

Diplodocus herd any more often than a pride of lions surges into a group of elephants—which is almost never. This is not to say that sauropods were not occasionally on the menu for Morrison theropods. Young *Diplodocus* calfs or injured or elderly adults would have been in great peril if they strayed too far from the protection of the herd. In that case, the whiplash tail probably did little to thwart the striking carnivores, which would have enjoyed an ample feast.

Apatosaurus fossils are rarely found in great concentrations in the Morrison Formation, however. Unlike the herding *Diplodocus*, *Apatosaurus* seems to have been a more solitary dinosaur, moving around the Morrison terrain as isolated animals or, at most, in small groups of two or three individuals. However, there does seem to have been an association between *Apatosaurus* and *Stegosaurus,* the plated ornithischian described later in this chapter. In most places where the bones of *Apatosaurus* have been found in the Morrison Formation, fossils of *Stegosaurus* also have been recovered. This association is probably more than a coincidence. Both *Apatosaurus* and *Stegosaurus* were probably solitary low browsers. Where low-growing shrubs grew in profusion on the Morrison plain, both dinosaurs would have found plentiful food. Since the teeth of these two dinosaurs are much different, and their feeding behavior was almost certainly dissimilar, there was probably little competition for food between them. In fact, we might even imagine *Apatosaurus* eating the softer fronds of ferns and leafy ginkgoes, while *Stegosaurus* might have preferred the coarser cycads growing in the same area. Perhaps the fellowship between *Apatosaurus* and *Stegosaurus* had other dimensions beside the lack of competition for food. There may have been some type of interaction between these two types of dinosaurs that allowed them to resist predators more successfully when they were together than when they were on their own. This, of course, is pure speculation, but the fossil record does suggest that there was a closer affiliation between

these two herbivores than between any other pair of Morrison dinosaur genera.

There are three known species of *Apatosaurus*: *A. ajax*, *A. excelsus*, and *A. louisae*. The distinctions between the various species involve differences in size and variations in the detailed anatomy of skeletal elements such as vertebrae and limb bones. Since all three species are based on incomplete specimens, paleontologists can't be positively certain that each species is actually a unique form, reproductively isolated from the other two. In any case, the three species of *Apatosaurus* are all more similar than they are different; what has been written here about the genus would apply equally well to all three species. If we could have visited the Morrison plain during the late Jurassic, perhaps the differences between the species of *Apatosaurus* would have been more obvious to us than are the variations in their fossils.

⑤ BAROSAURUS

Barosaurus is the largest of the three most common Morrison diplodocids, though it was less abundant and is represented by less complete fossil material than either *Diplodocus* or *Apatosaurus*. *Barosaurus* was about 80 feet long and stood more than 14 feet tall at the hips. However, it possessed a relatively slender build, much like *Diplodocus*, and probably weighed between 25–35 tons, a weight range not unlike the smaller but bulkier *Apatosaurus*.

The most distinctive feature of *Barosaurus* was its extremely long neck, which comprised about half of its total length. While no complete necks of *Barosaurus* have been discovered, their necks appear to have had the same number of cervical vertebrae (fifteen) as other diplodocids. The lengthening of the neck in *Barosaurus* was the result of the extreme elongation of the cervical vertebrae, which are about 33 percent longer than those of *Diplodocus*. The slender limb bones of *Barosaurus* are so similar to those of *Diplodocus* as to be virtually indistinguishable. In fact,

Barosaurus may not be as uncommon as scientists commonly think: many isolated limb bones that have been identified as the remains of large individuals of *Diplodocus* may actually belong to *Barosaurus*. Unless the limbs are found with portions of the distinctive neck, it would not be easy to tell the difference between a large *Diplodocus* and a small *Barosaurus*. The tail of *Barosaurus* probably tapered to the whiplash tip typical of other diplodocids, but only the front half of the tail is known. Based on the structure and size of the known caudal vertebrae, it appears that *Barosaurus* had a somewhat shorter tail than did *Diplodocus*.

Though *Barosaurus* remains seem to be rare in the Morrison Formation throughout most of western North America, this genus is relatively well represented at Dinosaur National Monument in northeastern Utah. In addition to the numerous preserved skeletal elements from this spectacular site, scientists have discovered a natural impression of skin in the sandstone that surrounded some of the *Barosaurus* fossils. The impression reveals skin that was knobby with many prominent folds, like the skin of the modern gila monster (*Heloderma suspectum*), a large lizard from the American Southwest. This fossil skin impression suggests that *Barosaurus*, and possibly most other dinosaurs as well, possessed a coarse granular integument much different from the scale-covered skins of most living reptiles.

In spite of the apparent scarcity of its fossils in the Morrison Formation, *Barosaurus* was a highly successful sauropod during the late Jurassic. Fossils of this dinosaur also have been discovered in the famous Tendaguru Formation (also late Jurassic) of Tanzania, indicating that it occupied an enormous geographic range. Even though western North America was closer to Africa in the Jurassic Period than it is now, *Barosaurus* still must have roamed over an immense tract of land covering at least several thousand miles. As shall be seen, *Barosaurus* is not the only Morrison dinosaur to surface in Africa. There appear to have

been few barriers to the dispersal of dinosaur populations between North America and Africa during the time that the Morrison and Tendaguru formations were being deposited.

OTHER MORRISON DIPLODOCIDS

Aside from *Diplodocus*, *Apatosaurus*, and *Barosaurus*, the Morrison Formation has produced remains of several other diplodocid dinosaurs, or at least of sauropods that seem to be closely related to this family. None of these miscellaneous diplodocids are represented by material that is sufficiently complete to allow paleontologists to develop any comprehensive reconstructions of their anatomy; nonetheless, what we do know about them suggests that some were very impressive creatures. The fragmentary remains also expand the known diversity of the family Diplodocidae beyond the three genera described thus far.

Dystrophaeus was the first dinosaur ever discovered in Utah. A portion of the forelimb and a few bones from the front foot were found by John S. Newberry in 1859 as he accompanied the U.S. Army Corps of Topographical Engineers expedition led by Captain John N. Macomb through southeastern Utah (Barnes, 1990). In 1877, these fossils were studied by famous dinosaur paleontologist Edward D. Cope, who applied the name *Dystrophaeus viaemalae* to them. Unfortunately, very little additional material belonging to this genus and species has been unearthed since the original discovery. The forelimb of *Dystrophaeus* is rather slender, as in *Diplodocus*, and the foot bones are of a generalized diplodocid type. It may be that *Dystrophaeus* is actually a species of *Diplodocus*, but additional material will have to be found before scientists can be sure. The question may be resolved soon, as Utah State Paleontologist David Gillette has begun a study of some additional fossils recovered from Newberry's original site in 1989 (Gillette, 1993).

Outside of Utah, several other diplodocids,

or diplodocid-like sauropods, have been found in rocks of the Morrison Formation. Since these dinosaurs likely roamed great distances, they probably occupied portions of Utah even though their fossils have not yet been positively identified from localities within the state. *Amphicoelias* is one such Morrison dinosaur described by Cope (1877) from Colorado. It is known on the basis of extremely fragmentary fossils representing a portion of a shoulder, forelimb, pelvis, and two vertebrae from the back. *Amphicoelias* is very similar to *Diplodocus* and may actually be a member of that genus.

Supersaurus (Jensen, 1985a), known from the Morrison Formation of western Colorado, was apparently an enormous diplodocid sauropod, close to 125 feet long and weighing some 50 or 60 tons. *Supersaurus* is known only from several pelvic bones, about a dozen caudal (tail) vertebrae, a few dorsal (back) vertebrae, and a scapulocoracoid. This latter bone is equivalent to the shoulder blade (scapula) and collar bone (clavicle) of humans and, in *Supersaurus*, it was over eight feet long! Among all known sauropod dinosaurs, *Supersaurus* is most similar to the diplodocids, but its placement into the family Diplodocidae is not absolutely certain. Until new material is discovered, it could be best to think of *Supersaurus* as an immense, overgrown *Diplodocus.*

Another gigantic late Jurassic diplodocid was discovered by David Gillette in New Mexico and named *Seismosaurus halli.* This large sauropod is known on the basis of a single partially articulated skeleton consisting of more than thirty vertebrae from the tail, sacrum, and back, along with portions of the pelvis, chevron bones, and some ribs (Gillette, 1991). The tall neural spines of the sacral vertebrae and the divided neural spines of the vertebrae of the back are the clearest indications that *Seismosaurus* belongs to the family Diplodocidae. Other aspects of its anatomy, however, differ from those of the more common members of that family. The pelvis of *Seis-*

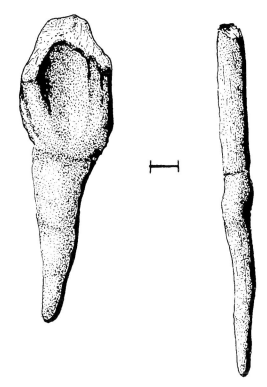

Figure 5-8. A spatulate tooth of *Camarasaurus* (left) compared to a peg-like tooth of *Diplodocus* (right). Note the curving spoon-like shape of the *Camarasaurus* tooth and the large wear surface on the crown. Scale bar=10 mm (about 1/2 inch).

mosaurus is more massive than that of other diplodocids, and the individual bones that comprise it have more robust form. The caudal (tail) vertebrae are heavier than in other diplodocids and have neural spines that are nearly erect, as contrasted with those of *Apatosaurus* and *Diplodocus*, which slant somewhat to the rear. *Seismosaurus* appears to have been around 120 feet long, and the heavy construction of its pelvis and tail suggests a sauropod of impressive mass, perhaps 40 or 50 tons. No *Seismosaurus* remains have yet been found in Utah, but it almost certainly accompanied the herds of other sauropods as they moved about the broad alluvial plain of Morrison time.

⑤ Family Camarasauridae

The camarasaurid sauropods are generally smaller but bulkier sauropods than the diplodocids. In addition, the skulls of the Camarasauridae are rather heavy and blunt in comparison to the lighter skulls and elongated snouts of

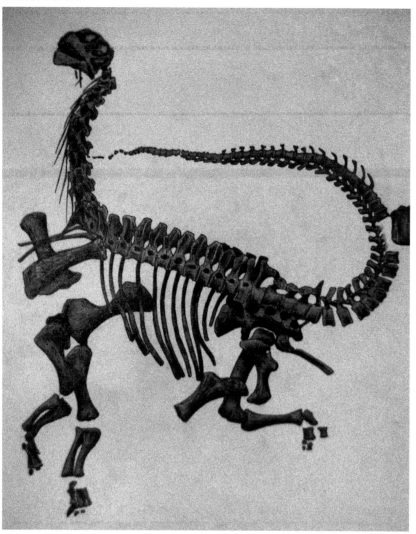

Photo 21. The remarkably complete skeleton of a juvenile *Camarasaurus* from Dinosaur National Monument.

rasauridae include a relatively short neck consisting of about twelve cervical vertebrae, neural spines divided by a U-shaped trough, relatively low neural spines rising from the sacral vertebrae in the hip region, and forelimbs that are somewhat longer in relation to the hind limbs than is the case in the Diplodocidae. The forefeet of the camarasaurids were less splayed than those of the diplodocids, as the elongated foot bones were arranged in an arc rising from the base of the toes toward the "wrist" and ankle. The tails of camarasaurids were relatively short and thick, consisting of about fifty vertebrae, below which simple, blade-like chevron bones were suspended.

The family Camarasauridae appears to be a less diverse assemblage of sauropods than the Diplodocidae. Only two or three North American genera can be confidently placed in the Camarasauridae; however, several other camarasaurids are known from other continents. Though they may be less diverse than the diplodocids, the camarasaurids, particularly the namesake genus *Camarasaurus*, are by far the most common dinosaur found in the Morrison Formation. Russell (1989) has estimated that about one of every five dinosaur bones ever recovered from the Morrison sediments belongs to *Camarasaurus*.

CAMARASAURUS

the diplodocids. Perhaps the most important characteristic of the Camarasauridae in understanding their habits and behavior is their teeth. Unlike the feeble teeth of the diplodocids, camarasaurid teeth are large and robust, shaped somewhat like a spoon, and bear relatively large wear surfaces (Figure 5-8). These dental features suggest that the camarasaurids made much greater use of their teeth to process plant matter than did the diplodocids. The nostrils of camarasaurids are placed high on the skull, as is the case with the diplodocids, but they are much larger and are usually located a little farther forward. Other features that typify the family Cama-

Camarasaurus was a medium-sized sauropod, about 50 feet long, that stood some 12 feet high at the hips, and probably weighed between 25–30 tons as a mature adult. The remains of *Camarasaurus* are remarkably abundant in the Morrison Formation of Utah and adjacent states. Consequently, *Camarasaurus* is perhaps the best-known sauropod dinosaur in the world. As our knowledge of its anatomy has developed over the past century, some of the earliest sauropod remains described from the Morrison Formation, such as "*Morosaurus*" and "*Uintasaurus*," are now known to be specimens of *Camarasaurus*. The number of *Camarasaurus* fossils known to science

Photo 22. Skull and neck vertebrae of *Camarasaurus* at Dinosaur National Monument. John Telford.

is large, probably in the thousands, allowing pale-ontologists to make some very detailed recon-structions of this dinosaur. At least three different species of *Camarasaurus* have been identified from the Morrison Formation, differing slightly from each other in body proportions and minor anatomical details. Nearly all Utah specimens have been identified as *Camarasaurus lentus*, and it is on this species that the following discussion is based.

The skull of *Camarasaurus* is large and mas-sive, but not very long. The lower jaw is particu-larly heavy and expands toward the front. The snout and lower jaw are both strongly curved, giv-ing *Camarasaurus* its unique brusque snout (Fig-ure 5-9). The nostrils of *Camarasaurus* are very large in comparison to those of the diplodocids and are located high above the eyes and well for-ward of them, opening outward to either side of the skull. The teeth of *Camarasaurus* are compar-atively large, spoon-like in shape, and are posi-tioned along the entire margin of the jaws. The large teeth commonly exhibit prominent wear surfaces produced when the upper and lower teeth contacted each other during chewing. The teeth are firmly set into sockets along a deep groove in the jaws.

The skeleton of *Camarasaurus* (Figure 5-10)

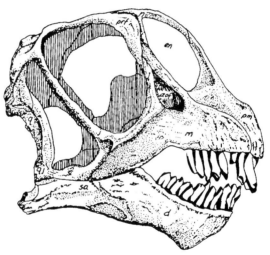

Figure 5-9. Skull of *Camarasaurus*. The large nostrils (en) opened well above, and in front of, the eyes of this blunt-faced sauropod.

is of typical sauropod form, but it is proportioned much differently than in the diplodocids. The neck, consisting of only a dozen or so vertebrae, is shorter and more corpulent, or thick, than the slender neck of *Diplodocus*. The cervical vertebrae of the neck, as well as the bones elsewhere in the spinal column, have deep side pockets known as pleurocoels. Many dinosaurs have these weight-saving cavities, but they are particularly well de-veloped in *Camarasaurus*. The tail is also short and relatively blunt. In some specimens of *Cama-rasaurus*, the caudal vertebrae in the forward por-tion of the tail are fused together into a solid

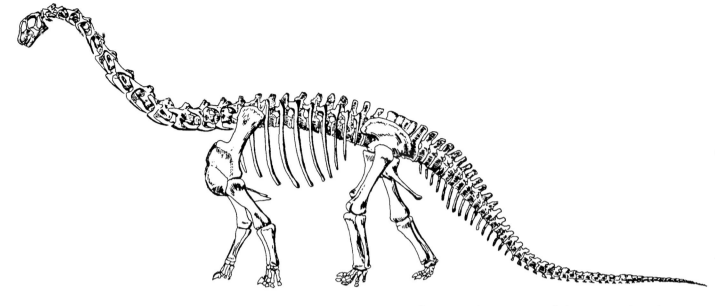

Figure 5-10. *Camarasaurus* skeleton, approximately 60 feet long, as reconstructed by Gilmore, 1925.

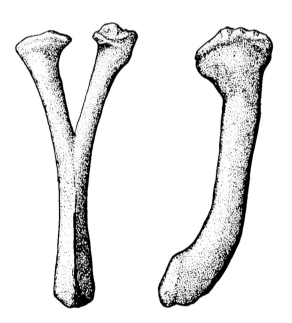

Figure 5-11. The Y-shaped chevron bones from the tail of *Camarasaurus*. Compare with Figure 5-4, illustrating the chevron bones typical of the diplodocid sauropods.

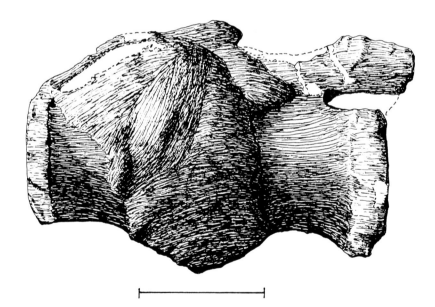

Figure 5-12. Fused caudal vertebrae of *Camarasaurus*. Two separate caudal vertebrae are firmly fused by the growth of bone tissue around the point of articulation. Scale bar=10 cm (4 inches). Based on a photograph from Rothschild and Berman, 1991.

mass of bone (Rothschild and Berman, 1991; Figure 5-12). This condition would have resulted in a pronounced stiffening of the tail just behind the rump. This suggests that the relatively short tail of *Camarasaurus* was carried high above the ground, at least for those individuals that exhibit the fusion of caudal vertebrae. A similar fusion of caudal vertebrae is sometimes seen in *Diplodocus* (Rothschild and Berman, 1991). Contrary to some popular depictions, there is no strong evidence that either of these sauropods habitually dragged their tails behind them like a dead snake. Since the caudal vertebrae are fused in only some specimens, this feature might be linked to the sex of the dinosaur. It seems plausible that males might have possessed the stiffened tail for defense against predators and competition for mates, while the more flexible tails of females might have been better suited for reproductive posturing and egg laying. The chevron bones in the tail of *Camarasaurus* are, as is the case in all camarasaurids, blade-like and divided at the upper end where they join the caudal vertebrae (Figure 5-11). *Camarasaurus* forelimbs are longer in relation to the hind limbs than are those of the diplodocids. This difference in forelimb/hindlimb proportions is reflected in the nearly level positioning of the back of *Camarasaurus*, as compared with the slight forward slope along the backs of most diplodocids. The hind foot of *Camarasaurus* had five widely splayed toes; the innermost toe was the largest and bore a large curved claw. The bones of the middle feet (the metacarpals and metatarsals, fore and aft), however, were more elongated than in the diplodocids and were arranged in an arcuate (curving) pattern between the toes and the ankles (or "wrists").

At Dinosaur National Monument, one of the most complete dinosaur skeletons ever discovered was excavated in the early 1900s. This famous skeleton is that of a juvenile *Camarasaurus*, and it is one of the most notable dinosaur treasures that have been collected in Utah. The young *Camarasaurus* was only about 17 feet long, less than half

the normal adult length of this genus. Remarkably, 90 percent of the skeleton was preserved and most of the bones were still articulated. The small *Camarasaurus* must have become quickly buried following its premature death, for there is little sign of scavenging, decomposition, or postmortem transportation of the bones of this extraordinary specimen. The fossils at Dinosaur National Monument are preserved in a lens of sandstone in the Brushy Basin Member that accumulated as a sandbar in a river channel. Within the sandstone body, about fifteen feet thick, there are at least three bone-producing horizons (Lawton, 1977). Fiorillo (1994) has suggested that the bones in these horizons were buried over a relatively short period of time, perhaps only a few months. The remarkable specimen of the juvenile *Camarasaurus* from Dinosaur National Monument probably arose from the nearly immediate burial of the carcass soon after the death of the young sauropod. The young camarasaur must have died very close to, or perhaps even on, the sandbar in the river channel.

Camarasaurus obviously was adapted to feed on different kinds of plants from those that sustained the diplodocids. The robust teeth would no doubt have been able to withstand powerful crushing forces that would have snapped the delicate teeth of *Diplodocus*. Fiorillo (1991) microscopically examined the wear surfaces of *Camarasaurus* teeth and found coarse scratch marks and pits, indicating that relatively tough plant material was processed and chewed with them. Unlike the diplodocids that used their teeth primarily for raking vegetation into the mouth or stripping it from branches, *Camarasaurus* probably chewed leafy food thoroughly before passing it through the digestive tract. Although its neck was relatively short, it was flexible, and a *Camarasaurus* could probably have lifted its head a little higher than was comfortable for the diplodocids. Given the differences in their teeth, body size, and posture, it is highly doubtful that *Camarasaurus* competed with the diplodocids for the same food

Plate 6.
The Jurassic
environment:
Dinosaur National
Monument 150
million years ago.
A bone-littered
sandbar along an
ancient river cap-
tures dinosaur
carcasses drifting
downstream.

Plate 7. *Camarasaurus* mother and young feeding along the banks of a late Jurassic Utah stream.

resources. Most likely, *Camarasaurus* was a high browser and fed by nipping off the fronds of tree ferns or the leaves of cycads that grew well above the ground. This more tree-like, or arborescent, vegetation may have been tougher and more fibrous than the lower-growing shrubs that provided the bulk of the diplodocid diet. Based on the overall abundance and geographic distribution of *Camarasaurus* and the diplodocid sauropods in the Morrison Formation, it certainly seems that they could have been compatible companions who roamed together across the broad alluvial plain.

There seems to have been considerable variation between *Camarasaurus* species during the late Jurassic. At least three species of *Camarasaurus* populated the Morrison habitat in western North America: *C. supremus*, *C. grandis*, and *C. lentus*. These species differ from each other in size, details of skeletal anatomy, configuration of the pelvis, and general proportions. A fourth species has recently been descibed (McIntosh and others, 1996) on the basis of fossils that were orginally thought to indicate a separate genus, *Cathetosaurus*.

⑥ CATHETOSAURUS (OR CAMARASAURUS LEWISI?)

In 1988, James Jensen described a partial skeleton of what appeared to be a camarasaurid sauropod from the Morrison Formation of western Colorado. On the basis of a nearly complete series of cervical vertebrae, a dozen dorsal vertebrae, some twenty ribs, most of the sacrum and pelvis, forty-three caudal vertebrae, and a partial right forelimb, the genus *Cathetosaurus* was established (Jensen, 1985a). The fossils studied by Jensen seemed to represent an animal that was more similar to *Camarasaurus* than to any other known sauropod, but the animal had some very unusual features that suggested it might have been able to support itself, at least occasionally, in a bipedal stance. Though *Cathetosaurus* was not a particu-

larly large sauropod (weighing about 10–15 tons), its pelvis was more massive than is typical for *Camarasaurus*. In addition, the pelvis was rotated forward around the hip socket and the hip blades (ilia) were braced to the sacral portion of the backbone by a very odd network of plates and struts of bone. The tail was unusually deep and thick. To Jensen, these features suggested that the pelvis, the sacral vertebrae, and part of the tail were designed to withstand the great vertical load or stress on the spinal column that would result from a bipedal stance. The genus name coined by Jensen, Cathetosarus, literally means "perpendicular reptile," in allusion to the inferred ability of this sauropod to periodically rear up on its hind legs. This interpretation of the anatomy of *Cathetosaurus* suggested that this sauropod was an arboreal forager that could gain access to higher vegetation by standing up on the toes of its hind feet. This type of behavior has recently been postulated for many other types of sauropods, but the evidence for it in *Cathetosaurus* was reasonably convincing. No remains of *Cathetosaurus* have yet been found in Utah, but Jensen's original discovery was made only a short distance east of the Utah-Colorado line, so we may safely assume that this unique sauropod also lived in Utah.

The validity of *Cathetosaurus* has been questioned recently by some researchers (McIntosh and others, 1996) who point out that some of the unique characters seen in the skeleton may be attributable to the advanced age of the individual. The atypical fusion and ligamentous bracing of portions of the sacrum in *Cathetosaurus* may be features that become enhanced in old age, just as humans sometimes experience bone fusions and loss of flexibility in the spine as we age. *Cathetosaurus* may therefore represent a large, old *Camarasaurus* individual. However, the attachment of the chevron bones to the tail, a cleft in the neural spines of the sacral vertebrae, and the positioning of the ilium of *Cathetosaurus* is unlike any known species of *Camarasaurus* (McIntosh and others, 1996). This new study suggests that *Cathetosaurus* actually represents a fourth species of *Camarasaurus*, namely *C. lewisi*, and does not signify a separate genus, as was originally proposed by Jensen in 1988. Because *Cathetosaurus* is so similar to *Camarasaurus* in terms of its overall skeletal architecture, this interpretation seems sensible.

☉ Family Brachiosauridae

The family Brachiosauridae includes some of the most immense land animals that ever lived on the earth. These gigantic sauropods had relatively long skulls, not unlike the diplodocids, but with large bulging nostrils placed high on the face, a feature somewhat reminiscent of the camarasaurids (Figure 5-13). The teeth of the brachiosaurids were large, lining the entire margin of the jaws, and had a unique chisel-like form. The thirteen cervical vertebrae were highly elongated, giving the brachiosaurids the longest necks of any dinosaur. The neural spines of the cervical vertebrae were not bifurcated, or forked, and each vertebra possessed very long ribs that extended along the lower neck, probably to anchor large neck muscles and ligaments. The tails, in contrast to the enormous necks, were relatively short and strongly tapered. Perhaps the most distinctive feature of the brachiosaurids was the unusual proportions of their limbs. The front limbs were significantly longer than the hind limbs, giving the relatively short back a pronounced upward tilt from the hips to the shoulders. This limb structure, coupled with the animals' extremely long necks, made the brachiosaurids probably look somewhat like overgrown reptilian giraffes (Figure 5-14). Because of this unique form, the forelimbs of the brachiosaurids carried much more weight than did those of other sauropods. Consequently, the front legs are massive and columnar, proportioned much like the forelimbs of an elephant. The shoulder girdle of brachiosaurids, which transmitted the weight of the body to the elephantine forelimbs, was more massive than in most other sauropods. In addition, the front feet

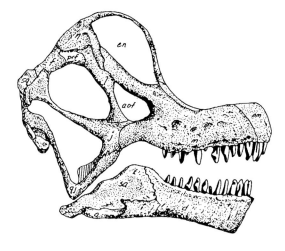

Figure 5-13. Skull of *Brachiosaurus*. Note the very large nostril (en) located high on the skull. The smaller opening below the nostril is the antorbital fenestra (aof). The teeth are large and chisel-shaped in the brachiosaurid sauropods.

are well designed to support the enormous load they carried. The toes were formed from massive bones and were widely spread to distribute the immense weight. The middle foot bones (metacarpals) were very long and positioned almost vertically to resist the crushing forces applied to them. Thick pads of shock-absorbing cartilage were present in the soles of the feet and between the limb bones to cushion the pounding that would have resulted from the movement of such large beasts. The brachiosaurids were truly ponderous creatures; the largest of them would have made *Camarasaurus* look runty in comparison.

In general, brachiosaurids are very uncommon in the Morrison Formation of western North America. No brachiosaurid remains have yet been recognized among the fossils collected from Utah exposures of the Morrison Formation, but they are known from localities in western Colorado. The Grand Valley and Uncompahgre Plateau regions of Colorado, only thirty miles or so from the Utah border, are among the few places in North America where brachiosaurid remains have been discovered. Moreover, at least several different types of brachiosaurids are represented among the Morrison fossils excavated from that region. *Brachiosaurus altithorax* was first identified from Morrison exposures near Grand Junction, Colorado, in the early 1900s (Riggs, 1903, 1904). In more recent years, several

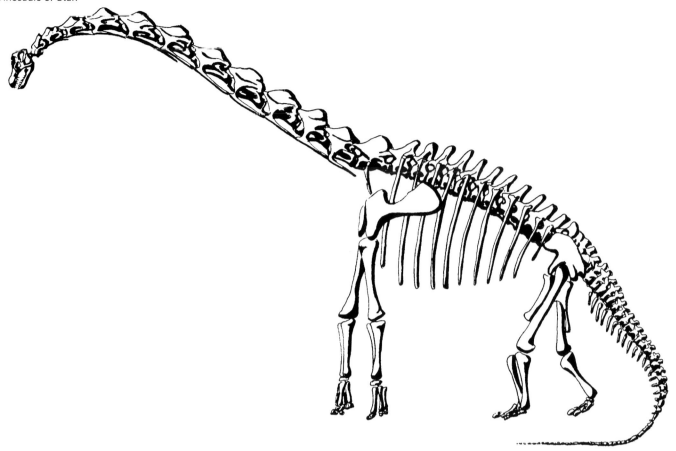

Figure 5-14. Skeleton of *Brachiosaurus*. The long forelimbs lifted the shoulders well above the hips, giving this sauropod its unique giraffe-like appearance. The extremely long neck was angled upward, allowing the largest of the brachiosaurids to feed on vegetation some fifty feet above the ground. Based on reconstuction of Norman, 1991, cited in Chapter 1.

other brachiosaurids have been uncovered at the nearby Dry Mesa Quarry in the Uncompahgre Plateau by scientists from Brigham Young University (Jensen, 1985a,b; Miller and others, 1991). Included in the more recent discoveries is the enormous brachiosaurid *Ultrasaurus*, which may have exceeded 100 feet in length and might have weighed more than 125 tons! Even the better-known *Brachiosaurus* was considerably larger than most of its sauropod contemporaries, reaching a length of around 75 feet. The long necks of the brachiosaurids, coupled with their giraffe-like stance, would have allowed one to raise its head 45 feet or more above the ground.

The unique anatomy of the brachiosaurid sauropods seems to suggest that these sauropods were especially well adapted to the niche of a high browser. No other dinosaur could have competed with them for the foliage crowning the tallest of

the Jurassic trees. The brachiosaurids were clearly very successful in this ecologic niche, for their remains have been found in North America, east Africa, and Europe. It seems that wherever there were tall trees in the late Jurassic, there were probably brachiosaurid sauropods nipping at their highest leaves. This provides a partial explanation for why the remains of brachiosaurids are unknown in Utah but do occur in nearby western Colorado. As has been mentioned, during the late Jurassic most of eastern Utah was occupied by the lowland basin in which the Morrison sediments were deposited. In western Colorado, however, the low terrain probably rose to the east toward small "islands" of higher ground that represented the eroded remains of the late Paleozoic–early Mesozoic Uncompahgre Uplift (Figure 5-3). Though there is no geological evidence that western Colorado was actually mountainous during

Plate 8. *Brachiosaurus,* with its high nostrils and large, blade-like teeth.

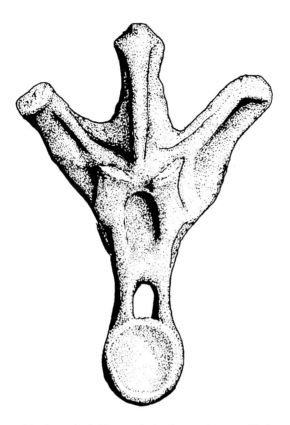

Figure 5-15. Dorsal vertebrae of *Haplocanthosaurus*. Lateral flanges of bone, the transverse processes, extend outward and upward from the vertical neural spines on the vertebrae from the back. Based on specimens illustrated in McIntosh and Williams, 1988.

this time, the hilly terrain in that region was likely to have been several hundred (or thousand) feet higher than the lower portions of the Morrison basin to the west in Utah. At these higher elevations, where water was more plentiful, the plant communities may well have been dominated by taller tree-like ferns, ginkgoes, and conifers. Such habitats would have been preferred by the brachiosaurids, if scientists are correct in interpreting their overall anatomy as a reflection of their high-browsing habits. Any brachiosaurid that might have wandered to the lower ground in Utah would have found less food available and would have had to compete with the lower-browsing diplodocids and camarasaurids for it. Thus, the scarcity of brachiosaurid remains in the Morrison Formation of Utah may be the result of the restriction of brachiosaurids to the loftier settings of the surrounding highlands. This hypothesis might be further verified if brachiosaurid remains could be found in western Utah and eastern Nevada where highlands more elevated than

those of western Colorado are thought to have existed during the late Jurassic. Unfortunately, however, sedimentary rocks of late Jurassic age have not been found in that region. This explanation therefore must remain, at least for the time being, a plausible but unverified notion. Nonetheless, in spite of their rarity, the brachiosaurids were probably an important part of the dinosaur community that existed in the Utah region during the late Jurassic.

◎   Family Cetiosauridae

The cetiosaurids represent a small group of relatively unspecialized sauropods. This family includes fewer genera than either the Diplodocidae or the Brachiosauridae, and paleontologists are still uncertain about the precise relationships between the various types of cetiosaurs. In general, the cetiosaurs are a rather poorly defined group of modest-sized sauropods. The neural spines on the vertebrae of the back and neck are undivided and possess relatively simple, oval pleurocoels. The necks appear to have been relatively short. The neural spines of vertebrae in the back region have flanges or extensions of bone called the transverse processes that extend outward and upward to connect with the heads of the ribs (Figure 5-15). In comparison to other sauropods, this configuration of the transverse processes is one of the few distinctive characteristics of the cetiosaurs. The neural spines of the vertebrae in the hip region are low, as in the Camarasauridae, and the caudal vertebrae are relatively short and of simple form. Few skulls of cetiosaurs are known, but the animals appear to have had spatulate teeth that were smaller and less massive but more numerous than those of the brachiosaurids or camarasaurids. The limbs are massive, as in all sauropods, but they do not appear to be especially distinctive or specialized in any of the known cetiosaurs. The cetiosaurs were fairly common worldwide during the early Jurassic, but they seem to have become less abundant in the late Jurassic when the more specialized brachiosaurids, diplodocids, and camarasaurids developed.

Haplocanthosaurus is the only cetiosaur known from the Morrison Formation (Hatcher, 1903; McIntosh and Williams, 1988). The placement of *Haplocanthosaurus* into the family Cetiosauridae is a bit speculative, but this dinosaur certainly does not exhibit the distinguishing features of any other sauropod family. *Haplocanthosaurus* is most common in the Garden Park area of Colorado, where at least two different species have been identified, *H. priscus* and *H. delfsi*. In Utah, fragmentary remains of a sauropod that may represent *Haplocanthosaurus* have been collected from the Morrison Formation at the Cleveland-Lloyd Quarry in Emery County. In addition, some of the many isolated sauropod bones found in numerous other sites in Utah may be from *Haplocanthosaurus*. So, while the evidence of *Haplocanthosaurus* in Utah is admittedly weak, it at least suggests that this sauropod might have lived among the far more common camarasaurids and diplodocids during the late Jurassic.

Haplocanthosaurus was not a large sauropod. A fully grown adult was probably about 45 feet long and weighed about 8 tons. The short neck and the general form of its teeth suggest that *Haplocanthosaurus* may have fed on the same vegetation, and in the same manner, as *Camarasaurus*. If that was the case, then paleontologists might interpret the rarity of *Haplocanthosaurus* in Utah exposures of the Morrison Formation as a reflection of the superior adaptation of *Camarasaurus* to a similar ecological niche. In many ways, *Haplocanthosaurus* was a primitive holdover during the late Jurassic, a "living fossil" in its time. If we could return to Utah in the late Jurassic, we might notice an occasional *Haplocanthosaurus* among the herds of sauropods. It perhaps would have been very rare and we might be tempted to bestow "endangered species" status on it. And endangered it was, for *Haplocanthosaurus* was the last known survivor of its lineage. After the late Jurassic, it and all other cetiosaurids (as well as many other sauropods) vanish from the fossil record.

Other Morrison Herbivores: The Ornithischians

The great sauropods were no doubt the primary herbivores during Morrison time, but there are other plant-eating dinosaurs represented by the fossils excavated from this formation. The miscellaneous herbivores all belong to the order Ornithischia and include the plated stegosaurs, the bipedal ornithopods, and the armored ankylosaurs. None of the ornithischian dinosaurs known from the Morrison Formation rivals the great sauropods in abundance or diversity; nonetheless, they are all fascinating creatures in their own right and warrant more than passing mention.

⑥ Suborder Stegosauria
Family Stegosauridae

The stegosaurids are one of the most familiar of all late Jurassic ornithischian dinosaurs. It is likely that no set of dinosaur toys has ever been produced that didn't include the familiar *Stegosaurus*, with its arched back bristling with triangular bone plates. The basic architecture of the stegosaurids has inspired numerous mythical monsters in science fiction movies for decades. I have always been impressed with the creativity of the originators of the "Godzilla" movies—they managed to combine characteristics of stegosaurs, theropods, and sauropods to come up with a fire-breathing carnivore as large as a skyscraper that hauled an impressive array of plates and spikes along its back. The basis for that latter characteristic of Godzilla was, of course, the stegosaurids.

There are about ten genera in the family Stegosauridae (Galton, 1990). This family belongs to a larger group of ornithischians known as the Thyreophora, or "shield bearers," in reference to the bony armor possessed by these quadrupedal

Photo 23: There are actually several different bone beds in the Morrison Formation at Dinosaur National Monument. In addition to sauropods, the remains of other herbivorous dinosaurs such as *Stegosaurus*, *Camptosaurus*, and *Dryosaurus* have been found there. John Telford.

herbivores (Sereno, 1989). Within the Thyreophora, the stegosaurs are related to other armored ornithischians such as the ankylosaurs, a group most common in the Cretaceous Period, and the primitive early Jurassic forms like *Scelidosaurus* discussed in Chapter 4. The stegosaurs are the most common late Jurassic thyreophoran dinosaurs, although in some places their remains are found in Cretaceous strata as well.

All stegosaurids have a dorsal row, or rows, of bony armor that extended along the back, projecting upward from the spinal column. This armor may include both plates and spikes of various shapes, sizes, and arrangements in the many genera of stegosaurids. The skulls of stegosaurids are elongated, small, and narrow, with the eyes set well back toward the rear of the head (Figure 5-16). The teeth are small and of very simple leaf-like form (Figure 5-17). The stegosaurids were exclusively quadrupedal herbivores and were mostly medium-sized dinosaurs, only rarely exceeding 25 feet in length.

◐ STEGOSAURUS

Stegosaurus is one of the best known of all stegosaurids and was the most widespread and abundant armored dinosaur in North America during the late Jurassic. The skull of *Stegosaurus* was relatively small in proportion to its body size and was long, narrow, and low (Figure 5-16). The eyes were set back toward the rear of the skull and the large nostrils were located at the tip of the snout, opening on each side. A toothless beak, formed by the upper premaxillary bone and lower predentary bone, adorned the tip of the snout. The teeth of *Stegosaurus* were small and leaf-shaped, with numerous ridges and denticles (Figure 5-17). These teeth would probably have been effective in shredding fibrous or tough plant tissues.

The back of *Stegosaurus* was strongly arched upward, reaching a maximum height just above the hips (Figure 5-18A). The vertebrae of the mid-back region were tall and had upward-directed transverse processes (Figure 5-18B). The ribs attached to these processes at nearly right angles to form a deep, but narrow, rib cage. The neck was relatively short and the head was carried low to the ground. The hind limbs of *Stegosaurus* were much longer than the forelimbs and were massive and pillar-like to support most of the weight of the animal. There were three robust toes tipped with hoof-like claws on each hind foot. The short forelimbs were constructed of stout bones that had prominent ridges for the attachment of strong muscles in the upper "arms" and shoulder. The five toes of the forefeet had smaller hoof-like claws.

The armor plates and spikes along the back of *Stegosaurus* are, to most people, its most distinctive feature. The size, shape, and pattern of the plates appear to have varied somewhat among the several known species of *Stegosaurus*, but there are some consistent similarities among them all. The plates extend from just behind the skull and continue in a row, or rows, along the entire neck, back, and about three-fourths of the tail. The neck plates are small and more or less rectangular in shape, increasing in size along the back to the hips, where the largest of the bone plates were located. The plates of the back generally become more triangular in shape toward the hips and, in some species, tapered to a sharp point directed upward. In the forward portion of the tail, the plates become smaller but have relatively broad bases. The spikes were restricted to the end

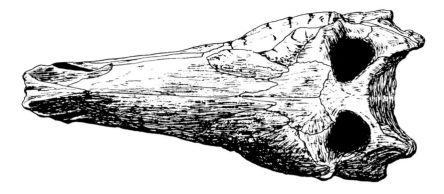

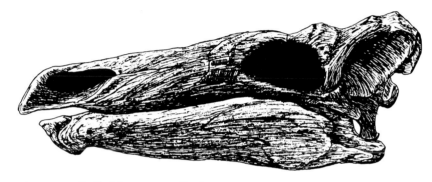

Figure 5-16. Skull of *Stegosaurus*. The low, narrow skull of *Stegosaurus* was about 18 inches long and tipped with a sharp-edged beak. Redrawn from Gilmore, 1914.

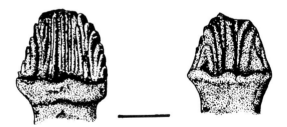

Figure 5-17. The small teeth of *Stegosaurus*. Scale bar=4 mm (.16 inch). From Galton, 1990.

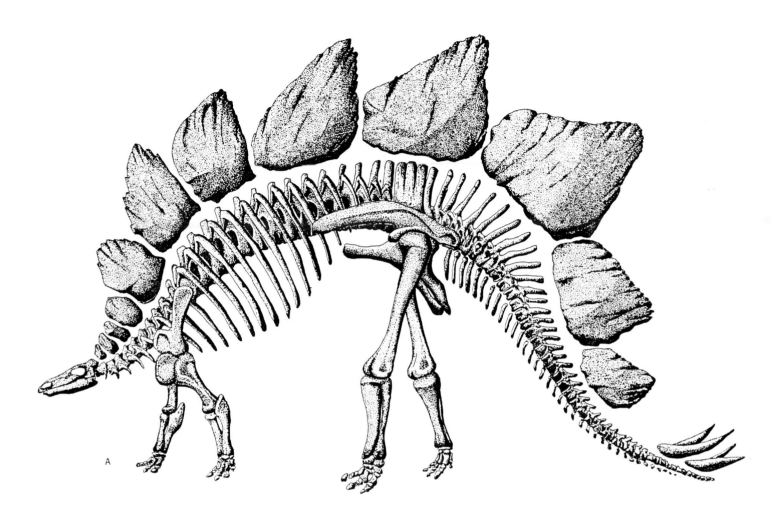

Figure 5-18. A: Skeleton of *Stegosaurus ungulatus*, based on the restoration of Gilmore, 1914. Note the highly arched back that supports the distinctive plates. The forelimbs were much shorter than the hind limbs, giving this dinosaur its crouching posture. B: A dorsal vertebra from *Stegosaurus*. The high neural arches and upward flaring transverse processes are typical of the stegosaurs. Bar=10 cm (4 inches). Redrawn from Galton, 1990.

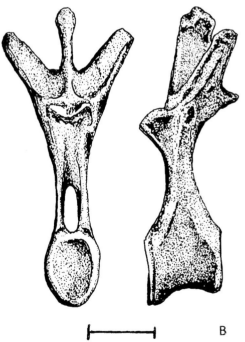

of the tail. The number of spikes appears to have been variable in different species, but there were at least four and perhaps as many as eight or more.

The function of the plates in *Stegosaurus* has been the subject of considerable disagreement and discussion among paleontologists ever since the first specimens of this genus were described in the 1890s. The plates have been variously regarded as defensive devices (see, for example, Gilmore, 1914), display structures (see Colbert, 1961), or as providing a thermoregulatory mechanism for adjusting the animal's body heat (Farlow and others, 1976; de Buffrenil and others, 1986). Perhaps the most revealing clue in this puzzle is the detailed structure of the plates. The plates have very thin walls of bone surrounding a "spongy" center that was probably full of blood when the animal was alive. Moreover, the surfaces of the larger plates usually have sinuous channels, suggesting that a network of blood vessels may have existed at the surface of the plates. It doesn't make sense that the plates would have been so thin and supplied with such copious amounts of blood if they functioned as defensive organs. The plates could have been easily damaged during an attack of a large theropod. Any *Stegosaurus* that suffered significant damage to its plates might have easily bled to death. Also, the plates were attached just beneath the skin and were anchored into the shallow muscles along the back. Because they were not rigidly connected to the bones of the back, the plates would have been easily deflected, offering little resistance to an attacking carnivore.

It seems far more likely that the plates of *Stegosaurus* were used to warm or cool the body. On warm days, or following periods of exertion, the plates could have been positioned into the breeze. The overheated blood that flowed through the plates and at their surfaces could have been cooled in this way. When its body temperature fell below the optimal range, *Stegosaurus* might have been able to elevate its core temperature by facing the plates toward the sun in a manner similar to the way lizards warm themselves on a cold day by basking in the sunlight. It is also possible, of course, that the plates served more than one function; but it does not seem likely than they were used primarily for defense. We might think of the plates as primarily thermoregulatory structures that could also have been used to attract mates or to communicate species identity to other stegosaurs.

Almost as controversial as the function of the plates is their precise arrangement along the back of *Stegosaurus*. This issue remains unsettled for one simple reason: no *Stegosaurus* skeleton has ever been discovered that has the full set of plates in their original position. Because the plates were not connected to the skeleton, they quickly became scattered and repositioned when the skin and muscles decayed after the death of an animal. Sometimes, in partial skeletons representing a *Stegosaurus* carcass laying on its side, the preserved plates are found overlapping one another. This might suggest that there were two rows of plates; alternately, however, we might interpret the overlap of the plates as a consequence of the displacement of a single row of plates along the back. Czerkas (1987) reviewed the various theories of plate arrangement and concluded that *Stegosaurus* most likely possessed a single row of plates. Although Czerkas's concept has become popular and is featured in several recent reconstructions of *Stegosaurus*, it does contradict the primitive archosaur pattern of paired rows of dermal plates in the skin. Crocodiles still retain this pattern and, until more complete and intact specimens of *Stegosaurus* are discovered, scientists at least must acknowledge the possibility of a paired row of plates garnishing the humped back of this ornithischian.

As slow-moving herbivores, the stegosaurs would have been under the constant threat of attack from the carnivorous theropods of Morrison time (discussed in the next chapter). If the plates offered little protection and flight was not possi-

Plate 9. *Stegosaurus* and *Ceratosaurus.* The muscular tail of *Stegosaurus,* studded with sharp spikes, would have been effective in deterring attacks from predators approaching this slow-moving dinosaur from the rear.

ble, how then did *Stegosaurus* defend itself? This was almost certainly the function of the tail spikes. The spikes were long and covered by a tough sheath that tapered to a sharp point. They could clearly inflict a serious wound. In addition, the spikes were angled upward and outward from the top of the tail in such a manner that the thrashing of the tail from side to side would have produced a dangerous situation for any animal approaching from the rear. But what about predators that might have approached from the side or front? Remember that *Stegosaurus* had most of its weight centered over the hips, and the shoulders were heavily muscled. The forelimbs of *Stegosaurus* seem to have been well designed to deliver a powerful sideways push to the front of the body. Such a rapid lateral movement of the forward portion of the body would have allowed *Stegosaurus* to pivot swiftly around the hips, redirecting its tail toward the attacking predator. We could well envision a *Stegosaurus* under attack quickly whirling around while wildly flailing its tail back and forth. The image is not unlike the behavior of a porcupine that bristles its quills and slaps its tail at any threatening animal. In defending itself, a *Stegosaurus* might have behaved a bit like an immense porcupine. In addition to the tail spikes, many small, circular plates of bone were imbedded in the skin covering the neck and belly regions of *Stegosaurus*. These small plates, known as dermal ossicles, afforded at least some protection to these otherwise vulnerable portions of the body by making the skin less penetrable to the teeth and claws of predators.

Stegosaurus has always been cited as a dim-witted or stupid creature. This perception stems from the ridiculously small brain that it evidently possessed. Studies of well-preserved skulls of *Stegosaurus* indicate that the cavity housing the brain was indeed tiny in comparison to the body size. The average *Stegosaurus* brain was about the size of a golf ball and weighed two or three ounces; yet this miniature brain controlled a body weighing several tons! Partly because its puny

brain seems so feeble in comparison to the large body, a popular notion has developed that *Stegosaurus* may have had a "second brain" located in the hip region. Paleontologists have noted that the tunnel-like cavity in the backbones that house the nerve-laden tissue of the spinal cord is significantly enlarged as it passes through the sacral vertebrae in the hip region of *Stegosaurus*. This cavity is called the sacral plexus, and it has a total volume of about ten times the brain cavity in the skull. Was this a "second brain," as it is popularly described? Probably not. The sacral plexus is not a unique feature of *Stegosaurus*. In fact, most vertebrate animals (including humans) have such an expansion of the dorsal nerve cord as it passes through the pelvic region, though it is often less pronounced than it is in *Stegosaurus*. It most cases, the sacral plexus seems related to the branching from the spinal cord of nerves that control the muscles of the hip and tail. In some animals, we know that the sacral plexus is partially filled with fat, evidently being stored for future use. In no living animal does the sacral plexus contain the type of complex nervous tissues that comprise the vertebrate brain. In the case of *Stegosaurus*, the expansion of the nerve cord in the hip region is probably related to the massiveness of the hind limb and tail muscles, which may have required numerous nerve branches and a store of fat to be used in times of nutritional stress. Thus, *Stegosaurus* was probably every bit as dim-witted as it has been portrayed as being. Though its brain was obviously large enough to coordinate its movement and overall respiration, that was about all it could do. A *Stegosaurus* would not have made a good pet… it almost certainly lacked the ability to learn behaviors the way many modern mammals can. Even my witless dogs could have easily outsmarted any *Stegosaurus*.

About a half-dozen species of *Stegosaurus* have been described by paleontologists, but only two seem to have been common in Utah. *S. ungulatus* was the larger and evidently more common of the two. Its remains have been found in the Morrison Formation in Colorado, Wyoming, and Utah. *S. ungulatus* was generally 15–25 feet long, with relatively long hind limbs, a high rump, large dorsal plates, and as many as eight tail spikes. The smaller species of *Stegosaurus*, *S. stenops*, was usually less than 15 feet long, possessed relatively short limbs and a lower rump, and had four tail spikes. The largest individuals of *S. ungulatus* might have weighed as much as 6 tons, while the smaller *S. stenops* normally weighed between 1 and 2 tons. Both species were clearly low-vegetation browsers and seem well adapted to subsist on coarse and tough vegetation. As noted earlier in this chapter, *Stegosaurus* is commonly associated with the diplodocid sauropods, particularly *Apatosaurus*, in many Morrison fossil quarries. Because the teeth and jaws of these two groups of dinosaurs are so dissimilar, it is not likely that they competed for the same food resources. *Stegosaurus*, with its shredding teeth and chopping beak, probably consumed plant fodder that the diplodocids could not process with their diminutive, weak teeth.

⑥ **Suborder Ankylosauria**

Stegosaurus was not the only armor-plated ornithischian roaming the Morrison plain. In several Morrison dinosaur localities, small circular-to-rectangular plates of bone with a raised keel have been found that might indicate the presence of primitive members of the suborder Ankylosauria. These fragments of dermal armor are quite different from the plates, spikes, and ossicles associated with the remains of *Stegosaurus*. However, the ankylosaurs are best known from the late Cretaceous Period, when these gigantic and heavily armored herbivores were widely distributed throughout the world. Few ankylosaurs are known from the Jurassic Period. The origin of the ankylosaurs remains uncertain, but the well-developed bony armor, quadrupedal posture, and other traits suggest that

they are more closely related to the *Scelidosaurus-Stegosaurus* group than they are to other ornithischians. Nevertheless, the skulls and skeletal features of the ankylosaurs are much different from those of the stegosaurs, so the divergence between these two groups of dinosaurs must have occurred early in their evolutionary histories.

The nature of mysterious ankylosaur-like plates found in the Morrison Formation was illuminated by the recent discovery in this formation of the oldest ankylosaur in North America. Kirkland and Carpenter (1994) have identified the partial remains of the primitive ankylosaur *Mymoorapelta maysi* from Morrison outcrops near the Utah-Colorado border. *Mymoorapelta* was a small quadrupedal herbivore that had a well-developed bony plate covering the hip region and triangular plates projecting outward on either side of the tail. Elsewhere on its body, *Mymoorapelta* evidently had many circular-to-oval plates, or scutes, imbedded in the skin. Small isolated scutes similar to those of *Mymoorapelta* are also known from several other localities in Utah, indicating that this ankylosaur, or a close relative, was widely distributed across the central interior basin during late Jurassic time. The skull is missing in the specimen described by Kirkland and Carpenter and only a few bones of the limbs were found. However, it is clear that *Mymoorapelta* is a primitive member of the suborder Ankylosauria, and this discovery documents the presence of such armored dinosaurs in the Morrison fauna. So, while the armored ankylosaurs were certainly not very abundant in Utah during Morrison time, this group of dinosaurs had definitely taken the first evolutionary steps toward the success that awaited them in the Cretaceous Period.

⑥ **Suborder Ornithopoda**

The ornithopod ornithischians are a large and diverse group of bipedal and semi-quadrupedal herbivores that exhibit many advanced specializations. The climax of ornithopod evolution occurred during the late Cretaceous, when they became the most successful dinosaur herbivores on a global scale. The ornithopods include the familiar "duck-billed" dinosaurs such as *Edmontosaurus*, *Corythosaurus*, and the crested *Parasaurolophus*, which all might serve as good examples of basic ornithopod design. However, this subclass includes many other types of herbivorous dinosaurs that are less specialized than the duck-billed representatives. In the late Jurassic, the true duck-billed dinosaurs (families Hadrosauridae and Lambeosauridae) had not yet evolved from their more primitive ancestors. Among the suborder Ornithopoda in the late Jurassic, we find instead several different groups of more primitive character such as the iguanodontids, hypsilophodontids, and fabrosaurids. Such groups traditionally have been considered to represent families of ornithopod dinosaurs, but there is still some uncertainty about which primitive ornithopods belong in which families. Several schemes of classification have been recently proposed for these groups (see, for example, Weishampel and Heinrich, 1992; Sues and Norman, 1990), but the categories are not always consistent. Despite the comparatively primitive character of the late Jurassic ornithopods and the confusion about their classification, they were still highly successful during their time and were an important element in the Morrison ecosystem. Let's examine a few of the ornithopods known from the Morrison Formation.

⑤ Family Iguanodontidae

The iguanodontids were all relatively large, heavily built, and mostly bipedal herbivores. Their skulls were long and only moderately deep, with relatively simple teeth and a beak-like snout. An elongated recess formed a "cheek pocket" on each side of the skull, a feature that would become even more prominent in the later hadrosaurs and lambeosaurs. The limbs were stout and massive, and the toes were tipped with hoof-like struc-

tures. The hind limbs were clearly larger than the forelimbs, but the iguanodontids could probably support their bodies in either a bipedal or quadrupedal posture. All iguanodontids have a "thumb" on the manus ("hand") that was shaped like a spike and projected inward from the other four digits. This unique thumb is one of the most distinguishing characteristics of the iguanodontids.

⑥ *CAMPTOSAURUS*

Camptosaurus is the most common of the Morrison ornithopods and the only member of this suborder that can be regarded as abundant and widespread. The remains of *Camptosaurus* have been found in many sites across Utah, Colorado, and Wyoming, including the Cleveland-Lloyd Quarry and Dinosaur National Monument. Compared to other iguanodontids, *Camptosaurus* was of modest size, with most specimens exhibiting a length of about 15–18 feet and weighing between 1,500 and 2,200 pounds. Occasionally, unusually large *Camptosaurus* fossils are found that suggest that the biggest individuals might have grown to 28 feet in length and attained a body weight closer to 3 or 4 tons. The skull of *Camptosaurus* was long and low, with a toothless beak-like tip formed from the premaxilla and predentary bones (Figure 5-19). The well-developed cheek pockets in the skull suggest that *Camptosaurus* thoroughly chewed its food with its small, leaf-shaped teeth.

The hind limbs of *Camptosaurus* were powerful and no doubt supported most of the animal's weight and provided the main propulsion for the body (Figure 5-20). The four large toes of the hind foot were equipped with hoof-like claws. The forelimbs were smaller than the hind limbs but were still relatively stout. The thumb spike of *Camptosaurus* was comparatively small and the other four digits of the manus had small, pointed, hoof-like claws. These features, coupled with the solid construction of the wrist, suggest that

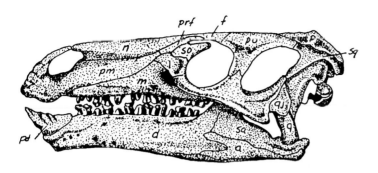

Figure 5-19. Skull of *Camptosaurus*.

Camptosaurus frequently supported itself in a quadrupedal fashion even though it was fully capable of a bipedal stance. Since the beak and teeth of *Camptosaurus* indicate that it was probably a low-browsing herbivore, it is reasonable to envision *Camptosaurus* feeding in a quadrupedal posture and using the hind limbs alone while walking or running from place to place.

Camptosaurus teeth are relatively small, but they appear to be well designed for shredding leafy vegetation. Its short neck and modest body size prevented *Camptosaurus* from reaching high-growing vegetation. The neck was rather flexible, however, and, with its quadrupedal feeding stance, *Camptosaurus* was probably very efficient as a forager among the low-growing late Jurassic shrubs. It probably fed at about the same level as *Stegosaurus*, but it may have selected the more tender plant tissues as its primary food. Unlike *Stegosaurus*, however, *Camptosaurus* does not appear to have possessed any defensive armor to protect itself from the fearsome predators of the Jurassic. The thumb spike, which might have been used as a defensive weapon in other iguanodontids, is so small and weakly developed in *Camptosaurus* that it probably could not have inflicted a very serious wound on an attacking theropod. Furthermore, though it could move efficiently in a bipedal stance, *Camptosaurus* was not particularly well designed for speed; many late Jurassic theropods probably could have outrun it, at least for short distances.

We might wonder how *Camptosaurus*, without protective armor and with limited abilities for flight, managed to survive the attacks of carnivores. There are at least two plausible possibilities. First, *Camptosaurus* probably spent a great deal of time feeding in the dense foliage of the more forested areas of the Morrison basin. In this shadowy environment, protective coloration may have helped conceal *Camptosaurus* individuals from predators. Such natural camouflage is employed by many browsing mammals in the modern world and would have been particularly valuable to *Camptosaurus* when it was feeding in a head-down posture. Since skin does not readily fossilize, the coloration or patterning of the skin (integument) of *Camptosaurus* remains unknown. It is at least possible, though, that this ornithopod had mottled patches or bars of color that would have made it less visible in the late Jurassic shrubbery. Another effective means of defense might have been herding or other group behavior that enabled bands of *Camptosaurus* to detect the approach of predators and to confuse them when they attacked. Many of the herding animals in modern grassland and forested habitats employ this mechanism of survival. It rarely prevents the loss of animals from the herd, but it certainly limits the success of the predators to a tolerable level that enables the herd, as a whole, to survive. In the absence of armor or any extreme specializations for speed, it is likely that *Camptosaurus* depended primarily on camouflage or group behavior, or both, to survive the attacks of dinosaur predators.

Ⓖ *IGUANODON*(?)

Iguanodon was one of the first dinosaurs ever discovered. Gideon Mantell applied this name to some fragmentary fossils found in England in 1825. The name, meaning "iguana tooth," was inspired by the leaf-like teeth of *Iguanodon*, which bear a strong resemblance to those of the modern iguana in that they have long ridges leading to small denticles along the cutting edge. The teeth are not dissimilar to those of *Camptosaurus*, and

Plate 10. *Camptosaurus* feeding in the shrubs. Protective camouflage and herding behavior may have helped these gentle herbivores survive in a world filled with rapacious predators.

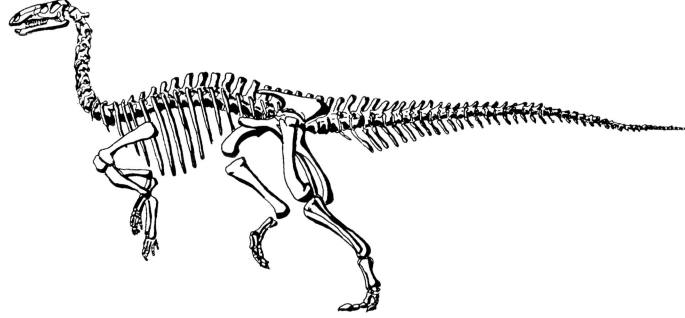

Figure 5-20. Skeleton of *Camptosaurus dispar*, based on the drawing of R.T. Bakker from Norman and Weishampel, 1990. This reconstruction shows *Camptosaurus* in a bipedal running stance; but the animal was also capable of supporting its body in a quadrupedal posture. This species of *Camptosaurus* was about 15 feet long and stood about 4 feet high at the back.

other skeletal similarities unite *Iguanodon* and *Camptosaurus* within the family Iguanodontidae. *Iguanodon* was thought be a strictly European dinosaur for many years following its discovery. Recently, though, its remains were reported from the Morrison Formation of western Colorado (Armstrong and others, 1987). This was a surprising discovery because it suggested that *Iguanodon* lived in North America in the late Jurassic, millions of years earlier than the European *Iguanodon*, which occurs in early Cretaceous deposits. Was the Morrison specimen the world's oldest *Iguanodon*? Maybe. The Morrison fossils were very limited, however, consisting of a portion of the jaw and a few loose teeth. *Iguanodon* was so similar to *Camptosaurus* that it is not easy to distinguish between the two ornithopods with such limited fossil material. Though additional *Iguanodon*-like material was later recovered from the site, it was not sufficient to prove that the specimen was not *Camptosaurus*. Many paleontologists are still not sure if the western Colorado fossils really do represent *Iguanodon*. Though no *Iguanodon* fossils have yet been positively identified in Utah, its possible occurrence in western Colorado suggests that it also could have lived in

Utah during the late Jurassic. Let's briefly examine the differences between *Iguanodon* and *Camptosaurus*, if for no other reason than to learn how the two dinosaurs differed from each other. Perhaps someday new fossil discoveries will allow scientists to settle the "Morrison *Iguanodon*" issue once and for all.

Overall, *Iguanodon* was similar in basic design to *Camptosaurus*, but it was substantially larger. An adult *Iguanodon* attained a body length of as much as 35 feet, nearly twice as long as an average *Camptosaurus*. *Iguanodon* also seems to have been more advanced than *Camptosaurus* in that it had a much more prominent thumb spike, one less toe (three) on each hind foot, and an intricate system of criss-crossing tendons that helped to strengthen the back and tail. The skull of *Iguanodon* was deeper and longer than that of *Camptosaurus* and contained more and larger teeth. The forelimbs of *Iguanodon* are proportionally larger than those of *Camptosaurus* and the forefeet are more robust. These features suggest that *Iguanodon* may have assumed a quadrupedal posture more frequently than did *Camptosaurus*.

⑥   Family Hypsilophodontidae

The hypsilophodontid ornithischians were mostly small (roughly 6–15 feet long), bipedal herbivores that were most common in the late Jurassic and early Cretaceous periods. Most hypsilophodontids were lightly built creatures with slender, long hind limbs that were well designed for running. The forelimbs are smaller than the hind limbs and have five-finger hands that lack the hoof-like claws of the iguanodontids. The tails of hypsilophodontids were generally braced by a basket-like network of tendons that would have made them quite rigid in life. The beam-like tail was probably used as a counterbalancing stabilizer that would have enhanced the maneuverability of the hypsilophodontids as they ran. The skulls of hypsilophodontids are small, with a narrow horny beak at the tip. The small teeth are somewhat variable in form, from leaf-shaped to triangular to chisel-like in the dozen or so different genera of hypsilophodontids. However, the bones of the snout are weakly joined in such a way that the maxilla (upper cheek bone) could pivot outward past the lower jaw while a hypsilophodontid chewed its food. This transverse movement between the upper and lower teeth probably allowed the hypsilophodontids to thoroughly process their plant food into a easily digested pulp.

⑥   *DRYOSAURUS*

Dryosaurus is by far the most common and well-known member of the hypsilophodontid group known from the Morrison Formation in Utah and adjacent regions of western North America (Galton, 1981, 1983; Shepherd and others, 1977). However, several skeletal features of *Dryosaurus* are different from the general hypsilophodontid pattern (see discussion below), leading to some confusion or debate about its family-level classification. Some paleontologists consider *Dryosaurus* to be an advanced member of the family Hyp-

silophodontidae (Galton, 1983), while others place it in a separate category known variously as the Dryosauridae (Sues and Norman, 1990) or the Dryomorpha (Sereno, 1986). Still other paleontologists have suggested that *Dryosaurus* is an iguanodontian, closely related to *Camptosaurus* (Weishampel and Heinrich, 1992).

However *Dryosaurus* is classified, it is a very interesting member of the Morrison dinosaur fauna. Originally named *Laosaurus altus* by O.C. Marsh in 1878, *Dryosaurus* was a relatively small, bipedal herbivore, ranging in length from about 6 feet to 10 feet or more. An adult *Dryosaurus* would have weighed about 200 pounds and stood some 3–4 feet tall at the hip. The skull of *Dryosaurus* was small and delicate, similar to those of the hypsilophodontids (Figure 5-21). However, unlike the true hypsilophodontids, *Dryosaurus* had no teeth on the bone (the predentary) that forms the lower tip of the snout. The leaf-shearing teeth of *Dryosaurus* are small, with prominent ridges on the flat surfaces and small denticles along the edges (Figure 5-22). These teeth are more elongated and triangular in shape than those typical of the true hypsilophodontids. Worn surfaces on the teeth of *Dryosaurus* indicate that it chewed its food thoroughly, using the flexible upper jaws to move the upper and lower teeth past each other in a manner similar to the that of the more typical hypsilophodontids. The snout of *Dryosaurus* was relatively blunt, suggesting that it might have browsed close to the ground.

Dryosaurus was evidently a speedy little dinosaur. It had long and well-muscled hind limbs (Figure 5-23). The hind feet had only three functional toes, rather than the four that is the case in most other hypsilophodontids. Because it results in a decrease in the frictional contact between the foot and the ground, the reduction of toes is usually interpreted as an adaptation for swift running. Furthermore, the vertebrae in the middle of the back of *Dryosaurus*, from the hips to the shoulders, were braced by bony tendons that would have strengthened the spine. This feature,

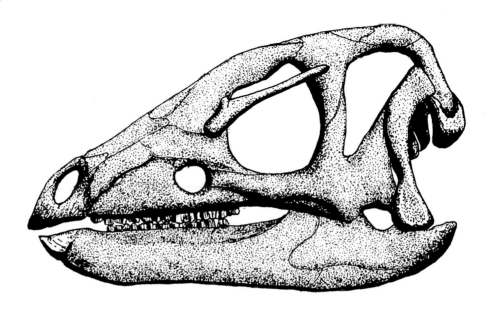

Figure 5-21. Skulls of an adult *Dryosaurus* (top) and a baby of the same genus (bottom). The adult skull is about 20 cm (8 inches) long, while the smaller baby had a skull about half that size. The eyes were relatively larger and the face was relatively shorter in the baby. Sketch of baby skull modeled after Carpenter, 1994.

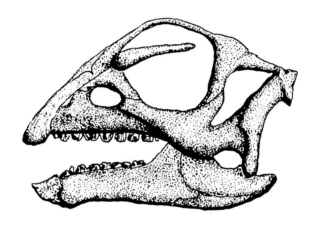

Figure 5-22. Typical upper teeth of *Dryosaurus* (right) and of *Hypsilophodon*, a hypsilophodontid (left). The teeth of *Dryosaurus* are longer and have a prominent ridge on one side, one of several differences between it and the true hypsilophodontids. From Sues and Normal, 1990.

Plate 11.
A *Dryosaurus* nest
in the Morrison
interior basin.

Figure 5-23. Skeleton of *Dryosaurus altus*, as reconstructed by Gregory S. Paul (in Sues and Normal, 1990). *Dryosaurus* was a swift runner, with large hind limbs and a rigidly braced back.

also seen in other bipedal dinosaur herbivores, would have helped transfer the force of the hind limbs to the body, an additional specialization for speed.

Perhaps the most intriguing aspect of *Dryosaurus* is the frequency with which fossils representing small babies of this genus have been found. From a site in western Colorado at least 2,500 bone fragments have been found associated with eggshell fragments. About 90 percent of these small bones represent baby dryosaurs, ranging in size from embryos to immature adults (Scheetz, 1991). It seems likely, though not certain, that many of the eggshell fragments from this locality represent the remains of *Dryosaurus* eggs from a nest. In addition, at Dinosaur National Monument, where some of the best *Dryosaurus* fossils in the world have been recovered, a 10-cm (4-inch)-long baby dryosaur skull was discovered in 1922 and recently reconstructed by K. Carpenter (1994). From these discoveries, paleontologists have a reasonably good idea what a baby *Dryosaurus* looked like. The tiny baby skulls had large eyes compared to the adult and the snout was less elongated (Figure 5-21). These distinctions between adult and baby dryosaurs are similar to those of many other animals, particularly birds, in which the young often appear to have large eyes and short faces. As they matured, the baby dryosaurs probably followed the same

pattern that we see in modern birds and mammals—that is, the head grows faster than the eyes, while the adult snouts develop from the lengthening of the skull. In this way, babies gradually lose their infantile proportions. Depending on its age, a baby *Dryosaurus* was probably not much larger than a modern robin and would easily have fit into the palm of your hand.

Even though paleontologists have discovered fossils of the babies of several different dinosaurs in recent years, such fossils remain relatively rare. The frequency of juvenile *Dryosaurus* remains in the Morrison Formation of Utah and nearby regions is unusual. Perhaps the conditions on the broad alluvial plain were well suited to those required by *Dryosaurus* for successful mating and nesting. Recently, an embryo of *Camptosaurus* was also discovered at Dinosaur National Monument (Chure and others, 1994). It thus appears that at least two types of ornithopod dinosaurs found favorable breeding and nesting conditions on the lowland plains of Utah during the late Jurassic. For some reason, it seems that the other larger dinosaurs preferred to nest elsewhere, because embryos and juveniles of other genera are much less common in the floodplain and river-deposited sediments of the Morrison Formation in eastern Utah and western Colorado. Maybe the relative abundance of ornithopod babies in this region is just the result of chance discoveries. On the other hand, perhaps it was the combination of such factors as the abundance of food, the ability to conceal the nest, the ease of finding mates, and the favorable climate that created near-optimal conditions for the ornithopods to procreate on the Morrison plain. One thing is certain: the breezes that drifted across the late Jurassic landscapes of eastern Utah would have commonly carried the chirps and squeals of baby dinosaurs.

☙ OTHNIELIA

Othnielia, named for the illustrious American paleontologist Othniel C. Marsh (Galton, 1977), is a poorly known bipedal herbivore that seems to be a member of the family Hypsilophodontidae. Our knowledge of the skeletal anatomy of *Othnielia* is limited by both its rarity and the fragmentary nature of the few partial skeletons that have been discovered.

This dinosaur has been known by several other names, including "*Nanosaurus rex*" and "*Laosaurus gracilis.*" In addition, there is some lingering disagreement among paleontologists about the family-level classification of *Othnielia*, which is not surprising given the limited information scientists have concerning its skeletal characteristics. In this book, *Othnielia* will be described as a hypsilophodontid, because it seems most similar to that group of dinosaurs.

The scrappy remains of *Othnielia* known to date suggest that its skeleton was similar to, but substantially smaller than, *Dryosaurus*, with a length not exceeding about 7 feet. In life, *Othnielia* probably weighed no more than about 40 or 50 pounds as a full-grown adult and of course would have been smaller as a juvenile. It had primitive, leaf-shaped teeth and evidently lacked the well-developed cheek pouches that were common in the more advanced ornithopods. It seems that *Othnielia* favored the sheltered environments where it coexisted with other small creatures (Russell, 1989).

Other Ornithopods and Small Animals of the Morrison

In addition to the ornithopod dinosaurs already described, there are indications from the Morrison fossil record that at least one other member of this suborder existed in Utah during late Jurassic time. *Nanosaurus* was a tiny ornithopod dinosaur about two feet long that weighed perhaps two pounds. This bird-sized herbivore is known from late Jurassic localities in Colorado but has yet to be identified with certainty from Utah exposures of the Morrison Formation. The overall skeletal architecture of *Nanosaurus* seems to be very primitive, but its anatomy is so poorly known that there is no consensus among paleontologists as to which family it should be placed in. *Nanosaurus* is most commonly regarded to be a member of the Fabrosauridae, a very primtive family of ornithischian dinosaurs. Alternately, *Nanosaurus* might represent an unspecialized member of the Hypsilophodontidae. Also, some paleontologists regard *Nanosaurus* and *Othnielia* as small and large variants of the same species.

Although *Nanosaurus* is poorly known and not yet documented from Utah exposures, it can serve as a reminder of an important fact about the Morrison ecosystem: even though the late Jurassic is referred to as the "Golden Age of Sauropods," there were many smaller creatures that played equally important roles in the ecological drama that continued in eastern Utah for some 10 million years in the late Jurassic Period. That, in comparison to our knowledge of the sauropods, we know so little about the small creatures that populated the Morrison plain does not mean that these smaller animals were unimportant or uncommon. This situation is probably a reflection of the historical bias toward the collecting of large fossils that was discussed in Chapter 1. Gradually, scientists are learning more about the many kinds of small animals—dinosaurs and non-dinosaurs—that were important elements of the overall Morrison fauna. Some recent work (for example, Callison, 1987) demonstrates that there was a rich fauna of lizards, primitive mammals, pterosaurs, turtles, crocodiles, and snakes that lived with the dinosaurs in the Morrison basin. A thorough review of all these non-dinosaur vertebrates is beyond the scope of this exploration of Utah dinosaurs, but their importance as vital elements in the ecological system that supported the larger dinosaurs should not be overlooked.

Up to this point, there also has been no mention of the animals that were positioned at the top of the Morrison food chain—the theropods. All of the herbivorous dinosaurs, along with the smaller non-dinosaur vertebrates, represented an enormous food base for creatures designed to consume flesh. Responding to the virtually unlimited opportunities for predation, the theropods of the Morrison represent a fascinating assemblage of fearsome creatures cloaked in tooth and claw. They will be the focus of our next peek into the late Jurassic world of Utah.

THE THEROPOD DINOSAURS represent to
many people the quintessential prehistoric
monsters. The perception of them as colossal
eating machines with a fierce demeanor and sav-
age nature has been fostered by countless portray-
als in movies and books that project such a
ferocious image. From Arthur Conan Doyle's *Lost
World*, published in 1914, to the current *Jurassic
Park* and *The Lost World* by Michael Crichton, we
seem to love our fear of theropods. They are
everybody's favorite dinosaur villains.

In reality, the theropods were fascinating
creatures that exhibit many remarkable adaptations for survival and success as predators in the
Mesozoic world. As a group, the suborder
Theropoda is enchanting for reasons other than
the sense of terror evoked by their perceived fe-
rocity. They are wondrous examples of the
efficiency of natural selection in driving the
process of adaptation and change in living systems. In many ways, the theropods represent a
conservative lineage of dinosaurs, because they all
consistently retained the bipedal stance and carnivorous habits of the earliest dinosaurs and dinosaur ancestors. Other groups of dinosaurs,
such as the sauropods and ornithischians, radi-
cally modified these original characteristics as
they became specialized for the variety of herbivorous roles they played in the Mesozoic ecosystem. But not the theropods. Throughout the
entire era of dinosaur dominance, they never
abandoned the basic traits of the earliest members of the Dinosauria. However, if we closely examine the details of theropod design from the
earliest and most primitive carnivores, such as
Herrerasaurus, to the most advanced forms, such
as *Tyrannosaurus* and other Cretaceous predators,
we observe an amazing amount of variation on
the general themes of flesh eating and bipedal
movement.

Consequently, the theropods represent a
highly differentiated group of dinosaur predators,
and their individual specializations for greater
meat-eating efficiency are amazingly varied. So
numerous are the variations on the general theme
of bipedal carnivory among the theropods that
their classification has been a subject of constant
debate among paleontologists. Reflecting the
complexities and variations in their form, a confusing snarl of taxonomic categories for the
theropod dinosaurs has become established over
the past century.

The suborder Theropoda was established in
1881 by O.C. Marsh to encompass all the carnivorous dinosaurs known at that time, which, of
course, were only a few. As more and more fossils
of carnivorous dinosaurs were discovered, it became necessary to subdivide the Theropoda into
smaller groups. The earliest subdivision was
based on size, more than on any other feature.
Thus, the Coelurosauria was established as an infraorder to accommodate the smaller carnivores,
while the larger forms were placed into the infraorder Carnosauria. Several new orders and other
taxonomic groups were added later as the diversity of the theropods steadily increased as a consequence of continued research and collecting.
Various infraorders, families, and subfamilies
were established as the need arose, and soon the
classification of the theropods was a confusing
weave of taxonomic threads that often obscured
the true relationships between the various groups.

The basis of the modern taxonomy of the
theropod dinosaurs was established when Gauthier revised the classification of the entire suborder in 1986 (Gauthier, 1986; Rowe and Gauthier,
1990). In this modern classification, the theropods are divided into two broad groups on the
basis of sets of characteristics that are considered
to be either primitive or advanced. The set of
primitive features make up the basic blueprint for
the entire suborder, while the more advanced (or
derived) groups within the Theropoda are distinguished by evolutionary innovations that are superimposed upon the older, primitive framework.

This approach to classification, based on the
distribution of primitive and derived characteristics, is known as cladistics and has become the

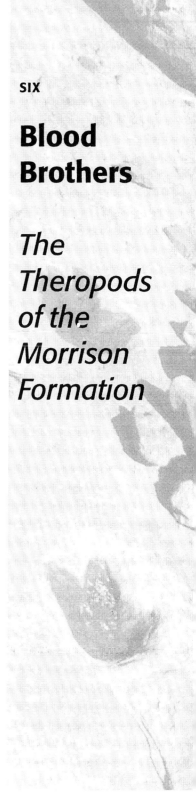

SIX

Blood Brothers

The Theropods of the Morrison Formation

dominant method of subdividing the various dinosaur taxa, or groups. Earlier schemes of classification that stressed overall morphological (form and structural) similarity (such as the size distinctions between the "coelurosaurs" and "carnosaurs") have become less popular because they often resulted in the grouping together of creatures that were probably not closely related in a evolutionary sense. The "coelurosaurs," for example, is a category that includes many different theropods that are not actually very similar or closely related to one another, except in terms of size.

The cladistic approach has allowed the development of a system of classification that more accurately represents the true evolutionary relationships between the various groups of theropods by attempting to deemphasize superficial similarities such as size. While cladistic classifications are now used, or are being developed, for all groups of dinosaurs, their use in theropod classification has been well accepted for at least a decade. It is beyond the purpose of this book to fully explore the contrasts between the traditional morphological and the modern cladistic classifications, but the almost universal acceptance of cladistic techniques among paleontologists stems from the fact that the categories they produce are less subject to individual judgment and make a much stronger statement about ancestry and evolution than did the orthodox taxonomy of the past. Gradually, as the modern cladistic classification of the theropods and other dinosaur groups is refined, some of the confusion created by unnatural assemblages such as the "coelurosaurs" is beginning to clear.

In Chapter 1 it was mentioned that the suborder Theropoda is divided into two broad groups: the Ceratosauria and the Tetanurae. These two groups are defined according to the distribution of primitive and derived characteristics among the theropods and, as such, represent groups of dinosaurs that share a common evolutionary history. Such a group is called a clade. Thus, the Tetanurae and Ceratosauria technically are not infraorders or families, because they are not established on the basis of overall morphological similarity but instead reflect the primitive characteristics of some theropods and the specialized (or derived) nature of others. The Ceratosauria is the primitive clade and consists of only about ten different genera, while the more specialized Tetanurae represent a larger set of derived and highly varied theropods, among which at least sixty-five genera are recognized.

At least ten different theropods have been identified from the Morrison Formation in western North America (see Table 1) and eight of these are known from Utah sites. The Morrison theropods are a diverse array of predators ranging from gigantic beasts such as *Torvosaurus* to the unpretentious *Ornitholestes*, which looked a bit like an overgrown, bipedal lizard, about three feet long. The variety observed among the theropods identified in the Morrison Formation suggests that there was some degree of specialization among them for specific prey animals, different hunting strategies, and variable habitats. Each of the Morrison theropods went about their carnivorous ways in their own distinctive style, and, evidently, the food base of prey animals was large enough to accommodate several different approaches to carnivory.

Ceratosauria

The primitive Ceratosauria are defined by several characteristics that serve to separate the group from the more advanced tetanurine theropods. The skulls of the ceratosaurs are relatively heavy and long, with teeth that extend backward to at least the position of the eye socket, or orbit (Figure 6-1). As in almost all theropods, the individual teeth of ceratosaurs are curved toward the rear, flattened to a blade-like form, and have small serrations along the cutting edges, much like a steak knife. The skull is commonly ornamented by bony crests, ridges, or blade-shaped horns that are developed to varying degrees in individual specimens.

The vertebrae of the backs of ceratosaurs had distinctive triangular transverse processes that projected outward and back from the vertical neural spines (Figure 6-2B). The cervical vertebrae were robust and had two pockets, or pleurocoels, to conserve weight. The necks of ceratosaurs appear to have been thick, muscular, and flexible. Elsewhere in the skeleton, the ceratosaurs exhibit numerous fusions of individual bones in the ankles, feet, and pelvis (Figure 6-2A). These fusions are thought to represent an adaptation for running, since they would have resulted in stronger limb bones and a more rigid bracing of the hind limbs to the pelvis. The pubis, which projects forward and down from the center of the pelvis, tapers to a blunt tip in the ceratosaurs and lacks the expanded "boot" seen in the tetanurine theropods. The pubis of ceratosaurs is also distinctive in that the plate-like portion of it in front of the hip socket has a small circular opening, or embayment, that is not observed in the Tetanurae.

One of the most intriguing aspects of the ceratosaurs is the common observation that the skulls and other skeletal elements of the individual species seem to have had two forms. This dimorphism is usually expressed by distinct differences in the ornamentation on individual skulls and the proportions of both the limb bones and the vertebrae of the back. The relatively small, slender, and less bulky bones of the "gracile" form may signify sexual differences, presumably the female ceratosaurs. The larger, heavier, and more prominently ornamented bones observed in the more robust variant might represent the males. Or perhaps the females might have been the larger form. In any case, the dimorphism commonly seen in ceratosaurs does not seem to reflect the age of the animals, because the robust and gracile forms can be recognized in bones of varying size.

Sexual dimorphism is the most logical inter-

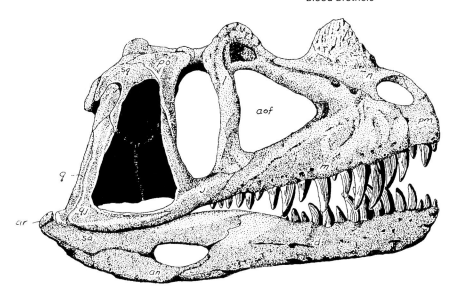

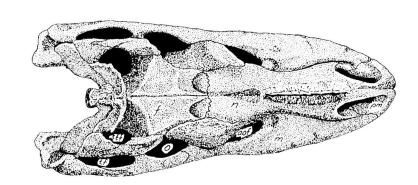

Figure 6-1. Skull of *Ceratosaurus nasicornis*. Note the blade-like horn on the snout and the prominent brow ridges. Based on specimen illustrated by Gilmore, 1920.

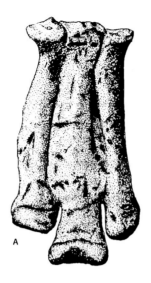

Figure 6-2. A: Fused foot bones (metatarsals) of *Ceratosaurus*; and B: dorsal vertebrae of *Ceratosaurus*, in ventral view. Note the wing-like transverse processes that are strongly deflected toward the rear. Adopted from Gilmore, 1920.

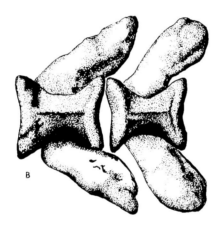

grounds, flashing their prominent crests as display organs to attract females or subdue rivals.

The ceratosaurs were mainly a late Triassic and early Jurassic group of theropods. By the late Jurassic, and throughout the ensuing Cretaceous Period, the tetanurnine theropods were the dominant dinosaur predators on a global scale. Such late Triassic and early Jurassic predators as *Coelophysis* and *Dilophosaurus* represent fairly specialized members of this clade that lived during the climax of ceratosaur history. It is not surprising, then, that only one of the Morrison theropods belongs to this group. *Ceratosaurus*, the namesake genus of the entire clade, is the last of the ceratosaurs. Despite its relatively young age, *Ceratosaurus* seems, paradoxically, to be the most primitive member of the Ceratosauria.

⑥ CERATOSAURUS NASICORNIS

Ceratosaurus is not particularly common in the Morrison Formation of Utah, but enough of its remains have been discovered to indicate that it prowled the interior basin along with several other more advanced theropods. *Ceratosaurus* is the largest of the Ceratosauria, reaching an adult length in excess of 20 feet. Such a full-grown *Ceratosaurus* would have weighed approximately 1 ton and might have stood about 7 feet tall at the hip.

The skull of *Ceratosaurus* was large, lightly constructed, and relatively narrow (Figure 6-1). There were about sixty teeth in the upper and lower jaws of *Ceratosaurus*. Since the teeth of theropods were continuously shed or broken and replaced, some of these teeth were large and some were small, depending on the time of replacement for each individual tooth. The teeth are of typical theropod form, curving slightly toward the rear, with fine serrations along the cutting edges. The bone that forms the tip of the snout, the premaxilla, of *Ceratosaurus* held three robust teeth that were somewhat less blade-like in shape than those that lined the jaws farther back. The tooth row

pretation of the variation in the fossils of ceratosaurs. If the ceratosaurs were sexually dimorphic, then certain behavioral attributes can be reasonably postulated. The males may have used their horns and crests to compete with each other for mates. It is also likely that the ceratosaurs had a "breeding season," during which time individuals would gather to acquire mates, lay eggs, and perhaps nurture the hatchlings. The males may have acquired more vivid colors, as many modern lizards and birds do, during the breeding season. It is fascinating to envision what male ceratosaurs might have looked like as they were flushed with color while strutting around the breeding

Plate 12.
A male
Ceratosaurus,
with prominent
horns on the nose
and over the eyes.

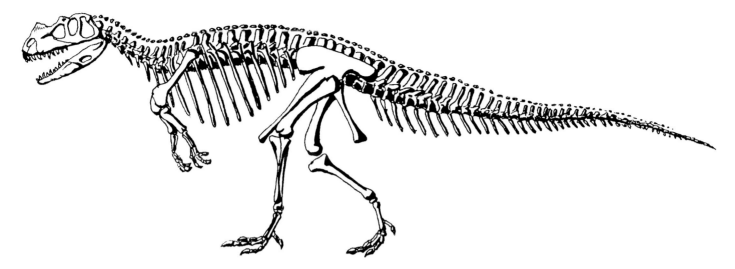

Figure 6-3. Skeleton of *Ceratosaurus*. This theropod had a broad, flattened tail and small knobs of bone (epaxial osteoderms) along its back. Based on reconstruction of Czerkas and Czerkas, 1991; cited in Chapter 1.

did not extend back beyond the orbit (eye socket) in *Ceratosaurus*. Perhaps the most distinctive feature of the *Ceratosaurus* skull is a prominent blade-like horn that decorated the snout just above and behind the nostrils. The preserved portion of this horn, likely covered by a tough sheath of proteinaceous material in life, represents the minimum actual dimensions of the horn. The species name *nasicornis*, meaning "nasal horn," is a literal allusion to what must have been a conspicuous bony adornment.

In addition to the nose horn, there are other protrusions of bone on the skull of *Ceratosaurus*. Just above and forward of the eyes, a pronounced ridge on the upper end of the lachrymal bone produced an obtrusive "brow" over the eyes. This brow ridge may have been covered by unpreserved horny material and, if so, would have been even more noticeable in life than it is in the fossil skulls of *Ceratosaurus*. The nose horn and brow ridges are among those features of *Ceratosaurus* that are subject to the sexual dimorphism exhibited by all ceratosaurs. Those skulls with especially prominent horns and crests probably represent the males, which might have used them in mating displays or to signify species membership or dominance within a group. The neck of *Ceratosaurus* was relatively short, but was thick and muscular. The powerful neck may have been

useful in feeding, in the competition for mates, and for displays of the cranial ornamentation.

The skeleton of *Ceratosaurus* was well designed for the speed it needed to capture prey. The hind limbs were long, massive, and probably heavily clad in muscle (Figure 6-3). The bones of the middle hind feet (metatarsals) were fused for extra strength and rigidity (Figure 6-2A), while the three bones comprising the pelvis were also fused into a solid mass. Such fusions are not uncommon in the Ceratosauria as a group and probably allowed for the strengthening of those portions of the skeleton that received the great stresses developed during running. The neural spines and chevron bones associated with the caudal vertebrae of *Ceratosaurus* were relatively long. This suggests that the tail of *Ceratosaurus* was deeper and more flattened from side to side than were those of most other theropods. A deeper and more massive tail would have increased both the stability and the maneuverability of *Ceratosaurus* while it was running. The small forelimbs of *Ceratosaurus* ended in hands that had four functional digits or "fingers," but it is unlikely that the slender limbs could have developed a very powerful grip. *Ceratosaurus* evidently possessed a series of small bones in the skin, aligned in a row along the neck, back, and tail. These bones, referred to as epaxial osteoderms, would have created a knobby ridge along the back of *Ceratosaurus*, a unique feature with respect to other late Jurassic theropods.

Like several other Morrison dinosaurs, *Ceratosaurus* seems to have been widespread in North America and eventually reached other continents as well. The Tendaguru Formation of Tanzania has produced the remains of a ceratosaur that is remarkably similar to Utah's *Ceratosaurus*. Migration between North America and east Africa during the late Jurassic was evidently unobstructed for several different Morrison dinosaurs.

Tetanurae

All Morrison theropods other than *Ceratosaurus* belong to the Tetanurae, the group that represents advanced, or derived, carnivores. The Tetanurae is a much larger clade than the Ceratosauria and has been subdivided into many smaller groups. In general, the Tetanurae all possess unique specializations that reflect biological innovations superimposed on the set of basic characteristics that define the more primitive Ceratosauria.

Overall, the Tetanurae are more birdlike than are the Ceratosauria. In fact, most paleontologists place the birds, traditionally classified as the Class Aves, within the tetanurine clade. Though it seems to most people that birds and theropod dinosaurs are quite different creatures, there actually is a great deal of similarity between them in the construction of the hind limbs and skulls. The skulls of tetanurine theropods are more lightly built than those of the ceratosaurs; they are composed of individual bones that are relatively slender and less massive. In addition, there are more openings in the skulls of tetanurine theropods than in those of ceratosaurs, reducing the weight of the head even more. In the Tetanurae, the sixty-odd bones than make up the skull are generally more loosely connected than related bones are in the ceratosaurs, giving the skulls a high degree of flexibility that facilitated the chewing and

swallowing of food. There are usually (but not always) fewer teeth in the jaws of the tetanurine theropods than in the ceratosaurs, and they were all positioned forward of the orbit. The overall flexibility and delicacy of the skull, along with the reduction and relocation of teeth, are two of the features that suggest a close relationship between the tetanurine theropods and the birds.

The hind limbs of the Tetanurae are large and powerful, as in the Ceratosauria, but the bones of the pelvis, ankles, and feet are not as firmly fused together. The proportions of femur (thigh bone), tibia and fibula ("shin" bones), and the foot bones are more birdlike than in the ceratosaurs. In addition, the muscle-attachment scars preserved on the pelvic and hind limb bones of the Tetanurae indicate that muscles were concentrated higher in the hip region. This redistribution of muscle mass would have increased the leverage between the various muscles and the limb bones they operated, considerably enhancing the running abilities of the tetanurine theropods. The relatively long foot would have given the tetanurine theropods a longer stride and a more powerful spring when bounding forward. The lower (distal) end of the pubic bone in the Tetanurae was expanded into a prominent bulb, known as the "boot" or "foot." This expansion of the pubis was probably for the insertion of abdominal muscles that would help stabilize the spine as it flexed up and down during locomotion. This up-and-down bending of the spine is also seen in many of the most adept mammal runners in today's world. Such fleet mammals as cheetahs, antelope, and jackrabbits bend the spine while they run to gain extra distance and power with each stride. The tetanurine theropods probably flexed their backs in much the same way as they raced after prey animals. The forelimbs of the Tetanurae are generally smaller and/or more slender than those of the Ceratosauria, with hands that have fewer digits, usually two or three, than the four-fingered hands of *Ceratosaurus*.

The origin of the Tetanurae has been an enduring mystery. Paleontologists assume that they must have evolved from a more primitive ceratosaur ancestor in (perhaps?) the late Triassic, but they seem to explode on the scene in the late Jurassic, by which time several different types are already present. The diversity of late Jurassic tetanurines suggests a lengthy period of earlier evolution, but such a group of derived theropods is virtually unknown from older strata. Many more theropod fossils from the early Jurassic and late Triassic are needed before scientists can begin to understand the origins of the Tetanurae. In any event, the tetanurine theropods were clearly the dominant meat eaters of the late Jurassic in Utah and adjacent regions. In the Cretaceous Period, after *Ceratosaurus* died out, the tetanurine theropods held exclusive dominion over the predatory ecologic niches in the global dinosaur community.

As the Tetanurae rose to dominance beginning in the late Jurassic, many highly specialized lineages evolved and the resulting array of derived theropods became incredibly diverse. Numerous subdivisions of the Tetanurae have been established by paleontologists to accommodate the many specific types. The older terms Carnosauria and Coelurosauria have now been redefined in cladistic terms on the basis of unique sets of derived characters within each group. Thus the Carnosauria are no longer considered to be just "large" theropods, as opposed to the "small" Coelurosauria. The carnosaurs and the coelurosaurs are considered to be "sister taxa," which probably share a common ancestor but are distinguished from each other by different sets of derived characteristics. It is true, however, that the Carnosauria are mostly larger theropods, while the Coelurosauria are mostly small- to medium-sized predators. However, size is not the sole criterion for the definition of these two clades within the Tetanurae; for example, several different carnosaurs were relatively small predators. This illustrates that the adoption of a cladistic classification does not mean that scientists necessarily

abandon all older taxonomic groups, but simply that they can redefine them in ways that are, from the evolutionary perspective, more meaningful.

Carnosaurs of the Morrison Formation in Utah

All of the larger tetanurine theropods of the Morrison Formation, and some of the smaller ones, are placed within the Carnosauria clade. At least two families of carnosaurs are known from this formation: the Allosauridae and the Megalosauridae. Fragmentary fossils indicate that other groups, such as the family Tyrannosauridae, may also have been present. The carnosaurs are characterized by relatively massive skeltons, constructed of bones that were robust and heavy in comparison to those of the coelurosaurs. The carnosaurs had large and relatively boxy heads, a relatively short neck, and short forelimbs that were much smaller than the hind limbs.

Family Allosauridae
ALLOSAURUS FRAGILIS

Allosaurus was by far the most common theropod in Utah during the late Jurassic. This genus name was first formalized by O.C. Marsh in 1877, but the animal we describe as *Allosaurus* has also been referred to as *Antrodemus, Poicilopleuron, Creosaurus, Epanterias,* and several other names coined over the past century. One reason for the proliferation of names for *Allosaurus* is the unusual abundance of this theropod in exposures of the Morrison Formation throughout western North America. Its remains are so abundant in Utah that this fierce predator has been designated as the official Utah state fossil. At least forty-four individuals of this species are represented by bones recovered at the Cleveland-Lloyd Quarry in Emery County. Although it is much less common at Dinosaur National Monument, one of the most spectacular skeletons of *Allosaurus* ever discovered came from that site in northeastern Utah.

Elsewhere in Utah, partial skeletons or isolated bones of *Allosaurus* have been found in dozens of places throughout the eastern and south-central portions of the state. Most *Allosaurus* specimens occur in the Brushy Basin Member, but an articulated (skeletally intact) specimen has recently been discovered in the Salt Wash Member at Dinosaur National Monument (Hubert and Chure, 1992).

The amazingly abundant fossils of *Allosaurus* suggest that there were swarms of these theropods pursuing prey animals across the Morrison basin for millions of years during the late Jurassic. Partly because of its extreme abundance in Utah exposures of the Morrison Formation, *Allosaurus* has become one of the best-known dinosaurs. Knowledge of the skeletal anatomy of *Allosaurus*, presented in such classic works as that of J.H Madsen, Jr. (1976b), surpasses that of all but a few other dinosaurs. In addition, *Allosaurus* fossils are known from several different horizons within the Morrison Formation, suggesting that it may have been the dominant theropod in Utah and adjacent regions from about 150 million years ago (at the Cleveland-Lloyd Quarry; Bilbey-Bowman, 1986) to about 127 million years ago (at the Dry Mesa Quarry in western Colorado; Britt, 1991), a period exceeding 25 million years! The designation of *Allosaurus* as the Utah state fossil is certainly appropriate—it is the state's signature fossil.

Allosaurus was the largest common theropod of the late Jurassic, with the largest individuals reaching a length of about 43 feet, standing some 8–9 feet tall at the hips, and weighing at least 2 tons. It was well designed for filling the ecologic niche of a large carnivore, exhibiting many refinements of the basic theropod body plan. The skull of *Allosaurus* (Figure 6-4) was proportionally shorter than that of *Ceratosaurus*, but it was still over three feet long in the larger specimens. As in other tetanurine theropods, the skull was lightly constructed, with numerous openings and hollow cavities. The bones that comprised the skull for-

ward of the eyes were slender and strut-like, while those at the back of the head were more robust. *Allosaurus* seems to have had a few more teeth than did *Ceratosaurus*, but they were all positioned far forward in the jaws, in front of the eye socket. Illustrating this tetanurine trait of concentrating the teeth in the front part of the mouth, the bone at the tip of the snout in *Allosaurus*, the premaxilla, bears five teeth, while in *Ceratosaurus*, the same bone has only three teeth.

Allosaurus possessed two prominent brow ridges on the lachrymal bone above and forward of the eyes, with a deep hollow cavity at the base of each. The lachrymal bone is similar to some of the other lightweight bones in the skull of *Allosaurus* in that it has thin walls, hollow pockets, and several small openings. A very interesting aspect of the skull of *Allosaurus* is the loose joints between some of the bones at the lower base of the skull (the quadratojugal and quadrate) and between several bones comprising the back portion of the lower jaw (dentary and angular-surangular bones). These flexible joints probably allowed *Allosaurus* to expand its gullet as it swallowed large chunks of food, or perhaps entire animals, in a manner akin to the way modern snakes can ingest objects larger than their heads.

Judging from the size and shape of the cervical vertebrae, the neck of *Allosaurus* appears to have been powerful and quite flexible. However, the neck appears to have had a natural upward S-shaped curve and was evidently not capable of being completely straightened, due to the way the cervical vertebrae interlocked (Madsen, 1976b). In the shoulder region, the vertebrae of the backbone have tall neural spines and horizontal transverse processes that suggest strong ligaments and powerful muscles along the back. The caudal vertebrae have shorter neural spines and chevron bones than did those of *Ceratosaurus*, indicating that *Allosaurus* had a less flattened tail, with a more circular cross-section. The tail probably projected horizontally behind the hips to help counterbalance the body and facilitate changes

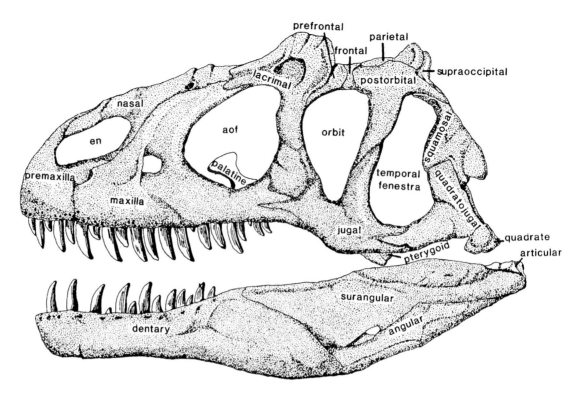

Figure 6-4. Skull of *Allosaurus*. In comparison to *Ceratosaurus*, the skull of *Allosaurus* was deeper, with more numerous openings, such as the small circular hole, the maxillary fenestra, between the external nares (en) and the antorbital fenestra (aof). In addition, the teeth do not extend back to the orbit in *Allosaurus*, as they do in the ceratosaurs. Based on Madsen, 1976b.

in direction while *Allosaurus* was moving (Figure 6-5).

The hind limbs of *Allosaurus* are massive. The largest bone of the hind leg, the femur (thigh bone), was bowed slightly toward the front. The curvature of this bone probably allowed it to bend slightly to accommodate some of the stress that would have been produced during locomotion. The feet of *Allosaurus* had five toes, though only three of these supported any weight. The fifth toe, on the outside of the foot, was merely a vestigial splint of bone, while the fourth toe was too small to reach the ground in a normal walking or running stance (Figure 6-6). The pelvis of *Allosaurus* is typical of other tetanurine theropods in that the bony elements—the paired pubes, ischia, and ilia—are not consistently and solidly fused. Madsen (1976b) points out that some of the pelvic bones, especially the pubes, of *Allosaurus* from the Cleveland-Lloyd Quarry are fused together, while others are not. This suggests that the variable degree of pelvic fusion may represent sexual differences; females may have pos-

sessed the less-fused pelvic bones in order to expedite egg-laying, similar to the way in which female mammals (including humans) loosen the pelvic bones as part of the birth process. The overall structure of the hind limbs, pelvis, and back of *Allosaurus* would clearly have enabled it to run efficiently, but its adaptations for speed are less pronounced than those in several other theropods.

The forelimbs of *Allosaurus* were small in comparison to the powerful hind legs. The hands had only three fingers, each tipped with a sharply pointed and curving claw. However, the bones of the fingers have many pits and roughened surfaces for the attachment of ligaments and muscles. These features suggest that the forelimbs and hands of *Allosaurus* were useful grasping organs that could develop a relatively powerful grip. *Allosaurus* most likely used its hands during feeding, when attacking prey animals, during mating, or on any other occasion that demanded the manipulation of objects.

While *Allosaurus* was a well-adapted preda-

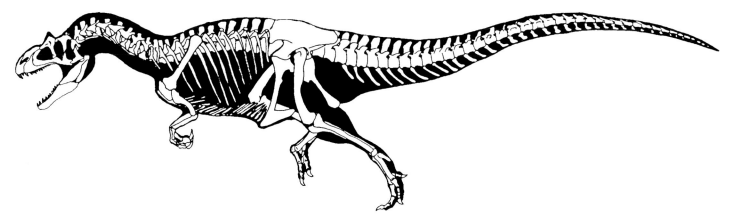

Figure 6-5. Skeleton of *Allosaurus*, as reconstructed by Paul, 1987. Note the S-shaped curve in the neck and the horizontal position of the tail and back in this running posture.

tor, it does not seem to have had the power or the speed to individually overtake and subdue large late Jurassic prey animals such as the sauropods or speedy prey such as *Dryosaurus*. Some paleontologists have suggested that *Allosaurus* may have employed pack hunting or ambush strategies to successfully capture large and/or elusive herbivores. Also, *Allosaurus* may have selectively hunted the slower prey animals such as *Camptosaurus* or *Stegosaurus*. Since the famous Cleveland-Lloyd Quarry in central Utah offers some insight into the feeding behavior of *Allosaurus*, it is well worth a brief pause in this review of Morrison theropods to explore the nature of this remarkable fossil accumulation.

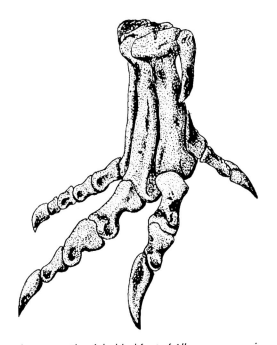

Figure 6-6. The right hind foot of *Allosaurus*, seen in oblique internal view. There were only three functional toes in the hind foot of *Allosaurus*, each tipped with a curving claw. Redrawn from Gilmore, 1920.

◆   THE CLEVELAND-LLOYD DINOSAUR QUARRY: AN *ALLOSAURUS* TRAP

T HE CLEVELAND-LLOYD DINOSAUR QUARRY is located about twenty-five miles south of Price, Utah, and is situated in the Brushy Basin Member of the Morrison Formation. Named for the nearby town of Cleveland and for Malcomb Lloyd, a benefactor who sponsored some of the early work at the site, this locality has had a long and colorful history of excavation that encompasses more than sixty years. The various phases in the development of the Cleveland-Lloyd Quarry have been summarized by many people (Stokes, 1985; Madsen, 1987; and Miller and others, 1996). Though the history of the quarry is in-

Plate 13. *Allosaurus*, the terror of the late Jurassic. This fierce predator was the most common theropod in the Morrison basin.

teresting, our main concern here is the insights the site offers concerning *Allosaurus* and other Morrison predators. The Cleveland-Lloyd Quarry is an exceptional dinosaur locality for several reasons, and it is no overstatement to refer to it as one of the most important fossil sites in the world. In recognition of its unique attributes and importance, the quarry was designated as a U.S. National Natural Landmark in 1968. Today, it is managed by the U.S. Bureau of Land Management, and numerous paleontological investigations are still under way. Research at the Cleveland-Lloyd Quarry, and on the bones it has already produced, will doubtless continue for many years before the full potential of the site is exhausted.

Well over 10,000 bones have been excavated from the fine-grained sediments at the Cleveland-Lloyd Quarry, among which at least nine genera of dinosaurs can be recognized. What is perhaps most remarkable about the Cleveland-Lloyd Quarry is that the vast majority of the bones preserved there belong to theropod dinosaurs. The remains of *Allosaurus* are the most abundant, with at least forty-four individuals, ranging in size from small juveniles to large adults, represented by the material currently available for study. The remains of *Ceratosaurus* also have been identified at the site, though they are much less common there than is *Allosaurus*. The *Ceratosaurus* material appears to represent a new species of that genus (Madsen, personal communication, 1996). In addition, other smaller theropods, such as *Marshosaurus* and *Stokesosaurus* (described later in this chapter) are represented by isolated bones collected from the quarry (Madsen, 1974; 1976a). Fossils representing the herbivorous sauropods or ornithischian dinosaurs are much less common, but they do indicate the presence of such familiar late Jurassic forms as *Camptosaurus*, *Stegosaurus*, *Camarasaurus*, and perhaps a few other herbivores.

The dominance of theropod remains at the Cleveland-Lloyd Quarry is very unusual; by

virtue of their position at the top of the terrestrial food pyramid, we would normally expect a very small number of carnivores to be supported by many herbivorous prey animals. This is certainly the pattern observed among mammals in the modern world wherever natural populations of predators coexist with their prey. For example, the vast herds of antelope and wildebeest in Africa support comparatively few lions, cheetahs, and hyenas. In a similar way, immense numbers of caribou in Alaska and adjacent regions sustain only a relatively small number of arctic wolves. These proportions appear to be reversed at the Cleveland-Lloyd Quarry. For some reason, many more carnivorous theropods were preserved at this site than would be expected in a random sample of the late Jurassic dinosaur community.

Photo 24. The Cleveland-Lloyd Quarry in Emery County. The visitor center and quarry buildings are located at the base of the distant slope, which exposes the mudstones of the Brushy Basin Member of the Morrison Formation. The blocks of sandstone in the foreground were eroded from thin stream deposits interbedded with the mudstone. About fifty individuals of *Allosaurus* are represented by the bones preserved at the Cleveland-Lloyd Quarry. John Telford.

The preservation of dinosaurs at the Cleveland-Lloyd Quarry was clearly, and uniquely, a non-random process. No other Morrison fossil locality has yielded dinosaur remains with such a skewed proportion of predators and prey. Everywhere else across the broad area covered by the Morrison Formation—at Dinosaur National Monument, at Como Bluff and the Howe Quarry in Wyoming, and at the sites in western Colorado—the fossils of herbivorous dinosaurs are the most abundant. What special circumstances prevailed at the Cleveland-Lloyd Quarry to cause the normal predator-prey ratio to be shifted so drastically?

The sediments that entomb the bones at the Cleveland-Lloyd Quarry offer some clues that help us understand the nature of this unique locality. Unlike those at Dinosaur National Monument, the bones at the Cleveland-Lloyd Quarry are preserved in a very fine-grained, clay-rich mudstone, interbedded with, and capped by, thin layers of limestone. The mudstones contain the clay mineral montmorillonite, which probably represents small grains of volcanic ash that either drifted or were washed into a body of shallow water (Bilbey, 1992). The matrix material surrounding the bones at the Cleveland-Lloyd Quarry has also produced the remains of turtles, freshwater snails, and charopytes, tiny fossils representing a type of green algae. These accessory fossils provide evidence of standing water in the area where the dinosaur bones became concentrated. None of the bone-producing sediments at the Cleveland-Lloyd Quarry appear to have been deposited by swift rivers or large streams as is the case at Dinosaur National Monument. Stokes (1985) has suggested that the most likely environment of sediment deposition at the Cleveland-Lloyd Quarry was a bog or perhaps a swampy cove of a shallow lake. Some of the ashy sediments at the Cleveland-Lloyd Quarry contain mineral grains that can be dated radiometrically. These dates suggest that the sediments were deposited about 147 million years ago (Bilbey, 1992).

Thus, it is likely that the theropods of the Cleveland-Lloyd Quarry were preserved in a bog or swampy pond. But why were so many predators attracted to this site? Imagine a likely scenario. The clay in the soft mud would have absorbed water from the bog and, when it was moistened, the sediment would have been a sticky, soft, and slippery ooze. Even today, when these types of sediments become saturated by rain, they are transformed into a mushy gumbo of almost frictionless mud. (My truck has been immobilized by such mud on more than one occasion when I was foolish enough to attempt travel on the dirt roads of the San Rafael Swell in a rainstorm!) Any dinosaur that might have ventured into the bog would no doubt have become deeply mired in the soft, slippery mud. Imagine a *Camptosaurus* buried knee-deep in the Cleveland-Lloyd bog. Slipping and sliding, struggling to extricate itself from the slimy ooze, this unfortunate creature would surely have attracted the attention of any theropods in the neighborhood. Taking advantage of a partially immobilized prey animal, the first allosaur on the scene would probably have dashed into the bog without hesitation to help itself to a "free lunch." The initial attack would have raised bellows of distress from the *Camptosaurus*, unable to employ its usual methods of evasion. The commotion might have drawn the attention of other allosaurs in the area, who might have joined in the feast. Also, recall that some paleontologists have speculated that *Allosaurus*, because of its apparent inability to outrun swift prey, might have practiced group hunting or ambush techniques in acquiring prey. Such predatory behavior would certainly have been useful to the allosaurs that lurked around the bog at the Cleveland-Lloyd site lying in wait for approaching herbivores. Once the prey animal was stuck in the bog, the attacking theropods may have begun to battle each other for a share of the meal. Something like a feeding frenzy may have ensued, wherein numerous allosaurs (and other theropods) large and small swarmed over the carcass of the poor prey animal that was hopelessly

Figure 6-7. Map of a portion of the Cleveland-Lloyd Quarry. The individual bones are completely disarticulated and scattered. From Madsen, 1976b.

trapped in the sticky mud. The *Camptosaurus* in this scenario would certainly have met its end, while it is likely that at least some of the theropods may have perished in battles with each other or have sustained mortal injuries that prevented them from escaping from the bog after the attack.

Such scenarios, in which a single trapped prey animal attracted numerous predators, were probably repeated many times as the sediments at the Cleveland-Lloyd Quarry accumulated. Sometimes the victim of the attack was a *Camptosaurus*, others times it may have been a *Stegosaurus* or a small *Camarasaurus*. The remains of earlier feeding frenzies were trampled and scattered by subsequent struggles that occurred in the bog. In this manner, the skeletons of dinosaurs, both predator and prey, became disarticulated (separated from each other) and the individual bones were dispersed throughout the soft mud. This is probably the primary reason why the bones found at the Cleveland-Lloyd site are, for the most part, rarely articulated (Figure 6-7). The bones from this locality do not exhibit any signs of wear that would suggest their transportation in streams or rivers prior to their burial. Most of the damage that has been observed in the bones appears to have occurred during death or while the carcasses were dismembered by predators or scavengers.

Paleontologists generally regard the Cleveland-Lloyd Quarry as a "predator trap," similar in many ways to the famous Rancho LaBrea tar pits of Pleistocene age in southern California. In the tar pits of California, large Ice Age prey animals such as mammoths, giant ground sloths, and horses became mired in the sticky tar that seeped into several small ponds some 30,000 years ago. The immobilized prey evidently lured many predators into the gummy asphalt. Some 90 percent of the fossils recovered from the tar pits are of carnivorous Ice Age mammals such as the sabre-toothed cats (*Smilodon californicus*), dire wolves (*Canis dirus*), short-faced bears (*Arctodus simus*), and others. The Cleveland-Lloyd Quarry produces the bones of dinosaur predators in similar proportions and may have attracted and trapped *Allosaurus* and other Jurassic predators in much the same way as the asphalt in Ice Age California doomed so many carnivorous mammals of that period.

One might wonder why the Cleveland-Lloyd herbivores were drawn into the lethal bog in the first place. What would have enticed *Camptosaurus*, *Stegosaurus*, or *Camarasaurus*, all of which are represented by fossils from the mudstone, to the spot where they met their end? Recall that the climate across the Morrison basin in late Jurassic time was probably strongly seasonal, with periods of drought alternating with rainy seasons. During the dry intervals, plant food for herbivores would probably have become more concentrated in those places where water remained available as the smaller streams dried up and the plain became barren and dry. Stokes (1985) has suggested that the bog or pond at the Cleveland-Lloyd site may have been fed by nearby springs. If this is a correct supposition, then it is likely that the bog may have contained water even during the height of the late Jurassic drought cycles. This is because groundwater is less immediately affected by climatic cycles than is surface water. Even today, in regions that experience drought conditions, springs often continue to flow for a time after the streams in the area have dried up. As water became scarce during the Jurassic dry cycles and the vegetation began to wither, the herbivorous dinosaurs would have become increasingly desperate for both food and water. A spring-fed bog, with its more permanent supply of water, would have attracted many dinosaurs. Ironically, the dinosaur herbivores may have ventured into the fatal bog as a response to their desperate need for food and water. If so, it was their survival instinct that ultimately led to their death.

An interesting twist on the story of the Cleveland-Lloyd site came in 1987 when Dee Hall of Brigham Young University discovered a nearly complete dinosaur egg among the scattered bones

Plate 14.
A feeding frenzy
at the future site
of the Cleveland-
Lloyd Dinosaur
Quarry.

of *Allosaurus* and other dinosaurs (Madsen, 1991). The preserved egg was small, only about ten centimeters (four inches) long, and was crushed so that the embryo inside could not be positively identified. Since *Allosaurus* is by far the most common dinosaur represented by the bones excavated from the Cleveland-Lloyd site, the egg quite likely belongs to this genus. The discovery of the egg was surprising because it does not seem likely that dinosaurs would have laid eggs in a muddy bog such as that in which the sediments at this site accumulated. The relatively small size of the egg, however, coupled with its occurrence in bog sediments, suggests that the egg was never laid. Instead, it most likely was developing inside the body of a female dinosaur that perished in the bog. After death, the premature egg evidently became preserved along with the bones of the mother dinosaur. This scenario also explains why the embryo within the egg was not identifiable: the egg had not developed long enough for the bones of the baby dinosaur inside to grow to the point where the preservation (and identification) of them was possible.

There are some indications that other members of the family Allosauridae were present in western North America during the late Jurassic. In the panhandle of Oklahoma, the Morrison Formation has produced a few bones of a gigantic theropod that was much larger than *Allosaurus*. This huge predator is known as *Saurophaganax* (Chure, 1995), and it had a femur as large as those of some sauropods. The vertebrae of *Saurophaganax* are unusual in that they have ridges and struts of bone that run upward from the base of the neural spines, a feature not seen in other theropods. Otherwise, the few bones known from *Saurophaganax* seem to be much like those of *Allosaurus*, except for their gigantic dimensions. *Epanterias*, known primarily from Colorado, Oklahoma, and Wyoming localities, appears to be another large allosaurid from the Morrison Formation. *Epanterias* was a very large theropod,

though it was considerably smaller than *Saurophaganax*. The differences between *Epanterias* and *Allosaurus* seem to be very subtle, leading some paleontologists to regard the two names as synonyms for the same animal. Because the genus *Epanterias* was established on the basis of incomplete fossil material, it will be difficult to resolve this confusion until more complete fossils are found. Even though *Epanterias* and *Saurophaganax* have not yet been positively identified in Utah and the anatomy of neither is well known, it appears that the family Allosauridae may have been represented by more than one genus during the late Jurassic. The packs of allosaurs that roamed Utah might have been accompanied by some very large and terrifying kin: the "Addams Family of the Jurassic."

Family Megalosauridae
TORVOSAURUS TANNERI

Torvosaurus is a large Morrison theropod first discovered by Galton and Jensen (1979) at the Dry Mesa Quarry in western Colorado. Subsequently, it has been identified from bones preserved at Dinosaur National Monument in Utah and from two localities in Wyoming (Britt, 1991). The genus was originally based on only a few bones, but paleontologists' understanding of the anatomy of *Torvosaurus* was greatly improved by the recent work of Britt (1991), who offered a much more detailed and complete description of this theropod than was previously available. Still, paleontologists remain divided on how to classify *Torvosaurus* at the infraorder or family level. For example, Britt (1991) considers *Torvosaurus* to be a member of the Ceratosauria, while Molnar and others (1990) describe it as a possible carnosaur belonging to the Tetanurae. This uncertainty reflects the generally primitive nature of many of the skeletal features of *Torvosaurus*; it may be thought of as either a relatively advanced ceratosaur or a relatively primitive carnosaur.

Torvosaurus, however it is classified, was a

large and powerful predator. It reached an adult length of about 30–35 feet and was, for the most part, heavily built. The skull (Figure 6-8) was over three feet long, with a relatively narrow snout. The upper and lower jaws contained about sixty large blade-like teeth, up to 15 cm (6 inches) long, that were all positioned in front of the orbit, as in the Tetanurae. However, as in the case of *Ceratosaurus*, the skull lacked the additional opening, the preantorbital fenestra, seen in most tetanurine theropods.

The body of *Torvosaurus* was massive, bulky, and muscular. In particular, the forelimbs seem to have been powerful, with a massive humerus, or upper arm bone. The cervical vertebrae were connected by means of "ball-and-socket" joints, with concave sockets developed on the rear of each neck vertebra to receive the forward-facing balls. This suggests that *Torvosaurus* had a very flexible neck. The cervical vertebrae were lightened by deep lateral pockets, or pleurocoels, on the sides and air-filled chambers inside. The vertebrae of the back were also connected to one another with ball-and-socket joints. The length of the tail is unknown, but it was probably about as long as the tail of *Allosaurus* (Britt, 1991). No complete hind limbs are known for *Torvosaurus*, but from the available fragments they appear to have been similar to the general theropod design, with muscular thighs that tapered to a slender foot.

Torvosaurus remains are much less common in the Morrison Formation than are those of *Allosaurus*. Even though *Torvosaurus* was widely distributed across the Morrison basin, it would probably not have been encountered very often. It would, however, have been a fearsome sight. Most individuals of *Torvosaurus* were significantly larger than *Allosaurus* and were certainly well adapted to pursue, subdue, and consume large prey animals. Even the larger prey animals such as the sauropods would most likely have become alarmed at the sight of a *Torvosaurus*.

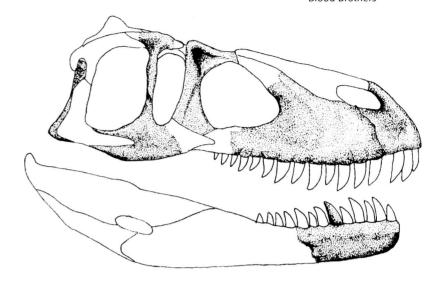

⑥   Family Tyrannosauridae
STOKESOSAURUS CLEVELANDI

Among the many bones excavated at the Cleveland-Lloyd Quarry during the early 1960s were two ilia (blade-like hip bones) and a premaxilla (bone at the tip of the snout) that clearly belonged to the Theropoda, but were different from those of any known late Jurassic species. James H. Madsen, Jr., described these unique elements in 1974 as a new species and genus, *Stokesosaurus clevelandi*, named in honor of the late William Lee Stokes, one of Utah's most renowned geologists, and for the site where the bones were discovered (Madsen, 1974). Even though additional material belonging to *Stokesosaurus* has been found elsewhere in the Morrison Formation since Madsen's original description was published (for example, Britt, 1991), most of its skeleton remains unknown. Nonetheless, it now appears that one of Madsen's original interpretations of *Stokesosaurus* was correct: it represents one of the earliest mem-

Figure 6-8. Skull of *Torvosaurus*, as reconstructed by Britt, 1991. This reconstruction is based on bones (shaded) collected from western Colorado. The total length of the skull is approximately 45 inches, or nearly four feet. For comparison, the front lower jaw bone (dentary) of an average *Allosaurus*, drawn at the same scale, is represented below.

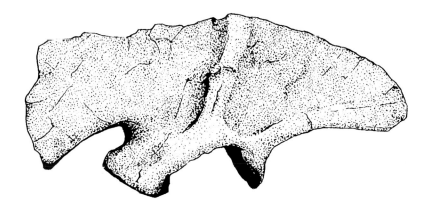

Figure 6-9. Left ilium of *Stokesosaurus clevelandi* from the Cleveland-Lloyd Quarry. Note the prominent ridge that rises vertically from the margin of the hip socket, or acetabulum. Scale bar=5 cm (2 inches). Based on a photograph from Madsen, 1974.

bers of the family Tyrannosauridae, the lineage that would culminate 70 million years later in *Tyrannosaurus*, the most menacing predator to ever live on land.

Even though *Stokesosaurus* is related to the tyrannosaurids, it was not a large dinosaur. The ilium is only about ten inches long from front to back. The teeth at the tip of the snout were about an inch long. These observations suggest that *Stokesosaurus* was probably only about 6–8 feet long, stood a little less than 3 feet high at the hips, and might have weighed around 100 pounds. The ilium is distinctive in that it has a prominent ridge on the outside surface that runs vertically from just above the hip socket to the upper edge (Figure 6-9). This ridge may have divided masses of muscles that were attached to the ilium. The premaxilla of *Stokesosaurus* held four teeth, a characteristic similar to the tyrannosaurids and different from either *Allosaurus* (five premaxillary teeth) or *Ceratosaurus* (three premaxillary teeth). *Stokesosaurus* is most similar to the tyrannosaurids that became dominant in the late Cretaceous Period, but it is some 70 million years older than other members of this family. Since the origins of the family Tyrannosauridae are obscure, *Stokesosaurus* is an extremely important dinosaur. It may eventually help paleontologists understand how this group of amazing predators evolved.

Stokesosaurus appears to have been wide-spread during the late Jurassic, but it was not a particularly common predator. Since only a few fossils of this genus have been found, scientists can't be sure about its maximum size, limb structure, body proportions, running ability, hunting strategies, and other characteristics. The relatively small size of the *Stokesosaurus* fossils known thus far suggest that it probably specialized on the smaller prey animals that inhabited the Morrison plain. The small animals that *Stokesosaurus* probably pursued will be discussed later in this chapter.

⑥ Coelurosaurs of the Morrison Formation

The Coelurosauria, as redefined by Gauthier (1986), include a great variety of generally small and lightly built tetanurine theropods that are, as a group, much more birdlike than the carnosaurs. As we have seen in the case of *Stokesosaurus*, not all carnosaurs were large predators. Also, among the coelurosaurs there are a number of genera that included individuals as large as some carnosaurs. It is the unique features of the skulls and skeletons of coelurosaurs, not their overall size, that are now used to distinguish this group from the Carnosauria. While it is beyond the scope of this book to completely review all the features that define the Coelurosauria, their birdlike traits include a light skull with additional openings (especially in the palate), elongated and slender forelimbs and hands, and feet that are longer and narrower in form than those of the carnosaurs.

The Coelurosauria consist of several different groups of birdlike theropods. Most of these groups are best known from late Cretaceous strata, so coelurosaurs are not very abundant in the Morrison Formation. However, it now appears that at least some of the late Cretaceous coelurosaur families originated in late Jurassic time. Thus, the rare coelurosaurs of the Morrison Formation represent some of earliest members of their respective lineages.

Plate 15. *Ornitholestes* fleeing from *Allosaurus*.

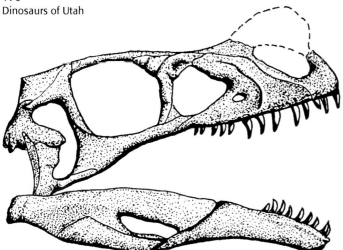

Figure 6-10. Skull of *Ornitholestes*. The total length of this small skull is a little over 15 cm (6 inches). The blade-like septum (dashed outline) above the nose is suggested by the ridges on the nasal bones, but it has not been found completely preserved in actual skulls. Based on the reconstruction of Paul, 1988.

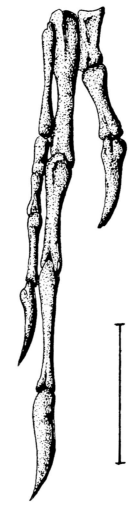

Figure 6-11. Hand of *Ornitholestes*. Note the highly elongated fingers and the reversed form of digit 1, the "thumb," which could have been opposable to the other two fingers. Bar=5 cm (2 inches). After Osborn, 1916.

⑥ ORNITHOLESTES

Ornitholestes was a small and graceful theropod no longer than about 6 feet, with a body weight of around 30 pounds. Its skull was very light, with large openings between the thin-walled bones. The orbit was particularly large, suggesting that *Ornitholestes* had unusually large eyes that might have given it acute vision. The teeth of *Ornitholestes*, placed forward in the jaws, were mostly blade-like and serrated like the teeth of other theropods (Figure 6-10). Toward the rear, the teeth became somewhat more conical with less pronounced serrations along the edges (Paul, 1988). The nasal openings of *Ornitholestes* were very large and evidently were separated by a blunt crest or blade of bone reminiscent of the nose horn of *Ceratosaurus*.

Like other coelurosaurs, *Ornitholestes* had relatively long forelimbs. The hands bore three fingers, two of which were very long. The first digit of the hand was relatively short and appears to have been opposable to the other two (Figure 6-11). The structure of the hand suggests that *Ornitholestes* had a strong grip and at least some ability to manipulate objects. Only portions of the hind limbs, feet, pelvis, backbone, and tail of *Ornitholestes* are known. On the basis of these incomplete remains, it appears that *Ornitholestes* was a swift and agile animal. *Ornitholestes* seems to have been built for speed, though it was probably not as fast as some of the Cretaceous coelurosaurs. Moreover, its minimal weight probably allowed it to change directions easily. These features suggest that *Ornitholestes* hunted small and elusive prey, which might have been captured with the prehensile hands rather than with the jaws.

The diet of *Ornitholestes* probably consisted of small animals such as lizards, mammals, and early birds. In fact, the name *Ornitholestes* means "bird robber," in reference to this possible mode of hunting. Perhaps *Ornitholestes* also lurked around the nesting areas of larger dinosaurs, waiting for a chance to steal a hatchling. If so, the adaptations for speed make perfect sense. After all, if an animal is going steal babies from the nest of such dinosaurs as *Allosaurus*, it had better be able to run! Imagine the pursuit that might have followed the theft of such a hatchling by *Ornitholestes*. Clutching the shrieking baby in its hands, the "bird robber" would race away while the mother allosaur followed, frantically trying to save her offspring. If, with her longer stride, she managed to gain ground on the fleeing *Ornitholestes*, the thief would probably veer sharply to one side while the less agile allosaur stumbled to redirect its pursuit. After a time, the allosaur would become exhausted from the chase, while *Ornitholestes* disappeared over the horizon to find a safe place to consume its stolen meal.

Ornitholestes was first discovered in Wyoming in 1900, but little well-preserved and complete material belonging to this dinosaur has surfaced since that time. Fragmentary remains of *Ornitholestes* are now known from several sites in Colorado and possibly from the Cleveland-Lloyd Quarry (Stokes, 1985) in Utah. However, it should be remembered that the fossils of small dinosaurs are much less likely to be discovered than are the remains of larger creatures. Also, the bones of *Ornitholestes* and other coelurosaurs were much more delicate than those of the carnosaurs. The relative fragility of coelurosaurian material strongly reduces the probability of its fossilization, compounding the problem of nondiscovery related to the small size. It is likely that *Ornitholestes* was more common during the late Jurassic than the relatively rare fossils preserved in the Morrison Formation might suggest. Russell (1989) has estimated that *Ornitholestes* might have comprised about 6 percent of the dinosaurs present during the late Jurassic in North America, even though its remains represent only 0.6 percent of the fossils collected from rocks of this age. These estimates make some sense because there are usually many more small animals than large animals in modern terrestrial vertebrate commu-

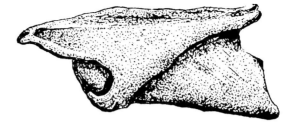

Figure 6-12. Cervical vertebrae of *Coelurus fragilis*, in side view (top) and front view (bottom). Bar=2 cm (3/4 inch). Redrawn from original sketch of Marsh, 1881.

nities. *Ornitholestes* individuals, along with their other coelurosaurian relatives, were probably fairly common in Utah during the late Jurassic.

ⓖ *COELURUS*

Coelurus was a close relative of *Ornitholestes*. In fact, ever since the first discoverey of *Coelurus* remains from Wyoming in the late 1870s, paleontologists have been debating whether or not *Coelurus* and *Ornitholestes* represent the same genus. Recently, John H. Ostrom of Yale University has undertaken a thorough study of the available fossil material of these two genera and has concluded that they are not the same dinosaur genus (Ostrom, 1980). This ongoing debate reflects both the fragmentary nature of the fossils used to define the two genera and their general similarity to each other.

Coelurus was a small theropod about 8 feet long, 2 feet tall at the hip, and weighing around 30 pounds. These dimensions are very close to those of *Ornitholestes*. However, *Coelurus* was evidently a better runner, with longer hind limbs and a lighter and more graceful neck. Its cervical verte-

is discovered, paleontologists can only regard *Coelurus* as a small *Ornitholestes*-like theropod that might have been seen occasionally on the late Jurassic plains of western North America.

⑥ Family Dromaeosauridae?
MARSHOSAURUS BICENTESIMUS

The remains of *Marshosaurus* were first discovered at the Cleveland-Lloyd Quarry and were described by James H. Madsen, Jr., in 1976 (Madsen, 1976a). Britt (1991) has identified *Marshosaurus* fossils from the Morrison Formation at Dry Mesa in western Colorado, demonstrating that this theropod was not restricted to central Utah during the late Jurassic. The genus is known only from isolated bones, including the ilium, pubic and pelvic bones, and several tooth-bearing bones of the skull, such as the premaxilla, maxilla, and dentary. With such limited knowledge of the skeleton, it is difficult to assign *Marshosaurus* to any specific family of theropods; however, it does not appear to represent any of the groups that have been discussed thus far.

Marshosaurus appears to be most similar to various members of the family Dromaeosauridae, an assemblage that includes the vicious "raptors" that have become familiar in popular culture since the release of the movie *Jurassic Park*. However, some uncertainty persists concerning the family-level classification of *Marshosaurus*, and some paleontologists are reluctant to assign this theropod to the Dromaeosauridae. For example, Molnar and others (1990) describe *Marshosaurus* as a "problematic carnosaur," while Britt (1991) questioningly places it in the family Dromaeosauridae. If it is a dromaeosaur, *Marshosaurus* is the earliest known member of its lineage to appear in Utah. As will be seen in the next chapter, the Dromaeosauridae became well established in Utah in the early Cretaceous Period, some 30 million years after the Morrison sediments were deposited.

Marshosaurus was a small theropod, but was

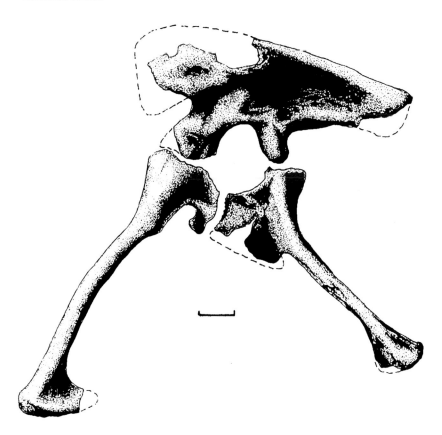

Figure 6-13. Pelvis of *Marshosaurus bicentesimus*, from the Cleveland-Lloyd Quarry of Emery County, Utah. Redrawn from Madsen, 1976a. Scale bar=5 cm (2 inches).

brae are very lightly constructed, with ribs (or rib facets) that are fused to the body of the neck bones in the form of a somewhat cylindrical collar (Figure 6-12). The caudal vertebrae are unusual in that they have large internal air spaces. These hollow tail bones provide the basis of the name of the genus—*Coelurus* means "hollow tail." No skull of *Coelurus* has been identified, but it was probably similar to the lightweight skull of *Ornitholestes*.

Coelurus remains a very poorly understood theropod. Its fossils are extremely rare in the Morrison Formation and always have been fragmentary. The classification of *Coelurus* at the family level remains in doubt and paleontologists are still unsure about its relationships with other coelurosaurs. In addition to the original Wyoming discovery, it has been identified in Colorado (Gilmore, 1920; Britt, 1991) and in Utah (Norman, 1990). Until more complete material

about twice as large as *Coelurus* or *Ornitholestes*. The pubic bone has a slight forward curve and small "boot" that is unlike that in other late Jurassic theropods (Figure 6-13). *Marshosaurus* appears to have had more teeth than did *Allosaurus* or *Ceratosaurus*, and the details of their serrations and placement in the jaw are different from those of the larger theropods (Madsen, 1976a). The detailed morphology of the premaxilla and maxilla of *Marshosaurus* and the way they were joined to each other are similar in some respects to that of the dromaeosaurs ("raptors") *Deinonychus* and *Velociraptor*, but the bones of *Marshosaurus* are larger. In addition, *Deinonychus* and *Velociraptor* are both Cretaceous theropods and are much more recent than *Marshosaurus*, casting some doubt on the closeness of their relationship. *Marshosaurus* may not have been the only dromaeosaur inhabiting the Morrison plain during the late Jurassic. Britt (1991) discovered several teeth that have dromaeosaur affinities at Dry Mesa in western Colorado, but the precise identity of the tooth bearers cannot be established until more remains of them are found.

◈ Family Ornithomimidae

The family Ornithomimidae ("bird mimickers") include some very interesting coelurosaurs that probably looked much like large reptilian ostriches. The ornithomimids had very long hind limbs, with extremely elongated mid-foot bones (metatarsals). The great lengthening of the metatarsals lifted the ankle high above the ground, as in an ostrich or emu, and increased the stride of these swift predators. The forelimbs of the ornithomimids are very long and slender, with elongated fingers. The long arms and hands would have been much more useful in grasping and manipulating objects than were the stubby forelimbs of the carnosaurs. Ornithomimid skulls are small and narrow but have a relatively large braincase and enlarged eye sockets. All ornithomimids had a toothless beak that contributed to

their general birdlike appearance. The edges of the beak appear to have been very sharp, capable of cutting through animal flesh in the same manner that hawks and eagles use their beaks to rip prey apart without the aid of teeth.

The ornithomimid theropods are most common in the late Cretaceous, but the earliest members of this group seem to have made their appearance in North America in the late Jurassic Period. Galton (1982) reported the occurrence of *Elaphrosaurus*, a primitive ornithomimid, in the Morrison Formation of Colorado. Only the upper arm bone (humerus) of *Elaphrosaurus* was found at the site, and very little material belonging to this genus has surfaced from the Morrison anywhere else. What is known about *Elaphrosaurus* is derived mainly from African specimens and suggests that it was a graceful animal with long, slender limbs. The toes and fingers of *Elaphrosaurus* were also elongated. However, the size and shape of the ilium and humerus are different in *Elaphrosaurus* than in other ornithomimids, leading some paleontologists (for example, Barsbold and Osmolska, 1990) to consider its family-level classification uncertain. Even though it has not yet been positively identified from Utah, the occurrence of *Elaphrosaurus* in the Morrison Formation of the Rocky Mountain region is significant for two reasons: it adds support to the idea that there was a high degree of faunal interchange between North America and Africa during the late Jurassic, and it suggests that the ornithomimids originated in North America long before the late Cretaceous Period, when their remains became much more abundant.

◈ Family Troodontidae
KOPARION DOUGLASSI

The latest dinosaur discovered from the Morrison Formation is *Koparion douglassi*, named by Daniel Chure in 1994 on the basis of teeth discovered in the Brushy Basin Member at Dinosaur National Monument (Chure, 1994). Though this

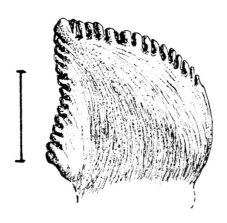

Figure 6-14. A tiny tooth of *Koparion douglassi* from the Morrison Formation of Dinosaur National Monument. Based on a photograph of the type specimen, Chure, 1994. Scale bar=1 mm (1/24 inch).

genus and species is based on a single small tooth, that tooth is clearly different from those of any other theropod known from the Morrison. *Koparion* had tiny teeth, only about 2 mm (less than .1 of an inch) tall. The tooth is curved toward the rear and has small denticles lining the front and back edges (Figure 6-14). The largest denticle is positioned at the apex of the tooth and is aligned with the smaller denticles along the back edge of the tooth. The crown of the tooth has a slight constriction at its base (Chure, 1994). These details of such a tiny tooth may seem trivial, but they are very important. They serve not only to distinguish this tooth from those of all other Morrison theropods but also to document the presence of a new family of predators among the Morrison carnivores: the fascinating troodontids.

The troodontids (family Troodontidae) are a rare family of theropod dinosaurs formerly known only from the Cretaceous strata of North America and Asia (Osmolska and Barsbold, 1990). The troodontids were small and highly specialized theropods with very long hind limbs, grasping forelimbs, and a very lightly constructed skull. All troodontids have many small teeth, with relatively large hooked denticles similar to those of *Koparion*. The braincase of the troodontids was very large relative to their body size. In fact, these dinosaurs could be considered the "brainiest" of all: they had the highest ratio of brain size to body size (known as the EQ, or encephalization quotient) of any known group of dinosaurs. The large

orbits (eye sockets) of the troodontids faced more directly forward than did those of any other group of dinosaurs, suggesting that they had excellent stereoscopic vision and could see very well in dimly lit habitats such as the shadowy floor of Mesozoic forests. In such environments, the good depth perception afforded by the placement of the eyes would also have been advantageous in finding and seizing prey animals that might have scampered through the tangle of shrubs and limbs.

These specialized characteristics of the troodontids seem to suggest an "intelligent" theropod, a selective predator that hunted small animals in forested settings where good visual acuity, agility, and cunningness would have been necessary to catch prey. Was *Koparion* an "intelligent" dinosaur? Until more of its skull and other parts of the skeleton are found, we can't be sure. However, if the rest of its skeleton is as similar to the troodontids as are its teeth, then *Koparion* probably could have easily outwitted any of its contemporaries of the late Jurassic. *Koparion* might have lurked motionless in the shadowy forests on the Morrison plain of Utah, its glistening reptilian eyes watching for movement among the leaves. No motion would have gone undetected and it would have responded to the slightest rustling. Moving silently forward, its head bobbing and weaving to keep the small prey in sight, *Koparion* might have deliberately approached its unsuspecting target from a direction calculated to conceal its approach. At just the right instant, *Koparion* might have lunged toward the animal, grasped it in its dextrous hands, and momentarily held the wriggling creature before its large eyes. *Koparion* might have paused as it rolled the prey around in its hands. Was it studying the animal? Was it deciding whether to eat it or release it? Was it thinking at all? Maybe.

◆ COELUROSAUR CUISINE: SMALL ANIMALS OF
THE MORRISON FORMATION

EVEN THOUGH THE small carnivorous
coelurosaurs are not particularly common in
the Morrison Formation, there are enough indications of their presence that we might wonder
what specific animals they captured as food. None
of these smaller theropods from the late Jurassic
Period of Utah seem to have been capable of successfully attacking the large prey animals, even if
they hunted in groups or packs. The large herbivores such as *Camptosaurus*, *Stegosaurus*, and the
sauropods were probably the prime targets of the
carnosaurs. A stegosaur would probably have had
little to fear from *Koparion* or *Ornitholestes*.

In addition to dinosaur fossils, the Morrison
Formation in Utah and nearby regions has produced the remains of many different small creatures that might have been pursued by the
coelurosaurs. Turtles were evidently common in
the ponds, lakes, and streams of the late Jurassic
plain. For example, two different turtles, *Glyptops
plicatus* and *Dinochelys whitei*, are known from
Dinosaur National Monument (Chure and Englemann, 1989; West and Chure, 1984). These turtles,
or close relatives of them, are known from many
other sites in the Morrison Formation throughout Utah and Colorado. In addition, the remains
of lizards and snakes are also fairly common in
the Morrison Formation (Callison, 1987;
Prothero and Estes, 1980). Several different crocodiles are also present in the late Jurassic sediments
of Utah, but their remains are usually very fragmentary. The fossils of amphibians (frogs, salamanders, and others) are very rare in the
Morrison Formation, but they do occur in places
(Chure and Englemann, 1989). Stokes (1957) reported tracks of a small pterosaur from the Morrison Formation of northern Arizona; however,
some scientists have suggested that these kinds of
tracks were actually made by a crocodilian reptile
(see Padian and Olsen, 1984; cited in Chapter 4).

Several different kinds of fish are known from

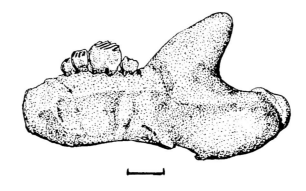

the Morrison Formation, including lungfish, possibly freshwater sharks, and heavily scaled bony
fish (Kirkland, 1987; Chure and Englemann,
1989). Though none of the Morrison coelurosaurs
exhibit adaptations for exclusive fish eating, they
might have occasionally taken advantage of fish
left stranded when ponds or lakes dried up.

No bird fossils have yet been positively identified from the Morrison Formation, but such fossils are exceedingly rare in rocks of any age owing
to their typically delicate construction. Paleontologists suspect that birds were well established by
the late Jurassic and that there may have been several different kinds of birds soaring through the
Utah skies in the company of the pterosaurs. Also,
small rat-like mammals appear to have been relatively common in the Morrison basin during the
late Jurassic, though they are known primarily
from tiny isolated teeth. Nonetheless, the assemblage of primitive mammals included many
different types, including multituberculates, tri-
conodontids, and symmetrodontids, among others (Bakker and Carpenter, 1990; Clemens and
others, 1979; Chure and Englemann, 1989;
Prothero and Jensen, 1983). As the names of these
groups of mammals suggest, each is distinguished
by the unique morphology of their teeth (see, for
example, Figure 6-15). Though they are represented by meager fossil material, the small mammals of the Morrison Formation all appear to
have been rodent-like animals that might have
been an important food source for the small and
agile coelurosaurian theropods.

Figure 6-15. Inner view
of the teeth and lower
jaw of *Zofiabaatar pul-
cher*, a multituberculate
mammal from the Morri-
son Formation. Multitu-
berculates had strong
ridges sweeping across
the surface of their tiny
teeth. Note the scale bar
(equal to 1 millimeter, or
1/24 of an inch) that in-
dicates this entire jaw
was less than one-half
inch long. This multitu-
berculate is one of about
fifty different small,
rodent-like mammals
known from the Morri-
son Formation. From
Bakker and Carpenter,
1990.

Thus, it appears that the small coelurosaurs might have survived on a mixed diet of small mammals, lizards, snakes, and perhaps even birds, fish, young crocodiles, and insects. Catching such small prey would require much different specializations than those necessary for pursuing the great herds of sauropods or subduing a large stegosaur. The coelurosaurs of the Morrison Formation, in contrast to the large carnosaurs and ceratosaurs, had to be quick, agile, dexterous, and perhaps even "smart" to survive by catching and consuming such small, evasive, and easily concealed prey. As will be seen in the coming chapters, this fundamental division between large and powerful carnivores and small and crafty predators persists until the end of the Mesozoic Era, but with different genera filling the two roles. In spite of their prominent differences, the hulking carnosaurs and the lithe coelurosaurs were collaborators in maintaining the ecological balance between predators and prey across the Morrison lowland of Utah. Together they limited the populations of the large and small herbivores to sustainable levels for at least 10 million years. They were the "blood brothers" of the Jurassic.

W HEN THE Jurassic Period ended, about 144 million years ago, eastern Utah was populated by a diverse array of dinosaurs. The great sauropods moved across the Morrison plain in herds and as solitary individuals, while other dinosaur herbivores foraged in the more heavily forested areas. Using a variety of hunting strategies and anatomical specializations, the large and small theropods maintained the overall ecological balance through predation, thus preventing herbivore overpopulation. The rivers flowing from the distant highlands carried sand, silt, and mud into the basin, depositing it across the lowlands in different places at different times as their courses periodically shifted in response to seasonal changes in the climate and the undulations of the landscape.

This ecosystem had been operating for millions of years when the sun rose on the first day of the Cretaceous Period, and nothing seems to have changed very much with that event. In fact, the Jurassic-Cretaceous boundary is often difficult to identify in the sedimentary rock sequences of the Colorado Plateau region. In places it appears that the sediments of the Brushy Basin Member of the Morrison Formation continued to accumulate well into the earliest part of the Cretaceous Period. For example, some researchers (Kowallis and others, 1986; and Kowallis and Heaton, 1987) have reported ages as young as 125 million years for zircon crystals from the volcanic ash of the Brushy Basin Member in the area around Capitol Reef National Park in central Utah. These dates are calculated by means of the density of tiny defects in the crystals produced by subatomic particles ejected from the nucleus of radioactive atoms such as uranium. Known as fission-track dating, this technique is not always as reliable, or as precise, as other methods of determining the ages of volcanic ash. Nonetheless, the dates provide at least a suggestion that the sediments of the upper portion of the Morrison Formation may be early Cretaceous in age.

Whatever the exact age of its uppermost lay-

ers may be, the Morrison Formation is always capped by a surface of erosion, an unconformity, that separates it from the overlying strata. Sometimes the unconformity at the top of the Morrison Formation is a distinct undulating surface with several feet of relief that truncates or visibly cuts off the layers beneath it (Figure 7-1). In other places, the unconformity is so subtle that it might be easily overlooked without careful inspection. In most places in eastern Utah, several hundred feet of soft mudstone and sandstone rest on the unconformity at the top of the Morrison Formation. These overlying sediments are generally similar to those of the Brushy Basin Member and are known throughout most of Utah as the Cedar Mountain Formation, named by Stokes (1944, 1952) for the highest point in the northern San Rafael Swell of Emery County. East of the Colorado River, in extreme eastern Utah and western Colorado, similar sedimentary rocks overlying the Morrison Formation are referred to as the Burro Canyon Formation. As an expression of the overall similarity of the Cedar Mountain/Burro Canyon sequence to the underlying Morrison sediments, these two formations were commonly mapped together as one unit prior to Stokes's detailed study.

Because the Cedar Mountain Formation and the Morrison Formation are so similar in general appearance to each other, and since the unconformity separating them may be subtle and indistinct, people exploring Utah's dinosaur country often have difficulty distinguishing the two formations. Only in the northern San Rafael Swell area, where about fifty feet of coarse conglomerate separates the Morrison Formation from the Cedar Mountain Formation, is it easy to identify the boundary between the two rock units. This pebble-cobble conglomerate was named the Buckhorn Conglomerate Member of the Cedar Mountain Formation by Stokes (1944, 1952) for the area around Buckhorn Reservoir, east of Cleveland, Utah. However, the Buckhorn Conglomerate is not very widely distributed and ei-

SEVEN

The Early Cretaceous

The (Un) Missing Links

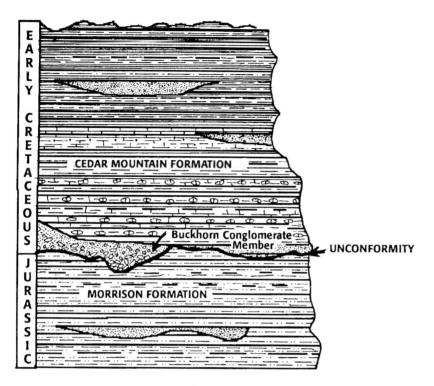

EARLY CRETACEOUS

CEDAR MOUNTAIN FORMATION

Buckhorn Conglomerate
Member

UNCONFORMITY

MORRISON FORMATION

JURASSIC

Figure 7-1. Generalized stratigraphy of the Morrison and Cedar Mountain formations, east-central Utah. A major unconformity separates these two formations almost everywhere in the northwest Colorado Plateau. The Buckhorn Conglomerate Member, at the base of the Cedar Mountain Formation, is either missing or represented by a relatively thin sandstone interval in areas beyond the northern San Rafael Swell.

ther disappears or thins to a generally inconspicuous sandstone layer beyond the northern San Rafael Swell area. In many places throughout eastern Utah the soft mudstones of the main body of the Cedar Mountain Formation rest directly on similar materials of the uppermost Morrison Formation. In these areas, however, a careful examination of the sediments in these units will reveal some differences that not only are useful in dividing the rock succession but also provide some important clues about the conditions during the early Cretaceous Period in east-central Utah.

First, the color banding in the Cedar Mountain Formation is usually less prominent than it is in the Morrison Formation. The Cedar Mountain mudstones generally have a drab gray or pale purple color in contrast to the bright red, white, lavender, and gray of the upper part of the Morrison Formation. In addition, the relatively broad and faded bands of color in the Cedar Mountain Formation are usually less distinct than are those of the Morrison. These differences in color banding render the Cedar Mountain badlands much

less scenic than the spectacular Morrison landscapes. Few tourists waste any film photographing Cedar Mountain badlands and no Hollywood producers have ever used them as a backdrop for western movies.

Gastroliths, the smooth and rounded stones that may represent the "gizzard stones" of dinosaurs, occur from place to place in the Morrison Formation; however, they are much more abundant in the Cedar Mountain Formation. In places, the weathered surfaces developed on exposures of the Cedar Mountain Formation are littered with hundreds of highly polished gastroliths, many with brilliant colors. The extreme abundance of gastroliths in the Cedar Mountain Formation can sometimes be helpful in distinguishing it from the underlying Morrison Formation. Exactly why gastroliths are so much more abundant in the Cedar Mountain Formation than in the Morrison remains a bit of a mystery. Though the Cedar Mountain Formation has produced the remains of several different types of dinosaurs, fossils of sauropods (the most likely dinosaurs to have possessed gizzard-like organs) are not particularly common. Perhaps many of the gastroliths that occur in the Cedar Mountain Formation are not "gizzard stones" at all; they may have developed their smooth form and polished surfaces by some mechanism other than gastric tumbling in the digestive system of a dinosaur. However they originated, the great abundance of gastroliths in the Cedar Mountain Formation is a unique characteristic of this early Cretaceous formation.

There is also a subtle, but very important, difference between the composition of the mudstones that comprise most of the Cedar Mountain Formation and the rock of the underlying Morrison Formation. In the upper part of the Morrison Formation (the Brushy Basin Member), the mudstones are composed primarily of clay minerals such as montmorillonite and illite, with minerals such as quartz and feldspar comprising a small fraction of the fine-grained sediment. Calcite, a mineral composed of calcium carbonate ($CaCO_3$) exists, but it is not usually very common in the Morrison mudstones. In the overlying Cedar Mountain mudstones, above the unconformity that caps the Morrison Formation, the mudstones are usually much richer in both calcite and dolomite [$CaMg(CO_3)_2$], a similar calcium-bearing mineral. The abundance of these minerals in the Cedar Mountain deposits has led geologists to refer to them as calcareous mudstones, meaning that the clay minerals are accompanied by significant amounts of calcium-bearing compounds. In addition, nodular masses of nearly pure calcite are extremely common in certain horizons in the Cedar Mountain Formation. These small nodules commonly weather out of the enclosing mudstones and accumulate on the surface as a loose blanket of small, irregularly shaped rocks. These calcite nodules often make maneuvering over Cedar Mountain slopes treacherous: it's a bit like trying to walk on a slope covered with marbles! Tying a pillow on your rump is not as absurd an idea as it sounds when walking over hills underlain by the Cedar Mountain Formation. In addition to the calcareous nodules, there are many more thin layers of solid limestone, composed almost entirely of calcite, in the Cedar Mountain Formation than there are in the underlying Morrison sediments. The Cedar Mountain Formation thus contains much more calcareous material, in several different forms, than is present in the Morrison Formation.

The significance of this increase in calcareous minerals in the Cedar Mountain Formation, is that it may be a reflection of changes in both the climate and the geography during the early Cretaceous Period. In the modern world, calcite and other carbonate minerals form abundant nodules in soils that develop from sediment under warm and dry climatic conditions. In many desert regions, the formation of calcite in the soil leads to the development of caliche, a crusty mass of calcium carbonate. Caliche forms in the soils of arid regions as both irregular lumps and as wavy layers

known as "hardpans." Both types of calcite are common in the Cedar Mountain Formation. Based on the geologic shift to more calcareous sediments in the Cedar Mountain Formation, it seems plausible to conclude that the climate of the early Cretaceous became more arid than it was during most of the preceding late Jurassic. If we examine the geological events that were taking place in adjacent regions of North America during the early Cretaceous Period, we can identify some reasons why this change in climate might have occurred.

In western Utah and eastern Nevada, the hilly terrain began to experience more serious geological disturbances following the close of the Jurassic Period (Schwans, 1987). Numerous studies of the early Cretaceous paleogeography and tectonics of the eastern Great Basin region (for example, Cowan and Bruhn, 1992; Allmendinger and others, 1985) suggest that compressional forces were intensified about 120 million years ago. The enhanced compression led to the crumpling of rock layers and the formation of low-angle thrust faults in the region around the Raft River Range of northwestern Utah, in the northern Wasatch Mountains area, and elsewhere in the eastern part of the Great Basin. This deformation, related to the compressive stresses produced by the subduction of an oceanic slab of rock beneath the western edge of North America, accelerated the uplift of the eastern Great Basin region that began in the late Jurassic. As the mountainous terrain rose, the older Mesocordilleran High was elevated to become a more prominent highland bordering the interior lowland of eastern Utah. The higher ground in eastern Nevada and western Utah took moisture from stormclouds passing inland from the west coast, just as the modern Sierra Nevada in California creates a rain-shadow desert across most of present-day Nevada. Little moisture remained in the air masses that passed over the early Cretaceous highland into the Colorado Plateau region. As the rains became less frequent in central and eastern Utah, the increasing aridity

Photo 25. The gray, nodular mudstones of the Ruby Ranch Member of the Cedar Mountain Formation in the San Rafael Swell. Frank DeCourten.

Photo 26. Gastroliths are abundant in most of the Cedar Mountain Formation of east-central Utah. John Telford.

led to the precipitation of calcium carbonate in the soils of the interior basin. The early Cretaceous uplift that led to the shift toward drier conditions in central Utah marks the transition of the Mesocordilleran High into what scientists call the Sevier Orogenic Belt. As will be seen in the next chapter, even more intense deformation would follow in the late Cretaceous Period as the Sevier Orogenic Belt evolved into a magnificent mountain system. Henceforth, the highlands of western Utah and eastern Nevada will be referred to as the Sevier Orogenic Belt, even though it was not nearly as prominent in the early Cretaceous as it would become some 30 million years later. As shall soon be seen, the early Cretaceous was a time of numerous transitions in the land and life of Utah. The first of those transitions occurred in western Utah as the Mesocordilleran High of the late Jurassic developed into the Sevier Orogenic Belt.

In addition to enhancing the aridity of eastern Utah, the uplift that affected the land in western Utah during the early Cretaceous also lifted the streambeds that were draining into the interior basin. In response, the rivers cut deeper channels through the rising land and scoured away at least some of the sediments that had been deposited earlier. In time, as the rivers shifted back and forth across the land, a broad erosion surface was developed. This surface of erosion is represented by the regional unconformity that in many places separates the Morrison Formation from the Cedar Mountain Formation. The rivers descending from the Sevier Orogenic Belt ran swiftly to the east down beds steepened by the uplift that was occurring in their headwater regions. Flowing with greater energy, the rivers could transport large pebbles and cobbles well beyond the eastern flanks of the Sevier Orogenic Belt. Eventually the streams flowed out of the mountainous terrain and across the gullied and scoured floor of the interior basin to the east. On this undulating surface, the pebbles and cobbles accumulated as the streams joined to form more

Photo 27. Outcrops of the Buckhorn Conglomerate Member of the Cedar Mountain Formation near Buckhorn Reservoir, Emery County. John Telford.

slow-flowing languid rivers that lacked the energy to carry the rubble any farther. The Buckhorn Conglomerate Member of the Cedar Mountain Formation originated from the accumulation of such materials transported from the highlands to the west. The smooth and rounded stones comprising the Buckhorn Conglomerate Member clearly show the effects of river transport and are primarily composed of chert and quartzite that sometimes have Paleozoic-age fossils preserved in them. This rock is a perfect match for the layers that were involved in the early Cretaceous deformation to the west as the Sevier Orogenic Belt emerged. In addition, the orientation of the pebbles in the Buckhorn Conglomerate suggests that most of them were deposited by streams flowing into central Utah from the west or southwest (Figure 7-2).

The Buckhorn Conglomerate Member is not particularly widespread in central Utah. Beyond the northwest San Rafael Swell region where this member was first defined, no massive conglomerates are present in the Cedar Mountain Formation. In places where the Buckhorn Conglomerate is missing, sheets of coarse, river-deposited sandstone commonly rest above the Morrison-Cedar Mountain unconformity. Thus, it appears that the Buckhorn Conglomerate represents a local accumulation of pebbles and cobbles that was deposited where the east-flowing ancient rivers first encountered the flatlands. In that area, where the flanks of the Sevier Orogenic Belt met the interior basin, a mound-like alluvial-fan complex would have developed. Beyond this pile of gravel, the streams transported smaller sand-sized grains across the broad floor of the basin, eventually de-

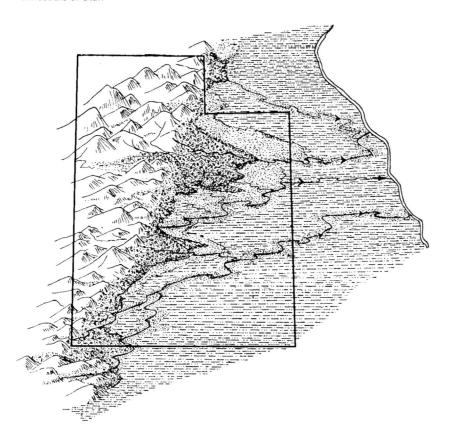

Figure 7-2. Early Creta-
ceous paleogeography
of Utah. Uplift during the
early phase of the Sevier
Orogeny in western Utah
created a prominent
highland that served as
the principal watershed
for the low plains of the
eastern and central por-
tions of the future state.
The streams that drained
the embryonic Sevier
Orogenic Highland de-
posited gravel in alluvial
fan complexes, sand
along the river channels,
and fine silt and mud on
the floodplains.

positing them on the eroded outcrops of the underlying Morrison Formation. Ultimately, as the
uplift of the Sevier Orogenic Belt temporarily
subsided, the eroded land in the basin had been
built up by the accumulation of layers of sand and
gravel, while the rivers had cut deeper channels
into the highlands to the west. These two factors,
erosion in the highlands and deposition of sediment in the basin (known to geologists as aggra-
dation), reduced the slope of the stream channels.
In response to the reduced slope of the streambeds, the rivers became more lethargic.

As early Cretaceous time progressed, the
now-sluggish rivers deposited fine silt and mud
on top of the coarse sand and gravel dispersed
earlier across the basin floor. Much of this fine
sediment was deposited across the plain during
flood events when the rivers breached their channels and spread out laterally over great distances.
Thus, the upper portion of the Cedar Mountain

Formation, the "main body," as it is referred to by
most geologists, is composed almost entirely of
calcareous mudstone that accumulated on the
floodplains bordering the slow streams. In time,
even the highest hills of the basin were buried under the mud and silt. In such areas, the Cedar
Mountain Formation would be relatively thin and
would rest directly on fine-grained mudstones of
the Morrison Formation. It would not be easy to
find the boundary between the two formations in
the locations where Cedar Mountain mudstones
buried hills carved into Morrison mudstones.

The main body of the Cedar Mountain Formation above the Buckhorn Conglomerate Member has recently been subdivided into four new
members (Kirkland and others, 1997). In ascending order, these newly established members are
the Yellow Cat Member, the Poison Strip Sandstone, the Ruby Ranch Member, and the Mussentuchit Member. All of these members are named
for Utah localities and reflect the varied nature of
the mostly fine-grained sediments that were deposited after the Buckhorn Conglomerate was
laid down. The distinctions between these various
members of the Cedar Mountain Formation involve subtle features such as the composition of
the clay minerals, the relative abundance of volcanic ash, and the amount of carbonaceous material in the sediments. A complete discussion of
the various members of the Cedar Mountain Formation is beyond the scope of this book, but
many additional details can be found in the work
by Kirkland and others (1997).

Historically, the Cedar Mountain Formation
has not been the source of very much information on dinosaurs or other prehistoric creatures.
Fossils of any kind are definitely less common in
the Cedar Mountain Formation than they are in
the underlying Morrison mudstones. However,
the Cedar Mountain Formation is not as bare of
fossils as it has often been portrayed in the geological literature of the 1950s and 1960s. It seems
that one reason this formation was overlooked for
so long is that many paleontologists were so daz-

zled by the abundance of dinosaur fossils in the Morrison Formation that they spent little time prospecting Cedar Mountain outcrops for fossils. Since the late 1980s, however, many new discoveries of fossil sites in the Cedar Mountain Formation have demonstrated that the formation is, in fact, rich in fossils, and the newly discovered material fosters some exciting new perspectives of the history of dinosaurs in Utah and adjacent regions of North America. At the risk of overstating things slightly, I regard the Cedar Mountain Formation of Utah to be one of the most exciting horizons in contemporary dinosaur research.

Dinosaur Fauna of the Cedar Mountain Formation

Until the late 1980s, very little was known about the dinosaur fauna of the Cedar Mountain Formation of Utah. In 1969, the first formal description of a Cedar Mountain dinosaur was published by Bodily (1969), who tentatively identified *Hoplitosaurus*(?), a quadrupedal and armored herbivore, from a site about twenty miles north of Moab. In the same region, the Dalton Well Quarry was developed by scientists at Brigham Young University, after it was discovered near the west side of Arches National Park in the 1970s (Galton and Jensen, 1979). This quarry is situated a few meters below the horizon that produced *Hoplitosaurus*(?), near the base of the Cedar Mountain Formation. The bones excavated from the Dalton Well Quarry are still under study and many more fossils could potentially be quarried from the site. In 1970, James Jensen described reptilian eggshell fragments from the Cedar Mountain Formation that were discovered near Castle Dale, Utah, on the west side of the San Rafael Swell (Jensen, 1970). In the mid-1980s, numerous small fossils were reported from what became known as the Rough Road Quarry, located in the northwest San Rafael Swell region east of Castle Dale.

The Rough Road Quarry and several other sites nearby have produced an amazing variety of fossils of both terrestrial and aquatic vertebrates. Small dinosaur teeth, crocodilian and turtle fossils, lizard and fish remains, and the teeth of several primitive mammals all have been recovered from this quarry (Nelson and Crooks, 1987; Nelson and others, 1984; Eaton and Nelson, 1991). The Rough Road Quarry is also significant in that it is situated very near the top of the Cedar Mountain Formation and is, therefore, younger than other fossil-bearing horizons in this formation.

The current surge of interest in the dinosaurs of the Cedar Mountain Formation began in earnest during the late 1980s, when researchers with the Utah Museum of Natural History discovered a concentration of bones in Emery County now known as the Long Walk Quarry (Figure 7-3). This site, which is still under study, is situated in the lower portion of the Cedar Mountain Formation, about forty-five feet above the top of the Morrison Formation. The Long Walk Quarry is thus intermediate in age between the younger (and higher) Rough Road Quarry and the older (and lower) Dalton Well Quarry. The Long Walk Quarry is still in an early stage of development and may ultimately yield thousands of fossils from its hard limestone bone bed.

James Kirkland (Dinamation International Society), Don Burge (College of Eastern Utah), and many collaborators and volunteers have provided the latest excitement in the study of Cedar Mountain dinosaurs. They have located several new quarries in the Cedar Mountain Formation, including the Gaston Quarry in Grand County, where the large dromaeosaur *Utahraptor* was first identified (Kirkland and others, 1993; Kirkland and Burge, 1994; Kirkland and others, 1995; Kirkland and Parrish, 1995). Meanwhile, Richard Cifelli of the Oklahoma Museum of Natural History has reported dinosaur and other reptile remains accompanying the fossils of small mammals that he has found in the upper Cedar Mountain Formation at Mussentuchit Wash in southern

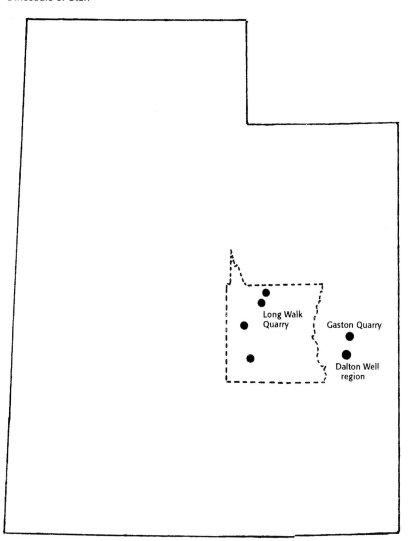

Long Walk
Quarry

Gaston Quarry

Dalton Well
region

Figure 7-3. Early Creta-
ceous dinosaur sites of
Utah. Most of these lo-
calities have been dis-
covered since the mid-
1980s, and other sites
will almost certainly be
found as current investi-
gations continue.

Utah's early Cretaceous dinosaur fauna than was possible only a decade ago. The story of early Cretaceous dinosaurs in Utah is, of course, still unfolding, and it is certain that many new types await discovery. Nonetheless, at this early stage of the study, scientists are beginning to recognize several different faunas that seem to be restricted to certain horizons within the Cedar Mountain Formation. James Kirkland and several colleagues have suggested that three distinct faunas can be recognized among the dinosaur remains excavated from this formation in Utah (Kirkland and others, 1997; Kirkland and Parrish, 1995; Kirkland and others, 1993). The review that follows is based on the model of Kirkland and others (1997), but is modified to include some unpublished discoveries and non-dinosaur elements of the faunas. It would have been surprising to paleontologists of the 1960s that such a rich vertebrate fauna would ultimately be documented from the "unfossiliferous" Cedar Mountain Formation!

The Yellow Cat Fauna: The Basal Assemblage

The lower portion of the Cedar Mountain Formation in eastern Utah is known as the Yellow Cat Member, a sequence of mudstone layers interbedded with limestone and sandstone. Overlying the Yellow Cat Member in eastern Utah is a thin, pebbly sandstone sequence known as the Poison Strip Sandstone Member. In the strata of these two members are found the fossils of the earliest Cretaceous dinosaur fauna in the Colorado Plateau region. This fauna is probably around 125–120 million years old, some 20 million years younger than the dinosaurs that occur in the Morrison Formation immediately below. Elements of this fauna have thus far been found primarily in Grand County in such places as the Gaston Quarry, the Dalton Well site, and other nearby localities. This oldest assemblage of dinosaurs from the Cedar Mountain Formation has been named the Yellow Cat Fauna (Kirkland and others, 1997).

The most common dinosaurs in the Yellow

Emery County (personal communication, 1994; Cifelli, 1993). Eaton and Nelson (1991) have reported additional small mammal remains from the Cedar Mountain Formation along the west side of the San Rafael Swell. In addition to these sites, a virtual "bone rush" to the Cedar Mountain beds over the past few years has resulted in the discovery of numerous other localities that offer additional clues about the dinosaurs living in Utah during the early Cretaceous Period (Kirkland and others, 1997b).

All of this new information, much of it still of a preliminary nature, allows paleontologists to formulate a much more complete perception of

Cat Fauna appear to be armored nodosaurs similar to the European *Polacanthus* (some authors prefer the older name *Hylaeosaurus* for this dinosaur) or the North American form *Sauropelta*. Nodosaurs were common worldwide during the early Cretaceous but in most cases are known only from very fragmentary material. In the absence of well-preserved and complete skeletons, many different names have been applied to the fragmentary remains of nodosaurs. This uncertainty is reflected in the queried identification *Hoplitosaurus*? given by Bodily in 1969 in his report of the first nodosaur discovered from the Cedar Mountain Formation. We do know that these nodosaurs (family Nodosauridae of the suborder Ankylosauria) were large, squat, quadrupedal herbivores with dermal (skin) armor that covered most of the dorsal surface (neck, back, hips, and tail). None of the nodosaurs had the tail club that characterizes their later, and generally larger, relatives in the family Ankylosauridae, such as the familiar *Ankylosaurus*. The ribs in nodosaurs flared out from the spine in a nearly horizontal fashion before curving downward around the animals' barrel-shaped bodies. This feature gave the nodosaurs very broad and practically flat backs. No complete skeleton of any nodosaur has ever been found in the Cedar Mountain Formation of Utah, but fragmentary remains are common, particularly in the lowermost layers. Judging from the range in size of the incomplete nodosaur remains and the morphological variety of armor plates and scutes, there may have been several different types of nodosaurs in Utah during the early Cretaceous.

Hoplitosaurus? was the first armored dinosaur described from the lower Cedar Mountain Formation (Bodily, 1969). The identification was based on many armor scutes of various shapes and sizes, numerous tail vertebrae and armor, and a few partial limb elements. Other paleontologists (for example, Weishampel, 1990) have regarded these fragmentary remains as more similar to *Sauropelta*, a nodosaur known from the Cloverly

Formation of Wyoming and Montana. Kirkland (1991) reported additional nodosaur remains from the lower Cedar Mountain Formation that were similar to both *Sauropelta* and *Polacanthus*. In addition, a new armored dinosaur, *Gastonia*, has been recently discovered in the Yellow Cat sequence. It has yet to be described in detail. Thus, there still remains some uncertainty about the precise identity of the lower Cedar Mountain nodosaurs. For example, Pereda-Suberbiola (1994) concluded, on the basis of the shape of the plates on the tail and the height of the neural spines of the caudal vertebrae, that *Hoplitosaurus*? is probably a specimen of *Polacanthus*. It is highly probable that several different nodosaurs lived in Utah during the time the lower portion of the Cedar Mountain Formation was being deposited. Until the record is sorted out by paleontologists, it is probably best to review a few of the species most similar to the Yellow Cat types.

◊ *POLACANTHUS*

Polacanthus (Figure 7-4) was a low, flat-bodied quadruped, with a broad bony shield covering the hip region. About 13 feet long, this herbivore was further protected by two rows of spikes that extended along the neck from the head to the middle of the back. A second double row of smaller and more blunt spikes ran along the dorsal (upper) surface of the tail from just behind the hips to the tip. The limbs of *Polacanthus* are short and massive, indicating that it could not have been a very swift or nimble animal. Without the ability to outrun predators or to conceal its corpulent body, the need for protective armor in this nodosaur is obvious.

Polacanthus was a low browser and it would not be inappropriate to view its motion and habits as similar to those of *Stegosaurus* of the late Jurassic. As in most other nodosaurs, the hundreds of armor plates that covered the neck, back, hips, and tail of *Polacanthus* came in many different sizes and shapes. The hip shield was

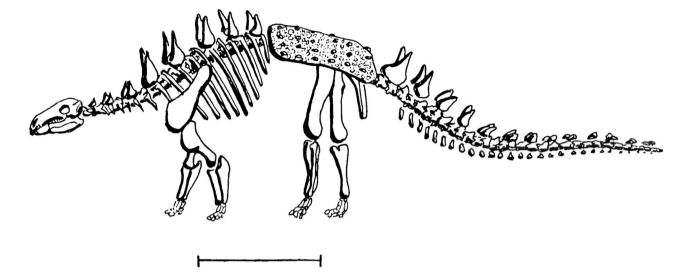

Figure 7-4. *Polacanthus*, an armored nodosaur from the Cedar Mountain Formation of east-central Utah. Note the paired rows of spikes protecting the neck, back, and tail. The hip region was shielded by an armor plate constructed of fused scutes of various sizes and shapes. Scale bar=1 m (about 3 feet). Based on data from Pereda-Suberbiola, 1994.

formed of many plates (dermal scutes) rigidly fused together. Elsewhere on the dorsal body surface, the scutes were isolated knobs or spikes embedded in the skin. After the animal's death, the unfused plates and spikes often became scattered as the carcass decayed. Even the fused plates in the hip shield could eventually break apart as decomposition and weathering proceeded. When these scutes are found as isolated fossils, it is difficult to know exactly what the original pattern of armor was, or even which nodosaur shed them. This is one reason for the uncertainty about the identity of the nodosaurs in the basal Yellow Cat Fauna.

Aside from the *Polacanthus* material, the lower Cedar Mountain Formation has produced fossils of an additional nodosaur, similar to *Sauropelta*. Scientists have a reasonably good idea about the skeletal structure of *Sauropelta* due to the fairly complete specimens of this genus that have been found in the Cloverly Formation of Wyoming and Montana (Carpenter, 1984). While most of the Cloverly Formation is probably slightly younger than the lower part of the Cedar Mountain Formation, fragmentary fossils of a similar dinosaur occur in the Poison Strip Sandstone Member. *Gastonia* was probably very similar to, and perhaps a relative of *Sauropelta*.

⑥ *SAUROPELTA*

Sauropelta was a large nodosaur, weighing over 3,000 pounds and exceeding 15 feet in length (Carpenter, 1984; Figure 7-5A). The skull was unarmored and triangular in shape, with a narrow snout and broad base. As in other nodosaurs, the small teeth (Figure 7-5B), confined mostly to the side of the jaws, are reminiscent of *Stegosaurus* teeth and were probably used in a similar manner to shear tough, low-growing vegetation. As reconstructed by Carpenter (1984), *Sauropelta* had several pairs of spikes protecting the neck, beginning just behind the head and extending to the shoulder region. Bony armor covered the entire upper body (dorsal) surface, but was particularly well-developed in the hip region, where it consisted of several rows of dome-shaped scutes surrounded by smaller knobs of bone. Evidently, *Sauropelta* did not have the tail spikes that characterize *Polacanthus*. Beneath the hip shield of *Sauropelta*, the pelvis was very broad (Figure 7-5C) and rigidly fused to the sacrum by means of strut-like sacral ribs. The limbs of *Sauropelta* were massive (Figure 7-5D) and the feet had five short and widely splayed toes to support the considerable weight. *Sauropelta* was, like *Polacanthus*, a slow animal, and the two nodosaurs probably spent a great

A

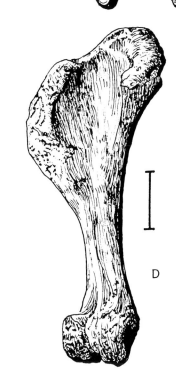

B

C

D

Figure 7-5. *Sauropelta*, an early Cretaceous nodosaur. A: Reconstruction of *Sauropelta*, based on Carpenter, 1984; B: a tooth of *Sauropelta*, scale bar= 1 cm (about 3/8 inch); C: the broad pelvis of *Sauropelta*, about 3 feet wide, seen in top view; D: the massive humerus of *Sauropelta* that helped to support the one-to-two-ton body. B and D based on illustrations of Coombs and Maryanska, 1990.

deal of time leisurely foraging through the low undergrowth of the early Cretaceous basin in east-central Utah. There is no evidence of gregarious behavior among the nodosaurs, because the isolated remains, wherever they have been found, seem to belong to single individuals.

Nodosaurs were not the only herbivores present in Utah during the early Cretaceous. At least two types of ornithopod dinosaurs have also been identified in the basal Yellow Cat Fauna. Recall that the ornithopods are bipedal herbivores such as *Camptosaurus* or *Dryosaurus* of the Morrison strata. In the late Cretaceous, the ornithopods are dominated by the hadrosaurs (family Hadrosauridae, or the "duck-bill" dinosaurs) with their broad snouts, elaborate dentition, and ornate crests, at least in some forms. During early Cretaceous time, the earliest hadrosaurs, or true duck-bill dinosaurs, to live in Utah have been identified in the Yellow Cat Fauna. Galton and Jensen (1979) reported the occurrence of a hadrosaur femur and remains of *Iguanodon ottingeri* from the lower portion of the Cedar Mountain Formation near Moab. Though it is not possible to identify the hadrosaur from a single poorly preserved femur (Figure 7-6A), this fossil may represent the remains of one of the earliest dinosaurs of its type

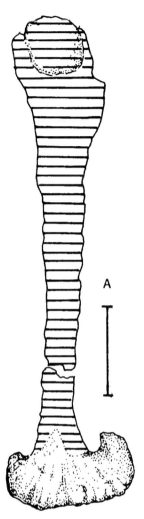

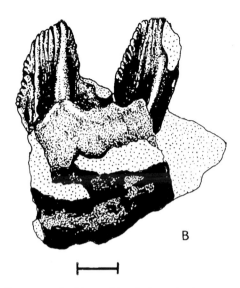

Figure 7-6. Ornithopod fossils from the lower Cedar Mountain Formation. A: A hadrosaur femur described by Galton and Jensen, 1979. Only the lower (distal) end of the femur was well preserved; ruling represents the badly weathered portion. Scale bar=20 cm (about 8 inches). B: A fragment of the maxilla with two teeth from *Iguanodon ottingeri*; redrawn from Galton and Jensen, 1979. Light stippling represents broken surfaces. Scale bar=20 mm (about 1 inch).

in North America. Moreover, the femur is over three feet long and evidently represents an animal between 25 and 30 feet in length, as large as any of the better-known hadrosaurs from the late Cretaceous. *Iguanodon ottingeri* is based on a single fragment of the maxilla (upper jaw) with two teeth preserved (Figure 7-6B). It is not surprising to find the remains of *Iguanodon* in the Cedar Mountain Formation, because this genus has also been identified in other early Cretaceous strata of western North America (for example, in South Dakota; after Weishampel and Bjork, 1989) and, as we saw in the preceding chapter, the Morrison Formation also has produced fossils tentatively identified as *Iguanodon*.

It should be pointed out that some paleontologists have questioned the identification of a new species of *Iguanodon* on the basis of such fragmentary material. Norman and Weishampel (1990) list *Iguanodon ottingeri* as a *nomen dubium* ("doubtful name"), while Weishampel and Bjork

(1989) assert that the fossil material is too fragmentary to be diagnostic even at the genus level. As is so often the case in dinosaur paleontology, more and better fossils of both *Iguanodon ottingeri* and the unnamed hadrosaur are needed before we can be certain about what kinds of ornithopods accompanied the nodosaurs in the basal Cedar Mountain Formation. Many other fossil specimens representing ornithopods from the lower Cedar Mountain Formation are currently under study, so a more complete understanding of these herbivores may soon be forthcoming. It is clear, even at this early stage in the investigations, that ornithopods were a significant part of the basal Cedar Mountain fauna, that they were relatively large animals, that several different types existed, and that at least some of them were more specialized than the relatively primitive forms of earlier Morrison strata.

In addition to the specific genera thus far described, the Yellow Cat Fauna of the Cedar Mountain Formation evidently included many other herbivores. Unfortunately, the material collected thus far from the lower members is far too fragmentary to allow its precise identification. Kirkland and others (1997b) include two different sauropods and a "sail-back" ornithopod among the Yellow Cat Fauna. Lungfish, bowfin-like fish, turtles, and crocodiles also have been identified in the Yellow Cat Fauna. But perhaps the most dramatic element of the dinosaur fauna from the lower Cedar Mountain Formation is a harrowing predator that must have stalked all of the herbivorous types—the menacing *Utahraptor*.

⑥ *UTAHRAPTOR*: TERROR OF THE EARLY CRETACEOUS

Without doubt, the most exciting of the many recent discoveries in the Cedar Mountain Formation was the identification of *Utahraptor ostrommaysi* (Kirkland and others, 1993) from the Gaston Quarry in the summers of 1991 and 1992. *Utahraptor* was discovered in Grand County in

Photo 28. The Yellow Cat/Gaston Quarry in the lower Cedar Mountain Formation near Moab. *Utahraptor* was first discovered at this site. Frank DeCourten.

the Yellow Cat Member of the Cedar Mountain Formation, about fifteen feet below the overlying Poison Strip Sandstone Member. *Utahraptor* was based on fragmentary fossils representing parts of the skull, a tibia, and claws from the foot and hand. This predator's fossils are also present at the Dalton Well Quarry, situated in the lower Cedar Mountain Formation, where additional claws from the hand and vertebrae from the tail were preserved. Though these remains of *Utahraptor* are far from complete, they provide a reasonably good basis from which to reconstruct the basic features of a most fascinating theropod.

Utahraptor is clearly a dromaeosaur (family Dromaeosauridae) or, to use a term than has become popular lately, a "raptor." The dromaeosaurs were fierce bipedal predators with long and powerful legs, a stiff counterbalancing tail, a large skull carrying many razor-sharp teeth, and greatly enlarged sickle-shaped claws on the second toes of the hind feet. These huge claws were raised off

the ground while the dromaeosaurs ran, but were attached through ligaments to powerful muscles higher in the leg. When activated, the large foot talon could rotate downward through a wide arc with great force. Coupled with a raking or kicking motion of the hind limb, the dromaeosaurs could inflict deep gashes in the flanks or belly of prey animals. The sharp claws of the hand were also well suited for grasping prey by stabbing through the hide with a forceful grip.

The best-known dromaeosaur from North America is *Deinonychus* (Figure 7-7), originally discovered in the Cloverly Formation along the Wyoming-Montana border. *Deinonychus* was a wide-ranging predator, and some of the fragmentary dromaeosaur remains in the Cedar Mountain Formation are very similar to this genus. *Deinonychus* was a small, quick, and birdlike predator that may have employed pack-hunting strategies in attacking large prey animals that lived in its area. In Montana, the remains of sev-

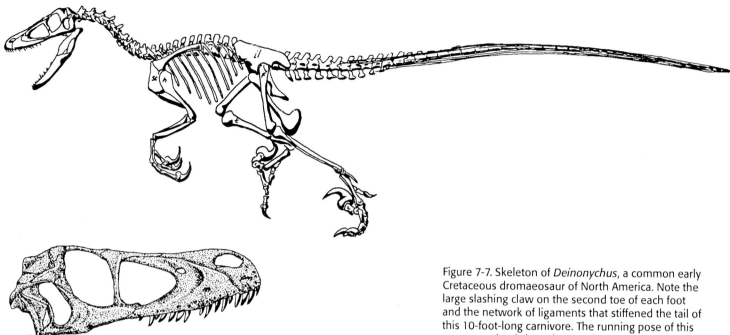

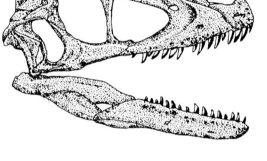

Figure 7-7. Skeleton of *Deinonychus*, a common early Cretaceous dromaeosaur of North America. Note the large slashing claw on the second toe of each foot and the network of ligaments that stiffened the tail of this 10-foot-long carnivore. The running pose of this reconstruction is based on Paul, 1988.

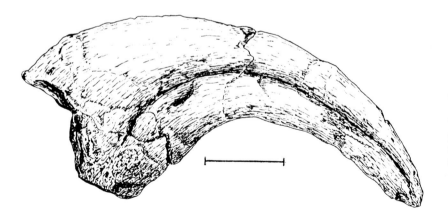

Figure 7-8. Claw from the foot of *Utahraptor*, based on a drawing by Rick Adleman in Kirkland and others, 1993. Note the prominent groove on the side of this claw from the second toe of the right foot. This groove helped to secure the horny sheath that covered the bone, forming a talon well over a foot long. Scale bar=25 mm (1 inch).

eral *Deinonychus* individuals have been found in direct association with a nearly complete skeleton of *Tenontosaurus*, a primitive ornithopod, in a manner that clearly suggests pack hunting (Ostrom, 1990; Ostrom and Maxwell, 1995). *Velociraptor*, a diminutive late Cretaceous dromaeosaur from Asia, evidently preferred smaller prey, but it could still attack creatures larger than itself. A partial skeleton of *Velociraptor* has been found still clutching the small ceratopsian *Protoceratops*. These two findings demonstrate that the dromaeosaurs were capable of hunting a wide range of prey animals, including relatively large herbivores.

Despite their viciousness, *Deinonychus*, *Velociraptor*, and other dromaeosaurs were generally rather small animals. Few dromaeosaurs exceeded about 10 feet in length, and full-grown adults generally weighed less than about 200 pounds. For dramatic effect, the raptors of the movie *Jurassic Park*, based on *Velociraptor*, were greatly exaggerated in size (but probably not in attitude). Or were they? Ironically, at the same time that this popular motion picture was thrilling audiences around the world, *Utahraptor* remains were being excavated in eastern Utah. What emerged from the Gaston Quarry was a dromaeosaur closer to the movie creatures' dimensions. Measured along the outer curve, the preserved claw on the second toe of *Utahraptor* is nearly 23 cm (9 inches) long, almost twice as large as that of *Deinonychus* (Figure 7-8). In life, the bony portion of this foot claw was covered by a horny sheath that would have formed a sharp talon about 14 inches long. The other preserved elements of *Utahraptor* (caudal vertebrae, premaxilla, foot and hand bones) from Utah sites are also much larger than their counterparts in *Deinonychus* or any other dromaeosaur (Kirkland and others, 1993). Based on the size of recovered bones, *Utahraptor* was probably around 20 feet long and weighed perhaps 1,000 pounds. This clearly makes *Utahraptor* the largest known dromaeosaur in the world. As Kirkland and others

(1993) have suggested, comparing *Utahraptor* to *Deinonychus* is like comparing a polar bear to a jackal, at least in terms of size.

With such a large body size, *Utahraptor* was clearly capable of overpowering and subduing relatively large prey animals. This dromaeosaur may not have been limited to the pack-hunting techniques that were evidently employed by the smaller members of its family. Moreover, the hand claws of *Utahraptor* are almost as large as the fearsome foot claws and are significantly narrower than those of most other dromaeosaurs (Kirkland and others, 1993). This suggests that the hands of *Utahraptor* had sharp-edged claws potentially useful in cutting and ripping flesh from the carcass of a prey animal. Although we cannot rule out the possibility of pack hunting for *Utahraptor*, there is no strong evidence for it, and it certainly seems that this large dromaeosaur could have functioned effectively as a solitary predator. The early Cretaceous basin of eastern Utah probably supported a variety of prey animals that could have been the targets of *Utahraptor* attacks. The ornithopods described earlier would certainly have been tempting to *Utahraptor*. The nodosaurs, even with their protected dorsal surfaces, might also have suffered from *Utahraptor* assaults, particularly if the powerful carnivores could overturn them to expose the vulnerable belly region. As shall be seen in the next section, small sauropods are also known from the Cedar Mountain Formation and these could have provided an additional food source. In view of its size and specializations, it is difficult to envision any herbivore that would not have been distressed by the approach of even one, not to mention a hungry group of these swift, snarling raptors. *Utahraptor* was the terror of the early Cretaceous!

The age of the basal fauna of the Cedar Mountain Formation can only be estimated, because no datable minerals have been found in the strata that produce the fossils in the lowermost portion of the formation. The dinosaurs thus far documented in the basal fauna seem to compare

Plate 16.
A pack of
Utahraptors
attacking a
nodosaur.

best with similar assemblages from the Wealdon Marl of southern England and the Lakota Formation of South Dakota (Kirkland, 1995; Kirkland and others, 1993). These two formations are thought to be of Barremian age (middle early Cretaceous), about 125 million years old. If the basal Cedar Mountain Formation is Barremian in age, as seems probable on the basis of the nodosaur and dromaeosaur fauna it contains, then the unconformity at the top of the Morrison Formation in eastern Utah encompasses about 20 million years of unrecorded time. What type of dinosaurs, if any, existed during this gap in the rock record may never be known.

The Ruby Ranch Fauna: The Middle Assemblage

Above the lowermost beds, the Cedar Mountain Formation is dominated by fine-grained mudstone and shale and contains thin interspersed lenses of limestone and channel-deposited sandstone. These fine-grained sediments of the main body of the formation are now known as the Ruby Ranch Member (Kirkland and others, 1997a). Fossils of any kind are relatively rare in the Ruby Ranch Member, but enough dinosaur material has been collected to suggest a fauna different from that which characterizes the lower portions of the Cedar Mountain Formation. The most important site producing fossils of the Ruby Ranch Fauna is the Long Walk Quarry in Emery County (Kirkland and others, 1993; 1997). Other fossil localities in the Ruby Ranch Member near the Colorado River and along the west side of the San Rafael Swell have produced additional material, but it is very fragmentary and not generally very well preserved. The Ruby Ranch Fauna is the most obscure of the three dinosaur assemblages known from the Cedar Mountain Formation.

The Long Walk Quarry, opened in 1987 and still active, has thus far produced the remains of at least three different kinds of dinosaurs (De-Courten, 1991; Kirkland and others, 1997) from a

hard limestone layer that probably represents a temporary pond or small lake that developed on the arid plains of the central Utah basin. There are literally thousands of bones preserved in the limestone "bone bed," but the process of removing the delicate fossils from the hard limestone matrix requires very delicate and time-consuming work. Researchers at the Utah Museum of Natural History are continuing the slow process of preparing fossils from more than a dozen large blocks of limestone that were retrieved from the Long Walk Quarry during the late 1980s. Since the Long Walk Quarry is potentially the most productive of the localities producing fossils of the Ruby Ranch Fauna, a great deal of new information is likely to emerge as the research continues.

Thus far, the fossils from this site are dominated by the remains of small sauropods, a type of dinosaur that was previously unknown in the Colorado Plateau region in the early Cretaceous Period. The sauropod fossils appear to have come from both adults and juveniles, possibly of the same species. A larger adult sauropod is represented by several large vertebrae (dorsal, sacral, and caudal), ribs, teeth, broken skull elements,

Photo 29. The Long Walk Quarry in the Ruby Ranch Member of the Cedar Mountain Formation. Note the hard limestone bone bed emerging from the soft calcareous mudstone. This site still contains thousands of bones and is potentially the largest fossil accumulation of all localities in the Cedar Mountain Formation. Frank DeCourten.

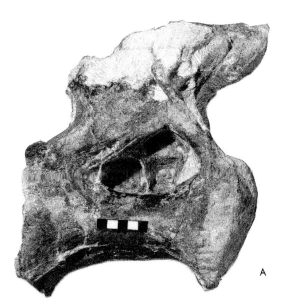

A

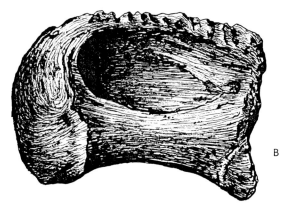

B

Figure 7-9. Juvenile vertebrae of *Pleurocoelus* from Utah and Maryland. A: Photograph of a dorsal vertebra from the Long Walk Quarry; scale bar=5 cm (about 2 inches). B: Dorsal vertebra of *Pleurocoelus* from the Potomac Group (early Cretaceous) of Maryland, as illustrated by Marsh, 1888, redrawn at the same scale as Figure 7-7A. Note the wrinkled upper surface of both vertebrae. The ridges on this surface interlocked with grooves in the base of the neural spine complex. In adults, this ridge-and-groove joint is solidly fused.

Figure 7-10. A spatulate tooth of an adult *Pleurocoelus* from the Long Walk Quarry. Overall length of the tooth is about 75 mm (3 inches).

and limb fragments. A juvenile specimen is known from dorsal vertebrae that have lost the unfused neural spines (Figure 7-9A) and jaw fragments with small teeth, some of which are still unerupted from the bone. Though the remains of the sauropods from the Long Walk Quarry are fragmentary, the bones are very well preserved and it is clear that they are most similar to the remains of *Pleurocoelus*, a small sauropod that was previously known from Maryland (Marsh, 1888; Lucas, 1904), Montana (Ostrom, 1970), and Texas (Gallup, 1974, 1989; Langston, 1974). Unfortunately, all *Pleurocoelus* fossils are very fragmentary and, to this day, most of that animal's skeletal anatomy is still not known. Nonetheless, the juvenile dorsal vertebrae from the Long Walk Quarry are almost identical to those from Maryland described by Marsh (1888; Figure 7-9B). The teeth of the Long Walk Quarry sauropod also are very similar to those of *Pleurocoelus* from the Cloverly Formation of Montana (Ostrom, 1970; Figure 7-10). The remainder of the sauropod material from the Long Walk Quarry appears to be consistent with *Pleurocoelus*, insofar as the anatomy of that genus is known. Eventually, when more fossils are available for study, the Long Walk Quarry sauropods may prove to be a new genus or species. In any event, *Pleurocoelus* is undoubtedly a close relative of the Long Walk Quarry sauropods, if not in fact the same animal.

On the basis of fossils found in Texas, Langston (1974) reconstructed *Pleurocoelus* as a small camarasaurid or brachiosaurid sauropod (Figure 7-11). *Pleurocoelus* of the early Cretaceous in Utah most likely had a very similar appearance and size. These sauropods were much smaller

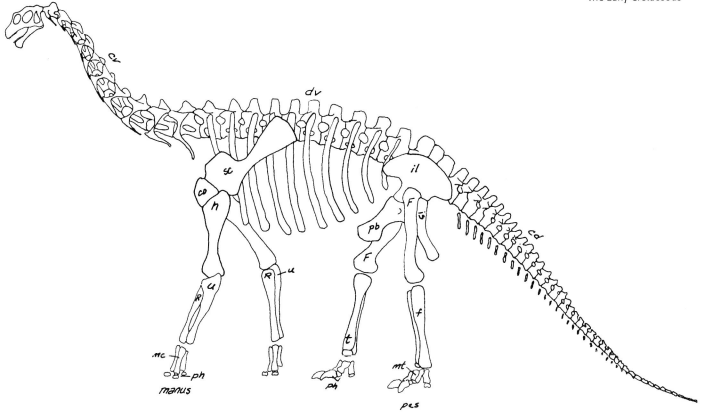

than their Jurassic predecessors; the largest individuals from the Long Walk Quarry were probably about 20 feet long. The baby sauropod may have been only about 9–12 feet long. The adults most likely weighed between 1 and 2 tons, while the baby was presumably no heavier than about 500 pounds. Thus, the sauropods from the Long Walk Quarry were not much larger than the nodosaurs that dominated the basal fauna of the Cedar Mountain Formation, but they evidently were capable of feeding on higher-growing foliage. In their general proportions, these Cedar Mountain sauropods were rather stubby animals with relatively short necks and tails and stocky bodies, much like *Camarasaurus* of the late Jurassic. In addition, the teeth of *Pleurocoelus* are spatulate (Figure 7-10), much like the teeth of the camarasaurids and brachiosaurids of the Morrison fauna. These features suggest that *Pleurocoelus* was a herbivore that browsed on relatively soft and leafy vegetation.

Since the Long Walk Quarry is the only Cedar Mountain site that produces abundant sauropod remains, it does not appear that *Pleurocoelus* (or a very similar relative) was widespread or particularly common in Utah during the early Cretaceous. The limited abundance and dispersal of sauropods in the Cedar Mountain faunas is not really very surprising, however. We might expect that the enhanced aridity of the early Cretaceous would have led to the severe restriction of forested areas that sustained the larger plants these herbivores required. It might be more than a coincidence that the sauropod bones found at the Long Walk Quarry come from a layer of sediment that was originally deposited in a body of standing water. The periphery of this small lake or pond was probably one of the few places where tree-sized plants might have been available to the hungry herbivores. We might conclude that the small sauropods stayed close to the moist and forested areas of the otherwise relatively barren

Figure 7-11. Reconstruction of *Pleurocoelus*. This 20-foot-long sauropod was much smaller than the late Jurassic giants, but was similar in form to *Camarasaurus*. The bones of *Pleurocoelus*, or a closely related sauropod, are the most common fossils found in the Long Walk Quarry. Modified from Langston, 1974.

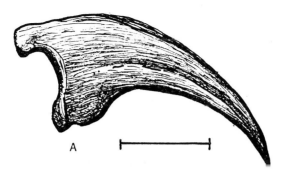

Figure 7-12. Theropod fossils of the middle fauna of the Cedar Mountain Formation. A: A claw (ungual III) from the foot of *Deinonychus*, very similar to that found in the Long Walk Quarry; scale bar=5 cm (2 inches); based on Ostrom, 1990. B: Large theropod tooth from the Long Walk Quarry as found in the limestone matrix. Black portion is the crown; shaded portion is a part of the root. Scale bar= 2 cm; total length of tooth is nearly 10 cm (4 inches).

landscape. If the sauropods were lured to the wooded fringes of such ponds for food, they would not, of course, always have enjoyed a tranquil feast. Life is never carefree for such a slow-moving and defenseless animal that comprises more than a ton of food for carnivores. The predators that lurked around the ponds of the early Cretaceous left a few fragmentary remains in the Long Walk Quarry that document the arrival of some new hunters in the Ruby Ranch Fauna.

At least two types of theropod dinosaurs are represented by the Long Walk Quarry material. A large curving foot claw demonstrates the presence of dromaeosaurs. This dromaeosaur was much smaller than *Utahraptor* but probably represents a carnivore much like *Deinonychus* from the Cloverly Formation of Montana. Until more dromaeosaur material is found at the Long Walk Quarry scientists cannot be sure about the exact identity of this theropod, but *Deinonychus* is a good guess at this point because the claw is almost identical to those of that genus (Figure 7-12A) and the Cloverly Formation is very nearly the same age as the Ruby Ranch Member of the Cedar Mountain Formation.

Even more exciting than the dromaeosaur claw was the discovery at the Long Walk Quarry of a much larger and completely different type of theropod tooth than those of the dromaeosaurs (DeCourten, 1991; Kirkland and Parrish, 1995; Figure 7-12B). These blade-like teeth are up to 10 cm (4 inches) long, with prominent serrations on the front and back edges. In general, the teeth appear be similar to those of *Allosaurus* of the late Jurassic or *Acrocanthosaurus*, known from early Cretaceous deposits in Texas and Oklahoma (Stovall and Langston, 1950). However, the two teeth thus far recovered from the Long Walk Quarry are somewhat larger than the average tooth size for either of these theropods, indicating that the dinosaurs that possessed them were probably gigantic predators. Since it is not generally possible to identify early Cretaceous theropods from the teeth alone, paleontologists can't be sure exactly what genus and species is represented by these large teeth from the Long Walk Quarry; they do know, however, that the animals were big! All of the dromaeosaurs would have been dwarfed by the multiton carnivores represented by the Long Walk Quarry teeth. As is so often the case, additional fossils are needed from the Long Walk Quarry to reveal more about these intriguing theropods.

Overall, the Ruby Ranch Fauna of the Cedar Mountain Formation appears to be a mix of small sauropods, dromaeosaurs, and large theropods (sometimes referred to as "carnosaurs"). In addition, fragmentary remains of the primitive ornithopod *Tenontosaurus* have been identified in the Ruby Ranch Member from an undocumented site along the west side of the San Rafael Swell (Weishampel and Weishampel, 1983). Nodosaurs also may have been present in the Ruby Ranch Fauna, but the remains of such animals are not very common in the sauropod-dromaeosaur-"carnosaur" assemblage that has been found in the middle portion of the Cedar Mountain Formation. The age of the Ruby Ranch Member of the Cedar Mountain Formation is estimated to be about 110–105 million years, based on its similarity to the Cloverly fauna and the generally accepted age of that formation in Wyoming and Montana. Researchers still have much to learn about all the dinosaur faunas of the Cedar Mountain Formation, but the Ruby Ranch Fauna, known essentially from one site, is perhaps the most mysterious. In the years to come, the Long Walk Quarry will almost certainly produce many new and exciting clues about this fascinating but little-known chapter in the story of Utah dinosaurs.

The Mussentuchit Fauna: The Rich Upper Assemblage

Some of the most intriguing aspects of the paleontology of the Cedar Mountain Formation

concern the fossil fauna and flora that occur in the uppermost seventy feet. These strata, the youngest of the Cedar Mountain Formation, are known as the Mussentuchit Member, named for Mussentuchit Wash south of Interstate 70 in the central San Rafael Swell (Kirkland and others, 1997). The Mussentuchit Member consists mostly of drab gray mudstone that contains abundant carbonaceous material and lacks the calcareous nodules that are so abundant in the

Photo 30. A quarry in the Mussentuchit Member of the Cedar Mountain Formation in the central San Rafael Swell. This quarry was excavated by scientists from the Oklahoma Museum of Natural History and produced a great variety of fossils. Frank DeCourten.

lower horizons of the Cedar Mountain Formation. These strata not only have yielded evidence of a unique early Cretaceous dinosaur fauna but also have shed light on some significant changes that were beginning to affect the land of eastern Utah as the first half of the Cretaceous Period drew to a close. The carbonaceous matter in the Mussentuchit Member consists mostly of small bits of carbonized wood and microscopic masses of organic residues. This material, mixed with clay and carbonate minerals in the mudstones, creates a generally darker gray color in the upper beds as compared to the pastel purples and lighter grays that typify the lower portions of the formation. Accompanying this increase in organic material is a rather sudden increase in the abundance of plant fossils of all sizes in the uppermost Cedar Mountain Formation. Studies of the pollen recovered from the Mussentuchit Member (Tschudy and others, 1984) have revealed the presence of many different types of conifers, cycads, ferns, and flowering plants (angiosperms).

The advent of the angiosperms in the early Cretaceous was a major event in the history of the terrestrial biota because these plants would soon dominate the global flora, a distinction they hold to the modern day. The highly efficient mode of reproduction used by the angiosperms, coupled with the variety of tissues each possesses, created new food sources for herbivorous animals of all types. After the early Cretaceous, plant-eating vertebrates could respond to the new nutritional resources such as fruit and flowers that only the angiosperms produce. The evolution of every group of herbivorous creatures, from the dinosaurs to the insects, was strongly affected by the development of the flowering plants.

Even though the angiosperms became established in central Utah during the time that the Mussentuchit Member of the Cedar Mountain Formation was being deposited, they were by no means the most common plants. In Utah, the fossils of coniferous trees are abundant at many outcrops of the upper Cedar Mountain beds (Thayn

and Tidwell, 1984; Thayn and others, 1983). Perhaps the most characteristic element of the Mussentuchit flora, however, was the giant fern *Tempskya* (Tidwell and Hebbert, 1976). The distinctive dark-colored and fibrous wood of this tree-sized fern is so common in the uppermost Cedar Mountain Formation that petrified fragments of it sometimes form a loose pavement that litters the surface. Near the Long Walk Quarry, many large trunks of *Tempskya* are found high in the formation, still in vertical growth position—a genuine petrified forest of giant ferns!

The dramatic increase in the abundance of plant fossils suggests that the forested areas were expanding and the vegetation was becoming more dense during late Cedar Mountain time. There are even a few thin coal seams in the Mussentuchit Member that indicate profuse vegetation (Tidwell and others, 1983). This proliferation of trees and shrubs may signify a greater supply of water and generally less arid conditions across central Utah in late Cedar Mountain time. *Tempskya* is a fern, although it is an unusually large one. Like all ferns, *Tempskya* probably required a moist and humid habitat, and its great abundance in the upper Cedar Mountain Formation is a further indication of damp environments. Such a notable shift in the patterns of climate and vegetation would be interesting by itself, but there is even more to the story.

The carbonaceous nature of the sediments in the upper Cedar Mountain Formation seem to suggest more sluggish rivers and a more stagnant drainage system. If the rivers were flowing swiftly, much of the accumulated plant litter would have been washed downstream or would have been decomposed in the well-oxygenated water of ponds fed by the streams. Studies of the ribbons of sandstone left by rivers (the "paleochannels") in the upper Cedar Mountain Formation (Harris, 1980; DeCourten, unpublished data) suggest low-gradient channels with winding patterns that are typical of sluggish streams in the modern world. At first glance, however, the deduction that there were languid rivers seems to be at odds with the other modern interpretation of wetter climatic conditions. More plentiful water should, it would seem, increase the streamflow velocity rather than reduce it. The resolution of this interesting paradox involves an oceanic event that was occurring on a global scale near the end of the early Cretaceous. There is very good geological evidence that at this time the sea level began to rise everywhere on earth. This was just the beginning of a process that would continue in even more dramatic fashion into the late Cretaceous. As the sea level rose, the ancient Gulf of Mexico crept north into central North America, while the ancestral Arctic Ocean penetrated south, submerging the lowlands of modern Manitoba and Saskatchewan. Eventually, these two encroaching arms of the sea would meet to form the Western Interior Seaway of the late Cretaceous, splitting North America into two island continents.

Near the end of early Cretaceous time, this oceanic advance, or transgression, was just beginning. One way to slow a river down is to raise its base level, the elevation of its mouth. The ultimate base level for nearly all the world's rivers is sea level. If the seas rise, then the ultimate base level rises as well. This, in turn, decreases the elevation drop between the headwaters and the mouth of any river, causing it to flow with less energy. The transgression of the early Cretaceous seas did just that; as the advancing sea crept ever closer to Utah from the east and south, the rivers began to decelerate in response to the rising base level. The encroaching sea never reached central Utah during the early Cretaceous (Figure 7-2), but it came close enough to cause a reduction in the velocity of streamflow. With less vigorous rivers, less plant litter was flushed downstream and more organic matter began to accumulate in the sediments deposited in central Utah. The proximity of the advancing ocean may also be responsible for the increased moisture that is postulated from the conspicuous increase in the abundance of plant fossils in the carbonaceous

sediments. Coastal regions are generally wetter than regions farther inland, because the air moving onshore is more heavily laden with moisture evaporated from the surface of the nearby sea. Central Utah was becoming more "coastal" near the end of early Cretaceous time as the sea advanced to the west from the interior lowland of North America.

Thus, it appears that by the time the sediments of the Mussentuchit Member were deposited, the landscape of central Utah had experienced a significant change. Water was more plentiful in the swampy lowlands, and plant growth was much more luxuriant than had been the case on the semiarid plains during the earlier stages of the Cretaceous Period. Optimal dinosaur habitats developed under these improved conditions. This verdant terrain also sustained large populations of other terrestrial and semiaquatic vertebrates. The overall vertebrate fauna of the upper Cedar Mountain Formation, known as the Mussentuchit Fauna, is a comparatively rich and diverse assemblage that includes dinosaurs, lizards, semiaquatic reptiles such as crocodiles and turtles, amphibians, and several different types of primitive mammals. Attention here will focus on the dinosaurs of the Mussentuchit Fauna, but the mammals (Figure 7-13; Cifelli, 1993; Eaton and Nelson, 1991) are also a very interesting assemblage, including the world's oldest marsupial (Cifelli, 1993). The non-dinosaur reptiles are dominated by crocodiles and turtles (Nelson and Crooks, 1987) that thrived in the numerous streams and ponds in the swampy forests. Amphibians such as salamanders were plentiful (Gardner, 1995), and, because they cannot survive or reproduce outside of moist habitats, amphibians provide further evidence of marshy conditions in the uppermost Cedar Mountain Formation. Cifelli and Nydam (1995) and Nydam (1995) have discovered a diverse assemblage of lizards, including a large active predator that was probably close to three feet long (Figure 7-14).

With so many egg-laying reptiles around, it is

Photo 31. The winding ribbon of sandstone (middle distance) in the Cedar Mountain Formation represents an ancient stream channel that was filled with sand and gravel. Such channel deposits allow geologists to reconstruct the direction, speed, and size of the early Cretaceous rivers in central Utah. Frank DeCourten.

Photo 32. A large ornithopod footprint preserved on the bottom of a sandstone layer in the Mussentuchit Member of the Cedar Mountain Formation, Long Walk Quarry. Frank DeCourten.

little wonder that many eggshell fragments also have been found in the upper Cedar Mountain Formation (Jensen, 1970). Evidently, many reptiles (and perhaps birds) nested among the dense foliage of the swampland as the sediments of the upper Cedar Mountain Formation were deposited. Some of these shell fragments may be from dinosaur nests; however, until someone finds an embryo preserved inside, scientists can only speculate about what creatures laid the eggs. And there are many good candidates in the upper Cedar Mountain fauna.

The dinosaurs of the Mussentuchit Fauna are known primarily on the basis of very fragmentary material, but some relatively well-preserved and complete material has surfaced in recent years. Though a detailed description of the upper dinosaur fauna of the Cedar Mountain Formation is not yet possible, it does appear that it is a distinct assemblage compared to the faunas preserved lower in the formation. For example, Kirkland and Burge (1994) have reported a partial skeleton of a large hadrosaur similar to the European *Telmatosaurus* from the upper Cedar Mountain Formation of the northwest San Rafael Swell. This hadrosaur had a skull nearly 28 inches long that contained many teeth a little over 2.5 cm (1 inch) long. *Telmatosaurus* is not a well-known dinosaur, but it is considered to be one of the most primitive members of the Hadrosauridae. Isolated hadrosaurid teeth are fairly common in the uppermost Cedar Mountain Formation and it is likely that several different types of primitive duck-bills populated the well-watered and marshy land of central Utah near the end of early Cretaceous time.

There also have been sketchy reports of *Tenontosaurus*, a primitive iguanodontian, in the upper Cedar Mountain Formation (Kirkland and others, 1997), but the fossil material has not been described in detail and little is known about the stratigraphic occurrence of this specimen. The presence of *Tenontosaurus* in the Mussentuchit Member is reasonable, however, given that this

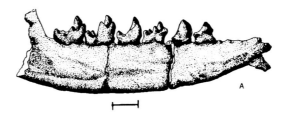
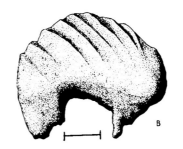
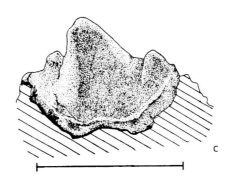

Figure 7-13. Mammal fossils from the upper Cedar Mountain Formation of Utah. A: A jaw fragment of *Kokopelia juddi*, the world's oldest marsupial, described by Cifelli, 1994; B: a multituberculate tooth, based on a photograph from Eaton and Nelson, 1991; C: a mammal tooth with three cusps reported by Nelson and Crooks, 1987. Scale bar=1 mm (1/24 inch) in all drawings.

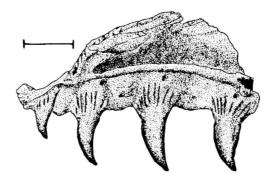

Figure 7-14. A lizard jaw from the upper Cedar Mountain Formation. This large predator was probably about 3 feet in length. From a drawing by N.J. Czaplewski in Cifelli and Nydam, 1995. Scale bar=5 mm (1/5 inch).

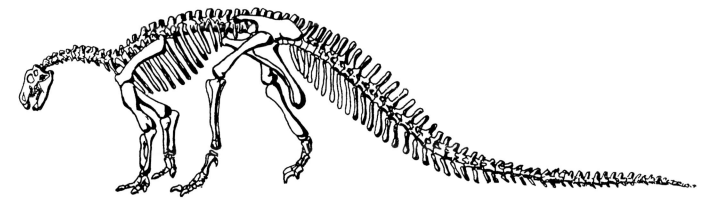

Figure 7-15. A *Tenontosaurus* skeleton, as reconstructed by Langston, 1974, on the basis of fossils found in Texas, Oklahoma, and Montana. This primitive iguanodontian ornithopod was common in western North America during the early Cretaceous and is probably present in the upper dinosaur fauna from the Cedar Mountain Formation. *Tenontosaurus* was about 20 feet long.

Figure 7-16. A large "iguanodontian" footprint from the upper Cedar Mountain Formation at a site near the Long Walk Quarry. Scale bar=5cm (2 inches).

primitive ornithopod is well known from the early Cretaceous strata of Oklahoma and Texas (Langston, 1974).

Tenontosaurus was a fairly large *Iguanodon*-like ornithopod, 15–20 feet long, with a deep and narrow skull that was nearly rectangular when viewed from the side (Figure 7-15). *Tenontosaurus* was a slow-moving browser that probably used a quadrupedal posture when feeding among the low-growing shrubs; but it could also walk or run bipedally when it was necessary. Further evidence of a *Tenontosaurus*-like ornithopod in the upper fauna comes from footprints discovered in the Mussentuchit Member near the Long Walk Quarry (Figure 7-16; DeCourten, 1991) that have been identified as "iguanodontid" tracks (Lockley and Hunt, 1995; Lockley and others, 1998). The morphology of these tracks indicates that the track maker was a large biped that had hind feet with three large toes that spread out to support a heavy body. Each of the toes appears to have been tipped with a blunt claw. This is precisely the kind of hind foot that a large iguanodontid dinosaur such as *Tenontosaurus* would have had. Despite the lack of abundant fossil data, then, it still seems likely that at least two types of ornithopods—primitive hadrosaurs and iguanodontids—are part of the Mussentuchit Fauna. In the near future new paleontological discoveries will probably provide the conclusive proof in the form of more complete skeletal material. It's only a matter of time.

Other herbivorous dinosaurs belonging to the Mussentuchit Fauna, all known from relatively fragmentary fossils, include the small nodosaurid *Pawpawsaurus*, a primitive crested hadrosaur, and a primitive ceratopsian, or horned dinosaur known only from teeth (Kirkland and others, 1997). An unknown small sauropod was also present in this fauna, but so far only a few tiny teeth from it have been found. The teeth appear to be similar to those of *Pleurocoelus* (or "*Astrodon*"), but otherwise little is known about this dinosaur. Lockley and others (1998) have recently identified the four-toed footprints known as *Tetrapodosaurus* in the Mussentuchit Member near the Long Walk Quarry. These tracks were presumably made by an ankylosaurid dinosaur, but without skeletal fossils it is impossible to identifiy the track maker with greater precision. Nonetheless, it appears that ankylosaurs or similar quadrupedal herbivores were present as part of the Mussentuchit Fauna.

The theropods of the upper Cedar Mountain fauna in Utah are not much better known than are the plant-eating dinosaurs. Like the prey animals they fed upon, their presence is indicated primarily by small teeth. Small theropod teeth have been recovered from the Rough Road Quarry (Nelson and Crooks, 1987) and from other sites near the top of the Cedar Mountain Formation (Kirkland and Parrish, 1995). However small and unimpressive these teeth may appear to be, they nonetheless provide evidence of an interesting assemblage of carnivores that appears to be unique among the Cedar Mountain faunas. Because they are known only from isolated teeth, none of the theropods of the upper Cedar Mountain fauna have yet been identified to the genus level. However, the tiny teeth that have been recovered belong to at least three different groups of theropods: dromaeosaurs, small tyrannosaurids such as the Asian form *Alectrosaurus*, and troodontids (Kirkland and Parrish, 1995).

Among these small carnivores, the presence

of dromaeosaurs is not surprising since their remains are present in all three of the Cedar Mountain faunas. Evidently, the foot-slashing mode of killing employed by the dromaeosaurs was a highly successful style of predation, one that could be directed toward a variety of prey animals throughout the early Cretaceous. The teeth of tyrannosaurids in the upper Cedar Mountain fauna probably belong to a smaller member of that family of theropods. *Alectrosaurus*, to which the tyrannosaurid teeth of the upper Cedar Mountain Formation have been compared by Kirkland and Parrish (1995), is a poorly known late Cretaceous genus. It appears to have been significantly smaller and more slender than *Tyrannosaurus*, its massive descendant from North America.

The troodontids are of interest because, as mentioned in the discussion of *Koparion* from the Morrison Formation, these small predators were probably the most intelligent of all dinosaurs. They were also swift and agile, with excellent stereoscopic vision. The teeth of troodontids are very unusual in that the denticles along the cutting edge are large with respect to the tooth size and tend to curve toward the tip. The slots between the denticles expand into circular depressions, known as blood pits, at the base. These and other features make it easy to distinguish the teeth of troodontids from those of other Cretaceous theropods. The appearance of perhaps several different troodontids in the upper Cedar Mountain fauna is characteristic. Other small theropod teeth from the Musseuntuchit Member have been referred to as *Paronychodon* and *Richardoestesia* (Kirkland and others, 1997b), but little is known about the skeletons and the overall morphology of these teeth-based genera.

Collectively, the small theropod teeth of the upper Cedar Mountain fauna suggest a diverse array of small carnivorous dinosaurs, none weighing much more than about fifty pounds, scurrying through the lush forests in pursuit of rodent-sized mammals, lizards, turtles, fish, eggs and hatchlings, and possibly birds. The hadrosaurs and probably *Tenontosaurus* ambled slowly though the undergrowth of the shadowy woodlands, grazing on the leaves of ferns, angiosperms, and other types of plants. The insects, reveling in the arrival of the angiosperms, would have buzzed through the heavy air searching for nectar among the world's earliest flowers. The swampy thickets would have visibly fluttered with the movement of so many different kinds of creatures. At least parts of central Utah probably looked, sounded, and felt a bit like the modern Everglades of Florida during the time represented by the upper Cedar Mountain Formation. The age of the upper fauna of the Cedar Mountain Formation can be estimated on the basis of the plant and animal fossils it yields, coupled with radiometric dates from volcanic ash present in one of the mammal-producing localities (Kirkland and Parrish, 1995; R. Cifelli, personal communication, 1995). The upper fauna is probably in the range of 100–90 million years, spanning the time from the late Albian to Cenomanian ages of the Cretaceous Period.

In east-central Utah, the Cedar Mountain Formation is capped by the Dakota Sandstone, a thin sequence of pebbly conglomerate, sandstone, shale, and siltstone. In most locations, the Dakota Sandstone rests on the Cedar Mountain Formation above a prominent unconformity, indicating a brief period of erosion after the deposition of the sediments that have produced the upper dinosaur fauna. The lower and middle horizons of the Dakota Sandstone have yielded the remains of small terrestrial and aquatic vertebrates, including mammals, fish, crocodiles, turtles, and dinosaurs (Eaton, 1993). The sparse dinosaur fossils from the Dakota Sandstone have not been studied in detail and little is known about the nature of the dinosaur communities they represent. Evidently, these animals lived in an environment much like that in which the uppermost Cedar Mountain sediments accumulated. The upper layers of the Dakota Sandstone, however, yield a completely

different assemblage of fossils, dominated by marine molluscs such as oysters and clams (am Ende, 1991; Eaton, 1993). From this evidence it is clear that the Dakota Sandstone records the steady incursion of the sea into south-central Utah from the east. The transgression of the Western Interior Seaway into central Utah following the deposition of the Cedar Mountain Formation submerged most of the dinosaur habitat that was formerly occupied by the creatures comprising the Cedar Mountain faunas. This mid-Cretaceous transgression is part of the Greenhorn Cycle, the earliest and greatest of several episodes of oceanic inundation that affected the Rocky Mountain region in the late Cretaceous Period (Weimer, 1983). Ultimately, the Greenhorn transgression resulted in a seaway that extended from northern Canada to the ancestral Gulf of Mexico, a distance of almost 6,000 miles (Figure 7-17). The Greenhorn seaway was about 1,000 miles wide, stretching from the foothills of the Sevier Orogenic Belt in western Utah as far east as Kansas and Iowa.

The development of the great Western Interior Seaway, initiated during the Greenhorn Cycle, ended the early Cretaceous chapter of dinosaur history in Utah by eliminating virtually all of the prime habitat these reptiles required. The dinosaurs that lived in Utah as the Greenhorn sea advanced either migrated to other areas beyond the state that were less affected by the encroachment or withdrew to higher terrain in the Sevier Orogenic Belt, where their remains were not preserved. However effective the Greenhorn transgression was in clearing Utah of dinosaurs, it was a temporary event. About 90 million years ago, in late Cretaceous time, the seas withdrew a short distance to the east, exposing a narrow strip of land between the Sevier Orogenic Belt and the receding shoreline. Eventually, dinosaurs returned to this low coastal plain. And when they did, the array of late Cretaceous dinosaurs was completely different from any of the faunas that had preceded them—yet another fascinating twist in the story of land and life in Mesozoic Utah.

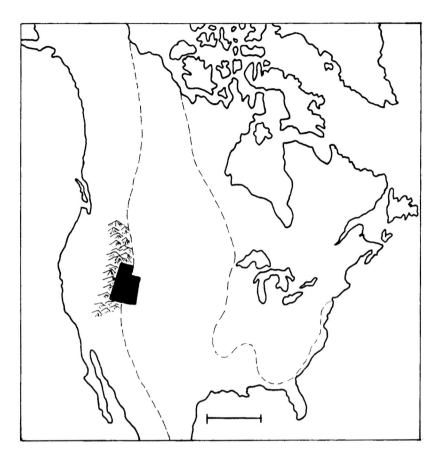

Figure 7-17. The Cretaceous Western Interior Seaway following the Greenhorn Transgression. The western margin of the seaway reached the foothills of the Sevier Orogenic Belt, submerging the lowland habitats occupied by the dinosaurs of the Cedar Mountain Formation.

Admittedly, scientific knowledge of the early Cretaceous dinosaurs of Utah is still a bit sketchy. The current wave of interest in the dinosaurs of the Cedar Mountain Formation began only about a decade ago and scientists still have much to learn from this heretofore-overlooked formation. The prospects of new discoveries from the Cedar Mountain Formation are very exciting because, in a broad sense, the early Cretaceous is an extremely important phase of dinosaur history in North America. As has been seen in Chapters 5 and 6, the late Jurassic (Morrison) fauna was dominated by sauropods, primitive ornithopods, stegosaurs, and large theropods. As shall be seen in the next chapter, the late Cretaceous fauna is characterized by highly specialized and advanced ornithopods, horned dinosaurs, small birdlike theropods, and very few sauropods.

Thus, the overall character of the dinosaur fauna of the late Cretaceous is utterly different from the assemblage of the late Jurassic. What was the pattern of faunal replacement between these two contrasting aggregations? How did it occurr? What events caused it? What was the pace and pattern of evolution and extinction among the various groups of dinosaurs during the faunal turnover? These are all compelling questions that currently have no certain answers. The Cedar Mountain Formation, along with other early Cretaceous strata in the West, may ultimately provide the keys to understanding this fascinating phase of Mesozoic history, because it was deposited at precisely the time when the great biotic shift was in progress. The overall Cedar Mountain dinosaur fauna has sauropods, but they are fewer and smaller than those known from the Morrison

Formation. It has primitive ornithopods different from those of the Morrison but less specialized and diverse than the duck-bills of the late Cretaceous. It has armored dinosaurs (the nodosaurs), but they are generally more primitive than their cousins, the highly evolved Cretaceous ankylosaurs. It has dromaeosaurs and small "carnosaurs" but scant indications of the ornithomimids or large theropods typical of the later Cretaceous.

The Cedar Mountain fauna is therefore a unique array of dinosaurs that bridges the gap between the better-known late Cretaceous and late Jurassic assemblages. Though current knowledge is limited, scientists can certainly recognize that the early Cretaceous dinosaurs of Utah are intermediate in age and character between two other great North American faunas. They were the dinosaurs that linked the late Jurassic forms to their late Cretaceous descendants. For generations, these were the "missing links" in the story of North American dinosaurs. Thanks to the efforts of paleontologists currently working in Utah, we are on the threshold of a new understanding of this mysterious and fascinating epoch. The links are not so "missing" after all. They can be found, if researchers look hard enough, in the gullies and canyons of east-central Utah, weathering out of the Cedar Mountain Formation.

UTAH STATE HIGHWAY 10, extending south from Price to Interstate 70, follows Castle Valley, a low strip of land between the eastern escarpment of the Wasatch Plateau on the west and the rolling incline of the San Rafael Swell rising to the east. The highway rises and falls gently as it passes though Huntington, Castle Dale, Ferron, Emery, and the barren lowlands that separate the towns. The land along the shoulders of the highway is a bleak expanse of gray soil, mantled here and there by a white mineral crust, that supports only a sparse cover of vegetation. Farming doesn't pay very well in Castle Valley, except where the streams falling from the mountainous plateau have washed better soil over the infertile gray dirt. The massive blue-gray shale, exposed in the low roadcuts along the highway, coupled with the lack of moisture in this desert region, are to blame for the failure of productive agriculture here. This shale is composed mostly of clay, heavily mineralized with alkaline salts. The minerals are drawn upward from the shale by water evaporating at the surface to leave the thin white crusts that fringe the gray hummocks. Some of the minerals in the shale, most notably selenium, have toxic effects on most plants and serve to enhance the sterility of the soil. Few grasses or shrubs can tolerate such a noxious soil chemistry, even if they could withstand the aridity. The clay in the "blue mud" has another interesting property: it swells whenever water is applied to it. When wet, the clay becomes impermeable and any additional water will flow over the surface rather than seeping in. As the clay expands in the rain, the gray soils of Castle Valley can become unbelievably slick. This is because the clay molecules can slide on one another with virtually no friction after they have absorbed water.

When traveling along the dirt roads of Castle Valley, it's wise to keep one eye trained on the weather. A surprise rainshower can quickly turn a dusty road to a quagmire of sticky mud. If you should become stranded in this manner in Castle Valley someday, one way to kill time while you're waiting for the mud to dry out is to crack open the hard nodules of limestone that occur more or less randomly in the shale. Chances are very good that you'll find a fossil of a late Cretaceous ammonite or a clam-like bivalve in the nodule (Figure 8-1). Such molluscan creatures were very common inhabitants of the late Cretaceous sea in Utah. Much of Castle Valley's present surface is the sediment that accumulated on its floor. These ancient sea-floor deposits are known as the Mancos Shale.

The Mancos Sea

The Mancos Shale is an extremely thick and widespread accumulation of mostly fine-grained marine sediments. In the Castle Valley region it is over 5,000 feet thick and includes many subdivisions, or members. Along the eastern escarpment of the Wasatch Plateau, the thick Mancos Shale forms a smooth slope that rises upward from the floor of Castle Valley to meet the ragged vertical cliffs hundreds of feet above. A similar slope is formed by the Mancos Shale at the base of the Book Cliffs, which extend east and south from Price. This enormous mass of late Cretaceous mud and silt extends eastward into western Colorado, where the name originated for such outcrops in the vicinity of the small town of Mancos. To the south, in the area around Bryce Canyon, similar offshore marine deposits are known as the Tropic Shale. Siltstone and shale very similar to the Mancos Shale extend north to Wyoming, where the shale is known variously as the Aspen, Mowry, and Hilliard Shale (along with other formations among these). In fact, deposits like the Mancos Shale accumulated over the entire area flooded by the Greenhorn and other oceanic transgressions of the late Cretaceous, from Canada to Mexico. All of these formations represent offshore, relatively deep-water marine environments. Collectively, they document over 20 million years of oceanic submersion in western North America.

EIGHT

The Late Cretaceous

Beasts of the Bayous

Photo 33. The Mancos Shale (lower gray slope) and the Mesaverde Group (upper cliffs) exposed along the east side of the Wasatch Plateau in the Castle Valley area. John Telford.

Because dinosaurs were strictly terrestrial animals, the Mancos Shale and the other late Cretaceous offshore marine deposits of Utah have not produced any dinosaur fossils. However, in addition to the abundant invertebrate fossils they contain, these sea-floor sediments occasionally yield the remains of sharks, fish, and marine reptiles. Among the fossils of marine reptiles, those of the plesiosaurs are the most abundant in the Mancos Shale and its equivalents in western North America. The plesiosaurs were large (up to 50 feet long) sea-going reptiles with paddle-like appendages and serpentine necks. The legendary Loch Ness monster, though it is almost certainly a completely mythical beast, was inspired by the plesiosaurs, the real sea monsters of the Mesozoic. Plesiosaur remains have been found in the open marine deposits of the Mancos Shale and its equivalents across western North America, including Wyoming, Colorado, and New Mexico (Breithaupt, 1985; Wells, 1952; Lucas and others, 1988).

In the Utah region, relatively short-necked plesiosaurs, known as pliosaurs, are known from fragmentary remains found occasionally in the Mancos Shale (Carter, 1991) and in the Tropic Shale of southern Utah (D. Gillette, personal communication, 1996). The pliosaurs (Figure 8-2) were excellent swimmers, with a compact and streamlined body, primarily propelled by a powerful tail. The limbs of pliosaurs were modified into fin-like appendages that helped to stabilize them in water and allowed some maneuverability as they pursued prey. The narrow jaws were lined with many sharp, conical teeth. The pliosaurs probably preyed primarily on fish and ammonites (a type of cephalopod and ancestor of modern squids and octopi), both of which were abundant in the Mancos sea.

In addition to the plesiosaurs, the Late Cretaceous seas of North America also contained turtles, sharks, huge marine lizards known as mosasaurs, and crocodilians (Nichols and Russell, 1990). Locally, shark teeth and fish fossils can sometimes be found in Utah exposures of the Mancos and related sediments (see, for example, Stewart and others, 1994), but otherwise the remains of the these vertebrates are not very common in the state. The preservation of marine vertebrates seems for some reason to have been

Plate 17.
Ichthyornis
feeding along the
beach of the late
Cretaceous
Mancos Sea.

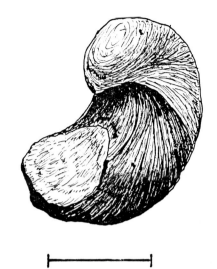

Figure 8-1. *Pyconodonte newberryi*, an oyster-like bivalve (top), and *Scaphites* (below), an ammonite from the Mancos Shale of Utah. These fossil molluscs are typical of the invertebrates that lived in the open marine environment of central Utah during the late Cretaceous. Scale bar=25 mm (1 inch).

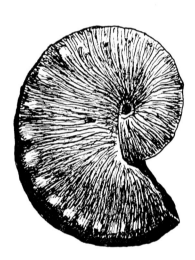

ern Utah during the late Cretaceous was probably muddy and turbid, as tiny silt grains suspended in the water sank very slowly toward the bottom. Perhaps the mosasaurs, fish, and turtles whose fossil remains are much more abundant to the east preferred the shallow, clear water that existed in that part of the seaway. Because the sea covered millions of square miles and had an enormous north-south reach, there also might have been climatic factors that controlled the distribution of vertebrates in the Western Interior Seaway. Major north-south zones of vertebrates in the marine basin were suggested by Nicholls and Russell (1990), and there might have been many smaller faunal provinces that influenced the geographic distribution of organisms on a smaller scale. Finally, it is likely that the shallow water of the Mancos Seaway in Utah might have been slightly fresher (lower in salinity) than was the water farther offshore. This is due to the high rate of freshwater runoff from the elevated mountainous terrain immediately west of the central Utah shoreline. The inflow of fresh water may have reduced the salinity to the point that the populations of fish and other food organisms on which the marine reptiles depended were minimal. All of these factors may have combined to limit the abundance of large sea-going reptiles in the portion of the Western Interior Seaway that extended into Utah. There is good geological and paleontological evidence that the environmental conditions such as turbidity, temperature, and salinity in this large seaway were anything but uniform (Kauffman, 1977). Thus, on the basis of the sparse fossils, scientists can conclude that marine reptiles occasionally swam through the seas of central Utah, but they did so less often and in smaller numbers than elsewhere in the Western Interior Seaway.

Even though the fossil assemblage from the Mancos Shale is dominated by marine creatures, occasionally the remains of terrestrial animals are encountered. Such fossils provide some clues about the life that populated the shore of the

more likely farther to the east, in the Colorado and Kansas area. Late Cretaceous marine sediments in that region have produced many spectacular vertebrate fossils. Since most of these marine vertebrates were active swimmers, and because there was no physical barrier to their movement in the Western Interior Seaway, the scarcity of their fossils in Utah probably reflects preservational factors or perhaps ecological preferences. Due to the proximity of the western edge of the great inland sea to the mountainous Sevier Orogenic Belt, the influx of sediment was much greater in the Utah portion of the seaway than it was farther offshore. The water that covered east-

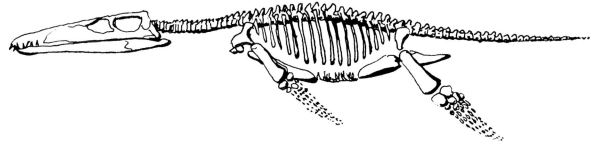

Mancos sea. We know that seabirds inhabited the edges of the Mancos sea, but they were different from the avian fauna of today. Lucas and Sullivan (1982) discovered the partial remains of *Ichthyornis* in the Mancos Shale of northwestern New Mexico, not far from Utah. *Ichthyornis* was a small bird, only about 8 inches high, and appears to have been a strong flier by virtue of its expanded sternum, L-shaped ribs, and modified fingers (Figure 8-3). In these features, *Ichthyornis* closely resembles the modern gulls and terns that are capable of flying great distances over land and water in coastal regions. Unlike its avian descendants, however, *Ichthyornis* had many small and sharply pointed teeth lining its elongated jaws. Because the remains of *Ichthyornis* in the West are found in marine deposits (the best specimens occurring in Kansas), it is regarded as a seabird that inhabited the margins of the Western Interior Seaway, feeding on fish and other marine organisms that it captured on flights over the water. Other birds known from the strata that accumulated in this seaway include *Hesperornis*, a large loon-like diving bird, and *Baptornis*, its smaller relative.

While most of what we know about the birds of the Mancos sea is based on fossils found in the center or eastern parts of the basin, it is plausible to imagine that the Utah shores were populated by great numbers of shorebirds. If we could have strolled along the beaches of central Utah in the late Cretaceous, we probably would have noticed great flocks of reptile-like birds soaring overhead

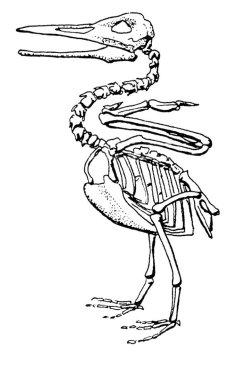

Figure 8-2. *Liopleurodon,* a pliosaur (short-necked plesiosaur) from the Jurassic of Europe. This well-known pliosaur is probably similar to the types of plesiosaurs that lived in the shallow coastal waters of the Mancos Sea in Utah during the late Cretaceous Period. The Mancos pliosaurs were large creatures, generally about 20–35 feet long. Skeletal reconstruction based on Padian, 1989.

Figure 8-3. *Ichthyornis,* a tern-like shorebird known from the Mancos Shale. Scale bar=75 mm (about 3 inches).

and bobbing in the surf. Occasionally, a pterosaur might have drifted by. Pterosaur remains are plentiful in the ooze deposited in Kansas at the same time that parts of the Mancos Shale were laid down. Though no well-preserved pterosaur fossils are known from the Mancos Shale, at least some of them probably lived along the western fringe of the seaway. The "bird"-watching would have been great in late Cretaceous Utah, but the flying creatures would have had a distinctly reptilian look.

Photo 34. The Mancos Shale, exposed in this butte near Hanksville consists primarily of soft, fine-grained sediments that accumulated as mud on the shallow sea floor. John Telford.

Very rarely, the Mancos Shale affords a glimpse of the larger creatures that lived along the coastal plain near the shore. Sandy sediments deposited along the shore of the seaway sometimes bear large trackways that could only have been made by a large terrestrial animal. The Ferron Sandstone Member of the Mancos Shale is one such track-bearing unit. In western Colorado, amazingly complete remains of a hadrosaur have been found in deposits like those that often produce ammonite and bivalve fossils (Wolny and others, 1990). The hadrosaurs ("duck-bills"), as will be seen later in this chapter, were highly specialized bipedal dinosaurs that were extremely successful almost everywhere in North America during the late Cretaceous. The hadrosaur discovered in the Mancos Shale of western Colorado appears to be most similar to *Kritosaurus*, a duck-bill with a prominent bump on its nose formed by the expansion of the nasal chamber. There almost certainly was more than a single species of hadrosaur along the edges of the Mancos sea in

the Utah region, since the low coastal plain was covered by dense jungles that could have supported many such herbivores. Their remains, however, are usually preserved in the sediment deposited on the adjacent coastal plain, not in muck that accumulated on the floor of the open ocean. The Colorado fossil probably represents a rare event in which a hadrosaur carcass was washed out to sea, eventually sinking to the bottom to become buried under Mancos mud. Such events would have been uncommon because the river that flushed this carcass offshore would normally accelerate its destruction by rolling and tumbling the decaying corpse. Even if the body, or a part of it, reached the sea, the sharks, predaceous fish, plesiosaurs, and mosasaurs inhabiting the Mancos Sea were voracious carnivores. It normally would not have taken these meat eaters long to find the remains and consume them. That the Mancos Shale yields so few dinosaur remains simply means that the chances of transporting intact remains from land, and avoiding the destruc-

Photo 35. A dinosaur trackway in the Ferron Sandstone Member of the Mancos Shale near Moore, Emery County. The trackway is exposed on the bottom of a large block that has fallen from the cliffs in the distance. The tracks were made by an unknown dinosaur walking along the edge of the Mancos Seaway. John Telford.

tive scavenging by marine carnivores, was virtually nil. It does not mean, as we shall soon see, that there were few dinosaurs ashore!

The Mountains Tremble: The Main Phase of the Sevier Orogeny

As the waters of the Mancos sea lapped quietly against the shore in central Utah, the mountains rising to the west were rumbling with intensified geological activity. It was in the late Cretaceous that the main phase of the Sevier Orogeny occurred, and this event brought dramatic changes to the mountainous terrain of western Utah and eastern Nevada. The effects of the Sevier Orogeny are well displayed in a north-south-trending belt that extends from the Mojave Desert region of southeastern California, through southeastern Nevada and western Utah, all the way to the area around Yellowstone National Park in Wyoming. Throughout this region, known as the Sevier Orogenic Belt, the earth's crust was intensely deformed several times during the late Cretaceous Period as compressive forces crumpled and splintered rocks of pre-Cretaceous age. This great geological disturbance was named for the Sevier Desert of Utah, where its effects are particularly striking (Armstrong, 1968). Elsewhere along the belt in Utah, tortured rock strata that yielded to the powerful geological forces of the Sevier Orogeny are exposed in the Wasatch Mountains (Bruhn and others, 1983; Yonkee, 1992), northwestern Utah (Jordan, 1981), central Utah (Lawton, 1985), and in the Bear River Range–Crawford

Mountains region in the extreme northeastern corner of the state (Royse and others, 1975).

All along the Sevier Orogenic Belt, pre-Cretaceous rocks were subjected to extreme compression during the late Cretaceous. As mentioned earlier, the deformation probably began on a much smaller scale as early as late Jurassic time. In the late Cretaceous, however, great folds formed in the rock strata as the squeezing compressional forces became amplified. The folds piled higher and higher upon one another, much like a small rug would behave if you slid it across a slick floor, jamming it against a wall. The "backstop" for the east-sliding slabs of rock was evidently the ancient edge of thick continental crust, mostly Precambrian in age, that runs almost north-south through central Utah (Pilcha, 1986). At times, the compressive forces also produced enormous low-angle fractures that allowed slabs of rock to move over each other like playing cards in a deck. These nearly horizontal fractures, referred to as thrust faults (or thrusts), further complicate the already bewildering pattern of folding seen in the rocks affected by the Sevier Orogeny. The thrusts originated several miles below the surface in western Utah and eastern Nevada; but, as the slabs above them were driven to the east, they eventually met the crustal buttress in central Utah. Here, along the north-south trend of the present-day Wasatch Mountains, the slabs of contorted rock piled up like shingles on a roof. As the great thrust sheets were forced over each other, and as the rocks in each slab were bent and crumpled, the land surface rose higher and higher. In time, a majestic mountain range developed in central Utah, with peaks reaching elevations from 15,000 to 20,000 feet and slopes that extended from Emery County to eastern Nevada. This was the Sevier Orogenic Belt at its grandest stage.

The source of the compression that created the Sevier Orogeny was the convergence of tectonic plates along the western edge of North America, which was actually situated in present-day central California during the late Cretaceous. As the North American Plate was forced to the west over sinking oceanic plates, the force of the resulting compression was transmitted inland, where it wrought the geological havoc so obvious in the pre-Cretaceous rocks of central Utah. But the deformation in the Sevier Orogenic Belt was not a continuous process throughout the late Cretaceous. At least four pulses of deformation affected the crust of western and central Utah from about 90 million years ago to about 60 million years ago (DeCelles and Mitra, 1995). These episodes of deformation in the Sevier belt may have been the consequence of periodic changes in the rate of convergence of the plates, the thickness of the plates, the angle of convergence, and the friction between the subducting oceanic plates and the overriding North American Plate. Scientists do know that the subduction along the western edge of North America during the Mesozoic Era was not a continuous and uniform process; instead, it occurred in several spurts and cycles (Ward, 1995). The rise of the Sevier Orogenic Belt in western Utah was clearly a sequential event. A period of rapid uplift through folding and faulting would elevate the land for a few million years. Then a period of quiescence would follow. Later, the compressive forces again were intensified and earthquakes would shake the region once more as the mountains heaved skyward. During the brief lulls (in geologic time) between the stages of active uplift, erosion would reduce the elevation of the Sevier mountains slightly as sediment was shed into the lower terrain to the east. However, whatever elevation was lost during the erosional interludes would be reclaimed as soon as the powerful compressional forces returned to lift the peaks to even loftier heights. When the Sevier Orogeny finally ended in the eastern Great Basin region, near the close of the Cretaceous Period, the earth's crust had been shortened by about sixty miles through the combination of the folding and thrusting. An immense amount of rock had been transported from the west to form the ragged peaks of Utah's most magnificent Mesozoic mountain system.

The Sevier Foreland Basin: Home of Utah's Late Cretaceous Dinosaurs

The Sevier Orogenic Belt is a classic example of a fold-thrust belt, the type of mountain system that evolves whenever the compressive forces generated by plate convergence are sufficiently powerful and long-lived. The uplift of the Sevier belt in the late Cretaceous steepened the gradient of rivers draining the elevated land and initiated vigorous erosion of the rising land. Even though the Sevier system rose faster than it was being worn down, a prodigious amount of sediment was shed from its surfaces during each pulse of uplift. The sediment was washed through the rugged canyons and flushed out onto the lower land adjacent to the mountain front. In the low ground of south-central Utah immediately east of the Sevier Orogenic Belt, thick layers of sand, gravel, and mud piled up. The low area adjacent to a developing fold-thrust belt that receives the erosional refuse from it is known as the foreland basin. The Sevier foreland basin was an elongated trough that extended in a southwest-northeast direction through central Utah parallel to, and just east of, the mountain system to which it was linked. During each pulse of uplift in the Sevier belt, a flood of debris spread out to the east, forcing the Western Interior (Mancos) Seaway back toward Colorado. The wedge-shaped masses of sediment that were deposited in response to the episodic uplift gradually built up a gently sloping coastal plain between the peaks to the west and the open sea to the east (Figure 8-4).

As each pulse of folding and thrusting in the Sevier Orogenic Belt lifted the mountains higher, additional sediment was shed into the foreland basin, adding weight to the surface of coastal lowlands. In response to the increased sediment load produced by the combination of uplift and erosion in the Sevier Orogenic Belt, the western edge of the foreland basin in Utah would periodically subside as the earth's crust sank under the weight of the additional geological litter. Farther east of the Sevier belt, in the middle of the Western Interior Seaway, there was less subsidence in the foreland basin because there was less loading of the earth's crust through deformation and sediment accumulation. As the western edge of the foreland basin subsided, eventually the sea crept back to the west over the sinking land, sometimes reaching as far as the foothills of the Sevier range. For at least the last 30 million years of the Cretaceous Period, this back-and-forth battle between land

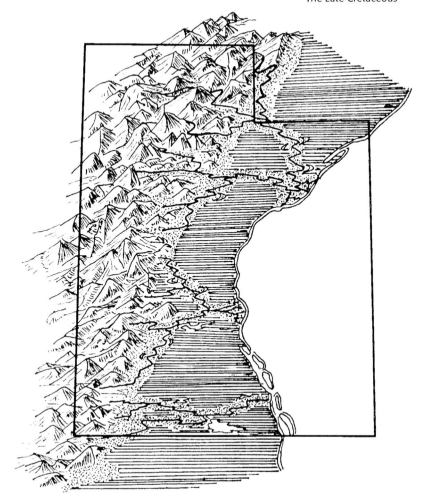

Figure 8-4. Late Cretaceous paleogeography of Utah. Dinosaurs lived primarily in central Utah on the low coastal plain that separated the mountainous Sevier Orogenic Belt to the west from the open seaway to the east.

Photo 36. Late Cretaceous synorogenic conglomerate in Emigration Canyon near Salt Lake City. These layers of conglomerate originated as part of a broad alluvial apron sloping from the Sevier Orogenic Belt to the east. The rock layers were tilted to their nearly vertical position by later mountain-building events.
Frank DeCourten.

and sea persisted. Several eastward withdrawals (or regressions) of the Western Interior Seaway were followed by westward advances (or transgressions). The regressions were linked to the cycles of uplift, while the transgressions peaked at times of geological tranquillity in the Sevier Orogenic Belt.

The coastal plain, that strip of nearly flat land between the rugged slopes of the Sevier belt and the open ocean, varied in width in rhythm with the cycles of transgression and regression. At times of peak regression (following a pulse of uplift), it was several hundred miles wide. During transgressions, much of the coastal plain was submerged by the advancing sea; in some places, at certain times, it may have been as narrow as only a few miles. Thus, the late Cretaceous coastal plain of central Utah was constantly changing. It was alternately buried by sediment from the west and submerged under the sea invading from the east. The record of these events is a thick and complex sequence of late Cretaceous sediments that accumulated along the western edge of the foreland basin (Figure 8-5). Each period of uplift in the mountains generated a great pile of gravelly rubble that was transported by streams down the eastern slopes of the Sevier belt. These gravelly deposits are known as synorogenic conglomerates because their deposition is linked to episodes of mountain building (technically known as an orogeny) to the west. Farther east, these coarse sediments grade into thinner tongues of finer-grained sandstone and mudstone deposited by rivers on the coastal plains. Along the western edge of the Western Interior (Mancos) Seaway, shoreline deposits included beach sand, deltaic mud and coal, and lagoonal silt. The sediments near shore extended as thin fingers to the east, where they eventually pinched out into thick accumulations of open marine deposits such as the Mancos Shale. The late Cretaceous sediments that accumulated in the Sevier foreland basin are thickest nearest their source and thin dramatically toward the east. In central Utah, just east of the

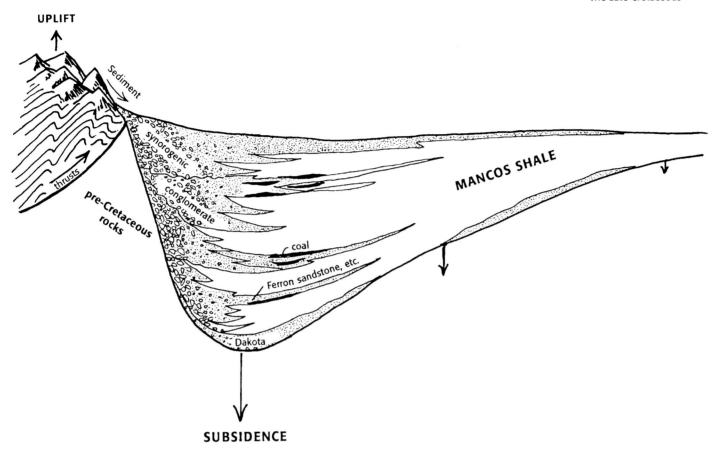

UPLIFT

Sediment

synorogenic conglomerate

pre-Cretaceous rocks

thrusts

coal

Ferron sandstone, etc.

Dakota

MANCOS SHALE

SUBSIDENCE

Sevier Orogenic Belt, the aggregate thickness of these sediments can exceed 18,000 feet. In Kansas, in the middle of the Western Interior Seaway, where subsidence was much less and the sediment source more distant, the late Cretaceous sediments are usually only around 1,000 feet thick. The thick late Cretaceous rock record of central Utah is also extremely heterogeneous and complex due to the active uplift in the nearby Sevier Orogenic Belt and the advancing-and-retreating oscillations of the Mancos seaway. Marine deposits, such as the Mancos Shale, interfinger with non-marine sediments in a complicated pattern that has taken geologists decades to unscramble.

In spite of its continual modulation, the coastal plain was an excellent habitat for dinosaurs. The high Sevier Orogenic Belt was a superb watershed, and the moisture it provided supported a lush jungle of trees and shrubs on the

coastal plain. The climate appears to have been warm and humid, due in part to the proximity of the sea. There was probably a year-round growing season, ensuring a stable supply of food to sustain the terrestrial ecosystem. Central Utah was a warm, lush, and flourishing garden during the late Cretaceous, a virtual paradise for a great variety of aquatic and terrestrial vertebrates, including dinosaurs. The abundant life on the coastal plain, especially when coupled with the extremely high rate of sediment accumulation, should have left us a rich fossil record of the dinosaurs that must have thrived in this environment. Surprisingly, however, though many dinosaur fossils have been found in the late Cretaceous rocks of south-central Utah, the fossils are not particularly abundant, well preserved, or complete. Only a few different types of dinosaurs are known from the rocks of the late Cretaceous coastal plain, and

Figure 8-5. Late Cretaceous sediments of the Sevier Foreland Basin. The cycles of transgression and regression, linked to the uplift of the Sevier belt and the subsidence of the basin, produced a complex interfingering of marine and nonmarine deposits. The late Cretaceous strata are thickest closest to the Sevier Orogenic Belt and thin noticeably to the east, where the foreland basin was subject to much less subsidence.

WASATCH PLATEAU-BOOK CLIFFS

KAIPAROWITS PLATEAU

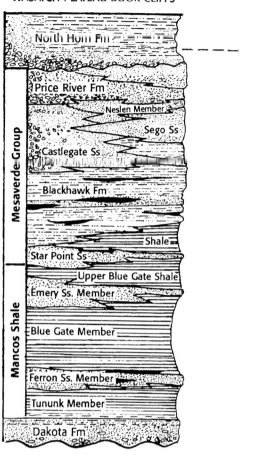

Figure 8-6. Late Cretaceous sedimentary rocks of central Utah (right) and southwestern Utah (left). The Tropic and Mancos formations represent the maximum stage of the earliest transgression of the Western Interior Seaway into Utah. Coastal plain sediments that contain dinosaur remains comprise portions of the Mesaverde Group (central Utah) and the Wahweap-Kaiparowits interval (southwestern Utah). The Mesozoic-Cenozoic boundary occurs within the North Horn and Caanan Peak formations.

most of those have been identified from very fragmentary fossil material. This relatively meager fossil record of Late Cretaceous dinosaurs in Utah is even more intriguing in light of the great abundance of dinosaurs in sediments of the same age in Alberta, Montana, Wyoming, and New Mexico.

One reason for the comparative scarcity of late Cretaceous dinosaur fossils in Utah may be that the narrow coastal plain, and consequently the dinosaur habitat it sustained, was generally too limited in size to support large populations of huge creatures. Another explanation may be that perhaps the ecological instability resulting from the repetitive transgression-regression cycles on the Utah coastal plain made it difficult for large vertebrates to gain a permanent foothold in this setting. In Montana and Alberta, the late Cretaceous environment was very similar to that of central Utah, but the coastal plains were much more expansive and less subject to the numerous cycles of marine inundation.

Late Cretaceous sediments accumulated on the coastal plain portion of the foreland basin everywhere east of the Sevier Orogenic Belt. However, there are two sequences of rock in Utah that have produced most of the fossils that document the dinosaur fauna of the time. In central Utah, the strata that rest above the Mancos Shale are known collectively as the Mesaverde Group. This package of rock layers is thick—up to 3,000 feet or more in some places—and is subdivided into several different formations. The principal formations of the Mesaverde Group in the area around Price are, in ascending order, the Blackhawk,

Castlegate, and Price River formations (Figure 8-6). Farther east, in the Book Cliffs northeast of Green River, the Mesaverde Group consists of as many as ten different rock units, including the Sunnyside Sandstone, the Sego Sandstone, and the Neslen Formation, among others. The sediments of the heterogeneous Mesaverde Group in central Utah were derived from the Sevier Orogenic Belt and deposited in a variety of nonmarine and marginal marine environments such as floodplains, braided stream systems, deltas, swamps, river channels, and tidal basins (Yoshida and others, 1996; Van Wagoner, 1995).

Farther south, in the Kaiparowits Plateau region between Lake Powell and Bryce Canyon, sediments of approximately the same age and type as the Mesaverde Group comprise the Straight Cliffs, Wahweap, and Kaiparowits formations (Figure 8-6). In these southern equivalents of the Mesaverde Group, the sediments originated from the southern portion of the Sevier Orogenic Belt and also from the Mogollon highlands to the south, in central Arizona. The Kaiparowits sequence is over 6,000 feet thick and consists mostly of river-deposited sediment, with less common deltaic, lagoonal, and offshore sand and mud deposits (Eaton, 1991).

Both the Mesaverde Group and the Kaiparowits sequence contain coal deposits that formed in swampy environments near the western shore of the late Cretaceous seaway. Carbon County is the heartland of Utah's coal industry, and in this area the chief deposits of coal are in the Blackhawk Formation, a deltaic formation within the Mesaverde Group. Coal is also found in central Utah in the Ferron Sandstone, an older deltaic wedge that extends into the Mancos Shale. In the Kaiparowits region, the coal occurs primarily in the Straight Cliffs Formation, though it is also present in the older Dakota Formation. The coal of the Kaiparowits Plateau region has not been mined as extensively as have the Mesaverde deposits of central Utah, but several mining ventures have been proposed for that area that target

the billions of tons of coal buried beneath the surface.

Coal is the result of the accumulation of plant debris—leaves, twigs, bark, etc.—in a stagnant body of water. Containing little oxygen, and with an acidic chemistry resulting from the generation of humic acids by the decaying vegetation, swamp water could be considered Mother Nature's pickling solution. The complete decomposition of the plant litter that falls into a swamp is prevented by the biologically hostile chemical environment. The layer of plant matter on the bottom of a swamp gets thicker and thicker with time. Eventually, these organic residues become buried under sand and mud when, for example, a nearby stream floods or shifts its course. Underground, the buried plant debris can become compressed and altered over millions of years into hard, black, combustible coal. The formation of coal thus requires three conditions: 1) abundant vegetation, 2) standing bodies of stagnant water on a poorly drained, nearly flat surface, and 3) eventual burial under additional layers of sediment. All three of these conditions existed on the narrow coastal plain in central Utah during the late Cretaceous, as indicated by the abundance of thick coal layers in the Mesaverde Group and the Kaiparowits sequence. In the modern world, we find similar conditions along the coast of Louisiana and Mississippi, where the climate is warm, where the vegetation is thick and jungle-like, and where the swampy land lies close to the ocean (Gulf of Mexico). The swamps and bayous of the modern Mississippi delta are probably very good modern analogues for the types of environments that must have existed on the narrow coastal plain of central Utah during the late Cretaceous Period. Plant fossils indicate that a lush forest of sequoia-like trees, magnolias, cypress trees, and palms rose above a floor carpeted with ferns and sphagnum moss on the ancient coastal plain of Utah (Nichols, 1995). The jungles that thrived on the swampland running through central Utah were populated by a rich fauna of verte-

Photo 37. A coal mine in late Cretaceous strata near Helper, Carbon County. The mine portals in the lower part of the photograph are in the gray, coal-bearing beds of the Blackhawk Formation. The massive cliffs along the skyline are exposures of the Castlegate Sandstone. John Telford.

brates including birds, turtles, fish, primitive mammals, and, of course, dinosaurs.

The presence of coal, an important fossil fuel, has promoted the intense study of Utah's late Cretaceous rock sequences by geologists (for example, Doelling, 1972, 1975; Olsen and others, 1995; Peterson, 1969; Franczyk and Pitman, 1989). Recent studies (Olsen and others, 1995; Nichols, 1995; Eaton, 1991) have placed the age of both the Mesaverde Group and the Kaiparowits sequence in the range of 90–75 million years. This corresponds to the Turonian through Campanian ages of the Cretaceous Period. In the course of some of these investigations, and sometimes during coalmining operations, people have come upon interesting fossils that provide information on the communities of dinosaurs that lived in the swampy areas on the coastal plain. Though the fossil material recovered thus far is not as abundant or complete as scientists might wish, it still provides an adequate basis for a glimpse at the dinosaurs that moved within the coal swamps—the beasts of the bayous.

Dinosaurs of the Mesaverde Group

Dinosaur bones are extremely uncommon in the formations of the Mesaverde Group. The Castlegate Sandstone produces an occasional scrap of bone along with mostly isolated footprints and fossil wood (Yoshida and others, 1996). However, dinosaur footprints are sometimes remarkably abundant in the sandstones that are associated with layers of coal in the Blackhawk Formation of the Mesaverde Group. Many footprints have been recovered from the working coal mines in Carbon and Emery counties, where they are most commonly encountered on the bottoms of sandstone layers that buried the coal. After the coal is removed, the lower surface of the rock layer above is exposed as the ceiling of the mine. The overhead surface can be decorated with hundreds of footprints that hang precariously from the ceiling. There are several accounts of coal miners being

injured by footprints that broke away from the ceiling and fell to the floor of the mine. Lockley and Hunt (1995) have documented hazards posed to coal miners from dinosaur footprints, including a 1969 fatality in western Colorado that resulted from injuries sustained when a miner struck his head on an overhead track. If the stories are true, then perhaps we can consider such injuries to be rare cases of human-dinosaur interaction. Even though the dinosaurs and the human miners are separated by at least 75 million years of time, the activity of the dinosaur was undeniably linked to the human injuries. Dinosaurs smashing people is a popular theme in science fiction, but it evidently has actually happened, albeit in a greatly delayed manner, in the coal mines.

People commonly refer to the objects on a coal mine ceiling as footprints; but, in fact, they are not footprints. In most cases, the actual footprint was impressed into the organic matter (peat) and mud on the bottom of the ancient swamps. This depression was later filled with sand or mud deposited by rivers that flowed into the bog. Eventually, the track-filling sediment hardened into the layer of sandstone or mudstone that rests above the coal (Figure 8-8). The "footprints" from Utah's coal mines are actually the inverted replicas, or casts, of the original footprints made in the underlying coal. In any case, the footprint cast can provide information on the gross foot morphology of its maker. In addition, when numerous footprints are preserved as a trackway on a coal mine ceiling, they record the movement of dinosaurs as they waded through the swamp. Through the analysis of these footprint casts, paleontologists can formulate some idea of the kinds of dinosaurs and other creatures that lived in the swamps and their relative abundance. In addition, some generalizations can be made about the behavior and locomotion of some of the dinosaurs in the swamp on the basis of the footprint evidence.

The most common trackways and individual footprints from the Mesaverde Group are those

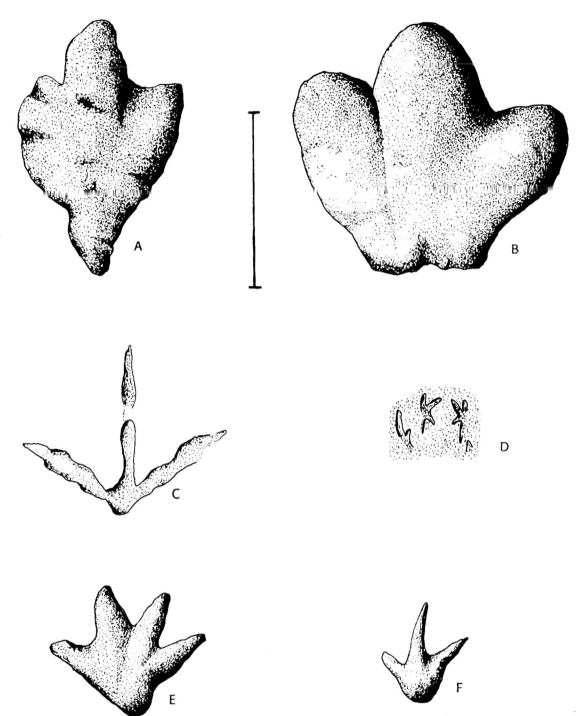

Figure 8-7. Dinosaur and other tracks from the Blackhawk Formation (Mesaverde Group) of central Utah. A and B: Large three-toed hadrosaur tracks. Scale bar = 0.5 m (20 inches); C: a bird track, about 8 cm (3 inches) long; D: tiny frog tracks, each a little less than 20 mm (1 inch) long; E: four-toed track probably made by a ceratopsian dinosaur, 40 cm (16 inches) long; F: a small theropod track with sharp claw impressions, about 28 cm (11 inches) long. A, D, E, and F based on photographs in Parker and Balsley, 1989; B and C after Lockley and Hunt, 1995.

evidently made by bipedal hadrosaurian dinosaurs that had a three-toed foot with blunt,
hoof-like claws (Figure 8-7A,B; Lockley and
Hunt, 1995; Parker and Rowley, 1989). The tracks
are most numerous in the coal-rich Blackhawk
Formation but are known from other horizons in
the Mesaverde Group as well. These presumed
hadrosaur tracks range in size from tiny prints,
less than an inch long, to gigantic tracks nearly
three feet in length. The larger hadrosaur tracks
signify the presence of some very large herbivores—they must have been made by an animal
that weighed more than ten tons! The large feet of
the hadrosaurs, with their three broad and widely
splayed toes, were well suited for supporting such
massive animals on the soft, spongy bottom of the
coal swamps. Nonetheless, these herbivores still
sank into the peat and mud as much as two feet as
they walked along, leaving the deep prints in
which the casting sediment later accumulated. In
some places, the density of hadrosaurian tracks in
the Mesaverde sediments is so great as to suggest
the movement of groups of dinosaur herbivores
through the swamps (Parker and Balsley, 1986;
Lockley and Hunt, 1995). Among the larger
hadrosaur footprints from Utah coal mines, tiny
tracks less than three inches long and commonly
oriented in a particular direction are also known
(Carpenter, 1992).

These observations suggest that herds of
hadrosaurs consisting of both juveniles and adults
were moving about the swampy lowland, possibly
migrating north and south, parallel to the late
Cretaceous shoreline (Carpenter, 1992). The
stride length of individual prints in the trackways
does not indicate rapid running but instead im-
plies a somewhat lazy saunter through the boggy
ponds. Some of these trackways veer around the
petrified remains of tree stumps and occasionally
reveal pauses or "resting stops" in the form of side-
by-side hind-foot prints that are unusually deep
(Parker and Balsley, 1986). Scientists infer from
this evidence that the hadrosaurs that left the coal
mine trackways were moving slowly together in

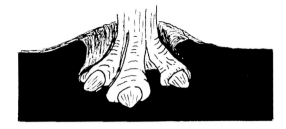

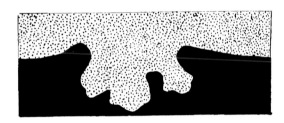

Figure 8-8. Formation of dinosaur tracks in the coal
swamps of the Mesaverde Group, central Utah. Foot
impressions were initially made in the peat and mud
of swamps (top). After the foot was withdrawn, a cavity remained open in the sticky sediment for a time
(upper middle). As streams flooded or shifted course,
sand and mud was washed into the pond, filling the
footprint (lower middle). The footprint casts are exposed millions of years later on the roofs of mines
when the coal beneath them is removed (bottom).

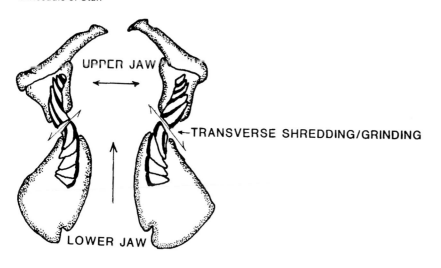

UPPER JAW

←TRANSVERSE SHREDDING/GRINDING

LOWER JAW

Figure 8-9. Cross-sectional view of hadrosaur teeth and jaws. The dental battery of the hadrosaurs consisted of hundreds of teeth that formed a grinding pavement in the mouth. The upper jaws could slide outward over the lower teeth to grind and mash plant material held in the large cheek pouches.

herds of perhaps several dozen individuals. Trampling through the swamps, they periodically paused to browse on the dense vegetation that must have been growing all around them.

Another clue to the identity of these track-making hadrosaurs was discovered recently in the form of skin impressions associated with fragmentary skeletal remains preserved in the Neslen Formation of the Mesaverde Group (Anderson and others, 1995). The skin of the hadrosaur was covered by tiny tubercles, or bumps, around 2.5 mm (.1 inch) in diameter, with larger rounded tubercles, up to about 13 mm (.5 inch) in size, located on the dorsal surface. Thus, the skin appears to have had a bumpy, beaded texture distinct from the folded, leathery skins of modern mammals such as hippos that live in rivers and ponds.

The identity of the large Mesaverde hadrosaurs has not yet been established with certainty, but they were probably similar to *Kritosaurus* (Figure 8-9) or *Gryposaurus*, which occur in strata of about the same age in Montana, New Mexico, and western Canada (Weishampel and Horner, 1990). However, neither of those hadrosaurs are commonly as large as the animals indicated by the biggest tracks from the Mesaverde Group of central Utah. More complete skeletal material will be required before paleontologists can be sure which hadrosaurs left the tracks pre-

served in the coal-swamp sediments of Utah. Unfortunately, well-preserved and complete skeletal fossils are very rare in the Mesaverde Group. However, as we have seen, remains of a hadrosaur very similar to *Kritosaurus* have been found in the Mancos Shale (Wolny and others, 1990), so scientists know that dinosaurs like it lived around the edges of the Western Interior Seaway. It is therefore likely that *Kritosaurus*, or hadrosaurs similar to it, left most of the footprints found in the coal mines of central Utah.

The hadrosaurs (family Hadrosauridae, or duck-bills) were derived from older and less specialized ornithopods such as *Camptosaurus* and *Iguanodon* of the late Jurassic Period. The hadrosaurs were extraordinarily successful and have left perhaps the best fossil record of any group of dinosaurs. Hadrosaur remains are incredibly abundant in late Cretaceous strata all over the world. Unlike their more primitive ancestors, the hadrosaurs had a highly specialized dentition that probably evolved in response to the increasing dominance and diversification of angiosperms in the global flora of the Cretaceous Period. All hadrosaurs had a broad, expanded, and toothless snout, the basis of their common name. Behind their "bills," the jaws contained hundreds of teeth arranged in side-by-side rows that formed very effective grinding surfaces. Each long, curving tooth in the dental arsenal had a layer of hard enamel on one side that created many small ridges on the grinding surface. As hadrosaurs chewed their plant food, the upper jaws could slide outward over the grinding surfaces formed by the lower rows of teeth (Figure 8-9). Deep cheek pockets allowed the hadrosaurs to hold a large mass of vegetation in their mouths as it was being pulverized. This motion, coupled with the unique arrangement of teeth, gave hadrosaurs the ability to turn virtually any plant material into a highly digestible pulp. In the heavily forested swamplands of the late Cretaceous in central Utah, the success of such efficient herbivores is certainly no mystery.

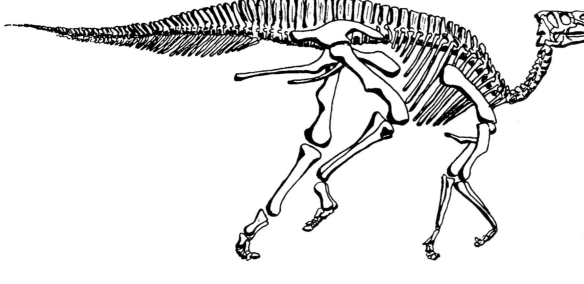

Figure 8-10. The skeleton of *Kritosaurus*, as reconstructed by Weishampel and Horner, 1990. This dinosaur is very similar to, or perhaps even the same as, the hadrosaurs that populated the late Cretaceous coal swamps of Utah. The average adult length of *Kritosaurus* was between 25 and 30 feet. On the basis of the footprints known from the Blackhawk Formation, some of the late Cretaceous hadrosaurs in Utah may have been considerably larger.

The family Hadrosauridae is divided into two subfamilies: the relatively primitive, flatheaded Hadrosaurinae and the more advanced Lambeosaurinae, all of which possessed some type of ornate bony crest on the skull along with other skeletal specializations. *Kritosaurus* (Figure 8-10) lacks any cranial decorations and therefore belongs to the Hadrosaurinae. *Kritosaurus* and other hadrosaurines had a broad, vertically flattened tail that might have assisted their movement through swamps and ponds. Though the forelimbs of the hadrosaurines were much smaller than the hind limbs, the "fingers" bore small hoof-like claws that indicate their use in locomotion and imply at least occasional quadrupedal movement. Such hadrosaurs often have been portrayed as semi-aquatic dinosaurs that spent most of their time in water, feeding on soft aquatic plants. This image might be a bit exaggerated, because the hadrosaurs were fully capable of processing tough non-aquatic vegetation as food and could move about effectively on dry land using a combination of bipedal and quadrupedal movement. The *Kritosaurus*-like hadrosaurs of the Utah coal swamps probably wandered continuously through the damp jungles in small groups, feeding as they went, walking over the spongy forest floor and wading or swimming though the bayous.

In addition to the numerous hadrosaur tracks, the Mesaverde sediments of central Utah have produced less-abundant footprints that reveal the presence of many other types of vertebrates in the late Cretaceous coal swamps. Birds lived among trees in the dense jungles, while frogs thrived in the ponds and peat bogs (Figure 8-7C,D; Robison, 1991). Rarely, four-toed impressions are found (Figure 8-7E), and these probably were made by quadrupedal, horned ceratopsian dinosaurs. Some of the smaller three-toed dinosaur tracks have very narrow toe impressions that end in sharp tips (Figure 8-7F). These were almost certainly made by small theropods that stalked the hadrosaur herds and other prey animals through the swamps. For years, a very large theropod print could be observed in the Blackhawk Formation near the dam at Joe's Valley Reservoir (Figure 8-11). This print was deeply impressed, indicating a relatively large animal, and had very narrow ridges made by the three sharp claws as they were pulled from the mud and peat. Sadly, this print disappeared in the early 1990s and its current whereabouts is unknown. It does suggest that there were some very large theropods in the swamps.

An intriguing twist in the story of the dinosaurs of the Mesaverde Group came in late

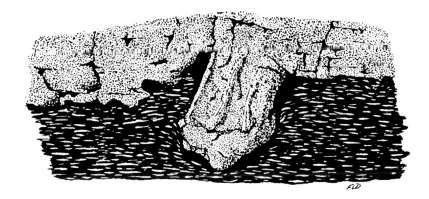

Figure 8-11. Sketch of a large theropod footprint from the Blackhawk Formation near Joe's Valley Reservoir, Utah. Note the sharp ridges on the footprint cast that correspond to grooves made by the sharp claws as they were pulled out of the mud and peat (black) surrounding the preserved print. This print is about 35 cm (14 inches) deep.

1994 when Scott Woodward of Brigham Young University and two colleagues reported the extraction of DNA from bone fragments found in the Blackhawk Formation (Woodward and others, 1994). The bone fragments came from a track-bearing layer of sandstone exposed on the roof of a coal mine after the coal below had been mined. The identification of the bone fragments as dinosaurian was based solely on their association with the track-bearing sediments of the Blackhawk Formation. The biochemical sequences on the small bit of DNA (nine segments of the code for one gene) did not seem to match any of the patterns known for humans, bacteria, birds, reptiles, or mammals. Woodward's discovery was highly publicized, at least in part because of the popular fascination over the possibility of regenerating extinct creatures from ancient DNA as hypothesized in the movie *Jurassic Park.* Among paleontologists, the report of dinosaur DNA received a cool reception. Some questioned the identification of the bone as dinosaurian; others were concerned with the possible chemical alteration of the original bone tissues and with the potential contamination of the fossil material with modern DNA. The latter are legitimate con-

cerns because the bone fragments were preserved in a geological environment that could have easily modified the original tissues and organic compounds and because the amount of DNA was so small and fragmentary that contamination would have been very difficult to avoid. About a year after Woodward's original report, other scientists concluded that the DNA was probably of human origin (Hedges and Schweitzer, 1995). The contamination of the fossil bone probably occurred during the handling of the original samples, as they were collected and prepared for analysis. Though this "discovery" of dinosaur DNA is no longer considered valid, it is nevertheless significant in that it represents a step forward in the application of powerful new analytical techniques to the study of dinosaur fossils. This type of research may be the wave of the future, and it may eventually reveal important new vistas to researchers. Only time will tell. We can be confident that Utah specimens will be important in the endless quest for new knowledge.

Because it is known primarily on the basis of footprints, skin impressions, and a few scraps of bone, the dinosaur fauna of the Mesaverde Group is still not understood in very great detail. It is clear, however, that the narrow coastal plain of central Utah was populated by a diverse array of dinosaurs, including huge hadrosaurs, ceratopsians, small theropods, and at least a few very large carnivores. Skeletal remains of this assemblage were not often preserved in coal swamps, and, when they were, the quality of preservation is usually very poor. This might be because of the destructive effects that acidic bog water has on bone tissues. The paucity of skeletal remains in the coal swamps might also be due to the effectiveness of scavengers in dismembering and destroying the remains of animals that died in the swampy environment. Luckily, south of the main coal swamp region of central Utah, in the area around the modern Kaiparowits Plateau, paleontologists find more abundant and better-preserved fossils of dinosaurs that lived on the coastal plain east of the Sevier Orogenic Belt. In that region, the strip of low land separating the mountains from the sea in the late Cretaceous was a little wider, and the chances were better for good fossilization of bone from terrestrial vertebrates. It is from the these deposits that scientists can add some details to the story of late Cretaceous dinosaurs in Utah.

Dinosaurs of the Straight Cliffs–Wahweap-Kaiparowits Sequence

In southern Utah, strata approximately equivalent in age to the Mesaverde Group of central Utah comprise the Straight Cliffs, Wahweap, and Kaiparowits formations. Though they have not been formally united as a group, here, for convenience, we will refer to these strata as the Kaiparowits sequence, after the Kaiparowits Plateau. The Kaiparowits sequence consists of sandstone, mudstone, shale, and coal that were deposited by rivers in swamps and lagoons and along the shore of the Western Interior Seaway. During most of the late Cretaceous, the coastal plain was relatively wide in southern Utah, and the dinosaurs and other terrestrial creatures had more prime habitat to occupy than was the case in central Utah. All three of the formations in the Kaiparowits sequence have produced the remains of dinosaurs. Overall, this dinosaur fauna is better known than is that of the Mesaverde Group, is comparatively rich and diverse, and is accompanied by the remains of many other vertebrates.

The Straight Cliffs Formation has yielded the fossils of turtles, crocodilians, dinosaurs, and mammals, along with marine invertebrates in the portions of the formation that were deposited in estuaries, lagoons, and bays near the coast (Eaton, 1991). Plant fossils of gymnosperms, ferns, mosses, and angiosperms are also common, especially microscopic grains of pollen (Nichols, 1995). The small, primitive mammals of the Straight Cliffs Formation have been extensively studied (Eaton and Cifelli, 1988; Eaton, 1995; Cifelli, 1990a) because their tiny fossils are relatively abundant; elsewhere in the world, mammal remains of the same age are very rare. The mammal fauna includes many varieties of small, rat- or rodent-like creatures, including symmetrodonts, multituberculates, and marsupials (Cifelli, 1990a; Eaton, 1995). There most likely were hordes of these mammals living in the mossy forests and beneath the fern thickets of the wide coastal plains. The dinosaur remains from the Straight Cliffs Formation have not been as intensely studied and are very fragmentary, consisting mainly of small, isolated teeth. Even from this meager data, however, it has been established that hadrosaurs and small theropods were present in southern Utah and were accompanied by the armored ankylosaurs (Parrish, 1991).

A similar assemblage of dinosaurs (hadrosaurs-theropods-ankylosaurs) also occurs in the Wahweap Formation of the Kaiparowits sequence (Parrish, 1991), but knowledge of it is limited by the isolated and fragmentary nature of the fossils. The dinosaurs of the Wahweap Formation were part of a rich vertebrate assemblage that included turtles, fish, mammals, and crocodilians (Eaton, 1991; Cifelli and Madsen, 1986). The Wahweap Formation was deposited by rivers draining eastward from the Sevier Orogenic Belt toward the Western Interior Sea across the broad coastal plain (Eaton and Cifelli, 1988). Sediment was deposited on floodplains, in stream channels, in sandbars, and in natural levees. The well-watered plain must have supported large populations of dinosaurs, but more fossil material is needed before scientists can form a more complete conception of the Wahweap fauna.

Dinosaur fossils are more abundant in the Kaiparowits Formation than in any other component of the Kaiparowits sequence. Nearly everything scientists know about the late Cretaceous dinosaurs of southern Utah is based on the study of fossils excavated from these strata. The Kaiparowits Formation is up to 2,800 feet thick and consists mostly of gray mudstone and weakly

Photo 38. The Straight Cliffs of south-central Utah. These cliffs, in the new Escalante–Grand Staircase National Monument, expose the late Cretaceous Straight Cliffs and Wahweap formations. Frank DeCourten.

Photo 39. A dinosaur excavation in the Kaiparowits Formation near Henrieville, Garfield County.
Frank DeCourten.

cemented, fine-grained sandstone. These deposits accumulated on the floodplains of the broad coastal plains and, to a lesser degree, on the boggy surfaces of deltas near the shoreline of the seaway. Where they are exposed, soft sediments of the Kaiparowits Formation weather into blue-gray badlands that are a fossil hunter's paradise. In the area known as "The Blues," along Utah Highway 12 between Tropic and Escalante, many well-preserved dinosaur fossils have been collected. In addition, the remains of turtles, crocodiles, primitive mammals, and many kinds of plants occur in the Kaiparowits Formation, sometimes in great abundance (Gregory and Moore, 1931; Gregory, 1951; Lohrengel, 1969, Cifelli, 1990b; Eaton, 1991). These fossils, particularly the mammals, have been used to establish the probable age of the Kaiparowits Formation as late Campanian, or about 75 million years (Eaton, 1991).

⑥ *PARASAUROLOPHUS*

Judging from the abundance of their fossils, hadrosaurs were the most common dinosaur herbivores of the Kaiparowits fauna. However, their fossil remains are usually rather fragmentary, consisting mostly of single bones, short vertebral series, skull fragments, and (rarely) a few articulated bones. There doubtless were many different genera comprising the hadrosaur fauna of the Kaiparowits Formation; however, thus far, *Parasaurolophus* is the only genus that has been clearly documented by diagnostic fossil material (Weishampel and Jensen, 1979). The remains of *Parasaurolophus* thus far collected from the Kaiparowits Formation are very scrappy, consisting of a few pieces of skulls, a few vertebrae, rib fragments, and other isolated material such as teeth. Fortunately, the skull elements reported by Weishampel and Jensen (1979) included a portion of the very distinctive crest that adorned the head of *Parasaurolophus* (Figure 8-12) and its relatives in the Lambeosaurinae, a group of specialized duck-bills with elaborate cranial ornamentation.

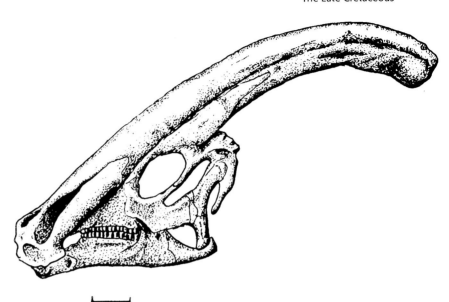

The lambeosaurs are considered to have been more specialized duck-bills than were the hadrosaurines. Their fossil remains are generally larger than those of their hadrosaur relatives, have more robust limbs, bear tall neural spines on the dorsal and caudal vertebrae, and possess a highly modified complex of nasal and facial bones that forms the large, hollow crests on their heads. *Parasaurolophus* was a large animal, up to about 35 feet long as an adult. It was also heavily built, with massive shoulders and pelvic girdle. The forelimbs were smaller than the hind limbs, but only modestly so, and the hands were tipped with blunt, hoof-like claws. These observations suggest that *Parasaurolophus* was a basic quadruped but could easily rear up on its hind legs as well. Like other hadrosaurs, the stiff tail of *Parasaurolophus* was flattened from side to side and seems well suited for propelling the animal through water. *Parasaurolophus* was an masterful plant eater, with elaborate batteries of teeth anchored to massive jaws that were powered by huge jaw muscles. The toothless bill of *Parasaurolophus* was expanded, but it was not quite as wide and duck-like as in the non-crested hadrosaurs.

The tubular bony crest on the skull of *Parasaurolophus* is its most peculiar characteristic

Figure 8-12. Skull of *Parasaurolophus*. The long snorkel-like crest was formed from the premaxillary and nasal bones that extended far behind the head. The post-cranial skeleton of *Parasaurolophus* was similar to, but more robust than, that of *Kritosaurus* (Figure 8-10). Scale bar=10 cm (4 inches). After Weishampel and Horner, 1991.

(Figure 8-12). This crest was formed from the grossly modified premaxillary and nasal bones that extend backward, projecting over the top of the head by as much as three feet. In addition, these bones are curved into a tubular form that surrounds a spacious nasal cavity inside. The function of the odd crests on the skulls of *Parasaurolophus* and other lambeosaurs has been a subject of great discussion among paleontologists for many years. These crests have been interpreted as defensive weapons, humidifiers, foliage deflectors, and accessory breathing devices for underwater feeding. For a variety of good reasons, none of these ideas for the primary function of the crests are currently favored by the majority of paleontologists. Instead, the crests are now generally regarded to have served primarily for communication between individual lambeosaurs in a group. The crest of *Parasaurolophus* was probably used for both visual and auditory signaling (Weishampel, 1981; Hopson, 1975). Because the size and shape of the crest in various types of lambeosaurs are unique to the species, its form would allow these dinosaurs to recognize members of their own genus and species. A stray *Parasaurolophus* could easily have distinguished the graceful, snorkel-crest of its own kind from, for example, the circular plate that decorated the heads of *Corythosaurus*, a lambeosaur relative. Within a group of *Parasaurolophus* individuals, communication might also have included sounds that were generated within the hollow tubes of their crests. Weishampel (1981) has shown that the hollow tubes in the crest formed a pathway for air brought in, and exhaled out, through the nose. By shunting air into different portions of the tubes, and controlling the rate of airflow, *Parasaurolophus* could have generated deep bellows and resonating calls. A trombone works on the same principle to create a variety of sounds. Perhaps different sounds were used to signal danger, to attract mates, to announce feeding opportunities, and to communicate with juveniles in a herd.

The sensible interpretation of the snorkel-crest of *Parasaurolophus* as a communication device fosters some interesting ideas about the appearance, sensory capabilities, and behavior of these dinosaurs. Such communicative capabilities only would have been useful in a group that remained within sight and sound of each other most of the time. This suggests strong herding behavior in *Parasaurolophus*. While the evidence for such clustering is weak in the remains excavated from the Kaiparowits Formation, fossils of other single hadrosaur genera do occur in great concentrations in Montana and in Mongolia (Weishampel and Horner, 1990). The hadrosaur bone beds in these areas suggest herds that consisted of many (perhaps hundreds of) adults and juveniles of the same genus and species. In all probability, *Parasaurolophus* also was a social animal, moving about in small groups or herds. If communication by means of sight and sound were important keys to survival for *Parasaurolophus*, then we could well assume that they had keen vision and good hearing. The relatively large eyes and the elaborate ear structure observed in well-preserved skulls of *Parasaurolophus* suggest that these duckbills could see and hear better than could many other dinosaurs. In addition, there is significant variation in the size and shape of the crests. In fact, these differences have been used to distinguish three species of *Parasaurolophus* in North America: *P. walkeri*, the standard genus, first known from Canada; *P. cyrtocristatus*, a species with a short and more strongly curved crest from New Mexico; and *P. tubicen*, a larger New Mexico form with a long, straight crest (Lucas, 1993; Weishampel and Horner, 1990).

It is doubtful, however, that there really were three different species of *Parasaurolophus* in North America during the late Cretaceous. Instead, these three "species" may likely represent males and females of the same species, probably *P. walkeri*. It would probably have been easy to distinguish males from females in a herd of

Parasaurolophus on the basis of the inferred sexual dimorphism of their crests: the longer crests probably signified males, while the shorter, bowed crests indicated females. If the development of the crest was a secondary sexual trait, then the juveniles probably had very small crests that developed variously, depending on gender, as the animals grew to maturity (Dodson, 1975).

What about color? If we accept the notion that the males and females could recognize each other by the size and shape of their crests, then it seems plausible that the tissues covering the crests may have been brilliantly colored, at least during the mating season when the males were competing for mates. Perhaps, as in the case of birds, there might have been mating rituals and displays that included the calls generated in the crests. Imagine the sights and sounds we might have witnessed during the *Parasaurolophus* mating season on the Kaiparowits coastal plain of Utah: bellowing males with crests ablaze with color cavorting through the herd, sparring with their two-ton competitors, and staging a grand spectacle for the sake of procreation.

In addition to *Parasaurolophus*, there were probably several other dinosaur herbivores in the Kaiparowits fauna. Fragmentary remains of ceratopsians, the horned quadrupeds with a bony frill extending behind the skull, are actually fairly common in the Kaiparowits Formation. Unfortunately, these ceratopsian fossils are far too fragmented to allow any firm identification of the genera and species they represent. As pointed out earlier, there were also other hadrosaurs in the Kaiparowits fauna. They might have been as abundant as *Parasaurolophus* in the late Cretaceous, but paleontologists cannot say much more about them until better fossils are found. Evidently, nodosaurs were also present, but nothing more about them has been determined since their isolated scutes were first reported by Gregory (1951) over forty years ago. The armored dinosaurs of the Kaiparowits Formation also in-

cluded several types of ankylosaurs (Parrish, 1991), but none have yet been identified to the genus level. Scientists still have a great deal to learn from the Kaiparowits Formation about this hadrosaur-dominated community of dinosaur herbivores.

ᛦ ORNITHOMIMUS

The remains of dinosaur predators are relatively rare in the Kaiparowits Formation. Only a few isolated theropod teeth, foot and tail bones, and vertebrae were known from these deposits prior to the mid-1980s (Gregory, 1951). The first, and currently the only, Kaiparowits theropod identified to the genus and species level was reported in 1985, when a nearly compete hind limb, partial pelvis, and many caudal vertebrae of *Ornithomimus velox* were discovered (DeCourten and Russell, 1985). *Ornithomimus* is the namesake genus for the family Ornithomimidae, a remarkably birdlike group of small theropods. The ornithomimids were small to medium-sized dinosaurs, with long slender legs, a lightly built skeleton, and a graceful neck that supported a small skull (Figure 8-13). In their general proportions, the ornithomimids bore an extraordinary resemblance to the modern ratite birds, such as ostriches, emus, and rheas. The snout of *Ornithomimus* was formed by a toothless beak, with sharp edges of bone where the teeth would normally be found.

The absence of teeth in *Ornithomimus*, coupled with the flexibility of the beak, has led some paleontologists to conclude that it was probably a omnivore, rather than a strict predator as might be implied by its classification as a theropod. This is a reasonable interpretation, because *Ornithomimus* also had well-developed forelimbs and a hand that could grasp and manipulate small objects. It had large eyes and, relative to its size, a very large brain. Furthermore, the elongated feet, ankles, and limbs of *Ornithomimus* were designed

Plate 18. *Parasaurolophus* in the dense Kaiparowits forests, with *Avisaurus* perched on tree limbs in the background.

Plate 19. *Ornithomimus* in the Kaiparowits jungles pursuing a rat-like ptilodontid multituberculate.

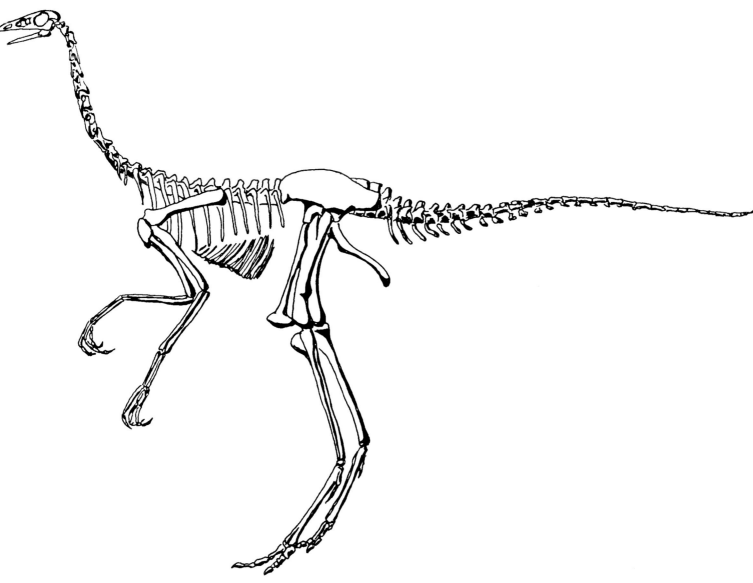

Figure 8-13. Skeleton of an ornithomimid dinosaur, patterned after *Struthiomimus* ("ostrich mimicker") from the late Cretaceous of western Canada. *Ornithomimus* from the Kaiparowits Formation was similar in size and appearence to this 10 to 12-foot-long ornithomimid.

for speed and mobility (Figure 8-14). This all suggests that *Ornithomimus* was a swift, stealthy animal that could exploit many different sources of food. The Kaiparowits ecosystem would have afforded a varied menu to a quick-moving, crafty omnivore like *Ornithomimus*. Lizards, insects, primitive mammals, the fruit of angiosperms, carrion, turtles, fish, and perhaps even the eggs and juveniles of dinosaurs may all have been included in the diet of these versatile creatures. Conversely, it is difficult to imagine *Ornithomimus*, only about 10 feet long and weighing

some 200 pounds, overpowering a large living prey animal such as a hadrosaur or ceratopsian dinosaur.

The ornithomimids were incredibly successful in the late Cretaceous. Their remains have been found throughout North America and much of Asia in sediments of roughly the same age as the Kaiparowits Formation of Utah. Closer to Utah, *Ornithomimus* is known from the late Cretaceous in New Mexico (Lucas, 1993), Colorado (DeCourten and Russell, 1985), Wyoming (Estes, 1964), and Canada (Russell, 1972). These little theropods were probably more numerous in Utah than their scant fossils might at first suggest. They seem to have been perfectly adapted for their role as an opportunistic omnivore and probably thrived on the coastal plains and in the bayous of central Utah. However, if we could have taken a safari to southern Utah during the late Cretaceous, we might not have seen *Ornithomimus* at all. It was probably a timid and secretive animal, perhaps even nocturnal, that would have detected us long before we noticed it. A muted screech and the rustle of foliage might have been our only hint of its presence in the jungles around us.

Other theropods in the Kaiparowits fauna are known only from very sparse, fragmentary, and isolated fossils; but *Ornithomimus* appears to have had some company. The remains of dromaeosaurs, troodontids, and carnosaurian theropods have been identified in the Kaiparowits fauna (Parrish, 1991). The dromaeosaurs were probably small descendants of early Cretaceous forms such as *Deinonychus* and *Utahraptor*. The troodontids were probably similar to the Canadian form *Troodon*, a small, swift, and brainy little predator. North American carnosaurs of the late Cretaceous included some fearsome predators such as *Albertosaurus* and *Tyrannosaurus*. Whether or not these genera lived in southern Utah during the late Cretaceous is still unclear, but something similar to them was probably terrorizing the herbivores on the Kaiparowits coastal plain. As is the case of the dinosaur herbivores, thus far scientists have only scratched the surface of what is proabably a rich theropod assemblage in the Kaiparowits Formation.

Ⓖ *AVISAURUS*: BIRD OR DINOSAUR?

In 1985, a portion of a small birdlike theropod foot found in the late Cretaceous sediments of Montana was named *Avisaurus archibaldi*, and a new family was proposed to accommodate the new genus (Brett-Surman and Paul, 1985). The specimen is only about 7.5 cm (3 inches) long

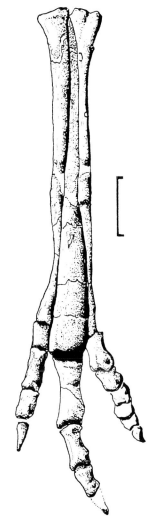

Figure 8-14. Foot of *Ornithomimus velox* from the Kaiparowits Formation of Utah. The metatarsals of the middle foot are highly elongated, similar to those of ostriches, giving this small theropod a long stride.

Figure 8-15. Middle Foot of *Avisaurus*. A more complete specimen of this creature from the Kaiparowits Formation demonstrates that it was a medium-sized bird, not a dinosaur. Scale bar=2.5 cm (1 inch). After Brett-Surman and Paul, 1985.

and consists of three metatarsals (middle foot bones), fused together toward the proximal (upper) end (Figure 8-15). This fossil exhibits several features that are unusual in late Cretaceous theropods, including a middle metatarsal (III) that is not concealed or pinched between the other two, a prominent bump on the second metatarsal, and a very thin fourth metatarsal. These features are similar to those commonly seen in some (but not all) bird fossils from the late Cretaceous. As is often the case when such limited fossil material is used to establish a new genus (not to mention a whole new family), paleontologists have vigorously debated the nature and validity of the *Avisaurus* classification. Is it a bird, a dinosaur, or something in between? If it is a dinosaur, then how is it related to other theropods? What were its habits? What ecological niche did it fill?

The *Avisaurus* controversy came to Utah in 1993 when a much more complete specimen was described from the Kaiparowits Formation (Hutchison, 1993). The Kaiparowits specimen was disarticulated and incomplete, but enough of it was recovered to determine that *Avisaurus* had a deep keel on its sternum, a well-developed furcula ("wishbone"), specialized hands with wing-supporting fingers tipped with sharp claws, and caudal vertebrae compressed into a birdlike structure known as a pygostyle (Hutchison, 1993). The Kaiparowits specimen clearly demonstrates that *Avisaurus* is a bird, probably related to the land birds known as the enantiornithines that flourished on several different continents during the late Cretaceous.

Avisaurus was a good flier, but it evidently lacked the endurance of modern birds. It probably spent a great deal of time on the ground or perching in trees, flying only when necessary to escape predators or to catch prey. Scientists assume that *Avisaurus* was a predator; however, it may have been a scavenging bird similar to a vulture, or an omnivore, like a raven. Unfortunately,

no one knows what the skull of *Avisaurus* was like since this part of the skeleton has never been found. Someday the rocks of the Kaiparowits Formation may yield additional fossils that will allow paleontologists to better understand this interesting bird. One thing, however, is certain: the forested floodplains and bayous of southern Utah were garnished with feathers in the late Cretaceous.

In summary, the late Cretaceous dinosaur fauna of Utah represents a unique array of animals that included hadrosaurs, ceratopsians, ankylosaurs, ornithomimids, and birds. Collectively, this dinosaur assemblage is much different from the nodosaur-sauropod-dromaeosaur-carnosaur community that preceded it in the early Cretaceous. The distinction between the early Cretaceous and late Cretaceous dinosaur faunas is probably a reflection of at least two factors: the shift to more swampy conditions in the late Cretaceous as the Western Interior Seaway encroached from the east, and the progressive evolution within the various dinosaur (and bird) lineages. The late Cretaceous dinosaurs were accompanied by lizards, turtles, fish, insects, and many primitive mammals. The coastal plain and swamplands supported a jungle of lush vegetation that thrived in the warm tropical climate.

About 70 million years ago, during the terminal age of the Cretaceous Period known as the Maastrichtian, renewed geological activity in the Sevier Orogenic Belt, coupled with new disturbances farther east, began to affect the landscapes of central and eastern Utah. Ultimately, the uplift that began at this time led to the complete withdrawal, or regression, of the Western Interior Seaway from Utah. The sea drained away into Colorado and Wyoming, and the coastal environment—the broad floodplains, the swamps, the lagoons, the bays, and the bayous—vanished with it. The rising land in and near Utah induced climatic changes that were superimposed upon the land even as the geological remodeling was in progress. As it always has, life responded to these changes. New plant communities developed in response to the changing conditions, and new types of animals appeared to replace those that either migrated or became extinct. Thus, a new chapter in the story of Utah dinosaurs began in Maastrichtian, or latest Cretaceous, time. It was, however, unlike any of the preceding episodes in this remarkable pageant of Mesozoic life: it was the final act of a 140-million-year natural drama. At the end of Maastrichtian time, the dinosaurs disappeared…completely and forever.

NINE

The Curtain Falls

Dinosaurs of the North Horn Formation

THE FINAL SLIVER of Mesozoic time, the last gasp of the dinosaurs, is known as the Maastrichtian Age of the Cretaceous Period. The Maastrichtian (sometimes also spelled "Maestrichtian") began approximately 74 million years ago and ended about 65 million years ago. The end of the Maastrichtian Age coincides with the closing of the last period of the Mesozoic Era, the Cretaceous, and the beginning of the first period of the Cenozoic Era, the Tertiary. The transition from Mesozoic to Cenozoic time is commonly known as the K-T interval, named for the periods of geological time (K = Cretaceous; T = Tertiary) that embrace it. Once the Maastrichtian Age of the Cretaceous Period was over, the dinosaurs vanished completely. No dinosaur fossils, except for some scraps probably eroded from earlier deposits, have ever been found in sediments of early Tertiary age. Because the age represents the last episode in such a grand story of vertebrate evolution, Maastrichtian deposits have been intensely studied on a global scale. Wherever the K-T boundary is recorded in the rock record, geologists and paleontologists have swarmed like a pack of hungry raptors, searching for clues to the mystery of the extinction of the dinosaurs and the events that occurred during their final days. From Italy to Denmark, from Spain to Montana, from New Mexico to Antarctica, and even from the deep ocean floor, scientists have scrutinized deposits at the K-T transition in great detail. Collectively, these scientists have documented the shifts in the fossil fauna and flora, analyzed the changes in sediment type and chemistry, and established the timing of the great transition with uncommon, if not perfect, precision.

The K-T interval is, without doubt, one of the most ardently studied phases in the 4.6-billion-year history of our planet. Despite this, there is still no universally accepted explanation for what caused the end of the era of dinosaurs. To be sure, there is no shortage of hypotheses concerning the extinction of the dinosaurs, but the data from the K-T interval, despite its prodigious vol-

ume, are still not sufficient to "prove" any one of them to the satisfaction of all scientists. We will return to the issue of dinosaur extinction later in this chapter, but first let us examine the K-T sediments in Utah and get acquainted with the last dinosaurs to live in the state.

The K-T Boundary in Utah

Unlike the case with some of the earlier phases of dinosaur history, Utah localities have not provided a wealth of information on the K-T transition. There is a good reason for this: during the Maastrichtian Age, most of the Utah landscape was in the midst of geological changes that did not favor either the continuous deposition of sediment or the preservation of dinosaur fossils. By the beginning of Maastrichtian time, the great Western Interior Seaway had regressed far to the east and north. The former coastal lowlands of central Utah were now far inland from the shrinking seaway, which had withdrawn to eastern Montana and adjacent regions. The great swamps dried out as water drained toward the distant, receding sea. Much of the lush vegetation that cloaked the former coastal plain withered, and the great era of coal deposition in Utah came to an end. As the swamps and bayous declined, the prime dinosaur habitat diminished as well. In the absence of swampy forests, the hadrosaur-ceratopsian dinosaur community could no longer thrive in Utah, at least to the degree that it had during the preceding Campanian Age. To the north, in Wyoming, Montana, and Alberta, where swampy coastal conditions persisted into the Maastrichtian Age, a rich assemblage of dinosaurs continued to flourish and diversify until the very end of the Cretaceous Period.

Perhaps the Maastrichtian dinosaur communities of this northern region included the descendants of Utah dinosaurs that migrated north, tracking the habitats to which they were so well adapted. When the seaside swamps withdrew from Utah, many area dinosaurs evidently followed the swamps east and north. The regression of the Western Interior Seaway in North America was not a local phenomenon: similar widespread regressions were occurring at the same time on a global scale. Everywhere in the world, dry land had appeared in continental lowlands that were formerly submerged by the great inland seas. By the end of the Maastrichtian Age, the distribution of land and sea began to look similar, though still not identical, to the pattern we see in the modern world. As the great regressions modified the patterns of land and sea, changes in climate were initiated on both the global and local scales. Now that the future state was far from the moderating effects of the withdrawn sea, the climate in Utah probably became a little less humid, and it also possibly became cooler. This climatic shift is just one of the many profound environmental changes that began near the end of the Cretaceous Period.

In Utah, the draining of the swamps linked to the regression of the sea was accelerated by at least two important geological disturbances. In fact, 75–70 million years ago, as Maastrichtian time was just beginning, Utah landscapes experienced what was probably the most significant period of upheaval of the entire Mesozoic Era. The Sevier Orogenic Belt in western Utah was in its final stages of deformation, and it went out with a bang! The last pulse of uplift in the Sevier belt in Utah created the structures now known as the Gunnison thrust system in central Utah and the Absaroka thrust system in northern Utah (DeCelles and Mitra, 1995; DeCelles and others, 1995; Wiltschko and Dorr, 1983). In addition to initiating these thrust faults, the intensified compressive forces of early Maastrichtian time also reactivated some of the older thrust faults and crumpled rock layers into large folds (Talling and others, 1995). This early Maastrichtian deformation elevated the mountainous Sevier Orogenic Belt one last time, invigorating the rivers that drained east into the foreland basin.

Even as the earth was shaking from the pow-

erful forces that thrust the Sevier belt skyward, new disturbances began to affect the land farther east during the Maastrichtian Age. In the Uinta Mountains, the San Rafael Region, and the Circle Cliffs area near Capitol Reef the land surface began to heave upward. The ascent of these areas east of the Sevier belt was subtle at first, but it accelerated steadily throughout latest Cretaceous to early Tertiary time. This uplift signified the beginning of the Laramide Orogeny, the widespread episode of mountain building that led to the creation of the modern Rocky Mountains. After its beginning in the latest Cretaceous, Laramide deformation continued across the Rocky Mountain region for at least 30 million years, well into the Eocene Epoch of the Tertiary Period.

At the conclusion of the Laramide Orogeny, the Uinta Mountains stood high along the Utah-Wyoming border and the San Rafael Swell bulged upward, rising higher above the surrounding lowlands than it does today. Elsewhere in Utah, the Circle Cliffs Uplift ascended, the Monument Uplift loomed high along the Utah-Arizona border, and the northern nose of the Uncompahgre Plateau slashed into Utah from southwestern Colorado (Goldstrand and others, 1993; Dickinson and others, 1988). Throughout the broader Rocky Mountain region, several major mountain systems were built during the Laramide Orogeny; they include the Front and Sawatch ranges of Colorado, the Bighorn and Wind River mountains of Wyoming, and the Beartooth Mountains of Montana. The deformation by which the Laramide Orogeny lifted these mountains was primarily high-angle compressional faults generated at relatively deep levels in the earth's crust. As the fault-forming compressional forces propagated through the crust, rock strata were also bent and crumpled to produce broad folds above the zones of displacement in the deeper basement rocks. Utah has many outstanding examples of such extensive Laramide folds, including the east flank of the San Rafael Swell (sometimes called the San Rafael Reef) and Comb Ridge, along the escarp-

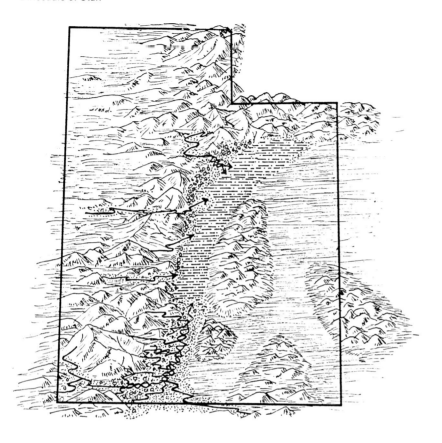

Figure 9-1. Maastrichtian paleogeography of Utah. About 70–65 million years ago an elongated interior basin existed in central Utah between the Sevier Orogenic Belt to the west and the San Rafael Swell and Circle Cliffs uplifts to the east. Rivers draining the highlands washed the gravel, sand, and mud of the North Horn Formation into this basin.

ment of the Monument Uplift in San Juan County. In the Uinta Mountains, the compressional faults actually broke through the surface and ancient rocks were pushed upward as a coherent block of fault-bounded rock. These rocks make up the core of the modern Uinta Mountains. While the mechanics of the Laramide Orogeny (deep faulting and folding) are much different from those of the Sevier Orogeny (shallow, "thin-skinned" thrusting and smaller folds), both mountain-building events were driven by compressional forces generated by the convergence of great rock plates along the western edge of North America. The difference in the style of deformation produced during the two orogenies probably reflects differences in the thickness and nature of the deeper crust and does not imply any significant change in the type of stresses that were produced by plate tectonic events of the Maastrichtian and early Cenozoic time periods. Many

geologists believe that the angle of subduction along western North America decreased dramatically during the Laramide Orogeny, allowing the compressive forces to be transmitted much farther inland from the western edge of the continent. This idea has merit because, generally speaking, there appears to be much less igneous activity of Laramide age than of Sevier age in western North America. This "magmatic gap" would be expected if in the latter orogeny the angle of subduction decreased to the point that the descending slab was not driven as deeply (or rapidly) into the hot mantle below as it was during earlier Cretaceous time.

In addition to their distinct styles of deformation, the Sevier Orogeny and the Laramide Orogeny are usually separated in both time and space throughout the Rocky Mountain and Great Basin regions. The Sevier Orogeny primarily affected the eastern Great Basin region from late Jurassic through Cretaceous time. The Laramide Orogeny followed the Sevier disturbance, affecting the Rocky Mountain area to the east during the latest Cretaceous and early Tertiary periods (Paleocene and Eocene epochs). In central Utah, however, the final stages of the Sevier Orogeny and the beginning of the Laramide Orogeny overlap both temporally and geographically. It was during Maastrichtian time that the overlap of these two orogenies was most conspicuous. At that time, uplift in the Sevier belt accompanied mountain building related to the beginning of the Laramide Orogeny across a broad area of central Utah, from the Wasatch and Uinta mountains area to the high plateaus in the southwestern corner of the state. The net effect of this geological ruckus was to transform the Sevier foreland basin of the earlier Cretaceous into a complicated terrain consisting of many rising uplifts separated by relatively small interior basins (Figure 9-1).

The rock record of these events is a rather complicated heap of conglomerates shed from the rising uplifts (both Sevier and Laramide), sandstones deposited by rivers flowing into the evolv-

Photo 40. Badlands eroded in the soft sediments of the North Horn Formation on the Wasatch Plateau. Frank DeCourten.

ing interior basins, and fine-grained siltstone and mudstone that accumulated on floodplains and lake bottoms. In the uplifted areas, such as the San Rafael Swell and the Uinta Mountain regions, the K-T transition is marked only by unconformities as rock was worn away from the rising land surfaces. It was only in the interior basins that developed east of the Sevier belt and between the ascending Laramide structures that sediment was deposited more or less continuously during the K-T interval. Even in the interior basins, there were periodic times of erosion or nondeposition that created small unconformities in the basin-filling rock sequences (Fouch and others, 1983; Goldstrand and others, 1993; Hintze, 1988). In addition, the strata that record the K-T transition in Utah are not always fossiliferous and commonly lack minerals that can be radiometrically dated. Since the K-T boundary is most clearly expressed by the distinct fossil assemblages before and after the faunal transition, it is next to impossible to

precisely locate the K-T boundary without abundant fossils. These factors make it difficult to locate a marker that separates Cretaceous strata from Tertiary deposits in most Utah rock successions that span the Mesozoic-Cenozoic boundary. In many places, no sediment at all was deposited at this time and only unconformities mark the threshold of the Cenozoic Era. In other localities, scientists can only approximate the position of the boundary in the complex, unconformity-ridden, and sparsely fossiliferous successions of conglomerate, sandstone, and mudstone.

Elsewhere in the Rocky Mountain region, where there was less geological chaos in progress, the K-T boundary is less difficult (but still not always easy) to locate. This is the case in New Mexico, Wyoming, and Montana, and it should come as no surprise that much of the research on the K-T transition has focused on rocks exposed in those areas. In Utah, the K-T boundary is probably preserved with the North Horn Formation of central Utah (Franczyk and Pitman, 1991; Spieker, 1960), the Canaan Peak and Grapevine Wash formations of southwestern Utah (Fillmore, 1991; Schmidt and others, 1991), the Evanston Formation of the Wasatch-Uinta Mountains region (Mullens, 1971; Ryer, 1976), and perhaps a few other less thoroughly studied rock units. Of these rock sequences, only the North Horn Formation has produced more than a few scraps of fossil bone. So, to glimpse the Maastrichtian dinosaur fauna of Utah, paleontologists look to the exposures of the North Horn Formation on the high Wasatch Plateau of central Utah. These rocks are the only source of abundant fossil material documenting the last participants in the 140-million-year cavalcade of Utah dinosaurs.

The North Horn Formation

The North Horn Formation was named for exposures on North Horn Mountain, not far from Joe's Valley on the Wasatch Plateau of central Utah (Spieker and Reeside, 1925; Spieker, 1946). In this area, the North Horn Formation consists of about 1,500 feet of soft red and gray siltstone and mudstone, interlayered with less-abundant sandstone and limestone. In the Wasatch Plateau region, the North Horn Formation rests on the underlying Price River Formation (of the Mesaverde Group), the last strata deposited in the Sevier foreland basin prior to its disruption during the Laramide Orogeny. In the San Pitch Mountains west of the Wasatch Plateau, the North Horn Formation is over 3,000 feet thick and contains thick sandstone units and great wedge-shaped masses of conglomerate along with finer-grained sediments typical of the exposures on the Wasatch Plateau (Talling and others, 1995). Core samples from oil wells in the western Uinta Basin indicate that the North Horn Formation extends in the subsurface north from the Wasatch Plateau into that area, where it is up to 2,500 feet thick. To the south, the North Horn Formation can be traced at least to the Capitol Reef National Park

area, beyond which it becomes buried under younger volcanic rocks that cover Boulder Mountain and other high plateaus. In the Bryce Canyon region, sediments typical of the North Horn interval cannot be recognized. In this southern area, the K-T boundary lies within the Canaan Peak Formation, which consists almost entirely of massive pebble and boulder conglomerate. The Canaan Peak rubble probably represents the coarse sediments flushed from highlands around the southern end of the interior basin in which the North Horn sediments accumulated. The North Horn Formation has not been identified east of the San Rafael Swell or in western Utah. The known extent of the North Horn Formation thus defines an elongated basin of sediment accumulation that stretched diagonally through central Utah (Figure 9-1; Franczyk and others, 1992; Franczyk and Pitman, 1991). This interior basin was some 130 miles long as it was situated parallel to, and just east of, the Sevier Orogenic Belt from the Uinta Mountains to the southern high plateaus of Utah. The North Horn basin was only about forty miles wide, bounded on the east by the San Rafael Swell and Circle Cliffs Uplift, both of which were actively rising during in the Maastrichtian Age. Elsewhere in Utah, Maastrichtian sediments accumulated in other small basins located between the Sevier and Laramide uplifts, but these deposits were either eroded later or are nonfossiliferous.

The sediments of the North Horn Formation were deposited by streams that drained the uplands adjacent to the basin and in lakes that formed from the water impounded within the enclosed lowland (Lawton, 1986; Olsen, 1995). Around the periphery of the basin, conglomerates in the North Horn Formation suggest there were swift rivers flowing across steep alluvial aprons that descended toward the lower part of the basin. In the middle of the basin, the rivers became more sluggish and deposited finer sand in the channels and spread mud and silt across the basin floor during flood events. The silty limestone layers of the North Horn Formation record the periodic development of ponds and lakes, some of them quite large, in the central portion of the basin. The presence of many fragmentary fossils of fish similar to gar pikes as well as fossils of turtles and crocodiles verifies the widespread aquatic habitats in the North Horn basin. In addition, fossils of freshwater clams and snails are abundant in many parts of the North Horn Formation, particularly in the lake-deposited limestones. For reasons that are not yet clear, plant macrofossils are not especially abundant in the North Horn Formation, but thin coal seams in these strata suggest that there was reasonably lush vegetation, at least at certain times in certain places, across the basin floor.

The terrestrial environment of central Utah during the Cretaceous-Tertiary transition was probably a well-watered lowland, nestled between rugged mountains to the west and hilly uplands to the east, north, and south. The basin floor was dotted with lakes and ponds, especially during the rainy seasons. Isolated clumps of vegetation developed wherever there was sufficient water to support trees and shrubs. The climate of the Maastrichtian–early Tertiary appears to have been from warm and temperate to subtropical (Robison, 1986). Lizard fossils, including some spectacularly well-preserved specimens, are quite abundant in the North Horn Formation (Figure 9-2; Gilmore, 1942a, 1942b, 1943). Among the lizards, the three-foot-long herbivore *Polyglyphanodon* was particularly common (Figure 9- 2). At least four different species of turtles are also known from the North Horn Formation, including the large tortoise-like *Basilemys* (Gilmore, 1946). The abundance of reptiles supports the concept of generally warm climatic conditions during the time represented by the North Horn Formation. Impressions of palm fronds in the part of the North Horn Formation bearing dinosaur fossils are also consistent with warm, subtropical conditions in the Maastrichtian floodplains of central Utah (Zawiskie, 1983).

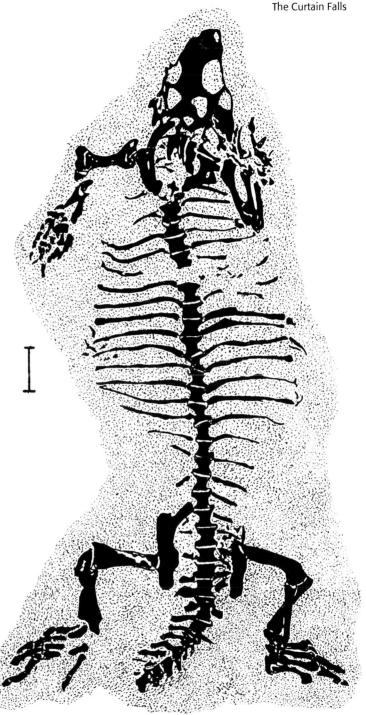

Figure 9-2. *Polyglyphanodon*, a large herbivorous lizard from the North Horn Formation of Utah. This genus was represented by more than a dozen articulated specimens, similar to that shown in this sketch. Based on a photograph of one of the original specimens in Gilmore, 1942. Scale bar=25 mm (1 inch).

Photo 41. A bone fragment weathering out of the North Horn Formation near Joe's Valley Reservoir. Frank DeCourten.

Figure 9-3. Paleocene (early Tertiary) mammal fossils from the North Horn Formation. A: A portion of the jaw of *Oxyclaenus pugnax*, about 3/4 of an inch long. B: Molar tooth of *Promioclaenus acolytus*, only about 1/8 of an inch tall. These small mammals are among dozens of genera that indicate an early Cenozoic age for the upper part of the North Horn Formation. Based on photographs from Robison, 1986.

Traces and casts of plant roots in soils preserved in the North Horn sediments indicate that some of the shrubs possessed long "tap roots," suggesting a low or fluctuating water table (Bracken and Picard, 1984). This, in turn, indicates that the climate of the Maastrichtian in central Utah may have been strongly seasonal. The presence of nodular caliche and red-colored soil horizons in parts of the North Horn Formation (Olsen, 1995) provides additional evidence that there were dry periods during the time represented by these sediments.

Soon after the North Horn Formation was first described, it attracted the attention of paleontologists because the lower portions of the formation contain many dinosaur fossils and the upper part produces abundant remains of a diverse mammal fauna. Dinosaur remains disappear from the rock succession above the lower beds and do not occur with the mammal fossils found in the upper part of the formation. Moreover, mammal fossils from the upper North Horn Formation, such as *Oxyclaenus*, *Promioclaenus*, and many others, indicate a Paleocene age, which was the earliest epoch of the Tertiary Period (Figure 9-3; Robison, 1986; Gazin, 1938, 1939, 1941; Archibald and others, 1983).

Therefore, the distribution of dinosaur and mammals fossils in the North Horn Formation suggests that the K-T boundary lies somewhere in the middle of this thick rock succession. The pattern of magnetic field reversals recorded in the sediments of the North Horn Formation reveals that it spans the interval from about 74–51 million years ago (Talling and others, 1994, 1995). These dates confirm that the K-T boundary, which occurred about 65 million years ago, is recorded somewhere in the middle of this rock sequence. Unfortunately, the middle beds of the North Horn Formation have produced far fewer fossils than the upper and lower portions, so the exact position of the K-T boundary has not yet been established. As geologists and paleontologists continue to study the North Horn Formation and its fossils, it may soon be possible to pinpoint the precise strata that were deposited during the K-T transition. For now, all we know is that this horizon exists somewhere in the middle, sparsely fossiliferous, portion of the formation. Nonetheless, the fossils from the North Horn Formation constitute the best record of the Mesozoic-Cenozoic faunal transition of any rock sequence in Utah. For dinosaur enthusiasts, the North Horn Formation is an especially intriguing rock unit, because the remains found in the lower beds reveal a Maastrichtian fauna much different from anything that preceded it.

Dinosaurs of the North Horn Formation

Dinosaur remains were first reported from the North Horn Formation of the Wasatch Plateau in the late 1930s and 1940s (Gilmore 1938; Spieker, 1946; Gilmore, 1946), following a series of paleontological expeditions to the area by the Smithsonian Institution beginning in 1937. During the Smithsonian expeditions of the late 1930s, interest was directed primarily toward the Paleocene mammal remains in the upper part of the formation (Gazin, 1938, 1939, 1941). The mammal fossils, and the stratigraphy of the rocks they are found in, have continued to attract a great deal of interest in more recent years (for example, Robison, 1986; Tomida and Butler, 1980). Unfortunately, few additional dinosaur fossils have emerged from the North Horn Formation in the fifty years since the first remains were excavated, although Jensen (1966) described eggshell fragments that were attributed to dinosaurs. Most of what is known about North Horn dinosaurs is based on the old specimens, but the search for additional clues continues every summer, high on the Wasatch Plateau.

Ⓖ *ALAMOSAURUS*

The best-represented dinosaur in the North Horn Formation is the sauropod *Alamosaurus sanjuan-*

ensis, first identified from Maastrichtian deposits near Ojo Alamo, New Mexico, by Charles W. Gilmore in 1922 (Gilmore, 1946b; Gilmore, 1922). During the Smithsonian expeditions, many *Alamosaurus* fossils were excavated from the North Horn Formation, including thirty articulated caudal vertebrae (representing nearly all of the tail), twenty-five chevron bones, portions of the pelvis and shoulder, an almost complete forelimb, and large sternal plates. Even though the skull, neck, main portion of the backbone, and most of the limbs were missing, the North Horn specimen is still one of the best ever found for *Alamosaurus*. In terms of its overall appearance, *Alamosaurus* was probably similar to the sauropods of the late Jurassic, but it was not as large as some of them. The forelimb of *Alamosaurus* was about 9–10 feet long and the total length of this dinosaur was probably not much more than about 35 feet. The long forelimb, with an elongated humerus, suggests a posture reminiscent of *Brachiosaurus*, in which the shoulders were higher than the hips. However, *Alamosaurus* also seems to have been a heavy-bodied sauropod, perhaps somewhat like the husky *Camarasaurus* of the Jurassic. In particular, the sternal plates (or "breast bones") were massive and heavy. This, along with the robust forelimb bones, suggests that *Alamosaurus* probably had bulky limbs and shoulders, an overall stocky build, and may have weighed 25–30 tons. No one knows what the neck of *Alamosaurus* was like, but the hefty proportions of its skeleton suggest that it might have been relatively short and thick. Although *Alamosaurus* was of modest size compared to the sauropod giants of the Jurassic, it was clearly the largest dinosaur of its time in North America. No other Maastrichtian dinosaur, including the fearsome *Tyrannosaurus rex*, came close to matching its bulk.

No skull of *Alamosaurus* has ever been discovered, but a few fragmentary teeth have been found in association with bones of this genus in New Mexico (Kues and others, 1980). The teeth are small and cylindrical, similar in a general way to the peg-like teeth of *Diplodocus*. In the absence of a skull, scientists cannot be certain about the placement of the nostrils or other details of the head. As has been seen earlier, the sauropods seem to have had a nasty habit of losing their heads soon after they died. *Alamosaurus* is merely one of many "headless" sauropods scientists study. Like other sauropods, though, *Alamosaurus* was certainly a browsing herbivore; but whether it fed on low-growing shrubs or tall trees remains unclear.

The caudal vertebrae of *Alamosaurus* are very distinctive, a fortunate circumstance for paleontologists studying the North Horn specimen, which had a nearly complete series of tail bones. The first caudal vertebra, located at the base of the tail immediately behind the rump, was of bi-convex form (rounded on both ends). All other caudal vertebrae have a ball-like knob on the rear surface and a deep socket on the front end (Figure 9-4). Vertebrae with such ball-and-socket joints, with the socket facing forward, are described by the term procoelous. In addition, the caudal vertebrae of *Alamosaurus* have neural spines that are consistently located on the front half of the main portion of the bone, or centrum. Another unique feature of *Alamosaurus* is the complete absence of the deep pockets, or pleurocoels, on the sides of the vertebral centra. In other sauropods, the pleurocoels are variously developed, but virtually all sauropods have them. Among the sauropods, procoelous caudal vertebrae, lacking pleurocoels, with anteriorly placed neural spines are very peculiar features that, in part, characterize the family Titanosauridae of the suborder Sauropodamorpha. Even though much of the anatomy of *Alamosaurus* is still unknown, the caudal vertebrae of the North Horn specimen clearly indicate that this sauropod belongs to the Titanosauridae, a family of dinosaurs not present in North America prior to the Maastrichtian Age. That a new family of sauropods suddenly appears in North America at the time the North Horn sediments were deposited is interesting, but the intrigue

grows if we consider the broader patterns of sauropod history on this continent.

We have seen that the late Jurassic was the "golden age of sauropods" in North America, a time when these gigantic herbivores were the dominant plant eaters. In early Cretaceous time, the sauropods declined dramatically, perhaps as a result of climatic variations, evolutionary changes among the plants, and competition from rapidly evolving ornithischian dinosaurs such as nodosaurs and ornithopods. Only one sauropod, *Pleurocoelus*, seems to have been widespread and relatively common in North America during the early Cretaceous. About 95 million years ago, just as the last half of the Cretaceous Period began, the sauropods seem to have completely disappeared from North America. No sauropod fossils have ever been found anywhere in North America in rocks equivalent in age to the Mesaverde Group of Utah. Instead, the large herbivore niche was evidently filled during this time by the hadrosaurs, accompanied by less-common hypsilophodonts, nodosaurs, and early ceratopsians. For at least 30 million years, until late Maastrichtian time, no sauropods appear to have lived anywhere in North America. This interval has been called the "sauropod hiatus" (Lucas and Hunt, 1989). The occurrence of *Alamosaurus* in the North Horn Formation is significant because it signals the reappearance of the sauropods after a lengthy absence from the continent. Even more interesting is the fact that *Alamosaurus* appears at about the same time in New Mexico (Gilmore, 1922; Lozinsky and others, 1984), Texas (Lucas and Hunt, 1989), Wyoming (Lucas, 1981), and Utah. Thus, when the sauropods (or at least their fossil remains) returned to North America after the hiatus, they emerged almost simultaneously in several different places in the Southwest. Sauropod remains are unknown from the rich Maastrichtian bone beds of Alberta and Montana, suggesting that *Alamosaurus* never spread north of Wyoming. Many questions arise for paleontol-

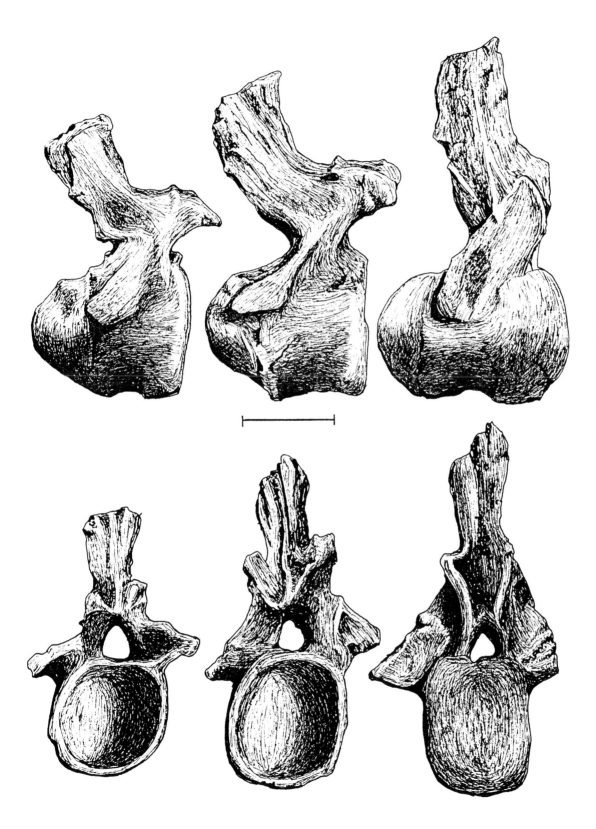

Figure 9-4. Caudal vertebrae of *Alamosaurus sanjuanensis*, from the North Horn Formation of central Utah. Lateral (top) and anterior (bottom) views of the caudal vertebrae 1, 2, and 3 (from right to left). Note the biconvex form of the first caudal vertebra, upper right, and the hollow sockets on the front (anterior) end of the second and third vertebrae. Another distinguishing feature of these vertebrae is the location of the upward projecting neural spines on the front (anterior) half of the main body, or centrum, of each vertebra. Based on photographs from Gilmore, 1946. Scale bar=15 cm (6 inches).

Plate 20.
An *Alamosaurus* herd
moves along the edge of
a large late Cretaceous
lake in central Utah.

ogists. How did *Alamosaurus* recolonize portions of North America after the hiatus? What caused the disappearance of sauropods after the early Cretaceous? What factors led to their return in the Maastrichtian?

Most paleontologists agree that *Alamosaurus* entered North America by migrating north from South America over a land connection between the two continents (Bonaparte, 1984; Lucas and Hunt, 1989). This explains the concentration of *Alamosaurus* in the Southwest and their absence in the northern part of North America. The view of *Alamosaurus* as an immigrant from the south makes sense for a different reason as well: the titanosaurids were widespread and abundant in the Southern Hemisphere during the sauropod hiatus that affected North America. Titanosaurid remains are found in late Cretaceous strata in Brazil, Uruguay, Chile, and Argentina. Elsewhere in the Southern Hemisphere, late Cretaceous titanosaurids are also known from India, Madagascar, and Laos (McIntosh, 1990). Several different titanosaurids are even known from Europe. In fact, the titanosaurids were one of the most abundant and successful groups of dinosaurs in the world during their time, though they were concentrated mainly on the southern continents. The only barrier to the dispersal of the South American titanosaurids was the ocean that completely surrounded that continent for much of the Cretaceous Period. To spread beyond South America, all the titanosaurids needed was a land bridge to facilitate their northern exodus. And that is exactly what developed in late Mesozoic time in the form of a volcanic arc that joined the two land masses of North and South America (Anderson and Schmidt, 1983).

Even though we often hear that North America and South America became joined only a few million years ago, the modern connection is only the most recent union between the Americas. After the late Mesozoic connection was established, and after *Alamosaurus* migrated over it, North America and South America became separated again until very late in the Cenozoic Era, when the current isthmus of Central America developed. This scenario suggests that the dinosaurs that ended the "sauropod hiatus" in North America were not descendants of the sauropods known from the Morrison or Cedar Mountain formations. Of course, this was already known, because *Alamosaurus* is a titanosaurid, not a diplodocid, camarasaurid, or brachiosaurid. Although its general appearance may have been similar to *Camarasaurus*, *Alamosaurus* was not the evolutionary progeny of any North American dinosaur that preceded it. That is why the skeletal features of *Alamosaurus* seem so distinctive to us in comparison to the more familiar late Jurassic sauropods of Utah. *Alamosaurus* evolved from different ancestors, in a different place, and under different ecological conditions.

The well-established view of *Alamosaurus* as an invader from South America spawns an interesting perception of the sauropod hiatus and provokes a bewitching question. If *Alamosaurus* is not a descendant of the Jurassic sauropods of North America, then the disappearance of these giant herbivores that initiated the sauropod hiatus was not just an out-migration, it was a genuine drop-dead extinction. If, for example, *Alamosaurus* were derived from a diplodocid ancestor, we could envision that this sauropod lineage persisted in South America (or somewhere else) and was reintroduced to Utah in the Maastrichtian Age. But, this is not the case. When the brachiosaurids, camarasaurids, and diplodocids vanished after the "golden age of sauropods" in North America, they were gone completely and forever. Taking this line of thought one step further, if the sauropod hiatus signifies a widespread sauropod extinction in western North America, then what caused it? What factors led to the extinction of the Jurassic sauropods and what conditions permitted an ecologically similar animal to thrive later in the Maastrichtian Age? Perhaps it was the changing climate, as mentioned previously. Maybe the comings and goings of sauro-

Figure 9-5. The teeth of ceratopsian dinosaurs. The teeth of ceratopsians were arranged in vertical rows (left, seen in cross-sectional view) that were firmly locked together in the jaw (right). The hard enamel surfaces joined to form a continuous blade-like cutting ridge along the edge of the jaws.

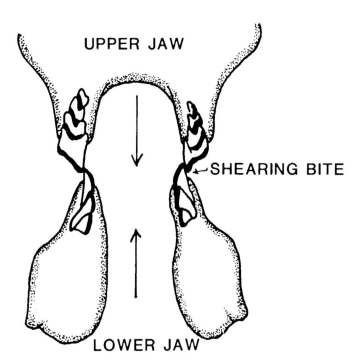

Figure 9-6. Chewing mechanism in ceratopsian dinosaurs. When ceratopsian dinosaurs chewed, plant matter was chopped into small bits as the cutting blade of the lower teeth passed inside the sharp edge formed by the upper teeth. Plant tissues caught between these blades were cleanly chopped.

pods in North America had something to do with the advances and retreats of the continental seas. Conceivably, it might be related to the changing composition of the global flora or the advent of the hadrosaurs and ceratopsians. No one knows the answers to these questions for sure, however, and the sauropod hiatus remains an unexplained phenomenon. Therefore, even though *Alamosaurus* was not the most imposing of the dinosaurs, and it certainly is not very common in Utah, it is still one of the most fascinating elements of the Maastrichtian fauna. About it, and the circumstances surrounding its appearance in the North Horn Formation, we still have much to learn.

⑥ *TOROSAURUS*

Along with *Alamosaurus*, the remains of at least eleven individual ceratopsian dinosaurs were found in the North Horn Formation during expeditions conducted by the Smithsonian Institution (Gilmore, 1946). Because it has been so commonly featured in movies, books, and toys, the most familiar ceratopsian is the quadrupedal herbivore *Triceratops* ("three-horn face"), with two prominent brow horns, an upward curving nose horn, and a broad frill extending over the neck from the back of the skull. These features are all typical of the Ceratopsia, but there are many other distinctive traits that define this clade (or infraorder) of ornithischian dinosaurs. Unique to the ceratopsians is a beak-like bone, the rostral, which joins the premaxilla at the tip of the snout (Figure 9-7). The surface of the rostrum is wrinkled and rough, indicating that a horny sheath covered the bone in life. The snout of ceratopsians was tipped with a vicious, sharp-edged beak that would have been extremely effective in chopping vegetation. Except for the closely related psittacosaurs, no other group of dinosaurs possessed such a parrot-like snout. The teeth of ceratopsians were arranged in vertical rows similar to the tooth batteries of the hadrosaurs (Figure

9-5), but they functioned in a unique manner. The tooth rows were locked together in such a way that they formed a continuous cutting blade along the edge of the jaws. In ceratopsians, the upper teeth passed just outside of the lower teeth each time the massive jaws were closed by powerful muscles anchored near the back of the head and on the frill. As the hard enamel edges of the teeth sheared past each other, vegetation was chopped into small pieces (Figure 9-6). Coupled with the beak at the snout, ceratopsian jaws were no doubt capable of chopping even the toughest vegetation, perhaps evoking an image of the modern mulching machines used to turn tree branches into wood chips. This is much different from the transverse grinding motion that the hadrosaurs employed in processing their plant food. To better envision the effect of the different ways of chewing in these two groups of ornithischians, think of the hadrosaurs swallowing a mashed pulp of plant matter, while the ceratopsians filled their gullets with material more like confetti.

In a manner similar to the hadrosaurs, the teeth of the ceratopsians are recessed inward, forming prominent cheek pockets on either side of the mouth. In life, the cheek pockets of ceratopsians were probably regularly stuffed with plant matter that was forced through the blade-like dental batteries. It would have been fascinating to watch a ceratopsian feed: swollen cheeks packed with stiff and stringy fodder, jaw muscles swelling at the base of the frill, and the beak continuously shearing off fronds and branches to replace the swallowed choppings. Because of the differences in their teeth and chewing styles, it is not likely that the ceratopsians and the hadrosaurs competed for the same food resources. Ceratopsians seem to have been well adapted to processing tough and/or fibrous vegetation, whereas the hadrosaurs might have preferred softer leafy food. Certainly the Maastrichtian fossil record, rich in both ceratopsians and hadrosaurs, indicates that these two ornith-

ischians were perfectly compatible with each other.

The nostrils of ceratopsians were very large and housed in a deep pocket just behind the beak. The paired nasal bones that form the upper part of the nostrils are usually fused, and a hump of bone that supported the nose-horn sheath projected upward. The nose-horn cores were as long as two feet in some species of ceratopsians (the actual horns would have been even longer in life), but they are barely noticeable in others. The brow horns are also variously developed in ceratopsians, but all arise from the bones that form the upper border of the orbit, or eye socket. The jugal (cheek) bones on the sides of the skull below the eye had a spike-like portion that projected out and down, giving ceratopsians two additional horn-like protuberances on the head. The characteristic head frill of ceratopsians was formed mainly by highly elongated squamosal and parietal bones. In other dinosaurs, these two bones normally make up portions of the top and back of the skull. Thus, the frills of ceratopsians developed as the back of the skull "grew" out over the neck. The frills may be nearly circular, heart-shaped, or triangular, and, in some genera, they are decorated with knobs of bone or spikes arranged around the periphery. In addition, many ceratopsians had circular or elliptical openings in the frills that probably served for the attachment of jaw muscles. The frills, horns, and massive skull bones gave the ceratopsians the largest heads of any land animal that ever lived. In the largest ceratopsians, the skulls were as long as nine feet, almost the size of a small car!

The vertebral column and limbs of the ceratopsians are well designed to support a large quadrupedal animal. The cervical (neck) vertebrae are large and partially fused to support the gigantic head. The backbone was arched upward and braced through the hip region by a network of bony rods. The tails of ceratopsians were relatively short and not particularly massive. The limbs are very robust and solidly attached to the

Plate 21.
A *Torosaurus* herd
feeding along a
wash descending
into a distant lake.

pelvis and shoulder girdle. The hind limbs are massive columns that were positioned vertically beneath the body; but there has been some controversy about the positioning of the forelimbs. Some paleontologists (for example, Johnson and Ostrom, 1991) argue that the forelimbs of the ceratopsians were splayed outward from the midline, while others assert that they were placed vertically beneath the body, similar to the hind limbs (Paul, 1991; Lockely and Hunt, 1995). The feet were very broad, with widely splayed toes tipped by large hoof-like claws. Overall, the skeletal architecture of the ceratopsians seems better designed for weight-bearing than for speed. Nonetheless, the ceratopsians could probably move quite effectively over land. Mass accumulations of ceratopsian remains, representing scores of juveniles and adults, are not uncommon in the Maastrichtian bone beds of Montana and Alberta (Currie and Dodson, 1984). Such bone beds suggest strong herding behavior among the ceratopsians, but whether they moved at a slow walk like elephants or galloped along like rhinos is still debatable. All together, the ceratopsians are a remarkable group of highly specialized ornithischians.

The fragmentary ceratopsian fossils described by Gilmore (1946) from the North Horn Formation were originally identified as *Arrhinoceratops? utahensis*. *Arrhinoceratops* is known from the Maastrichtian deposits of Alberta, but it is otherwise quite rare in North America (Tyson, 1981). *Arrhinoceratops* means "without nose horn face," in reference to the relatively small horn, actually a mere bump, on the noses of members of this genus. Lawson (1976) invalidated Gilmore's queried identification and, on the basis of the shape and sculpturing of the frill bones, determined that the North Horn material represented a species of *Torosaurus* ("bull reptile"). But the Utah material was different from other fossils of *Torosaurus*, which are found primarily in Montana, Wyoming, and South Dakota. Therefore, Lawson (1976) combined Gilmore's original species name with the correct genus name to -

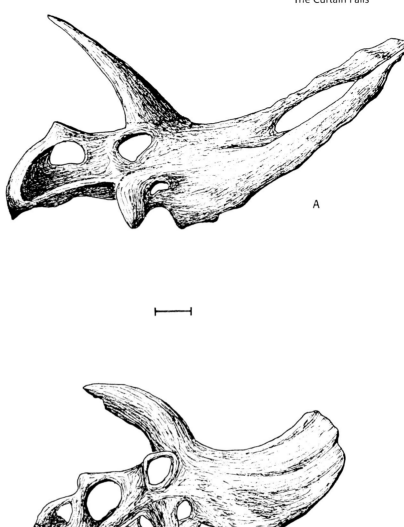

Figure 9-7. Skulls of *Torosaurus* and *Triceratops*. *Torosaurus* (top), known from the North Horn Formation of Utah, has a long perforated frill, well-developed brow horns, and a small nose horn. The smaller but more familiar *Triceratops* had a more circular and solid frill and shorter, thick horns that curved forward. Modified from sketches of Dodson and Currie, 1990. Scale bar=20 cm (about 8 inches).

designate the Utah specimen as *Torosaurus uta-hensis*.

Torosaurus is known only from the skull, but it appears to have been one of the largest ceratopsians ever identified. The skull of some specimens is more than 9 feet long. Using the better known, but generally smaller, *Triceratops* as a model for the post-cranial skeleton, full-grown *Torosaurus* individuals might have been about 25 feet long and weighed 10–15 tons. *Torosaurus* had a long, heart-shaped frill extending back from the skull at a rather low angle, completely covering the neck and shoulders. The frill was actually longer than the main portion of the skull, and had two openings separated by a bar of bone that formed a ridge running front to back along the midline (Figure 9-7A). The outer edge of the frill was smooth and unornamented. The morphology of the frill of *Torosaurus* is much different from that of the more familiar *Triceratops*, which had a relatively small, solid frill with a knobby border formed by small bones known as the epoccipitals (Figure 9-7B). The two brow horns of *Torosaurus* projected upward at a high angle from just behind the eyes and curved gently toward the snout at their tips (Lawson, 1976). The nose horn was a small, blunt cone that was positioned above and just behind the nostrils. Like other ceratopsians, *Torosaurus* had a prominent beak formed by a horny sheath that covered the curved rostral bone at the tip of the snout.

The larger ceratopsian dinosaurs (family Ceratopsidae) are subdivided into two distinct sub-families: the Centrosaurinae and the Chasmosaurinae (Lehman, 1990; Dodson and Currie, 1990). The Centrosaurinae are the smaller and presumably more primitive ceratopsids, having a relatively short frill in which the squamosal bone does not reach to the back edge. In addition, the Centrosaurinae usually have a nose horn that is larger than their brow horns and ornate frill margins. *Centrosaurus*, with its single large nose horn, and the spiky-frilled *Styracosaurus* are good examples of the Centrosaurinae. *Torosaurus*, on the other hand, exhibits the features that characterize the Chasmosaurinae: a long, relatively smooth-bordered frill in which the squamosal bones reach the back edge; brow horns larger than the nose horn; and a large body size. Accompanying *Torosaurus* in the Chasmosaurinae are *Triceratops*, *Chasmosaurus*, and *Pentaceratops*, plus a few other genera. The chasmosaurine ceratopsians are more specialized (that is, more "derived," in cladistic terms) than are the centrosaurs, and they are one of the very last groups of dinosaurs to evolve in the Mesozoic Era.

Three species of *Torosaurus* have been described: *T. latus*, the "northern" species known from Maastrichtian strata from Wyoming to Alberta; *T. gladius*, a somewhat larger individual with subtle differences in the shape of the frill and elsewhere; and *T. utahensis*, the North Horn species, which also occurs in New Mexico and Texas. The known differences between the three species have mainly to do with the size and shape of horns and frills. Some paleontologists, the author included, are skeptical about the validity of these species. In fact, I think that the morphology of the frills and configuration of the horns in ceratopsians have been, as a general rule, overemphasized in defining species of the various genera, and even in defining the genera themselves. The frills and horns were probably used in ritualistic displays and in sparring for mates. Recall that there is good evidence that the ceratopsians were herding animals. Communication between individuals is essential in animals that depend on a herd for protection and successful reproduction. In addition, it seems that the frills of most ceratopsians were too thin and, in some cases, too perforated with openings, to afford much protection from predators. Instead, it seems more reasonable to envision the frills as devices for signaling species membership and gender, establishing position in the social hierarchy of the herd, and attracting mates. The frills may also have been important in anchoring the powerful jaw muscles and increasing the leverage with which they operated the lower jaw. However, the muscle-attachment functions of the frill were probably of secondary importance, a "fringe" benefit of such an expanded skull. The large frills of ceratopsians would have been very effective in communicating with members of the herd. By tipping the snout or waving the head, ceratopsians could have sent visual signals to other members of the herd that would have been hard to miss. The highly ornamented edge of the frills in some genera, coupled with possible patterns of color in the skin covering the frill, also might have increased the visibility of the display.

In most herding animals, the males engage in nonlethal competition with one another for dominance and reproductive opportunities. This was probably the primary function of the horns in ceratopsian dinosaurs, just as it is in the case of many modern herding mammals such as bison and elk. If the horns and frills of ceratopsians evolved for communication, display, and mating purposes, then it is almost certain that the size and shape of these structures varied with age and gender, just as they do in all horned or antlered mammals of today's world. The antlers of male deer, elk, moose, and other game animals are so variable in form that trophy hunters have developed complicated formulas to "score" them. So, it is likely that at least some of the species that have been established for the various ceratopsian genera really represent male and female, or old and young, individuals of the same species. This may be the case in *Torosaurus*, especially since virtually nothing is known of the post-cranial skeletal anatomy. *T. latus*, *T. gladius*, and *T. utahensis* may all be the same species, or, at most, geographic variants of a single species. Because their species-level classification has traditionally emphasized horns and frills, the same may be true of other ceratopsian genera as well. For example, the sixteen different species of *Triceratops* that have been

described by paleontologists probably represent morphological variations of no more than two species, *T. horridus* and *T. prorsus* (Ostrom and Wellnhofer, 1990; Forster, 1996).

Alamosaurus and *Torosaurus* are the only North Horn dinosaurs currently identified to the genus level, but there were others in Utah during the late Maastrichtian Age. Gilmore (1946) reported a hadrosaur femur along with a few isolated skull bones that evidently belonged to a ceratopsian dinosaur that was distinct from *Torosaurus*. No identifiable hadrosaur material has been reported from the North Horn Formation since Gilmore's expeditions, so it is still uncertain what genus is represented by the femur. Jensen (1966) described several different types of fossil eggshells from the lower portion of the North Horn formation and attributed some of them to dinosaurs, but he could not identify the egg layers to the genus or species level because no embryos were preserved with the shell fragments. Fossil eggshell fragments are very common in the lower, dinosaur-bearing, portion of the North Horn Formation even to this day. Given the abundance of lizard and turtle remains in the North Horn, however, it is likely that many of these eggs were laid by non-dinosaur reptiles or perhaps even by birds. Reconstructions of the eggs based on the shell fragments preserved in the North Horn Formation, however, suggest that some of the eggs were too large to have been laid by the reptiles or turtles known from fossil bones (Jensen, 1966). These larger eggs might have been of dinosaurian origin, but they cannot be associated with any particular group. Until an intact egg is found with an identifiable embryo preserved inside, scientists can't be sure about the identity of the egg layers. Currently, the eggs prove only that reptilian (or avian) reproduction was occurring in the North Horn basin.

Except for several isolated teeth, a large hand claw, and a foot bone (Gilmore, 1946), theropod fossils have not been formally reported from the North Horn Formation. The fossils reported by Gilmore are too fragmentary to be identified with precision, but they do indicate that some large dinosaur predators accompanied *Alamosaurus*, *Torosaurus*, and the hadrosaurs during late Maastrichtian time. A few additional teeth, all isolated and fragmentary, have been found from the North Horn Formation and age-equivalent strata since Gilmore's investigations. These, along with unpublished reports and rumors of additional fossil material, suggest that the large North Horn theropods were similar to *Tyrannosaurus* and *Albertosaurus*, the most terrifying of all theropods. The very rare tooth fragments cannot be precisely identified to the genus level, and no technical description of them has been published, but paleontologists do know that large tyrannosaurids were present elsewhere in western North America during late Maastrichtian time. The North Horn, Evanston, or Canaan Peak formations may someday yield fossils sufficiently complete and well-preserved to establish the genera and species of such carnivores in the North Horn Formation.

Because the North Horn Formation and other late Maastrichtian strata of western North America produce the remains of the very last dinosaurs, the fossil assemblages from these rock units have been of great interest to paleontologists. A wealth of Maastrichtian dinosaur fossils has been collected in many different localities in the West, from New Mexico to Alberta. This material has allowed the recognition of three distinctive late Maastrichtian dinosaur faunas (Lehman, 1987). The North Horn Formation produces what is known as the *Alamosaurus* Fauna, named for the largest dinosaur represented in it. In addition to the namesake genus, this fauna contains *Torosaurus*, the hadrosaurs *Edmontosaurus* and *Kritosaurus* (both "holdovers" from the slightly older Campanian faunas), and the theropods *Tyrannosaurus* and *Albertosaurus*. All of the dinosaurs comprising the *Alamosaurus* Fauna have

either been positively identified or are presumed to have been present in the North Horn Formation. In addition to central Utah, the *Alamosaurus* Fauna also occurs in the late Maastrichtian sediments of New Mexico, West Texas, and southwestern Wyoming (Lehman, 1987). This unique congregation of late Maastrichtian dinosaurs appears to have been confined to the interior basins of southwestern North America.

Farther north, in central Wyoming, eastern Montana, the Dakotas, and Alberta, the *Triceratops* Fauna has been recognized in rocks equivalent in age to the North Horn Formation. This fauna is dominated by *Triceratops*, a ceratopsian absent from the *Alamosaurus* Fauna of Utah, along with hadrosaurs, the thick-skulled pachycephalosaurs, ankylosaurs, and large theropods. *Torosaurus*, a major element of the *Alamosaurus* Fauna in Utah and adjacent southern regions, was a very minor component of the *Triceratops* Fauna. The *Triceratops* Fauna evidently was adapted to low coastal environments quite dissimilar from the interior basin in which the North Horn Formation was deposited and where the *Alamosaurus* Fauna flourished.

Finally, the *Leptoceratops* Fauna, characterized by the diminutive protoceratopsian for which it is named, represents an upland assemblage that includes many of the same taxa, or elements, as the *Triceratops* Fauna, although in somewhat different proportions. The *Leptoceratops* Fauna is known only from a few localities in northwestern Wyoming and in Alberta, Canada, where hilly highlands existed during the late Maastrichtian Age.

The last dinosaurs to live in North America were thus dispersed in recurring assemblages that correspond to specific environments: the *Alamosaurus* Fauna in the interior basins, the *Triceratops* Fauna along the coastal lowlands, and the *Leptoceratops* Fauna in the interior uplands (Lehman, 1987). This biogeographic pattern is not really very surprising, because scientists would expect to see a similar pattern among any group of animals distributed over such a broad and environmentally varied region. In modern North America, researchers certainly have little difficulty recognizing the unique mammal faunas that exist in moist coastal lowlands, high alpine forests, semi-arid grasslands, and deserts, for example. We don't often expect to see a moose in a Louisiana bayou or a mountain goat in the prairies of Nebraska. There is, of course, some overlap among the modern mammal faunas, and it is usually most notable among the predators. Coyotes and mountain lions, for example, can survive almost anywhere—in swamps, in blistering deserts, in high mountains, not to mention the dry hills above urban Los Angeles. In a similar way, the dinosaur predators of the Maastrichtian Age such as *Tyrannosaurus* and *Albertosaurus* appear to have been present almost everywhere; but the herbivores appear to have been more restricted in consistent faunal assemblages adapted to specific environmental conditions. Similar biogeographic patterns probably existed throughout the Mesozoic Era for all the dinosaurs on every continent, but the extraordinarily rich fossil record of the late Maastrichtian Age of North America affords a rare opportunity to discern the faunal groupings. Many more dinosaur fossils will have to be collected from older rocks before paleontologists can formulate equally precise ideas about the biogeography of dinosaurs during the earlier periods of the Mesozoic Era.

Extinction: The Enduring Mystery

The fact that the dinosaurs ultimately became extinct is one of the most intriguing aspects of their existence in the Mesozoic Era. Many people, scientists and nonscientists alike, have become preoccupied by the disappearance of this group of reptiles and with attempts to understand their so-called "failure" some 65 million years ago. Personally, I view it somewhat differently; I see their remarkable success during most of the Mesozoic Era as the most fascinating element in the story

of the dinosaurs. Despite the perception of dinosaurs as obsolete biological relics of the past, they were more successful than any group of land animals in the earth's history. The dinosaurs survived, indeed, they thrived, during several periods of environmental change that might have ended the ecological reign of less resilient creatures. Even restricting attention to Utah alone, it has been seen that several different faunas of dinosaurs came and went throughout the Mesozoic Era as geological forces wrought changes in the land and the environment. The ability of the dinosaurs to successfully adapt to new conditions, and to do so for more than 140 million years, is clearly demonstrated by the Mesozoic fossil record of Utah. On a global scale, the evolutionary versatility and endurance of dinosaurs is even more impressive. Thus, it is not their extinction that should mesmerize us; rather, it is their extraordinary ability to survive so long as monarchs of the terrestrial ecosystem that should evoke our wonder. The dinosaurs are amazing not for the fact that they died but for the way that they lived.

Still, it is only natural to ponder the circumstances that finally ended the rule of the dinosaurs. What events could have happened, what changes could have occurred, that exceeded the proven abilities of the dinosaurs to adapt and survive? In view of their prior success in the face of profound environmental changes, the extinction of the dinosaurs is more than just a casual curiosity, it is a puzzling enigma. Consequently, every person interested in dinosaurs, whether they are paleontologists or not, eventually is drawn to consider the extinction issue. Some will consider it more than others, but it seems that almost everyone develops or subscribes to a theory on the matter. An enormous body of scientific literature deals with topics related to the extinction of the dinosaurs. Just listing the references would require a book as long as this one. In fact, such bibliographies have been compiled, and they are indeed book-sized (see Fouty, 1987). Good summaries of the dinosaur-extinction debate include those of Archibald (1996), Russell and Rice (1982), and Benton (1990). As these sources demonstrate, scores of theories have been proposed to account for the extinction of the dinosaurs. Some of the theories, such as one concerning alien beings from space, are easily dismissed or are utterly untestable. Many other theories summon plausible causes of extinction such as disease, asteroid impacts, geographic and climatic change, changes in plant communities, reproductive dysfunction, and dwindling gene pools. Each can find at least some support in the geological and paleontological data that can be brought to bear on the issue. But, the fact of the matter is that even now, at the end of the twentieth century, there is no single explanation for the demise of the dinosaurs that is universally accepted by even a simple majority of scientists.

Scientists' inability to completely understand the extinction of the dinosaurs after so much intense study stems from several factors. First, extinction, though a natural and ongoing biological process, is never as simple as many people assume. The death of an individual organism is much different from the death of an entire species, genus, or family. Remember that when the dinosaurs vanished, two taxonomic orders of reptiles disappeared forever. The search for a "killing mechanism" has sometimes centered on events that might well have caused the death of individual dinosaurs in some locality at some time, but how such mechanisms could have led to the extinction of larger taxonomic groups dispersed over a broad area is unclear. Extinctions, in general, are complex events in the history of life that result from the combined effects of numerous factors. The search for a "smoking gun" for the dinosaur extinction has often focused on identifying the event that led to the faunal turnover. In all likelihood, however, there were probably several different causes of the biotic stress that tipped the ecological scales against the dinosaurs at the end of the Cretaceous Period. The combined ecological effects of such well-

documented late Cretaceous phenomena as the widespread regression of the seas, a volcanic outburst, numerous mountain-building events, changing patterns of global geography, and climatic trends are not simple to assess. These factors may have operated to varying degrees in different locations at different times, further complicating the task of evaluating their overall global effect. Individually, none of these events is an adequate explanation for the demise of the dinosaurs; however, when considered together in terms of their complex interactions, they might have triggered the K-T biotic transition. In the modern world, it is sometimes difficult to distinguish a primary cause for the decline of a single endangered species; imagine how perplexing it might be to formulate a model for the disappearance of many different creatures 65 million years ago. It is probably unreasonable to expect that such a complex biological phenomenon would have a simple, single cause. It seems that modern human beings are reluctant to embrace complexity and uncertainty in many fields. We tend to champion solutions similar to those advocated by politicians in television sound bites: simple, easy answers that, on the surface, make sense but, when tested against reality, ultimately break down. The extinction of the dinosaurs was a complex event that, in all probability, had complex causes.

A second reason for difficulty is that the geological record of the extinction of the dinosaurs is really not very good. This is unquestionably the case in Utah, where a single formation (the North Horn) provides only meager information on the great K-T transition. And this situation is certainly not unique to Utah. In fact, most of what paleontologists know about the pace and detailed pattern of dinosaur extinction comes from the study of the K-T sediments in the eastern Montana region, specifically the dinosaur-bearing late Maastrichtian Hell Creek Formation and the overlying Paleocene Tullock Formation (Dodson and Tatarinov, 1990). Elsewhere in the world, as in Utah, the sediments that span the K-T transition usually either lack adequate numbers of dinosaur fossils, are complicated by unconformities, or are too imprecisely dated to tell scientists much about the events of the time. Even in the Hell Creek Formation, scientists have formed different interpretations about the timing of the extinction and the pattern of dinosaur abundance and diversity (see, for example, Sheehan and others, 1991, and Sloan and others, 1986). The imperfections of the geological record of the dinosaur extinction pose a very real challenge to researchers' attempts to fully understand this event. This is one reason why so many theories have been formulated and why it is not always possible to simply choose among them. In many cases, the imperfect data offer equivocal support for several different interpretations and extinction scenarios.

A third problem in the search for an explanation of the K-T extinction is that the mystery has become so attractive that specialists from many different scientific disciplines have directed their attention to it. In the long run, this is a good situation, because it may reveal insights that might ultimately lead researchers to a sound understanding of the event. In the short term, however, additional confusion can be expected as specialists familiar with only one aspect of the problem develop explanations for their data while ignoring, either through design or innocent nescience, the perspectives of other disciplines.

The recent and much-debated theory that the dinosaur extinction was caused by an asteroid impact offers a good example of this point. The theory emerged when concentrations of the rare element iridium were discovered in K-T sediments in Italy, and later in many other places in the world (Alvarez and others, 1980; Prinn and Fegley, 1987). For good scientific reasons, the iridium concentration was considered by the geologists and chemists who discovered it to be the result of the impact between the earth and an extraterrestrial body, a six-mile-wide asteroid. The extinction of the dinosaurs, which occurred at approximately the same time that the iridium-rich marine clay was deposited, was attributed to the impact. However, the actual paleontological record of dinosaurs in late Maastrichtian time was not studied by the originators of the asteroid hypothesis. In actuality, the imperfect paleontological record can be interpreted as either supporting the theory of asteroid impact or ontradicting it. The long debate between the "impactors" and the "non-impactors," which persists to this day, was triggered in part by the disregard of the paleontological data in favor of the geochemical evidence. However, paleontologists, exercising their traditional bias toward fossils, would probably never have discovered the iridium anomaly and might have remained ignorant of the very good evidence for an explosive event at the end of Cretaceous Period without the involvement of scientists from other disciplines. Thus, while multidisciplinary approaches to solving the mysteries of nature can result in new perspectives and are generally good, they are also complex, leading to the fact that it might take some time before solutions are developed that satisfy all of the available data. Currently, scientists from a broad spectrum of specializations are working to reconcile the paleontological, geological, astronomical, and chemical data that pertain to the K-T extinctions. No universally acceptable answers have yet emerged, and the extinction of the dinosaurs is as great a mystery now as it was decades ago.

In spite of the confusion and uncertainty, there are a few points regarding the K-T extinctions on which there is general agreement. First, it was not just the dinosaurs that disappeared. Many other groups of organisms experienced extinction or a severe decline in abundance or diversity at about the same time that the last of the dinosaurs vanished. The demise of the dinosaurs was just a part (albeit the most notable part) of a broader episode of extinction that seems to have been of global extent. Among the most prominent non-dinosaur victims of the K-T extinction were the pterosaurs, ichthyosaurs, plesiosaurs, marsupial

Plate 22.
Extinction.

mammals, the coiled ammonites, several groups of bivalve molluscs, and plankton that secreted tiny calcareous (calcium-bearing) shells.

There also were many other groups of animals, however, that not only survived the K-T events but appear to have flourished during this time of presumed biotic stress. The survivors include the crocodiles and turtles, amphibians such as frogs and salamanders, many lizards, small placental mammals, birds, bony fish, sharks, and plankton that possessed siliceous (containing silica) shells. Mysteriously, many of the survivors were living in the same or similar habitats as those occupied by victims of the K-T extinction. The undisputed selectivity of the K-T extinctions is the most difficult conundrum scientists face in understanding how the extinctions occurred. What happened to remove so many species of calcareous plankton in the sea but left those with silica shells unaffected? What events destroyed the populations of carnivorous marine reptiles but did not create unfavorable conditions for the sharks and other predatory fish? What caused the flying and gliding pterosaurs to vanish but allowed the birds that fluttered beside them to flourish? Why did the dinosaurs disappear from the swamps of Montana while the crocodiles and turtles in the same bogs thrived? It is extremely difficult to reconcile the selectivity of the K-T extinctions with any theory that proposes an abrupt and global ecological catastrophe such as an asteroid impact.

Because of its highly selective impacts, the overall severity of the K-T extinctions is difficult to assess because it depends on what taxonomic level and which groups of organisms are chosen to be analyzed. Because its primary victims (dinosaurs and other large reptiles) were such striking creatures, perhaps the severity of the K-T extinctions often has been overstated. For example, it is frequently alleged that the K-T extinctions claimed about 75 percent of all species on the earth (see, for example, Glen, 1990; Allaby and Lovelock, 1983; Raup, 1986). However, an analysis

of more than 100 species of terrestrial and aquatic vertebrates from the K-T boundary sequence in Montana indicates that 64 percent of them survived and only 36 percent became extinct (Archibald, 1991). Among families of fish, only eleven out of eighty-five (13 percent) became extinct during the K-T transition (Benton, 1989). Other studies suggest a similarly modest extinction for all groups of organisms on a global scale (Briggs, 1995). The K-T extinction, usually described as a "mass extinction," may not have been that massive after all. Even among the dinosaurs, our principal interest in this tangled debate, it should be remembered that most of the dinosaurs that ever lived on the earth became extinct long before the end of the Cretaceous Period. As has been seen in earlier chapters, there were several dinosaur extinctions during the Mesozoic Era, each eliminating some genera from the global fauna that existed at the time. In each case, except for the K-T event, the survivors diversified again following the extinction to give rise to new faunal assemblages.

Dinosaur extinctions of varying severity can be documented at the end of the Triassic, after the early Jurassic, just before the late Cretaceous, and, of course, at the end of the Cretaceous (the K-T extinction). While some 300 dinosaur genera are known, only a few such as *Triceratops*, *Torosaurus*, *Tyrannosaurus*, *Alamosaurus*, and *Edmontosaurus* died out during the K-T extinctions. All the others had disappeared millions of years earlier for completely different reasons. Because the last of the dinosaurs disappear at the end of Cretaceous, we often think of it as *the* dinosaur extinction when, in fact, there was no such thing. Also, we have no information at all on how the events of the K-T transition affected creatures such as the insects, worms, and microbes that no doubt constituted a major portion of the Cretaceous biosphere, just as they do now. It seems a bit premature to refer to the K-T event as a "mass extinction" when we are so uncertain about its effects on the worldwide biota. This is not to deny that something unusual occurred at the end of the Cretaceous Period; it is merely to suggest that our perception of it as a major biotic crisis might reflect our preoccupation with the dinosaurs and other large reptiles.

In addition to scientists' uncertainty about the causes and severity of the K-T extinction, there is also doubt about its pace. Was it a short event produced by a sudden catastrophe? Or was it a protracted decline resulting from the much slower progression of geological and biological processes? Data on the distribution, abundance, and diversity of dinosaurs during the last few million years of the Maastrichtian Age have been used to support both a sudden extinction scenario (Sheehan and others, 1991; Sheenhan and Fastovsky, 1992) and a slower-paced, more gradual decline (see, for example, Carpenter and Breithaupt, 1986; Hulbert and Archibald, 1995). In the Hell Creek Formation of Montana, which produces almost all of the known information pertaining to dinosaur extinction, the number of genera of dinosaurs is nineteen at the base, twelve in the uppermost sixty feet, and seven at the very top (Lucas, 1994). This general pattern suggests a gradual decline rather than an abrupt disappearance of the last dinosaurs. On a global scale, at least fifty species of dinosaurs existed about 6 million years before the end of the Cretaceous Period, but only around a dozen species are documented from strata deposited 2 million years prior to the K-T boundary layer. This suggests that an abrupt decline in diversity began well before the end of the Cretaceous. However, such tabulations can be misleading, because many of the species that are counted might be invalid (recall, for example, the comments on the species of *Triceratops* earlier in this chapter) and the dating of the deposits is only approximate. The basic problem here is, once again, the abundance and quality of the data. Paleontologists need many more fossils from additional localities preserved in well-dated sediments before a more certain

perception of the timing and pace of the dinosaur extinction can be formulated.

After more than a decade of vigorous, and sometimes acrimonious, debate, most scientists now agree that there is very good evidence that something very unusual occurred at the end of the Cretaceous Period. The evidence from K-T sediments for an exceptionally explosive event is compelling and includes not only iridium but also shattered ("shocked metamorphosed") quartz grains, tiny glassy spheres that probably represent droplets of liquefied rock, and soot-like globules of carbon thought to be the fallout from global wildfires (Bohor and others, 1984; Wolbach and others, 1988). Though none of these things have yet been found in the North Horn Formation of Utah, they have been detected in enough of the world's K-T deposits that they can no longer be dismissed. These discoveries all indicate that something very explosive occurred during the time that the last dinosaurs were struggling to survive. Perhaps that event was the impact of an asteroid. Some scientists (for example, Officer, 1994) consider these things to be evidence of unusually violent and widespread volcanic activity. The recent discovery of a large impact structure of K-T age in the Yucatan Peninsula of Mexico, along with deposits of rubble around the Gulf of Mexico attributed to the enormous waves generated by the impact, has stimulated additional discussion of the probability of an asteroid impact.

Some scientists (for example, Officer, 1994) continue to resist the idea of an asteroid impact at the end of the Cretaceous Period, however, explaining the unusual materials in the boundary sediments, and the wave-deposited debris, as the consequence of extremely violent volcanic activity and oceanic tempests related to either the volcanism or to powerful earthquakes that it might have generated (see, for example, Officer, 1994). As was learned in Chapter 1, the end of the Cretaceous was a time of extraordinarily intense volcanic activity worldwide, and the iridium, shocked quartz, and glassy droplets might conceivably have originated during such an unusual volcanic rampage. Recall also that at the end of the CretaceousPeriod a rapid global regression of the sea was under way. The falling sea level would have altered the pattern of land and ocean, inducing profound climatic changes in many locations around the world. The mixing of previously separated dinosaur faunas, as we have seen in the case of the appearance of *Alamosaurus* in North America, has been documented between other continents elsewhere in the world near the end of Cretaceous time. When isolated populations of animals are brought into contact with each other, disease epidemics almost always follow, as new pathogens are introduced into populations that have little resistance to them. Thus, in terms of the geological, biological, climatological, and (probably) even the astronomical events of the time, the terminal Cretaceous was a chaotic episode in the history of our planet. Any one of these phenomena might have caused the extinction of the dinosaurs, but it was probably the biotic stress that resulted from their combined effects that finally ended the dinosaurs' reign. If so, then researchers can make no simple statements about the agent of dinosaur extinction; many factors were involved in a complex and interconnected way. With more and better data on the K-T boundary events, scientists may someday be able to model these interactions and demonstrate exactly how the K-T extinctions occurred. In the meantime, one should be wary of short, sweet, singular answers to the mystery of dinosaur extinction. Such answers are, at best, oversimplifications; at worst, they are probably dead wrong.

Whatever ecological developments may have occurred during the K-T transition, after the middle portion of the North Horn Formation was deposited in Utah the days of the dinosaurs were over. In the subsequent epochs of the Tertiary Period, especially the Paleocene and Eocene, the fossil record of Utah is extraordinarily rich. Literally tens of thousands of fossils have been collected from the early Cenozoic strata in the High Plateaus, Uinta Basin, and other places in Utah. The study of these fossils reveals a magnificent menagerie of primitive mammals but discloses no hint of the dinosaurs. The world had passed from the "Age of Reptiles" to the "Age of Mammals."

TEN

Doing Paleontology

PALEONTOLOGISTS HAVE been studying dinosaur bones from Utah for nearly 150 years. During this time, many thousands of fossil bones have been collected and analyzed by hundreds of scientists from all over the world. In the preceding chapters, the results of this research have been summarized and a general portrait of Utah dinosaurs and the world they inhabited has been presented, at least as they are currently understood. After such a lengthy period of study, some might expect that little remains to be discovered. It may appear to some readers that the glorious days of dinosaur paleontology in Utah are, like the dinosaurs themselves, artifacts of the past. In fact, however, just the opposite is true: however substantial our current knowledge of Utah dinosaurs might seem, much more remains to be discovered than has been learned thus far. Many questions still exist about nearly every dinosaur that has been documented in the Mesozoic fossil record of Utah. In spite of the many years of dedicated work by scientists, the knowledge of Utah dinosaurs—their anatomy, their habits and habitats, and their evolution and history—is still severely limited. As is obvious from the earlier chapters of this book, scientists have many more questions than they have answers about Utah dinosaurs. This might prompt additional questions: Why have the results come so slowly? What might we anticipate in the years ahead? How do people become involved in the quest to solve the many mysteries that remain about Utah dinosaurs?

Vertebrate paleontology is a unique science, practiced by a rather peculiar breed of scientists. In the modern age of sophisticated analytical capabilities, vertebrate paleontology is still a field-based, outdoor science. To do vertebrate paleontology, you must have fossils; and fossils are not found in laboratories and libraries. There are, of course, many paleontologists who employ high-tech approaches to the study of fossils, such as the many computer-based techniques of imaging, analysis, and modeling. Scientists have learned a

great deal from the application of such technology, but the fossils themselves still represent the essential and fundamental data through which we gain insights on the vanished world of the dinosaurs. Recall from Chapter 2 that the process of fossilization produces numerous limitations in our basic data set. The fossil record is undeniably biased and fragmentary. Because of this, some questions may never be answered, at least to the degree of certainty that scientists might like. Other questions, however, might be resolved by more and better data; that is, when new fossils are discovered that help researchers formulate a better idea of some aspect of the Mesozoic world. Finding these fossils is not always easy or simple, even in a place like Utah where they are relatively abundant. The search for fossils can be a time-consuming endeavor, and this is one reason why the expansion of the knowledge of Utah dinosaurs has taken so long.

I am often asked how paleontologists go about the business of finding dinosaur bones. While each individual paleontologist has his or her own unique strategy for finding fossils, there are several steps in the process that are followed by most. First, the search for fossils is not a random quest to find just any dinosaur remains. Instead, specific fossils are targeted that will help answer a particular question. A paleontologist might be interested in learning more about the species of a certain ceratopsian dinosaur, let's say *Torosaurus*, for example. First, that scientist has to become acquainted with everything that is currently known about this genus. This stage of the investigation might require months of library research, compiling all the information on *Torosaurus* that has been published previously. The researcher would also contact specialists in ceratopsian dinosaurs to see if they have any additional information that would help resolve the questions. Perhaps other scientists may want to join the effort, at which point the project becomes a collaborative endeavor. You may notice in the technical literature on dinosaurs, much of which has been cited in the bibliography of this book, that single authors are relatively rare. Collaboration in vertebrate paleontology is a time-honored tradition, because for most questions, two (or three or four) heads are better than one. Eventually, the researchers may decide that their questions cannot be addressed by existing fossils, so they begin to plan an expedition to find the material that might help provide answers. If the questions concern *Torosaurus*, they would not plan an expedition to outcrops of the Morrison or Chinle formations, both of which are older than any known ceratopsian dinosaur. The researchers would concentrate on deposits of latest Cretaceous age (Maastrichtian), because it was during that time that the ceratopsian dinosaurs were abundant and diverse. As was discussed in the last chapter, the scientists might have several different rock units and places to choose from in selecting the site for their *Torosaurus* expedition. To make the best choice, a paleontologist might spend days, weeks, and even months compiling what is known about the stratigraphy, structure, and depositional environments of Maastrichtian strata in Utah. He or she might have to read scores of scientific papers, make dozens of phone calls, and visit several different libraries. Ultimately the research team can select, usually from several possibilities, a field location where sediments that accumulated at the right time, and under conditions favorable to the preservation of bones, are well exposed. In this step of the process, the scientists have improved their chances of finding fossils by targeting an area where rocks of the appropriate age and origin are most accessible.

At this stage, the researchers are ready to embark on their expedition. Many people envision that this expeditionary phase of the work is all that vertebrate paleontology is about; but, as we have already seen, it is just one step in a much longer process. The general public often perceives field paleontology as an "Indiana Jones" sort of adventure; however, in reality, it is most often much less glamorous. Because there is still no way to locate dinosaur fossils from satellites or airplanes, and no remote sensing techniques can reveal the presence of fossil bones over a broad area, the actual finding of scientific treasures requires walking…and walking…and walking. This means dealing directly with all the hazards and discomforts of any outdoor activity: heat, thirst, rugged terrain, rattlesnakes, insects, and weather, to name just a few. In addition, it is almost axiomatic that the best sites for the reconnaissance prove to be in very remote locations. Just getting within walking distance of the outcrops can be a challenge that requires some rough (and often dangerous) four-wheel-drive travel. I personally even have used horses a couple of times to prospect for fossils in especially rugged areas impassable to all-terrain vehicles. Unexpected problems, such as mechanical breakdowns (or injured horses) or violent and nasty thunderstorms, pose obstacles to an expedition that are not quickly or easily overcome. Once in a while, paleontologists get lucky and find significant fossils by almost stepping on them as they climb out of the truck. More commonly, however, the fossils are located only after days of laborious and exhausting reconnaissance.

Once fossils are located, a preliminary assessment of their significance is made. Usually, the exposed portion of skeletal remains allows the paleontologist to make a preliminary identification of the bones, estimate the quality of preservation, and determine whether or not the material warrants additional effort. Sometimes the paleontologist can't be sure about these things on the basis of the scrappy and weathered bone exposed on the surface, so some of the concealing sediment is carefully removed from the fragile fossils. If it appears that the fossils might provide some useful information, it is time to begin the excavation in earnest. The fossil bones normally are not "dug up," as is commonly thought. Instead, the fossils are left in a block of surrounding material that is isolated from the barren sediment by carefully digging and chipping a slot around the fossil-bearing rock. The isolation of the block may take days or weeks, depending on its size and delicacy, as brushes, dental tools, trowels, chisels, and ice picks are used to remove rock in small pieces. On rare occasions, the block and the fossils might be large and durable enough to allow power tools, such as concrete saws and pneumatic drills, to be used in this stage. Penetrating hardeners, usually various adhesives and glues thinned in a solvent, are applied to the delicate bones during the isolation process to protect them from the vibrations generated while the slots are cut. Once the fossil-bearing block is isolated, it is jacketed with a hard shell that will protect the fossils during removal and transport. The idea here is similar to that of a physician placing a cast on broken bone: the hard shell holds the rock and bone in place, preventing damage or dislocation of the materials inside. Traditionally, the jackets are made by dipping burlap strips in plaster and wrapping them around the block on top of a layer of paper, plastic, or foil that serves as a separator. If the block is large, strips of wood or lengths of steel rods ("rebar") can be used to strengthen the cast. Some paleontologists are beginning to use quick-catalyzing resins and expanding foams in place of plaster for jacketing blocks. After the hard shell is constructed and cured, the block is removed and transported back to a laboratory for further work. If a partial skeleton has been found, many blocks may be required for its complete retrieval. In some very productive dinosaur quarries, this effort may go on for many years before all of the fossils have been collected. This is the case in several Utah sites, such as the Cleveland-Lloyd Quarry, the Long Walk Quarry, the Dalton Well Quarry, and others. The field excavation phase may take a few days, or it may go on for decades. But the work is far from over!

The jacketed blocks are normally returned to what is known as a "preparation laboratory," which may be anything from an enclosed loading dock or garage to a gleaming high-tech workroom full of specialized equipment. In the preparation lab, the jackets are carefully opened and the

meticulous process of the cleaning of the rock matrix from the fossil bones begins. This step in the process involves the use of tools ranging from tiny probes to miniature sand-blasting machines to pneumatic chisels. This work, the "preparation" of the fossils, is agonizingly slow. Haste in this delicate operation usually results in damaged or destroyed fossils. As a general rule, paleontologists plan on at least a year of work in the lab to prepare what was collected in a few weeks during the field season. Even more time can be required if the fossils are particularly delicate or, as is the case in many museums and colleges, if a staff of trained, full-time preparators is not available. The preparation of fossil bones requires patience, skill, and tolerance for monotonous work. A good preparator can work wonders on fossil bones; an impatient or inexperienced one can easily ruin a priceless treasure.

After preparation, the cleaned fossils, which are usually just bone fragments, are restored by assembling the pieces into complete bones and sealing the cracks with a fixative to prevent deterioration. In general, paleontologists try to avoid filling in missing portions of the bones, because this may alter the original morphology in a way that might lead to the misinterpretation of its form. In most institutions that house fossil collections, the bones are inventoried and assigned a number in a collections data base. Important information accompanying the specimen, such as the geological horizon from which it was collected, the precise geographic location of the field site, the character of the enclosing rock matrix, and other details, are recorded in the computerized data base. The specimen then goes into storage until time is available for a detailed study of it, or a replica is made from it, or it goes on display in a museum exhibit.

This entire process in vertebrate paleontology, from the outset of the library research to the cataloging of the prepared fossils, may take decades. This is why so many dinosaur projects are in a seemingly perpetual "ongoing" state. For example, recall that bones were first discovered at Dinosaur National Monument in 1909 and at the Cleveland-Lloyd Quarry in the 1930s. Both of these sites are still producing new information and probably will continue to do so indefinitely. More recent discoveries in Utah, such as the Gaston and Long Walk quarries, are not likely to be exhausted during the lifetime of anyone reading this book. The point is: we can't expect quick answers to the many questions about Utah dinosaurs that can only be resolved by more and better fossils than are currently available. Eventually, scientists will know more and be able to inform us about the Mesozoic world and its inhabitants, but we must be patient. That is the nature of the game in vertebrate paleontology.

The study of dinosaurs is currently experiencing a renaissance of sorts. While the fossils will always be the essential data of these fascinating creatures, scientists are beginning to move beyond the simple desciption of new dinosaur types into fields of research that may open completely new vistas into the Mesozoic world. This expansion of knowledge and perspectives is attributable to several factors. First, over the past twenty years or so, there has been a dramatic increase in the number of scientists studying dinosaurs and dinosaur-related issues, such as the K-T extinction and Mesozoic paleobiogeography. Today, there are more paleontologists studying dinosaurs than at any time in history. Many of these scientists are engaged in studies designed to address more than just the skeletal anatomy of dinosaurs, which has been the traditional focus of research for over a century. Also, advances in technology have resulted in many new tools of analysis, such as CT-scanning devices and DNA-sequencing techniques, that were unheard of just a few decades ago. In addition, the cladistic method of classifying and analyzing dinosaur family trees has changed some older perceptions of dinosaur relationships that were based on the traditional morphometric approach. In combination, these factors are allowing scientists to confront such in-

teresting aspects of the dinosaurs as their behavior, their patterns of dispersal, their evolutionary histories, and their physiology in ways that were unimaginable in the early twentieth century. The future of dinosaur paleontology is promising, and we can look forward to many exciting discoveries. The nature of the dinosaur fossil record may not allow the complete resolution of all of the present mysteries about dinosaurs, but the present flurry of interest will almost certainly settle some of the debates. What is particularly appealing about the current frenzy of interest in dinosaurs is that almost anyone can play a role in it.

Vertebrate paleontology has traditionally been more accessible to a wider range of practitioners than most sciences have been. Many important discoveries have been made by amateurs with little or no academic background in the subject but with a compelling interest in the life of the past. It doesn't take much to find dinosaur bones and to make important contributions to paleontological knowledge. Imagine trying to discover a new subatomic particle in your garage, or unraveling the structure of DNA in your kitchen, or studying the surface of Neptune from your back porch. Success in such scientific efforts would be unlikely. But in vertebrate paleontology, where all knowledge is derived from fossils, a good pair of hiking boots along with the knowledge of what to look for and where to find it is all that is required for a breakthrough discovery to be made.

As has been described above, however, developing the full potential of a new discovery is not easy or simple. For this reason, it is important that people interested in becoming involved in the effort to expand the understanding of dinosaurs do so in collaboration with scientists in universities and museums. This is not because vertebrate paleontology is the sole domain of the "privileged" academics and/or their "elite" institutions. Paleontology is a science for all people. However, scientists with experience in field paleontology and with access to properly equipped laboratories can spare the amateur collector the cost and trouble of acquiring those things on his or her own. They can help the amateur target the search for new fossils and can assist in properly completing the various stages of work that will be required for any discovery to have full impact. In most museum and university programs in vertebrate paleontology, the involvement of volunteers is not only welcomed, it is desperately needed. This is because there are actually very few professional paleontologists in the world, perhaps fewer than 100. Most researchers work as college professors, as museum professionals, or in government agencies. This, of course, means that they have other tasks that seem to take up nearly all of their available time. Hence, they would accomplish little were it not for the volunteers willing to lend assistance in the lab and in the field. Since so few scientists are actually employed specifically as paleontologists, I suppose it is not inaccurate to view most of us as amateurs. We are, as a general rule, motivated by the same things that stir the amateur collector to action: the sheer excitement of exploring an ancient world and the thrill of discovering the unknown. Perhaps that is one reason why there has been such a strong professional-amateur bond throughout the history of vertebrate paleontology. We are all united by something much more powerful than the superficial distinctions such as academic degrees and professional status that separate us. In any event, no one should hesitate to contact paleontologists at your local museum or college about volunteer opportunities in paleontology. You'll almost always be welcomed aboard.

In many areas, there are organizations that can help make connections between professional paleontologists and amateurs. In Utah, the Utah Friends of Paleontology, a statewide association with numerous local chapters, has been heavily involved with paleontological excavations and community education for many years. Local chapters of such organizations are commonly based at community museums or colleges. A sim-

ple inquiry about organizations of this type will usually get you started on the right track. If there are no museums or colleges in your area, try calling the nearest one. One or more of your neighbors might already be involved in paleontology and can give you guidance in getting involved. For institutions and agencies in Utah that have active programs in paleontology, see the list at the end of this chapter. In other areas, check with your local equivalents to these organizations.

In addition to maximizing the value of your efforts, there is another reason for channeling your interest in paleontology through a volunteer organization or individual contact with an institution. The removal of vertebrate fossils from most public land is illegal, either by policy or statute, without a permit from the appropriate management agency. In Utah, a state composed predominantly of public land, collecting permits are issued by the state of Utah, U.S. Forest Service, U.S. Bureau of Land Management, National Park Service, and various tribal agencies for land within Native American reservations. Though the criteria and stipulations of the permitting process vary somewhat from agency to agency as well as over time, permits are rarely issued to private individuals. This is because there is growing concern over the looting and vandalism of dinosaur fossil sites by unauthorized private collectors. Laws protecting paleontological resources on public lands have not been as clearly defined as those protecting archaeological resources (such as ARPA, the Archaeological Resources Protection Act), but efforts are currently under way to clarify the prohibition against the private collection of what are, in reality, public resources that belong to everyone. This is a highly controversial topic, one that always generates heated debate between resource managers, amateur collectors, land owners, and professional paleontologists. The issue has come to a head recently because many private collectors are willing to pay substantial sums to acquire dinosaur bones for their personal collections. In short, a black market for dinosaur bones has developed similar to that which has led to the tragic vandalism of many archaeological sites in Utah and other regions. The furor over the protection of paleontological resources stems from the well-intended efforts to halt the loss of valuable scientific information as unscrupulous collectors convert public property to personal gain.

Any paleontologist who has spent much time in the field can relate stories of specimens lost or destroyed by vandals. Sadly, nearly all dinosaur paleontologists can offer many such testimonies. So, protecting paleontological resources on public land makes good sense; but exactly how best to do it without violating or restricting rights of access, or placing obstacles in the path of legitimate research projects, is at the center of all the contention. Currently, there are no uniform regulations that apply on a national level to all public land. As management agencies continue to address the issue, there may soon be consistent guidelines that will help reduce the threat of vandalism of dinosaur sites. Nonetheless, it is usually very difficult for private individuals, unaffiliated with a paleontological organization or academic institution, to secure a collecting permit for vertebrate fossils. Involvement with a museum, college, or recognized organization eliminates the problem of a permit and ensures that the best uses will be made of whatever new fossil material you locate.

Another benefit of channeling your interest in dinosaurs through an institution or organization, perhaps the most attractive advantage of all, is the people with whom you will come into contact. Vertebrate paleontology has traditionally attracted people with a wide range of interests in the natural world and with diverse talents. Maybe this results from the necessity in paleontology of applying concepts from a variety of scientific disciplines. After all, to fully understand the events documented in the fossil record, researchers need to master the fundamental ideas of biology, geology, chemistry, physics, and other sciences. My personal suspicion is that the unique nature of

paleontological inquiry requires even additional versatility. At times it is as important for paleontologists to be able to repair a broken fuel pump as it is to construct a cladogram. Most paleontologists can do both. Paleontologists need to develop skill in using dental tools on very delicate specimens, but they also have to confront problems of moving blocks of rock that weigh several hundred pounds. This multidimensional aspect of vertebrate paleontology breeds a unique genre of scientists, people fascinated by the innumerable intricacies of the natural world and possessing an uncommonly broad array of talents. In general, vertebrate paleontologists are fun to be around. Most tend to be generous with their knowledge, unassuming, and thrilled to share their zeal for prehistoric life with anyone. In a crowd of dinosaur paleontologists, you will probably encounter more colorful characters, more diverse viewpoints, and a wider range of personalities than is typical of society at large. You'll also develop a whole new dimension in your sense of humor, if you hang around long enough. Seen against the backdrop of millions of years of evolution and extinction, the conventions and customs of modern human society take on an almost comical aspect. Vertebrate paleontologists, by virtue of their unique perspective on the history of life and human existence, tend to see our world a bit differently from most folks. You will most likely enjoy their company.

So You Want to Be a Paleontologist?

Sooner or later, all paleontologists are asked how one prepares for a career as a dinosaur paleontologist. It is usually, but not always, younger people who ask this question. Fearful of quenching youthful enthusiasm, I normally respond with a reminder that paleontology is a unique discipline that requires academic preparation in the basic sciences and mathematics. Careers in paleontology are best built upon such a foundation of knowledge. However, it might be better advice to simply say, "Don't bother!" There are very few professional paleontologists, and opportunities for gainful employment in the field are severely restricted. This bleak employment outlook, despite the public frenzy over dinosaurs, seems to be getting worse, not better. Many museums that proudly display dinosaur skeletons in their exhibits don't have vertebrate paleontologists on the staff. Several research-grade fossil collections have been transferred from prestigious universities during the past decade, as more and more institutions eliminate or deemphasize paleontology as a part of the science curriculum. Funding for paleontological projects is becoming increasingly difficult to acquire in comparison with that for other scientific fields. This trend has been the subject of extensive discussions among paleontologists. The reasons for it are numerous and complicated, but the fact of the matter is that professional opportunities in paleontology are not likely to expand anytime soon.

So, should young (or older) people be discouraged from pursuing an interest that likely will not result in any viable career options for them? Absolutely not! Even if the chances of establishing a career in paleontology are very remote, a lifetime of wonder and awe is a more than adequate reward for all who seek to comprehend the life of past. Whether or not we get paid to participate in this intellectual journey is not nearly as important as simply doing it.

It is precisely the deficiency of opportunities in professional paleontology that makes the in-volvement of nonprofessionals so critical. Without the interest and commitment of the general public, the growth of knowledge about dinosaurs, or any other group of prehistoric creatures, would crawl along at a snail's pace. It might even eventually stop dead in its tracks, if the winds of academic fashion continue to blow against us. There are simply too few professionals to address the many questions and mysteries concerning the dinosaurs; and there will always be too few professionals for this task. So, the best way to join the excitement of exploring the prehistoric world is to get involved with the institutions and organizations that are struggling to keep paleontology alive. They need your help and, in turn, can provide an avenue for the fulfillment that comes from active participation in scientific work. To contribute to paleontology, you don't necessarily need to be a "professional." All you really need is the passion for learning about the history of life on our planet and the willingness to take the initiative to make contact with people sharing that fervor. Virtually anyone reading this book can make valuable contributions to this never-ending quest to resolve the mysteries of the past. You have already demonstrated, by your interest in Utah dinosaurs, the primary qualification for involvement in paleontology: the enthusiasm for learning about prehistoric life. And, that is all it really takes. An amazing world of discovery awaits you in the wild splendor of Utah's dinosaur country. Perhaps I'll meet you there.

Institutions and Organizations in Utah with Active Programs in Paleontology

Earth Science Museum
Brigham Young University
Provo, UT 84602
801-378-3680

Utah Museum of Natural History
University of Utah
Salt Lake City, UT 84112
801-581-4303

Museum of Natural Science/
Department of Geology
Weber State University
Ogden, UT 84408
801-626-6653

Dinosaur National Monument
P.O. Box 128
Jensen, UT 84035
435-789-2115

Cleveland-Lloyd Dinosaur Quarry
c/o River Resource Area
Bureau of Land Management
900 North 700 East
Price, UT 84501
435-637-4584

Utah Field House of Natural History
235 East Main Street
Vernal, UT 84078
435-789-3799

Office of the Utah State Paleontologist
Utah Geological and Mineral Survey
P.O. Box 146100
Salt Lake City, UT 84114-6100
801-537-3300

Gratitude is extended to the following authors and publishers for permission to reproduce the following artistic material:

PERMISSIONS

Geological Society of America for Figure 1-6, from Sereno, P.C. 1991. Ruling reptiles and wandering continents: A global look at dinosaur evolution. *GSA Today* 1, no. 7:141–45.

Museum of Northern Arizona for Figures 3-4A–C and 3-5A–D, F, from Colbert, E.H. 1972. Vertebrates from the Chinle Formation. *Museum of Northern Arizona Bulletin* 47:1–11; and for Figures 4-8A–D, from Colbert, E.H. 1981. A primitive ornithischian dinosaur from the Kayenta Formation of Arizona. *Bulletin of the Museum of Northern Arizona* 53:1–61.

Cambridge University Press for Figure 4-14, from Lockley, M.G. 1991a. *Tracking dinosaurs: A new look at an ancient world*. Cambridge: Cambridge University Press.

Utah Geological and Mineral Survey for Figure 6-7, from Madsen, J.H., Jr. 1976b. *Allosaurus fragilis*: a revised osteology. *Utah Geological and Mineral Survey Bulletin* 109.

ALLUVIAL APRON: a broad surface consisting of alluvium that slopes from a steep mountain front toward the lowlands. Alluvial aprons are also known as bajadas and result from the overgrowth and coalescence of adjacent alluvial fans.

ALLUVIAL FAN: a fan-shaped mass of alluvium deposited at the foot of a mountain where stream velocity decreases sharply.

ALLUVIUM: a general term for any sediment (clay, gravel, sand, etc.) deposited by flowing water.

AMMONITE: an extinct mollusc with coiled shell of the class Cephalopoda, order Ammonitida. Ammonites were abundant in the seas of the Mesozoic Era.

ANAPSID: a reptile belonging to the subclass Anapsida, which is characterized by the absence of temporal fenestrae in the skull. Turtles and tortoises are modern anapsids, but many other extinct types are known from the fossil record.

ANGIOSPERM: a flowering plant; the dominant type of plant in the modern flora.

ANTORBITAL FENESTRA: an opening on the side of the skull just in front of the eye. All archosaurs possess at least one antorbital fenestra.

ARBOREAL: living primarily in trees.

ARCHOSAURS: any diapsid reptile, living or extinct, that belongs to the infraclass Archosauria. The archosaurs include the crocodiles, dinosaurs, pterosaurs, and (according to some scientists) the birds.

BENTONITE: a clay-rich rock that forms from the weathering of volcanic ash.

BIVALVE: a name referring to the clams, oysters, and mussels of the class Bivalvia of the phylum Mollusca.

CALCITE: a carbonate mineral of composition $CaCO_3$; a common constituent of sedimentary rocks.

CALICHE: nodules or layers of calcium carbonate

$(CaCO_3)$ that form in the soil, usually under warm and dry climatic conditions.

CARNOSAUR: a large theropod, generally with very small forelimbs and a massive head.

CARTILAGE: a hard but flexible connective tissue that consists of collagen fibers, special cells, and cellular secretions. Cartilage is found on the ends of some bones (for example, ribs) or between bones that are connected in a joint. In the skull, vertebrae, and limb bones, cartilage may be converted to less flexible bone after maturity.

CAST: in paleontology, a fossil represented by rock or mineral mass that forms in a cavity within or around the original organic tissues.

CAUDAL: of or pertaining to the tail.

CENOZOIC: the era of "modern life," also known as the "Age of Mammals," encompassing approximately the last 65 million years of geologic time.

CERVICAL: of or pertaining to the neck.

CLADE: a cluster of organisms that share a common ancestor. A clade may consist of several taxonomic groups and may be recognized at several different levels of biological classification.

CLADISTICS: a method of categorizing organisms based on shared derived and primitive features. Cladistic analysis often reveals patterns of relationship that are not obvious from the morphology alone.

CLASS: a taxonomic category below the phylum and above the order; that is, a subdivision of a phylum and an aggregate of orders.

COAL: a sedimentary rock that consists of the compressed and altered remains of plant tissues such as leaves, twigs, bark, etc. Coal deposits usually represent swampy conditions where plant matter accumulated in thick layers.

CONGLOMERATE: a sedimentary rock that consists mostly of rounded particles larger than 2 mm (1/12 inch) in size. Conglomerates usually represent coarse sediment, such as gravel and pebbles, deposited by swift rivers.

COPROLITE: a rock composed of fossilized dung.

CORACOID: a roughly circular bone fused or otherwise attached to the lower end of the scapula in a dinosaur shoulder.

CRETACEOUS: the last period of the Mesozoic Era, from about 144–65 million years ago.

CREVASSE SPLAY: a mass of sand and silt that is deposited as a result of floodwater breaching the natural levee along a river channel.

CURSORIAL: capable of running efficiently; or, also, a skeletal feature specifically adapted to enhance running abilities.

DELTAIC: of or pertaining to deltas, the wedge-shaped masses of sediment that accumulate when rivers empty into a body of standing water. Many dinosaur fossils are found in deltaic sediments deposited along ancient coastal plains.

DIAPSID: a term that describes the two temporal openings in the skulls of dinosaurs and related reptiles; a member of the subclass Diapsida of the class Reptilia.

DISTAL: the lower, rearward, or far end of a bone or structure; cf. PROXIMAL.

DNA: an abbreviation for deoxyribonucleic acid, the complex molecule that carries the genetic code in all organisms. DNA molecules are formed from two strands of sugar molecules linked by phosphate units and connected to each other by unique pairs of organic molecules known as bases. This ladder-like structure is twisted into the form of the famous "double helix."

DORSAL: the upper, or skyward, direction; also, a term applied to the vertebrae of the spinal column between the hips and shoulders.

ECTOTHERMIC: a term describing the physiology of an animal that receives its body heat from external sources such as the sun. The common phrase "cold-blooded" is nearly synonymous with ectothermic, because such creatures have only limited ability to generate internal heat.

ENDOTHERMIC: a term applied to any animal capable of sustaining a high and uniform body temperature through the generation of internal (metabolic) heat. Endothermic creatures, such a modern mammals and birds, are not dependent on outside sources for body heat. In common language, the term "warm-blooded" is synonymous with endothermic.

FEMUR: the largest and uppermost bone of the hind limb; the "thigh bone."

FIBULA: a small, rod-like bone that lies against the tibia in the lower hind limb between the knee and the ankle.

FLUVIAL: of or pertaining to rivers. A fluvial sandstone, for example, is a sandstone consisting of grains deposited by a flowing stream.

FORMATION: a body of rock layers that has more or less uniform characteristics that allow it to be distinguished from other rock units adjacent to it.

GASTROLITHS: "stomach stones"; smooth, rounded, and highly polished stones produced in the gizzards or gizzard-like organs of some birds and reptiles.

GASTROPOD: a mollusc of the order Gastropoda, commonly referred to as snails.

GENUS, GENERA (pl.): the level of biological classification immediately above the species and below the family. Many dinosaurs are referred to by their genus name alone, such as *Diplodocus* or *Allosaurus*, even though several different species of each may be recognized.

GROUP: in geological usage, a group consists of several formations of similar lithologic character and origin.

GYMNOSPERMS: a large group of relatively primitive plants that produce "naked" seeds uncovered by tissue layers. Modern gymnosperms include the conifers, junipers, cycads, and ginkgoes.

GYPSUM: a sulfate mineral of the composition $CaSO_4\ 2H_2O$. Gypsum forms most readily by the evaporation of water from a lake, the ocean, or from soil. When present in sedimentary rocks, gypsum usually indicates dry climatic conditions in the prehistoric past.

INNER CORE: the innermost interior subdivision of the planet Earth. The inner core is composed mostly of solid iron and is approximately 1,500 miles in diameter.

JURASSIC: the middle period of the Mesozoic Era, extending from about 208–144 million years ago.

K-T: a common abbreviation used by geologists to designate the boundary between the Cretaceous Period (K) and the Tertiary Period (T). The K-T boundary is also the boundary between the Mesozoic and Cenozoic eras.

KINGDOM: the highest level of biological classification.

LACUSTRINE: of or pertaining to lakes. A lacustrine mudstone, for example, consists of silt and clay grains that accumulated on the floor of a lake.

LARAMIDE OROGENY: the late Cretaceous to early Cenozoic (approximately 70–35 million years ago) episode of mountain building that affected much of the Rocky Mountain region. In Utah, the Uinta Mountains, San Rafael Swell, and Capitol Reef areas were among the regions affected by uplift during the Laramide Orogeny.

LAVA: a common term for magma that erupts onto the earth's surface from an underground reservoir.

LEPIDOSAURS: any diapsid reptile belonging to the infraclass Lepidosauria, which includes the modern snakes and lizards, along with other extinct forms.

LIGAMENT: a band, sheath, or cord of strong but elastic tissue that connects bones or muscles. Ligaments commonly brace joints between bones, but they may also serve to connect muscles to bones.

MAGMA: molten rock generated by high temperatures beneath the surface of the earth; cf. LAVA.

MANTLE: the largest interior subdivision of the Earth, located between the thin crust and the core. The mantle is approximately 1,900 miles thick and contains nearly 80 percent of the mass of the planet Earth.

MARGINOCEPHALIA: a group, or clade, of ornithischian dinosaurs that possess skulls decorated by frills, spikes, or nodes. This group consists of the ceratopsian dinosaurs, the pachycephalosaurs, and their common ancestors.

MAXILLA: the (paired) bones of the upper jaw that contain the cheek teeth.

MEMBER: a subdivision of a formation.

MESOCORDILLERAN HIGH: a term that describes the highlands that existed from about early Triassic to middle Jurassic time in western Utah and eastern Nevada. The Mesocordilleran High was the precursor of the Sevier Orogenic Belt.

MESOTARSAL: a term that describes the simple hinge-like construction of the ankle of a dinosaur and other vertebrates.

MESOZOIC: the era of "middle life"; the great "Age of Reptiles," extending from about 245–65 million years ago.

METACARPAL: a bone in the middle portion of the "hand" or forefoot between the wrist and the fingers.

METAMORPHIC ROCKS: rocks that have undergone some change in chemistry, texture, or physical properties through the process of metamorphism.

METAMORPHISM: the process of altering the original characteristics of rocks through the effects of heat, pressure, and chemically active fluids and vapors.

METATARSAL: a bone in the middle portion, or "instep," of the foot between the ankle and the toes.

MOLD: as applied to fossils, an impression made in the surrounding rock by the surface of an organic structure such as a shell or bone.

NATURAL LEVEE: a elongated mound of sandy sediment that forms along the banks of rivers during flood events.

NEURAL SPINE: a blade or spike of bone that projects upward from the vertebrae that comprise the spinal column.

ORBIT: the opening in the skull that houses the eye; the eye socket.

ORDER: a taxonomic category between the class and the family; that is, a subdivision of a class, consisting of (usually) several families.

ORNITHISCHIA: an order of dinosaurs in which the pubis is positioned nearly parallel to the ischium so that both bones point down and back from the center of the pelvis. The ornithischian dinosaurs include the ceratopsians, the ornithopods, the stegosaurs, and the ankylosaurs.

ORNITHOPOD: any ornithischian dinosaur that belongs to the suborder Ornithopoda. This group includes all the bipedal, herbivorous types, such as "duck-bill" dinosaurs, hypsilophodonts, heterodontosaurids, hadrosaurs, and iguanodontids.

OUTER CORE: the fluid portion of the earth's core that surrounds the inner core. The outer core is composed of molten iron that circulates vigorously as it is heated by the inner core below.

PALEOZOIC: the era of "ancient life," from about 570–245 million years ago.

PERMINERALIZATION: a mode of fossil preservation in which the open spaces in porous organic tissue such as bone or wood are filled with mineral matter.

PHALANX, PHALANGES (pl.): a small bone, or bones, of the digits (fingers and toes).

PLEUROCOEL: a hollow pocket, or cavity, on the sides of vertebrae.

POINT BAR: a sandbar developed in the inside of a bend of a river where current flow is insufficient to transport sand-sized grains.

PREDENTARY: the bone that forms the tip of the lower jaw, or the "chin," in ornithischian dinosaurs.

PREMAXILLA: the bone that forms the tip of the snout in dinosaurs and other reptiles.

PROXIMAL: the forward, upper, or near portion of a bone or structure; cf. DISTAL.

PUBIS: one of the three bones that comprise the dinosaur hip. The pubis projects forward and down in the saurischian dinosaurs; in the ornithischians, it generally points down and back from the pelvis.

RADIOMETRIC DATING: the method of determining the absolute age of rocks that is based on the time-dependent decay of radioactive elements.

REPLACEMENT: a mode of fossil preservation involving the replacement of original organic tissues by secondary minerals such as calcite or silica.

SACRAL: of or pertaining to the pelvis or hip region.

SACRUM: that portion of the vertebral column to which the hip bones attach.

SANDSTONE: a granular sedimentary rock with particles between 2 mm and 1/16 mm in size.

SAURISCHIA: an order of dinosaurs characterized by a pelvis in which the three bones (ilium, ischium, and pubis) diverge in a triradiate pattern. The saurischian dinosaurs include the carnivorous theropods and the herbivorous sauropods.

SAUROPOD: any dinosaur belonging to the suborder Sauropodomorpha; a large quadrupedal, herbivorous dinosaur with a long neck and tail.

SCAPULA: a long, blade-like bone of the shoulder region. In many reptiles, the lower end of the scapula is fused to a smaller bone, the coracoid, to form the scapulocoracoid.

SCLEROTIC BONES: small plate-like bones that form a ring supporting the soft tissues of the eyeball.

SCUTE(S): a plate or disk of dermal bone imbedded in the skin.

SECONDARY PALATE: the bony roof of the mouth that separates the nasal cavity from the oral cavity.

SEVIER OROGENY: a mountain-building event, characterized by compressional faulting and folding, that elevated western Utah and adjacent parts of Nevada, Idaho, and Wyoming during late Jurassic through late Cretaceous time.

SEVIER OROGENIC BELT: the late Jurassic-Cretaceous mountain system produced in western Utah by deformation attributable to the Sevier Orogeny.

SHALE: an even-textured, fine-grained sedimentary rock consisting of mineral fragments smaller than 1/256 mm.

SPECIES: the lowest level of biological classification; it describes an array of organisms that are so similar to each other that they are capable of successful interbreeding.

STRATIGRAPHIC: of or pertaining to the sequence of layering in geological deposits.

STRATIGRAPHY: the study of layered rock sequences; usually, but not always, applied to sedimentary rocks.

SYNAPSID: any reptile that belongs to the extinct subclass Synapsida, characterized by a single temporal fenestra. The synapsids are commonly referred to as the "mammal-like" reptiles and are subdivided into numerous groups. The synapsids were most common in late Paleozoic and early Mesozoic (Triassic) time.

SYSTEMATICS: the study of the relationships and evolution of groups of organisms. Systematics is related to taxonomy but is generally broader in scope, as it is concerned with the relationships of named categories of organisms through time.

TAXON: a named group of organisms of any rank; a species, genus, order, etc.

TAXONOMY: the science of naming and classifying organisms; cf. SYSTEMATICS.

TEMPORAL FENESTRAE: the openings in the side or top of reptile skulls behind the eye socket.

THECODONTS: an archaic term that has been used to describe an unnatural group of primitive reptiles that included the ancestors of dinosaurs, birds, crocodiles, and pterosaurs.

THYREOPHORA: a diverse group of armor-bearing ornithischian dinosaurs including the stegosaurs and ankylosaurs.

TIBIA: generally, the larger of two bones in the lower hind limb between the knee and the ankle; the "shin" bone.

TRANSVERSE PROCESSES: paired flanges or plates of bone that extend outward from the main body of a vertebra. The transverse processes serve as attachment points for the ribs, brace the sacral vertebrae to the ilium, and anchor some of the back muscles.

TRIASSIC: the first period of the Mesozoic Era, extending from approximately 245–208 million years ago.

TURBINATE BONES: the thin, highly convoluted sheets of bone that are located in the nasal cavity of most vertebrates. The turbinate bones have both olfactory (related to smelling) and respiratory (related to breathing) functions.

UNGUAL: a term, technically an ungual phalanx, that is applied to the last small bone in the fingers and toes. The "unguals" are commonly modified into claws or hoof-like forms.

VENTRAL: the lower, or groundward, surface or direction.

VERTEBRA, VERTEBRAE (pl.): one of the bones that comprise the backbone from the neck to the tail.

VERTEBRATE: a term used to describe animals belonging to the subclass Vertebrata of the class Chordata; any chordate that possesses internal or external bone.

VOLCANIC ASH: a granular or powdery material that consists of small rock particles formed when magma is explosively discharged from a volcano as a fine mist.

BIBLIOGRAPHY

ONE: THE MESOZOIC WORLD

General Geology and Physiography of Utah

Baars, D.L. 1983. *The Colorado Plateau: A geologic history.* Albuquerque: University of New Mexico Press.
———. 1993. *Canyonlands country.* Salt Lake City: University of Utah Press.
Hintze, L.F. 1988. *Geologic history of Utah.* Brigham Young University Geology Studies Special Publication 7. Provo, UT: Brigham Young University.
Stokes, W.L. 1986. *Geology of Utah.* Utah Museum of Natural History Occasional Paper 6. Salt Lake City: Utah Museum of Natural History/Utah Geological and Mineral Survey.

Overview of the Mesozoic Era of North America

Dott, R.H., Jr., and Prothero, D.R. 1994. *Evolution of the earth.* 5th ed. New York: McGraw-Hill.
Herendeen, P.S., Crane, P.R., and Ash, S. 1994. Vegetation of the dinosaur world. In *Dino Fest*, Rosenberg, G.D., and Wolberg, D.L., eds., 347–64. Paleontological Society Special Publication No. 7.
Russell, D.A. 1989. *An odyssey in time: The dinosaurs of North America.* Ottawa: NorthWord Press and University of Toronto Press (in association with the Canadian National Museum of Natural History).
Sereno, P.C. 1991. Ruling reptiles and wandering continents: A global look at dinosaur evolution. *GSA Today* (Geological Society of America) 1, no. 7:141–45.
Wing, S.L., and Sues, H.-D. 1992. Mesozoic and early Cenozoic terrestrial ecosystems. In *Terrestrial ecosystems through time*, Behrensmeyer, A.K., et al., eds., 327–416. Chicago and London: University of Chicago Press.

Fossilization and the Fossil Record

Hubert, J.F., Panish, P.T., Chure, D.J., and Prostak, K.S. 1996. Chemistry, microstructure, petrology, and diagenetic model of Jurassic dinosaur bones, Dinosaur National Monument, Utah. *Journal of Sedimentary Research* 66, no. 3:531–47.
Lane, N.G. 1992. *Life of the past.* 3rd ed. New York: Macmillan.
Russell, D.A. 1995. China and the lost worlds of the dinosaurian era. *Historical Biology* 10:3–13.
Stearn, C.W., and Carroll, R.L. 1989. *Paleontology: The record of life.* New York: John Wiley and Sons, Inc.

Size of Dinosaurs

Callison, G., and Quimby, H.M. 1984. Tiny dinosaurs: Are they fully grown? *Journal of Vertebrate Paleontology* 3, no. 4:200–9.
Peczkis, Jan. 1994. Implications of body-mass estimates for dinosaurs. *Journal of Vertebrate Paleontology* 14, no. 4:520–33.

TWO: WHAT IS A DINOSAUR?

Dinosaur Classification

Benton, Michael J. 1990. Origin and interrelationships of Dinosaurs. In *The Dinosauria*, Weishampel, D.B., Dodson, P., and Osmolska, H., eds., 11–30. Berkeley: University of California Press.
Carpenter, K., and Currie, P.J., eds. 1990. *Dinosaur systematics: Approaches and perspectives.* Cambridge: Cambridge University Press.
Colbert, E.H. 1964. *Relationships of the saurischian dinosaurs.* American Museum Novitates No. 2181. New York: American Museum of Natural History.
Fastovsky, D.E., and Weishampel, D.B. 1996. *The evolution and extinction of the dinosaurs.* Cambridge: Cambridge University Press.
Lucas, S.G. 1994. *Dinosaurs: The textbook.* Dubuque, IA: Wm. C. Brown Publishers.
Maryanska, T. 1992. The dinosaur radiations. In *The ultimate dinosaur: Past, present, future*, Priess, B., and Silverberg, R., eds., 50–63. New York: Bantam Books.
Norman, D.B. 1991. *Dinosaur!* New York: Prentice Hall.
Novas, F.E. 1996. Dinosaur monophyly. *Journal of Vertebrate Paleontology* 16, no. 4:723–41.
Sereno, P.C. 1986. Phylogeny of the bird-hipped dinosaurs (Order Ornithischia). *National Geographic Research* 2:234–56.
White, T.E. 1973. Catalogue of the genera of dinosaurs. *Annals of the Carnegie Museum* 44:117–55.

General Information on Vertebrate Evolution and Biology of the Dinosaurs

Carroll, R.L. 1988. *Vertebrate paleontology and evolution.* New York: W.H. Freeman and Co.
Colbert, E.H., and Morales, M. 1991. *Evolution of the vertebrates: A history of backboned animals through time.* 4th ed. New York: John Wiley and Sons.
Coombs, W.P. 1990. Behavior patterns of dinosaurs. In *The Dinosauria*, Weishampel, D., Dodson, P., and Osmolska, H., eds., 32–42. Berkeley: University of California Press.
Farlow, J.O. 1990. Dinosaur energetics and thermal biology. In *The Dinosauria*, Weishampel, D., Dodson,

P., and Osmolska, H., eds., 43–55. Berkeley: University of California Press.

Fastovsky, D.E., and Weishampel, D.B. 1996. *The evolution and extinction of the dinosaurs.* Cambridge: Cambridge University Press.

Horner, J.R. 1995. Morphology and function of the enclosed narial chambers of lambeosaurid dinosaurs. *Journal of Vertebrate Paleontology* 15, supplement to no. 3:6A.

Ruben, J.A., Leitch, A., and Hillenius, W. 1995. Respiratory turbinates and the metabolic status of some theropod dinosaurs and *Archaeopteryx. Journal of Vertebrate Paleontology* 15, supplement to no. 3:50A.

Origin of the Birds, Birdlike Dinosaurs, and Pterosaurs

Chiappe, L.M. 1995. A diversity of early birds. *Natural History* 104, no. 6:52–55.

Novas, F.E., and Puerta, P.F. 1997. New evidence concerning avian origin from the late Cretaceous of Patagonia. *Nature* 387, no. 6631:390–93.

Ostrom, J.C. 1976. *Archaeopteryx* and the origin of birds. *Biological Journal of the Linnaean Society* 8:91–182.

Padian, K. 1989. Other Mesozoic vertebrates of the land, sea, and air. In *The age of dinosaurs*, Short Course Notes No.2, Culver, S.J., ed., 146–61. Knoxville, TN: The Paleontological Society.

Padian, K., ed. 1986. The origin of birds and the evolution of flight. *California Academy of Science Memoirs* 8.

Three: Dawn of the Utah Mesozoic

Earliest Dinosaurs of North and South America

Chatterjee, S. 1986. The late Triassic Dockum vertebrates and their stratigraphic and paleobiological significance. In *The beginning of the age of dinosaurs*, Padian, K., ed., 139–60. Cambridge: Cambridge University Press.

Lucas, S.G., Hunt, A.P., and Long, R.A. 1992. The oldest dinosaurs. *Naturwissenschaften* 79:171–72.

Novas, F.E. 1993. New information on the systematics and postcranial skeleton of *Herrerasaurus ischigualastensis* (Theropoda: Herrerasauridae) from the Ischigualasto Formation (Upper Triassic) of Argentina. *Journal of Vertebrate Paleontology* 14. no. 4:400–23.

Padian, K., ed. 1986. *The beginning of the age of dinosaurs.* Cambridge: Cambridge University Press.

Rogers, R.R., Swisher, C.C., and Sereno, P.C. 1993. The Ischigualasto tetrapod assemblage (late Triassic, Argentina) and the ^{40}Ar/^{39}Ar dating of dinosaur origins. *Science* 260:794–97.

Russell, D.A. 1989. *An odyssey in time: The dinosaurs of North America.* Ottawa: NorthWord Press and University of Toronto Press (in association with the Canadian National Museum of Natural History).

Sereno, P.C., and Arcucci, A.B. 1993. Dinosaurian precursors from the middle Triassic of Argentina: *Lagerpeton chanarensis. Journal of Vertebrate Paleontology* 13, no. 4:385–99.

Sereno, P.C., Forster, C.A., Rogers, R.R., and Monetta, A.M. 1993. Primitive dinosaur skeleton from Argentina and the early evolution of dinosauria. *Nature* 361:64–66.

Sereno, P.C., and Novas, F.E. 1993. The skull and neck of the basal theropod *Herrerasaurus ischigualastensis. Journal of Vertebrate Paleontology* 14, no. 3:451–76.

On the Moenkopi Formation

Baldwin, E.J. 1973. The Moenkopi Formation of north-central Arizona: An interpretation of ancient environments based upon sedimentary structures and stratification types. *Journal of Sedimentary Petrology* 23, no. 2:92–106.

Blakey, R.C. 1974. Stratigraphic and depositional analysis of the Moenkopi Formation, southeastern Utah. *Utah Geological and Mineral Survey Bulletin* 104:1–81.

Morales, M. 1987. Terrestrial fauna and flora from the Triassic Moenkopi Formation of the southwestern United States. *Journal of the Arizona-Nevada Academy of Science* 22:1–19.

———. 1993. Tetrapod biostratigraphy of the Lower-Middle Triassic Moenkopi Formation. In *The nonmarine Triassic*, Lucas, S.G., and Morales, M., eds., 355–56. New Mexico Museum of Natural History and Science Bulletin No.3.

Peabody, F.E. 1948. Reptile and amphibian trackways from the Lower Triassic Moenkopi Formation of Arizona and Utah. *University of California Bulletin of Geological Science* 28, no. 8:295–468.

Stewart, J.H., Poole, F.G., and Wilson, R.F. 1972. Stratigraphy and origin of the Triassic Moenkopi Formation and related strata in the Colorado Plateau region. U.S. Geological Survey Professional Paper 691.

Stokes, W.L. 1986. *Geology of Utah.* Utah Museum of Natural History Occasional Paper 6. Salt Lake City: Utah Museum of Natural History/Utah Geological and Mineral Survey.

The Paleontology and Stratigraphy of the Chinle Formation and Other Late Triassic Formations in the Utah Region

Ash, S.R. 1972. Plant megafossils of the Chinle Formation. *Museum of Northern Arizona Bulletin* 47:23–43.

Blakey, R.C., and Gubitosa, R. 1983. Late Triassic paleogeography and depositional history of the Chinle

Formation, southern Utah and northern Arizona. In *Symposium on Mesozoic paleogeography of the west-central United States,* Reynolds, M.W., and Dolley, E.D., eds., 57–76. Denver: Rocky Mountain Section of the Society of Economic Paleontologists and Mineralogists.

Camp, C.L. 1930. A study of the phytosaurs, with description of new material from western North America. *University of California Memoirs* 10:1–161.

Camp, C.L., and Welles, S.P. 1956. Triassic dicynodont reptiles: Part II, The North American genus *Placerias. University of California Memoirs* 13 (4): 255–348.

Colbert, E.H. 1947. Studies of the phytosaurs *Machaeroprosopus* and *Rutiodon. American Museum of Natural History Bulletin* 88:53–96.

———. 1972. Vertebrates from the Chinle Formation. *Museum of Northern Arizona Bulletin* 47:1–11.

Colbert, E.H., and Imbrie, J. 1956. Triassic metoposaurid amphibians. *American Museum of Natural History Bulletin* 110:399–452.

Dawley, R.M., Zairiskie, J.M., and Cosgriff, J.W. 1979. A rauisuchid thecodont from the Upper Triassic Popo Agie Formation of Wyoming. *Journal of Paleontology* 53:1428–31.

Dubiel, R.F. 1987. Sedimentology of the Upper Triassic Chinle Formation, southeastern Utah—paleoclimatic implications. *Journal of the Arizona-Nevada Academy of Science* 22:35–45.

Dubiel, R.F., Boldgett, R.H., and Brown, T.M. 1987. Lungfish burrows in the Upper Triassic Chinle and Dolores Formations, Colorado Plateau. *Journal of Sedimentary Petrology* 57 (3): 512–21.

Dubiel, R.F., Parrish, J.T., Parrish, J.M., and Godd, S.C. 1991. The Pangaean Megamonsoon—evidence from the Upper Triassic Chinle Formation, Colorado Plateau. *Palaios* 6:347–70.

Gillette, D.D. 1987. The age of transition: *Coelophysis* and the late Triassic Chinle fauna. In *Dinosaurs Past and Present,* vol.I, Czerkas, S., and Olsen, E.C., eds., 133–52. Los Angeles and Seattle: Natural History Museum of Los Angeles County/University of Washington Press.

Gregory, J.T. 1962. The genera of phytosaurs. *American Journal of Science* 260:652–90.

Heckert, A.B., Lucas, S.G., and Hunt, A.P. 1994. North America's most complete late Carnian dinosaur, a derived theropod from the Chinle Group in west-central New Mexico [abst.]. *Geological Society of America Abstracts with Programs* 26, no. 7:60.

Hunt, A.P., and Lucas, S.G. 1994. Ornithischian dinosaurs from the upper Triassic of the United States. In *In the shadow of the dinosaurs: Early Mesozoic tetrapods,* Fraser, N.C., and Sues, H.-D., eds., 227–40. Cambridge: Cambridge University Press.

Jacobs, L.L., and Murry, P.A. 1980. The vertebrate community of the Triassic Chinle Formation near St. Johns, Arizona. In *Aspects of vertebrate history,* Jacobs, L.L., ed., 55–72. Flagstaff: Museum of Northern Arizona Press.

Lockley, M.G., and Hunt, A.P. 1995. *Dinosaur tracks and other fossil footprints of the western United States.* New York: Columbia University Press.

Long, R.A., and Murry, P.A. 1995. Late Triassic (Carnian and Norian) tetrapods from the southwestern United States. *New Mexico Museum Natural History Bulletin* 4.

Lucas, S.G. 1991a. Revised Upper Triassic stratigraphy in the San Rafael Swell, Utah. In *Geology of East-Central Utah,* Utah Geological Association Publication 19, Chidsey, T.C., Jr., ed., 1–8.

———. 1991b. Sequence stratigraphic correlation of nonmarine and marine late Triassic biochronologies, western United States. *Albertiana* 9:11–18.

Lucas, S.G., DeCourten, F.L., and Hunt, A.P. 1993. Phytosaur from the Upper Triassic Chinle Group in the San Rafael Swell, east-central Utah. *New Mexico Museum Natural History Bulletin* 3:307–8.

Lupe, R. 1979. Stratigraphic sections of the Upper Triassic Chinle Formation, San Rafael Swell to the Moab area, Utah. U.S. Geological Survey Oil and Gas Investigation Chart OC-125.

Padian, K. 1990. The ornithischian form genus *Revueltosaurus* from the Petrified Forest of Arizona (Late Triassic: Norian; Chinle Formation). *Journal of Vertebrate Paleontology* 10, no. 2:268–69.

Repenning, C.A., Cooley, M.E., and Akers, J.P. 1969. Stratigraphy of the Chinle and Moenkopi Formations, Navajo and Hopi Indian Reservations, New Mexico and Utah. *U.S. Geological Survey Professional Paper* 521-B:1-34.

Riggs, N.R., Lehman, T.E., Gerhels, G.E., and Dickinson, W.R. 1996. Detrital zircon between headwaters and terminus of the Upper Triassic Chinle-Dockum paleoriver system. *Science* 273:97–100.

Rowe, T. 1979. *Placerias,* an unusual reptile from the Chinle Formation. *Plateau* 51 (4): 30–32.

Sawin, H.J. 1947. The pseudosuchian reptile *Typothorax meadei,* new species. *Journal of Paleontology* 21:201–38.

Schaeffer, B. 1967. Late Triassic fishes from the western United States. *Bulletin American Museum of Natural History* 135:287–342.

Stewart, J.H. et al. 1986. Late Triassic paleogeography of the southern Colorado Plateau: The problem of a source for voluminous volcanic debris in the Chinle Formation of the Colorado Plateau region. *Geology* 14 (7): 567–70.

Yen, T.-C., and Reeside, J.B. 1946. Triassic fresh-water

gastropods from southern Utah. *American Journal of Science* 244:49–51.

Four: The Early and Middle Jurassic: A Time of Transition

On the Jurassic-Triassic Extinction

Benton, M.J. 1986. The late Triassic tetrapod extinction events. In *The beginning of the age of dinosaurs: faunal change across the Triassic-Jurassic boundary*, Padian, K., ed., 303–20. Cambridge: Cambridge University Press.

———. 1989. Patterns of evolution and extinction in vertebrates. In *Evolution and the fossil record*, Allen, K.C., and Briggs, D.E.G., eds., 218–41. London: Belhaven.

———. 1991. What really happened in the late Triassic. *Historical Biology* 5:263–78.

Hallam, A. 1991, The end-Triassic mass extinction event. *Geological Society of America Special Paper* 247:577–83.

Olsen, P.E., and Galton, P.M. 1977. Triassic-Jurassic extinctions: Are they real? *Science* 197:983–86.

Olsen, P.E., and Sues, H.-D. 1986. Correlation of continental Late Triassic and Early Jurassic sediments, and patterns of the Triassic-Jurassic tetrapod transition. In *The beginning of the age of dinosaurs: faunal change across the Triassic-Jurassic boundary*, Padian, K., ed., 321–51. Cambridge: Cambridge University Press.

Padian, K. 1987. Patterns of terrestrial faunal change across the Triassic-Jurassic boundary and the rise of the dinosaurs [abst.]. *Geological Society of America Abstracts* 19, no. 7:797.

On Early-Middle Jurassic Rocks and Paleogeography of Utah and Adjacent Regions

Blakey, R.C., and Parnell, R.A., Jr. 1995. Middle Jurassic magmatism: The volcanic record in the eolian Page Sandstone and related Carmel Formation, Colorado Plateau. In *Jurassic Magmatism and tectonics of the North American Cordillera*, Miller, D.M., and Busby, C., eds., 393–411. Geological Society of America Special Paper 299.

Blakey, R.C., Peterson, F., and Kocurek, G. 1988. Synthesis of late Paleozoic and Mesozoic eolian deposits of the Western Interior of the United States. *Sedimentary Geology* 56:3–125.

Champan, M.G. 1993. Catastrophic floods during the middle Jurassic: Evidence in the upper member and Crystal Creek Member of the Carmel Formation, southern Utah. In *Mesozoic paleogeography of the western United States II, Pacific Section*, Dunne, G.C.,

and McDougall, K.A., eds., 407–16. Los Angeles: Society of Economic Paleontologists and Mineralogists.

Hintze, L.F. 1988. Geologic history of Utah. *Brigham Young University Geology Studies Special Publication* 7:44-52.

Imlay, R.W. 1980. Jurassic paleogeography of the conterminous United States in its continental setting. *U.S. Geological Survey Professional Paper* 1062.

Kocurek, G. 1981. Erg reconstruction: the Entrada Sandstone (Jurassic) of northern Utah and Colorado. *Palaeogeography, Palaeoclimatology, Palaeoecology* 36:125–53.

Middleton, L.T., and Blakey, R.C. 1983. Processes and controls on the intertonguing of the Kayenta and Navajo Formations, northern Arizona: Eolian-fluvial interactions. In *Eolian sediments and processes*, Brookfield, M.E., and Ahlbrandt, T.S., eds., 613–34. Amsterdam: Elsevier.

Miller, D.M., Hillhouse, W.C., Zartman, R.E., and Lanphere, M.A. 1987. Geochronology of intrusive and metamorphic rocks in the Pilot Range, Utah and Nevada, and comparison with regional patterns. *Geological Society of America Bulletin* 99:866–79.

Miller, D.M., and Hoisch, T.D. 1995. Jurassic tectonics of northeastern Nevada and northwestern Utah from the perspective of barometric studies. In *Jurassic magmatism and tectonics of the North American Cordillera*, Miller, D.M., and Busby, C., eds., 267–94. Geological Society of America Special Paper 299.

Olsen, H. 1989. Sandstone-body structures and ephemeral stream processes in the Dinosaur Canyon Member, Moenave Formation (Lower Jurassic), Utah. *Sedimentary Geology* 61, nos. 3–4:207–21.

Peterson, F. 1988. Stratigraphy and nomenclature of Middle and Upper Jurassic rocks, western Colorado Plateau. *U.S. Geological Survey Bulletin* 1633-B.

Peterson, F., and Pipiringos, G.N. 1979. Stratigraphic relations of the Navajo Sandstone to middle Jurassic formations, southern Utah and northern Arizona. *U.S. Geological Survey Professional Paper* 1035-B.

Pipiringos, G.N., and O'Sullivan, R.B. 1978. Principal unconformities in Triassic and Jurassic rocks, Western Interior United States—A preliminary survey: *U.S. Geological Survey Professional Paper* 1035-A.

Riggs, N.R., and Blakey, R.C. 1993. Early and middle Jurassic paleogeography and volcanology of Arizona and adjacent areas. In *Mesozoic paleogeography of the western United States II, Pacific Section*, Dunne, G.C., and McDougall, K.A., eds., 347–76. Los Angeles: Society of Economic Paleontologists and Mineralogists.

Thompson, A.E., and Stokes, W.L. 1970. Stratigraphy of the San Rafael Group, southwest and south-central Utah. *Utah Geological and Mineral Survey Bulletin* 87.

Young, R.G. 1987. Triassic and Jurassic rocks of the dinosaur triangle. In *Paleontology and geology of the dinosaur triangle*, Averett, W.R., ed., 5–20. Grand Junction. Museum of Western Colorado.

On the Paleontology of the Early-Middle Jurassic of Utah and Adjacent Areas

Attridge, J., Crompton, A.W., and Jenkins, F.A. 1985. Common Liassic southern African prosauropod *Massospondylus* discovered in North America. *Journal of Vertebrate Paleontology* 5:128–32.

Baird, D. 1980. A prosauropod dinosaur trackway from the Navajo Sandstone (lower Jurassic). In *Aspects of vertebrate history*, Jacobs, L.L., ed., 219–30. Flagstaff: Museum of Northern Arizona Press.

Brady, L.F. 1936. A note concerning the fragmentary remains of a small theropod recovered from the Navajo Sandstone in northern Arizona. *American Journal of Science* 31:150.

Brown, B. 1933. An ancestral crocodile. *American Museum Novitates* 638:1–4.

Camp, C.L. 1936. A new type of small bipedal dinosaur from the Navajo Sandstone of Arizona. *University of California Publications, Department of Geological Science Bulletin* 24:39–56.

Clark, J.M., and Fastovsky, D.E. 1986. Vertebrate biostratigraphy of the Glen Canyon Group in northern Arizona. In *The beginning of the age of dinosaurs: faunal change across the Triassic-Jurassic boundary*, Padian, K., ed., 1993, 285–301. Cambridge: Cambridge University Press.

Colbert, E.H. 1981. A primitive ornithischian dinosaur from the Kayenta Formation of Arizona. *Bulletin of the Museum of Northern Arizona* 53:1–61.

Colbert, E.H., and Mook, C.C. 1951. The ancestral crocodilian *Protosuchus. Bulletin of the American Museum of Natural History* 97:147–82.

Crompton, A.W., and Smith, K.K. 1980. A new genus and species of crocodilian from the Kayenta Formation (late Triassic?) of northern Arizona. In *Aspects of vertebrate history*, Jacobs, L.L., ed., 193–217. Flagstaff: Museum of Northern Arizona Press.

Galton, P.M. 1971. The prosauropod dinosaur *Ammonsaurus* and the crocodile *Protosuchus* and their bearing on the age of the Navajo Sandstone of northeastern Arizona. *Journal of Paleontology* 45:781–95.

Jenkins, F.A., Jr., Crompton, A.W., and Downs, W.R. 1983. Mesozoic mammals from Arizona: New evidence on mammalian evolution. *Science* 222:1233–35.

Lockley, M.G. 1991a. *Tracking dinosaurs:* A new look at an ancient world. Cambridge: Cambridge University Press.

———. 1991b. The Moab megatracksite: A preliminary

description and discussion of millions of middle Jurassic tracks in eastern Utah. In *Guidebook for dinosaur quarries and tracksites tour, western Colorado and eastern Utah*, Averitt, W.R., ed., 59–65. Grand Junction, CO: Grand Junction Geological Society.

Lockley, M.G., and Hunt, A.P. 1995. *Dinosaur tracks and other fossil footprints of the western United States.* New York: Columbia University Press.

Meszoely, C.A.M., Jenkins, F.A., and Schaff, C.R. 1987. Early Jurassic sphenodontids from northeastern Arizona [abst.]. *Journal of Vertebrate Paleontology* 7 (suppl.): 21A

Miller, W.E., Britt, B.B., and Stadtman, K.L. 1989. Tridactyl trackways from the Moenave Formation of southwestern Utah. In *Dinosaur tracks and traces*, Gillette, D.D., and Lockley, M.G., eds., 209–16. Cambridge: Cambridge University Press.

Morales, M., and Ash, S.R. 1993. The last phytosaur? In *The nonmarine Triassic*, Lucas, S.G., and Morales, M., eds., 356–57. New Mexico Museum of Natural History & Science Bulletin No. 3.

Padian, K. 1984. Pterosaur remains from the Kayenta Formation (?early Jurassic) of Arizona. *Palaeontology* 27 (2): 401–13.

———. 1987. Presence of the dinosaur *Scelidosaurus* indicates Jurassic age for the Kayenta Formation (Glen Canyon Group, northern Arizona). *Journal of Vertebrate Paleontology* 7, no. 3 (suppl.): 22A.

Padian, K., and Olsen, P.E. 1984. The fossil trackway *Pteraichnus*: not pterosaurian, but crocodilian. *Journal of Paleontology* 58:178–84.

Rowe, T. 1989. A new species of the theropod dinosaur *Syntarsus* from the early Jurassic Kayenta Formation of Arizona. *Journal of Vertebrate Paleontology* 9:125–36.

Stokes, W.L. 1957. Pterodactyl tracks from the Morrison Formation. *Journal of Paleontology* 31:952–54.

———. 1978. Animal tracks in the Navajo-Nugget Sandstone. *University of Wyoming Contributions to Geology* 16, no. 2:103–7.

Stokes, W.L., and Madsen, J.H., Jr. 1979. The environmental significance of pterosaur tracks in the Navajo Sandstone (Jurassic), Grand County, Utah. *Brigham Young University Geology Studies* 26:21–26.

Sues, H.-D. 1986. Relationships and biostratigraphic significance of the Tritylodontidae (Synapsida) from the Kayenta Formation of northeastern Arizona. In *The beginning of the age of dinosaurs: Faunal change across the Triassic-Jurassic boundary*, Padian, K., ed., 279–84. Cambridge: Cambridge University Press.

Sues, H.-D., Clark, J.M., and Jenkins, F.A., Jr. 1994. A review of the early Jurassic tetrapods from the Glen Canyon Group of the American Southwest. In *In the shadow of the dinosaurs: Early Mesozoic tetrapods*,

Fraser, N.C., and Sues, H.-D., eds., 1994, 284–94. Cambridge: Cambridge University Press.

Unwin, D.M. 1989. A predictive method for the identification of vertebrate ichnites and its application to pterosaur tracks. In *Dinosaur tracks and traces,* Gillette, D.G., and Lockley, M.G., eds., 259–74. Cambridge: Cambridge University Press.

Welles, S.P. 1954. New Jurassic dinosaur from the Kayenta Formation of Arizona: *Geological Society of America Bulletin* 65:591–98.

———. 1970. *Dilophosaurus* (Reptilia: Saurischia), a new name for a dinosaur. *Journal of Paleontology* 44, no. 5:989.

———. 1984. *Dilophosaurus wetherilli* (Dinosauria: Theropoda) osteology and comparisons. *Palaeontographica* Abt. A 185:85–180.

Winkler, D.A., Jacobs, L.L., Congleton, J.D., and Downs, W.R. 1991. Life in a sand sea: Biota from Jurassic interdunes. *Geology* 19:889–92.

FIVE: THE LATE JURASSIC:
THE GOLDEN AGE OF THE SAUROPODS

Western North America During the Late Jurassic

Allmendinger, R.W., and Jordan, T.E. 1984. Mesozoic structure of the Newfoundland Mountains, Utah: Horizontal shortening and subsequent extension in the hinterland of the Sevier Belt. *Geological Society of American Bulletin* 95:1280–92.

Allmendinger, R.W., Miller, D.W., and Jordan, T.E. 1984. Known and inferred Mesozoic deformation in the hinterland of the Sevier Belt, northwest Utah. *Utah Geological Association Publication* 13:21–34.

Armstrong, R.L., and Suppe, J. 1973. Potassium-Argon geochemistry of Mesozoic igneous rocks in Nevada, Utah, and southern California. *Geological Society of America Bulletin* 84:1375–92.

Hintze, L.F. 1988. Geologic History of Utah. *Brigham Young University Geology Studies Special Publication* 7. Provo: Brigham Young University.

Imlay, R.W. 1980. Jurassic paleogeography of the conterminous United States and its continental setting. *U.S. Geological Survey Professional Paper* 1062.

On the Stratigraphy and Paleoecology of the Morrison Formation

Dodson, P., Behrensmeyer, A.K., Bakker, R.T., and McIntosh, J.S. 1980. Taphonomy and paleoecology of the dinosaur beds of the Jurassic Morrison Formation. *Paleobiology* 6, no. 2:208–32.

Lockley, M.G., Houck, K., and Prince, N.K. 1986. North America's largest dinosaur tracksite: Implications for Morrison Formation paleoecology. *Geological Society of America Bulletin* 57:1163–76.

Lockley, M.G., and Hunt, A.P. 1995. *Dinosaur tracks and other fossil footprints of the western United States.* New York: Columbia University Press.

Peterson, F. 1988. Stratigraphy and nomenclature of Middle and Upper Jurassic rocks, western Colorado Plateau, Utah and Arizona. *U.S. Geological Survey Bulletin* 1633A-C: Ch. B, 13–56.

Peterson, F. and Turner-Peterson, C.E. 1987. The Morrison Formation of the Colorado Plateau: Recent advances in sedimentology, stratigraphy, and paleotectonics. *Hunteria* 2, no. 1.

———. 1989. *Geology of the Colorado Plateau, field trip guidebook T130, 28th International Geological Congress.* Washington, D.C.: American Geophysical Union.

Peterson, F., and Tyler, N. 1985. Field guide to the upper Salt Wash alluvial complex. In *Field guidebook to modern and ancient fluvial systems in the United States,* Flores, R.M., and Harvey, M.D., eds., 45-64. Third International Fluvial Sedimentology Conference, Colorado State University, Fort Collins.

Stokes, W.L. 1944. Morrison Formation and related deposits in and adjacent to the Colorado Plateau. *Geological Society of America Bulletin* 55:951–92.

Tidwell, W.D. 1990. Preliminary report on the megafossil flora of the Upper Jurassic Morrison Formation. *Hunteria* 2, no.8.

Turner, C.E., et al. 1991. Jurassic Lake T'oo'dichi': A large alkaline, saline lake, Morrison Formation, eastern Colorado Plateau. *Geological Society of America Bulletin* 103, no. 4:538–58.

Sauropod Dinosaurs of the Morrison Formation

Barnes, F.A. 1990. Utah's early place in paleontological history. *Canyon Legacy* 6:9–14.

Berman, D.S., and McIntosh, J.S. 1978. Skull and relationships of the Upper Jurassic sauropod *Apatosaurus* (Reptilia, Saurischia). *Bulletin of the Carnegie Museum of Natural History* 8.

Chure, D.J. 1983. The paleoecology of the Morrison Formation: Implications for sauropod dinosaur biology. *Geological Society of America Abstracts with Programs* 15, no. 5:286.

Coombs, W.P., Jr. 1975. Sauropod habits and habitats. *Palaeogeography, Palaeoclimatology, Palaeoecology* 17:1–33.

Cope, E.D. 1877. On *Amphicoelias,* a genus of saurian from the Dakota epoch of Colorado. *Proceedings, American Philosophical Society* 17:242–46.

Fiorillo, A. 1991. Dental microwear on the teeth of *Camarasaurus* and *Diplodocus*: Implications for sauropod paleoecology. Fifth Symposium on Mesozoic Terrestrial Ecosystems and Biota. *Contributions from the Paleontological Museum, University of Oslo* 364:23–24.

Fiorillo, A.R. 1994. Time resolution at Carnegie Quarry (Morrison Formation: Dinosaur National Monument, Utah): Implications for dinosaur paleoecology. *Contributions to Geology, University of Wyoming* 30, no. 2:149–56.

Gillette, D.D. 1991. *Seismosaurus halli*, gen. et. sp. nov.: A new sauropod dinosaur from the Morrison Formation (Upper Jurassic/Lower Cretaceous) of New Mexico, USA. *Journal of Vertebrate Paleontology* 11 (4): 417–33.

———. 1993. Type locality and stratigraphic position of *Dystrophaeus viaemalae* Cope 1879, the earliest sauropod dinosaur in North America. *Journal of Vertebrate Paleontology* 13 supplement to no. 3:37A.

Gillette, D.D., Bechtel, J.W., and Bechtel, P. 1990. Gastroliths of a sauropod dinosaur from New Mexico. *Journal of Vertebrate Paleontology* 9 supplement to no. 3:22A.

Gilmore, C.W. 1925. A nearly complete articulated skeleton of *Camarasaurus*, a saurischian dinosaur from the Dinosaur National Monument, Utah. *Memoirs of the Carnegie Museum* 10, no.3:347–84.

———. 1932. On a newly mounted skeleton of *Diplodocus* in the United States National Museum. *Proceedings of the U.S. National Museum* 81:1–21.

———. 1936. Osteology of *Apatosaurus* with special reference to specimens in the Carnegie Museum. *Memoirs of the Carnegie Museum* 11, no.4:175–300.

Hatcher, J.B. 1901. *Diplodocus* Marsh, its osteology, taxonomy, and probable habits, with a restoration of the skeleton. *Memoirs of the Carnegie Museum* 1:1–63.

———. 1903. Osteology of *Haplocanthosaurus*, with description of a new species. *Memoirs of the Carnegie Museum* 2, no. 1:1–72.

Jensen, J.A. 1985a. Three new sauropod dinosaurs from the Upper Jurassic of Colorado. *Great Basin Naturalist* 45:697–709.

———. 1985b. Uncompahgre dinosaur fauna: A preliminary report. *Great Basin Naturalist* 45:710–20.

Lawton, R. 1977. Taphonomy of the dinosaur quarry, Dinosaur National Monument. *Contributions to Geology, University of Wyoming* 15:119–26.

Madsen, J.H., Jr., McIntosh, J.S., and Berman, D.S. 1995. Skull and atlas-axis complex of the Upper Jurassic sauropod *Camarasaurus* Cope (Reptilia: Saurischia). *Carnegie Museum of Natural History Bulletin* 31.

McIntosh, J.S. 1990. Sauropoda. In *The Dinosauria*, Weishampel, D.B., Dodson, P., and Osmolska, H., eds., 345–401. Berkeley: University of California Press.

McIntosh, J.S., Miller, W.E., Stadtman, K.L., and Gillette, D.D. 1996. The osteology of *Camarasaurus lewisi*.

Brigham Young University Geology Studies 41:73–115.

McIntosh, J.S., and Williams, M.E. 1988. A new species of sauropod dinosaur, *Haplocanthosaurus delfsi*, sp. nov., from the Upper Jurassic Morrison Formation of Colorado. *Kirtlandia* 43:3–26.

Miller, W.E., Baer, J.L., Stadtman, K.L., and Britt, B. 1991. The Dry Mesa Quarry, Mesa County, Colorado. In *Guidebook for dinosaur quarries and tracksites tour*, Averett, W.R., ed., 31–46. Grand Junction, CO: Grand Junction Geological Society.

Parrish, J.M., and Stevens, K.A. 1995. Computer modeling of sauropod cervical vertebral function. *Journal of Vertebrate Paleontology* 15 supplement to no. 3:48A.

Riggs, E.S. 1903. *Brachiosaurus altithorax*, the largest known dinosaur. *American Journal of Science* Series 4, v. 15:299–306.

———. 1904. Structure and relationships of opisthocoelian dinosaurs, Part II, The Brachiosauridae. *Publications of the Field Columbian Museum of Geology* 2:229–48.

Russell, D.A. 1989. *An odyssey in time: The dinosaurs of North America*. Ottawa: NorthWord Press and University of Toronto Press (in association with the Canadian National Museum of Natural History).

Rothschild, B.M, and Berman, D.S. 1991. Fusion of caudal vertebrae in late Jurassic sauropods. *Journal of Vertebrate Paleontology* 11, no. 1:29–39.

Ornithischian Dinosaurs and Other Vertebrates of the Morrison Formation

Armstrong, H.J., Averett, W.R., Averett, M.E., McReynolds, E.S., and Wolny, D.G. 1987. Mid-Mesozoic paleontology of the Rabbit Valley area, western Colorado. In *Paleontology and geology of the dinosaur triangle guidebook*, Averett, W.R., ed., 37–43. Grand Junction, CO: Museum of Western Colorado.

Callison, G. 1987. Fruita: A place for wee fossils. In *Paleontology and geology of the dinosaur triangle guidebook*, Averett, W.R., ed., 91–96. Grand Junction, CO: Museum of Western Colorado.

Carpenter, K. 1994. Baby *Dryosaurus* from the Upper Jurassic Morrison Formation of Dinosaur National Monument. In *Dinosaur eggs and babies*, Carpenter, K., Hirsh, K., and Horner, J.R., eds., 288–97. Cambridge: Cambridge University Press.

Chure, D., Turner, C., and Peterson, F. 1994. An embryo of *Camptosaurus* from the Morrison Formation (Jurassic, Middle Tithonian) in Dinosaur National Monument, Utah. In *Dinosaur eggs and babies*, Carpenter, K., Hirsh, K., and Horner, J.R., eds., 298–311. Cambridge: Cambridge University Press.

Colbert, E.H. 1961. Dinosaurs, their discovery and their world. New York: Dutton.

Czerkas, S.A. 1987. A reevaluation of the plate arrangement of *Stegosaurus stenops*. In *Dinosaurs past and present, volume 2*, Czerkas, S.J., and Olson, E.C., eds., 83–99. Los Angeles and Seattle: Natural History Museum of Los Angeles County/University of Washington Press.

de Buffrenil, V., Farlow, J.O., and de Recqles, A. 1986. Growth and function of *Stegosaurus* plates: Evidence from bone histology. *Paleobiology* 12, no. 4:459–73.

Dodson, P. 1980. Comparative osteology of the American ornithopods *Camptosaurus* and *Tenontosaurus*. *Memoirs of the Geological Society of France* 139:81–85.

Farlow, J.O., Thompson, C.V., and Rosner, D.E. 1976. Plates of the dinosaur *Stegosaurus*: Forced convective heat loss fins? *Science* 192:1123–25.

Galton, P.M. 1977. The ornithopod dinosaur *Dryosaurus* and a Laurasia-Gondwanaland connection in the Upper Jurassic. *Nature* 268: 23–32.

———. 1981. *Dryosaurus*, a hypsilophodontid dinosaur from the Upper Jurassic of North America and Africa, postcranial skeleton. *Palaontologische Zeitschrift* 55:271–312.

———. 1983. The cranial anatomy of *Dryosaurus*, a hypsilophodontid dinosaur from the Upper Jurassic of North America and East Africa, with a review of the hypsilophodontids from the Upper Jurassic of North America. *Geologica et Palaeontologica* 17:207–43.

———. 1990. Stegosauria. In *The Dinosauria*, Weishampel, D.B., Dodson, P., and Osmolska, H., eds., 435–55. Berkeley: University of California Press.

Gilmore, C.W. 1909. Osteology of the Jurassic reptile *Camptosaurus*, with a review of the species and genus, and descriptions of two new species. *Proceedings of the United States National Museum* 36:197–332.

———. 1914. Osteology of the armoured Dinosauria in the United States National Museum, with special reference to the genus *Stegosaurus*: Smithsonian Institution, *United States National Museum Bulletin* 39.

———. 1925. Osteology of the ornithopodous dinosaurs from the Dinosaur National Monument, Utah. *Memoirs of the Carnegie Museum* 10:385–409.

Kirkland, J.I., and Carpenter, K. 1994. North America's first pre-Cretaceous ankylosaur (Dinosauria) from the Upper Jurassic Morrison Formation of western Colorado. *Brigham Young University Geology Studies* 40:25–42.

Norman, D.B., and Weishampel, D.B. 1990. Iguanodontidae and related ornithopods. In *The Dinosauria*, Weishampel, D.B., Dodson, P., and Osmolska, H., eds., 510–33. Berkeley: University of California Press.

Russell, D.A. 1989. *An odyssey in time: The dinosaurs of North America*. Ottawa: NorthWord Press and University of Toronto Press (in association with the Canadian National Museum of Natural History).

Sereno, P.C. 1986. Phylogeny of the bird-hipped dinosaurs (Order Ornithischia). *National Geographic Research* 2:234–56.

———. P.C. 1989. Evolution of the bird-hipped dinosaurs. In *The age of dinosaurs*, Short Courses in Paleontology No.2, Padian, K., and Chure, D., eds., 48-57. Knoxville, TN: Paleontological Society.

Scheetz, R.D. 1991. Progress report of juvenile and embryonic *Dryosaurus* remains from the Upper Jurassic Morrison Formation of Colorado. In *Guidebook for dinosaur quarries and tracksites tour*, Averett, W.R., ed., 27–29. Grand Junction, CO: Grand Junction Geological Society.

Shepherd, J.D., Galton, P.M., and Jensen, J.A. 1977. Additional specimens of the hypsilophodontid dinosaur *Dryosaurus altus* from the Upper Jurassic of western North America. *Brigham Young University Geology Studies* 24, part 2:11–15.

Sues, H.-D., and Norman, D.B. 1990. Hypsilophodontidae, *Tenontosaurus*, Dryosauridae. In *The Dinosauria*, Weishampel, D.B., Dodson, P., and Osmolska, H., eds., 498–509. Berkeley: University of California Press.

Weishampel, D.B., and Heinrich, R.E. 1992. Systematics of Hypsilophodontidae and basal Iguanodontia (Dinosauria: Ornithopoda). *Historical Biology* 6:159–84.

Six: Blood Brothers: The Theropods of the Morrison Formation

Theropod Dinosaurs of the Morrison Formation

Barsbold, R., and Osmolska, H. 1990. Ornithomimosauria. In *The Dinosauria*, Weishampel, D.B., Dodson, P., and Osmolska, H., eds., 225–44. Berkeley: University of California Press.

Bilbey-Bowman, S.A. 1986. Interpretation of the Morrison Formation as a time-transgressive unit. *North American Paleontological Conference, Abstracts with Programs* 4:5.

Britt, B.B. 1991. Theropods of Dry Mesa Quarry (Morrison Formation, late Jurassic), Colorado, with emphasis on the osteology of *Torvosaurus tanneri*. *Brigham Young University Geology Studies* 37:1–72.

Chure, D.J. 1994. *Koparion douglassi*, a new dinosaur from the Morrison Formation (Upper Jurassic) of Dinosaur National Monument; the oldest troodontid (Theropoda: Maniraptora). *Brigham Young University Geology Studies* 40:11–15.

———. 1995. A reassessment of the gigantic theropod *Saurophagus maximus* from the Morrison Formation (Upper Jurassic) of Oklahoma, USA. In *Sixth Symposium on Mesozoic Terrestrial Ecosystems and Biota, Short Papers*, Sun, A., and Wang, Y., eds., 103–6.

Galton, P.M. 1982. *Elaphrosaurus*, an ornithomimid dinosaur from the Upper Jurassic of North America and Africa. *Palaontologische Zeitschrift* 56:265–75.

Galton, P.M., and Jensen, J.A. 1979. A new large theropod dinosaur from the Upper Jurassic of Colorado. *Brigham Young University Geology Studies* 26, no. 2:1–12.

Gauthier, J. 1986. Saurischian monophyly and the origin of birds: In *The origin of birds and the evolution of flight*, Padian, K., ed. *Memoirs of the California Academy of Science* 8:1–55.

Gilmore, C.W. 1920. Osteology of the carnivorous Dinosauria in the United States National Museum, with special reference to the genera *Antrodemus* (*Allosaurus*) and *Ceratosaurus*. Smithsonian Institution, *United States National Museum Bulletin* 110.

Hubert, J.F., and Chure, D.J. 1992. Taphonomy of an *Allosaurus* quarry in the deposits of a late Jurassic braided river with a gravel-sand bedload, Salt Wash Member of the Morrison Formation, Dinosaur National Monument, Utah. In *Field guide to geologic excursions in Utah and adjacent areas of Nevada, Idaho, and Wyoming*, Wilson, J.R., ed., 375–81. *Utah Geological Survey Miscellaneous Publication* 92-3.

Madsen, J.H., Jr. 1974. A new theropod dinosaur from the Upper Jurassic of Utah. *Journal of Paleontology* 48, no.1:27–31.

———. 1976a. A second new theropod from the late Jurassic of east central Utah. *Utah Geology* 3, no. 1:51–60.

———. 1976b. *Allosaurus fragilis*: a revised osteology. *Utah Geological and Mineral Survey Bulletin* 109.

Molnar, R.E., Kurzanov, S.M., and Zhiming, D. 1990. Carnosauria. In *The Dinosauria*, Weishampel, D.B., Dodson, P., and Osmolska, H., eds., 169–209. Berkeley: University of California Press.

Norman, D.B. 1990. Problematic Theropda: "Coelurosarus". In *The Dinosauria*, Weishampel, D.B., Dodson, P., and Osmolska, H., eds., 280–305. Berkeley: University of California Press.

Osborn, H.F. 1916. Skeletal adaptations of *Ornitholestes, Struthiomimus, Tyrannosaurus*. *Bulletin of the American Museum of Natural History* 35:733–71.

Ostrom, J.H. 1980. *Coelurus* and *Ornitholestes*: Are they the same? In *Aspects of Vertebrate History: Essays in Honor of Edwin Harris Colbert*, Jacobs, L.L., ed., 245–56. Flagstaff: Museum of Northern Arizona Press.

Osmolska, H., and Barsbold, R. 1990. Troodontidae. In *The Dinosauria*, Weishampel, D.B., Dodson, P., and Osmolska, H., eds., 259–68. Berkeley: University of California Press.

Paul, G.S. 1988. The small predatory dinosaurs of the mid-Mesozoic: The horned theropods of the Morrison and Great Oolite—*Ornitholestes* and *Procer-*

atosaurus—and the sickle-claw theropods of the Cloverly, Djadokhta, and Judith River—*Deinonychyus, Velociraptor*, and *Saurornitholestes*. *Hunteria* 2:1–9.

Richmond, D.R., and Stadtman, K.L. 1996. Sedimentology of a *Ceratosaurus* site in the San Rafael Swell, Emery County, Utah. *Brigham Young University Geology Studies* 41:117–24.

Rowe, T., and Gauthier, J. 1990. Ceratosauria. In *The Dinosauria*, Weishampel, D.B., Dodson, P., and Osmolska, H., eds., 151–68. Berkeley: University of California Press.

Russell, D.A. 1989. *An odyssey in time: The dinosaurs of North America*. Ottawa: Northword Press, in association with the National Museum of Natural Sciences, Canada.

On the Cleveland-Lloyd Dinosaur Quarry

Bilbey, S.A. 1992. Stratigraphy and sedimentary petrology of the Upper Jurassic-Lower Cretaceous rocks at the Cleveland-Lloyd Dinosaur Quarry with a comparison to the Dinosaur National Monument Quarry, Utah. Ph.D. diss., University of Utah.

Hunt, A.P. 1986. Taphonomy of the Cleveland-Lloyd Quarry, Morrison Formation (Late Jurassic), Emery County, Utah—A preliminary report. *Proceedings, North America Paleontological Convention* 4:A21.

Madsen, J.H., Jr. 1987. The dinosaur department store. In *Paleontology and geology of the dinosaur triangle*, Averett, W.R., ed., 65–74. Grand Junction: Museum of Western Colorado.

———. 1991. Egg-siting (or) first Jurassic dinosaur egg from Emery County, Utah. In *Guidebook for dinosaur quarries and tracksites tour*, Averett, W.R., ed., 55-56. Grand Junction: Grand Junction Geological Society.

Miller, W.E., Horrocks, R.D., and Madsen, J.H., Jr. 1996. The Cleveland-Lloyd Dinosaur Quarry, Emery County, Utah: A U.S. natural landmark (Including history and quarry map). *Brigham Young University Geology Studies* 41:3–24.

Stokes, W.L. 1985. *The Cleveland-Lloyd Dinosaur Quarry, window to the past*. Washington, D.C.: U.S. Government Printing Office.

Small Animals of the Morrison Formation, Excluding Dinosaurs

Bakker, R.T., and Carpenter, K. 1990. A new latest Jurassic vertebrate fauna, from the highest levels of the Morrison Formation at Como Bluff, Wyoming: Part III, The mammals: a new multituberculate and a new pauradont. *Hunteria* 2, no. 6:4–8.

Callison, G. 1987. Fruita: A place for wee fossils. In *Pale-*

ontology and geology of the dinosaur triangle, Averett, W.R., ed., 91–95. Grand Junction: Museum of Western Colorado.

Chure, D.J., and Englemann, G.F. 1989. The fauna of the Morrison Formation in Dinosaur National Monument. In *Mesozoic/Cenozoic vertebrate paleontology: Classic localities, contemporary approaches*, Flynn, J.J., ed., 8–14. 28th International Geological Congress, American Geophysical Union, Washington, D.C.

Clemens, W.A., Lillegraven, J.A., Lindsay, E.H., and Simpson, G.G. 1979. Where, when, and what—A survey of known Mesozoic mammal distribution. In *Mesozoic mammals: The first two-thirds of mammalian history*, Lillegraven, J.A., Kielan-Jaworowska, Z., and Clemens, W.A., eds., 7–58. Berkeley: University of California Press.

Kirkland, J.I. 1987. Upper Jurassic and Cretaceous lungfish tooth plates from the western interior, the last dipnoan faunas of North America. *Hunteria* 2, no. 2.

Prothero, D.R., and Estes, R. 1980. Late Jurassic lizards from Como Bluff, Wyoming and their paleobiogeographic significance. *Nature* 286:484–86.

Prothero, D.R., and Jensen, J.A. 1983. A mammalian humerus from the Upper Jurassic of Colorado. *Great Basin Naturalist* 43, no.4:551–53.

Stokes, W.L. 1957. Pterodactyl tracks from the Morrison Formation. *Journal of Paleontology* 31, no. 5:952–55.

West, L., and Chure, D.J. 1984. *Dinosaur: The Dinosaur National Monument Quarry*. Jensen, UT: Dinosaur Nature Association.

Seven: The Early Cretaceous: The (Un)Missing Links

The Early Cretaceous History of Western North America

Allmendinger, R.W., Miller, D.M., and Jordan, T.E. 1985. Known and inferred Mesozoic deformation in the hinterland of the Sevier belt, northwest Utah. In *Geology of northwest Utah, southern Idaho, and northeast Nevada, Utah Geological Association Publication* 13, Kerns, J.G., ed., 21–34.

Cowan, D.S., and Bruhn, R.L. 1992. Late Jurassic to early Late Cretaceous geology of the U.S. Cordillera. In *The Cordilleran Orogen: Conterminous U.S., The Geology of North America*, vol. G-3, Burchfiel, B.C., Lipman, P.W., and Zobeck, M.L., eds., 169–203. Boulder, CO: Geological Society of America.

Schwans, P. 1987. Initial foreland flexure and sedimentation, Early Cretaceous, central Utah. *Geological Society of America Abstracts with Programs* 19 (7): 835.

Wiltschko, D.V., and Dorr, J.A., Jr. 1983. Timing of deformation in overthrust belt and foreland of Idaho, Wyoming, and Utah. *American Association of Petroleum Geologists Bulletin* 67 (8): 1304–22.

Yingling, V.L., and Heller, P.L. 1987. Timing and record of foreland basin development in central Utah during the initiation of the Sevier Orogeny. *Geological Society of America Abstracts with Programs* 19 (7): 902.

The Geology of the Cedar Mountain Formation

Crooks, D.M. 1986. Petrology and stratigraphy of the Morrison (Upper Jurassic) and Cedar Mountain (Lower Cretaceous) Formations, Emery County, Utah. M.S. thesis, Fort Hays State University.

Harris, D.R. 1980. Exhumed paleochannels in the Lower Cretaceous Cedar Mountain Formation near Green River, Utah. *Brigham Young University Geology Studies* 27, pt. 1:51–66.

Kowallis, B.J., and Heaton, J.S. 1987. Fission-track dating of bentonites and bentonitic mudstones from the Morrison Formation in central Utah. *Geology* 15:1138–42.

Kowallis, B.J., Heaton, J.S., and Bringhurst, K. 1986. Fission-track dating of volcanically derived sedimentary rocks. *Geology* 14:19–22.

Stokes, W.L. 1944. Morrison and related deposits in and adjacent to the Colorado Plateau. *Geological Society of America Bulletin* 41:951–92.

———. 1952. Lower Cretaceous in the Colorado Plateau. *American Association of Petroleum Geologists Bulletin* 36, no. 9:1766–76.

Vandervoort, D.S., and Schmidt, J.G. 1987. Evolution of early Cretaceous fluvial systems, hinterland of the Sevier Orogenic Belt, east-central Nevada (abst). *Geological Society of America Abstracts with Programs* 19 (7): 876.

Dinosaurs From the Cedar Mountain Formation

Bodily, N.M. 1969. An armored dinosaur from the lower Cretaceous of Utah. *Brigham Young University Geology Studies* 16:35–60.

Carpenter, K. 1984. Skeletal reconstruction and life restoration of *Sauropelta* (Ankylosauria: Nodosauridae) from the Cretaceous of North America. *Canadian Journal of Earth Science* 21:1491–98.

Coombs, W.P. 1978. The families of the ornithischian dinosaur order Ankylosauria. *Palaeontology* 21, part 1:143–70.

DeCourten, F.L. 1991. The Long Walk Quarry and tracksite: Unveiling the mysterious early Cretaceous of the dinosaur triangle region. In *Guidebook for dinosaur quarries and tracksites tour*, Averett, W.R., ed., 19-26. Grand Junction, CO: Grand Junction Geological Society.

Forster, Catherine A. 1984. The paleoecology of the ornithopod dinosaur *Tenontosaurus tilletti* from the Cloverly Formation, Big Horn Basin of Wyoming and Montana. *Mosasaur* 2:151–63.

Gallup, Marc R. 1974. Lower Cretaceous dinosaurs and associated vertebrates from north-central Texas in the Field Museum of Natural History. M.A. thesis, University of Texas.

———. 1989. Functional morphology of the hindfoot of the Texas sauropod *Pleurocoelus* sp. indet. In *Paleobiology of the dinosaurs*, Farlow, J.O., ed., *Geological Society of America Special Paper* 238, 71–74.

Galton, P.M., and J.A. Jensen. 1979. Remains of ornithopod dinosaurs from the Lower Cretaceous of North America. *Nature* 257:668–69.

Hatcher, J.B. 1902. Discovery of the remains of *Astrodon* (*Pleurocoelus*) in the Atlantosaurus beds of Wyoming. *Annals of the Carnegie Museum* 2:9–14.

Jensen, J.A. 1970. Fossil eggs in the lower Cretaceous of Utah. *Brigham Young University Geology Studies* 17, pt. 1:51–66.

Kirkland, J.I. 1991. A nodosaur with a distinct sacral shield of fused armor from the lower Cretaceous of east-central Utah. *Journal of Vertebrate Paleontology* 11, supplement to no. 3:40A.

Kirkland, J.I., and Burge, D. 1994. A large primitive hadrosaur from the Lower Cretaceous of Utah. *Journal of Vertebrate Paleontology* 14, supplement to no. 3:32A.

Kirkland, J.I., and Parrish, J.M. 1995. Theropod teeth from the Lower and Middle Cretaceous of Utah. *Journal of Vertebrate Paleontology* 15, supplement to no. 3:39A.

Kirkland, J.I., Britt, B.B., and Blows, W. 1993. The earliest Cretaceous (Barremian?) dinosaur fauna found to date on the Colorado Plateau. *Journal of Vertebrate Paleontology* 13, supplement to no. 3:45A.

Kirkland, J.I., Burge, D., and Gaston, R. 1993. A large dromaeosaur (Theropoda) from the Lower Cretaceous of eastern Utah. *Hunteria* 2, no. 10.

Kirkland, J.I., Britt, B.B., Madsen, S., and Burge, D. 1995. A small theropod from the basal Cedar Mountain Formation (Lower Cretaceous, Barremian) of eastern Utah. *Journal of Vertebrate Paleontology* 15, supplement to no. 3:39A.

Kirkland, J.I., Britt, B., Burge, D., Carpenter, K., Cifelli, R., DeCourten, F., Eaton, J., Hasiotis, S., Kirshbaum, M., and Lawton, T. 1997b. Lower to Middle Cretaceous dinosaur faunas of the central Colorado Plateau: A key to understanding 35 million years of tectonics, sedimentology, evolution, and biogeography. *Brigham Young University Geology Studies*, vol. 41, part II, 69–103.

Langston, W., Jr. 1974. Nonmammalian Commanchean

tetrapods. In *Aspects of Trinity division geology: Geoscience and man*, vol. 7, Perkins, B.F., ed., 77–102. Baton Rouge: Louisiana State University.

Lockley, M., and Hunt, A.P. 1995 *Dinosaur tracks and other fossil footprints of the western United States.* New York: Columbia University Press.

Lockley, M., Kirkland, J., DeCourten, F., and Hasiotis, S. 1997. Dinosaur tracks from the Cedar Mountain Formation of eastern Utah: a preliminary report. *Utah Geological and Mineralogical Survey,* in press.

Lucas, Frederick A. 1904. Paleontological notes: *Pleurocoelus* versus *Astrodon. Science* 19, no.480:436–37.

Marsh, O.C. 1888. Notice of a new genus of *Sauropoda* and other new dinosaurs from the Potomac Formation. *American Journal of Science* 35 (3): 85–94.

———. 1896. The dinosaurs of North America. *Sixteenth Annual Report of the U.S. Geological Survey, 1894–1895,* 1:143–415. Washington, D.C.: U.S. Geological Survey.

Nelson, M.E., and Crooks, D.M. 1987. Stratigraphy and paleontology of the Cedar Mountain Formation (Lower Cretaceous), eastern Emery County, Utah. In *Paleontology and geology of the dinosaur triangle,* Averett, W.R., ed., 55–63. Grand Junction: Museum of Western Colorado.

Nelson, M.E., Madsen, J.H., Jr., and Stokes, W.L. 1984. A new vertebrate fauna from the Cedar Mountain Formation (Cretaceous), Emery County, Utah. *Geological Society of America Abstracts with Programs* 16 (4): 249.

Norman, D.B., and Weishampel, D.B. 1990. Iguanodontidae and related ornithopods. In *The Dinosauria,* Weishampel, D.B., Dodson, P., and Osmolska, H., eds., 510–33. Berkeley: University of California Press.

Ostrom, J.H. 1970. Stratigraphy and paleontology of the Cloverly Formation (Lower Cretaceous) of the Bighorn Basin area, Wyoming and Montana. *Peabody Museum of Natural History Bulletin* 30.

———. 1990. Dromaeosauridae. In *The Dinosauria,* Weishampel, D.B., Dodson, P., and Osmolska, H., eds., 269–79. Berkeley: University of California Press.

Ostrom, J.H., and Maxwell, W.D. 1995. Taphonomy and paleobiological implications of *Tenontosaurus-Deinonychus* associations. *Journal of Vertebrate Paleontology* 15 (4): 707–12.

Parrish, J.M., and Eaton, J.G. 1991. Diversity and evolution of dinosaurs in the Cretaceous of the Kaiparowits Plateau, Utah (abst.). *Journal of Vertebrate Paleontology* 11, supplement to no. 3:50A.

Paul, G.S. 1987. The science and art of restoring the life appearance of dinosaurs and their relatives. In *Dinosaurs past and present,* Czerkas, S.J., and Olsen, E.C., eds., vol. 2, 4–49. Los Angeles and Seattle: Natural History Museum of Los Angeles County/University of Washington Press.

Pereda-Suberbiola, J. 1994. *Polacanthus* (Ornithischia, Ankylosauria), a transatlantic armoured dinosaur from the early Cretaceous of Europe and North America. *Palaeontographica Abt. A* 232, parts 4–6:133–59.

Stokes, W.L. 1987. Dinosaur gastroliths revisited. *Journal of Paleontology* 61 (6): 1242–46.

Stovall, J.W., and Langston, W., Jr. 1950. *Acrocanthosaurus atokensis*, a new genus and species of Lower Cretaceous Theropoda from Oklahoma. *American Midland Naturalist* 43 (3): 696–728.

Weishampel, D.B. 1990. Dinosaurian distribution. In *The Dinosauria*, Weishampel, D.B., Dodson, P., and Osmolka, H., eds., 63–139. Berkeley: University of California Press.

Weishampel, D.B., and Bjork, P.B. 1989. The first indisputable remains of *Iguanodon* (Ornithischia: Ornithopoda) from North America: *Iguanodon lakotaensis*. *Journal of Vertebrate Paleontology* 9 (1): 56–66.

Non-dinosaur Fossils from the Cedar Mountain Formation

Cifelli, R.L. 1993. Early Cretaceous mammal from North America and the evolution of marsupial dental characters. *Proceedings of the National Academy of Sciences*, USA 90:9413–16.

Cifelli, R.L., and Nydam, R.L. 1995. Primitive, heliodermatid-like platynotan from the early Cretaceous of Utah. *Herpetologica* 51, no. 3:286–91.

Eaton, J.G., and Nelson, M.E. 1991. Multituberculate mammals from the Lower Cretaceous Cedar Mountain Formation, San Rafael Swell, Utah. *Contributions to Geology, University of Wyoming* 29, no.1:1–12.

Gardner, J.D. 1995. Amphibians from the Lower Cretaceous (Albian) Cedar Mountain Formation, Emery County, Utah. *Journal of Vertebrate Paleontology* 14, supplement to no. 3:26A.

Nydam, R.L. 1995. Lizards from the early Cretaceous of central Utah. *Journal of Vertebrate Paleontology* 14, supplement to no. 3:47A.

Thayn, G.F. 1973. Three new species of petrified dicotyledonous wood from the Lower Cretaceous Cedar Mountain Formation of Utah. M.S. thesis, Brigham Young University.

Thayn, G.F., and Tidwell, W.D. 1984. Flora of the Lower Cretaceous Cedar Mountain Formation of Utah and Colorado, Part II, *Mesembrioxylon stokesi*. *Great Basin Naturalist* 44 (2): 257–62.

Thayn, G.F., Tidwell, W.D., and Stokes, W.L. 1983. Flora of the Lower Cretaceous Cedar Mountain Formation of Utah and Colorado, Part I, *Paraphyllanthoxylon utahense*. *Great Basin Naturalist* 43:394–402.

Tidwell, W.D., and Hebbert, N. 1976. *Tempskya* from the Lower Cretaceous Cedar Mountain Formation, Utah. *Brigham Young University Geology Studies* 22:77–98.

Tidwell, W.D., Bitt, B., and Robison, S. 1983. Paleoecology of a small lower Cretaceous swamp near Ferron, Utah. *Geological Society of America Abstracts with Programs* 15, no. 5:286.

Tschudy, R.H., Tschudy, B.D., and Craig, L.C. 1984. Palynological evaluation of the Cedar Mountain and Burro Canyon Formations, Colorado Plateau. *U.S. Geological Survey Professional Paper* 1281.

The Dakota Formation

am Ende, B.A. 1991. Depositional environments, palynology, and age of the Dakota Formation, south-central Utah. In *Stratigraphy, depositional environments, and sedimentary tectonics of the western margin, Cretaceous Western Interior Seaway*, Nations, J.D., and Eaton, J.G., eds., *Geological Society of America Special Paper* 260:65–83.

Eaton, J.G. 1993. Therian mammals from the Cenomanian (Upper Cretaceous) Dakota Formation, southwestern Utah. *Journal of Vertebrate Paleontology* 13:105–24.

Weimer, R.J. 1983. Relation of unconformities, tectonics, and sea level changes, Cretaceous of the Denver Basin and adjacent areas. In *Mesozoic Paleogeography of the West Central United States, Rocky Mountain Section*, Reynolds, M.D., and Dolly, E.D., eds., 359–76. Denver: Society of Economic Paleontologists and Mineralogists.

EIGHT: THE LATE CRETACEOUS: BEASTS OF THE BAYOUS

The Sevier Orogeny

Armstrong, R.L. 1968. Sevier orogenic belt in Nevada and Utah. *Geological Society of America Bulletin* 79:429–58.

Bruhn, R.L., Picard, M.D., and Beck, S.L. 1983. Mesozoic and early Tertiary structure and sedimentology of the central Wasatch Mountains, Uinta Mountains, and Uinta Basin. *Utah Geological and Mineral Survey Special Studies* 59:63–105.

DeCelles, P.G., and Mitra, G. 1995. History of the Sevier orogenic wedge in terms of critical taper models, northeast Utah and southwest Wyoming. *Geological Society of America Bulletin* 107:454–62.

Jordan, T.E. 1981. Thrust loads and foreland basin evolution, Cretaceous, western United States. *American Association of Petroleum Geologists Bulletin* 65:2506–20.

Lawton, T.F. 1985. Style and timing of frontal structures, thrust belt, central Utah. *American Association of Petroleum Geologists Bulletin* 69:1145–59.

Pilcha, F. 1986. The influence of preexisting tectonic trends on geometries of the Sevier Orogenic Belt and its foreland basin in Utah. In *Paleotectonics and sedimentation in the Rocky Mountain region, United States*, Peterson, J.A., ed., *American Association of Petroleum Geologists Memoir* 41:309–20.

Royse, F., Jr., Warner, M.A., and Reese, D.L. 1975. Thrust belt structural geometry and related stratigraphic problems, Wyoming-Idaho-northern Utah. In *Deep drilling frontiers of the central Rocky Mountains*, Bolyard, D.W., ed., 41–54. Denver: Rocky Mountain Association of Geologists.

Ward, P.L. 1995. Subduction cycles under western North America during the Mesozoic and Cenozoic Eras. In *Jurassic Magmatism and Tectonics of the North America Cordillera*, Miller, D.M., and Busby, C., eds., 1–41, *Geological Society of America Special Paper 299.*

Yonkee, W.A. 1992. Basement-cover relations, Sevier orogenic belt, northern Utah. *Geological Society of America Bulletin* 104:280–302.

The Mancos Shale and Equivalent Marine Strata

Briethaupt, B.H. 1985. Nonmammalian vertebrate faunas from the late Cretaceous of Wyoming. *Guidebook, 26th Annual Field Conference. Wyoming Geological Association.*

Carter, B. 1991. A plesiosaur from the upper Mancos Shale. In *Guidebook for dinosaur quarries and tracksite tours*, Averett, W.R., ed., 51. Grand Junction, CO: Grand Junction Geological Society.

Cobban, W.A. 1976. Ammonite record from the Mancos Shale of the Castle Valley-Price-Woodside area, east-central Utah. *Brigham Young University Geology Studies* 22, part 3:117–26.

Kauffman, E.G. 1977. Geological and biological overview: Western interior Cretaceous basin. *Mountain Geologist* 14, nos. 3–4:75–99.

Lucas, S.G., Hunt, A.P., and Pence, R. 1988. Some late Cretaceous reptiles from New Mexico. *New Mexico Bureau of Mines and Mineral Resources Bulletin* 122:49–60.

Lucas, S.G., and Sullivan, R.M. 1982. *Ichthyornis* in the late Cretaceous Mancos Shale (Juana Lopez Member), northwestern New Mexico. *Journal of Paleontology* 56, no. 2:545–47.

Nicholls, E.L., and Russell, A.P. 1990. Paleobiogeography of the Cretaceous Western Interior Seaway of North America: The vertebrate evidence. *Palaeogeography, Palaeoclimatology, Palaeoecology* 79:149–69.

Padian, K. 1989. Other Mesozoic vertebrates of the land, sea, and air. In *The age of dinosaurs*, Culver, S.J., ed., *Paleontological Society Short Courses in Paleontology* 2:146–61. Knoxville: Paleontological Society/University of Tennessee.

Stewart, J.D., Bilbey, S.A., Chure, D., and Madsen, S.K. 1994. Vertebrate fauna of the Mowry Shale (Cenomanian) in northeastern Utah. *Journal of Vertebrate Paleontology* 14, supplement to no. 3:47A.

Wells, S.P. 1952. A review of North American Cretaceous elasmosaurs. *University of California Publications in Geology* 29:47–144.

Wolny, D.G., Armstrong, H.J., and Kirkland, J.I. 1990. Hadrosaur skeleton from the Mancos Shale, western Colorado. *Journal of Vertebrate Paleontology* 10, supplement to no. 3:50A.

The Mesaverde Group

Anderson, B.G., Barrick, R.E., Droser, M.L., and Stadtman, K.L. 1995. Hadrosaur skin impressions from the upper Cretaceous Neslen Formation, east-central Utah: morphology and taphonomic implications. *Geological Society of America Abstracts with Programs* 27(4):2.

Carpenter, K. 1992. Behavior of hadrosaurs as interpreted from footprints in the "Mesaverde" Group (Campanian) of Colorado, Utah, and Wyoming. *Contributions to Geology, University of Wyoming* 29, no. 2:81–96.

Dickinson, W.R., Lawton, T.F., and Inman, K.F. 1986. Sandstone detrital modes, central Utah foreland region, stratigraphic record of Cretaceous-Paleogene tectonic evolution. *Journal of Sedimentary Petrology* 56:279–93.

Doelling, H.H. 1972. *Central Utah coal fields, Sevier-Sanpete, Wasatch Plateau, Book Cliffs, and Emery. Utah Geological and Mineral Survey Monograph* 3. Salt Lake City: Utah Geological and Mineral Survey.

Fouche, T.D., Lawton, T.F., Nichols, D.J., Cashion, W.B., and Cobban, W.A. 1983. Patterns and timing of synorogenic sedimentation in Upper Cretaceous rocks of central and northeast Utah. In *Mesozoic Paleogeography of the West-Central United States*, Reynolds, M.W., and Dolly, E.D., eds., 305–36. Second Rocky Mountain Paleogeography Symposium, Society of Economic Paleontologists and Mineralogists, Rocky Mountain Section.

Franczyk, K.J., and Pitman, J.K. 1989. *Evolution of resource-rich foreland and intramontane basins in eastern Utah and western Colorado. 28th International Geological Congress Guidebook* T324. Washington, D.C.: American Geophysical Union.

Hedges, S.B., and Schweitzer, M.H. 1995. Detecting dinosaur DNA. *Science* 268:1191–92.

Lockley, M., and Hunt, A.P. 1995. *Dinosaur tracks and other fossil footprints of the western United States*: New York: Columbia University Press.

Olsen, T., Steel, R., Hogseth, K., Skar, T., and Roe, S.-L. 1995. Sequential architecture in a fluvial succession: Sequence stratigraphy in the upper Cretaceous Mesaverde Group, Price Canyon, Utah. *Journal of Sedimentary Research* B65, no. 2:265–80.

Parker, L.R., and Balsley, J.K. 1986. Dinosaur footprints in coal mine roof surfaces from the Cretaceous of Utah. In *Abstracts with Program, First International Symposium on Dinosaur Tracks and Traces*, Gillette, D.D., ed., 22. Albuquerque: New Mexico Museum of Natural History.

Parker, L.R., and Rowley, R.L., Jr. 1989. Dinosaur footprints from a coal mine in east-central Utah. In *Dinosaur tracks and traces*, Gillette, D.D., and Lockley, M.G., eds., 361–66. Cambridge: Cambridge University Press.

Robison, S.F. 1991. Bird and frog tracks from the Late Cretaceous Blackhawk Formation in east-central Utah. In Geology of east-central Utah, Chidsey, T.C., ed., *Utah Geological Association Publication* 19:325–34.

Roehler, H.W. 1990. Stratigraphy of the Mesaverde Group in the central and eastern Greater Green River Basin, Wyoming, Colorado, and Utah. *U.S. Geological Survey Professional Paper* 1508.

Van Wagoner, J.C. 1995. Sequence stratigraphy and marine to nonmarine facies architecture of foreland basin strata, Book Cliffs, Utah, USA. In *Sequence stratigraphy of foreland basin deposits*, Van Wagoner, J.C., and Bertram, G.T., eds., *American Association of Petroleum Geologists Memoir* 64:137–223.

Weishampel, D.B., and Horner, J.R., 1990. Hadrosauridae. In *The Dinosauria*, Weishampel, D.B., Dodson. P., and Osmolska, H., eds., 534–61. Berkeley: University of California Press.

Woodward, S.R., Weyland, N.J., and Bunnell, M. 1994. DNA sequence from Cretaceous Period bone fragments. *Science* 226:1229–32.

Yoshida, S., Willlis, A., and Miall, A.D. 1996. Tectonic control of nested sequence architecture in the Castlegate Sandstone (Upper Cretaceous), Book Cliffs, Utah. *Journal of Sedimentary Research* 66, no. 4:737–48.

The Wahweap, Straight Cliffs, and Kaiparowits Formations

Brett-Surman, M.A., and Paul, G.S. 1985. A new family of bird-like dinosaurs linking Laurasia and Gondwanaland. *Journal of Vertebrate Paleontology* 5:133–38.

Cifelli, R.L. 1990a. Cretaceous mammals of southern Utah: III: Therian mammals from the Turonian (Early Late Cretaceous). *Journal of Vertebrate Paleontology* 10, no. 3:332–45.

———. 1990b. Cretaceous mammals of southern Utah: I: Marsupials from the Kaiparowits Formation (Judithian). *Journal of Vertebrate Paleontology* 10, no. 3:295–319.

Cifelli, R.L., and Madsen, S.K. 1986. An Upper Cretaceous symmetrodont (Mammalia) from southern Utah. *Journal of Vertebrate Paleontology* 6, no. 3:258–63.

DeCourten, F.L. 1979. Non-marine flora and fauna from the Kaiparowits Formation (Upper Cretaceous) of the Paria River Amphitheater, southwestern Utah. *Geological Society of America Abstracts with Programs* 10:102.

DeCourten, F.L., and Russell, D.A. 1985. A specimen of *Ornithomimus velox* (Theropoda: Ornithomimidae) from the terminal Cretaceous Kaiparowits Formation of southern Utah. *Journal of Paleontology* 59:1091–99.

Dodson, P. 1975. Taxonomic implications of relative growth in lambeosaurine hadrosaurs. *Systematic Zoology* 24:37–54.

Doelling, H.H. 1975. *Geology and mineral resources of Garfield County, Utah. Utah Geological and Mineral Survey Bulletin* 107.

Eaton, J.G. 1991. Biostratigraphic framework for the Upper Cretaceous rocks of the Kaiparowits Plateau, southern Utah. In Stratigraphy, depositional environments, and sedimentary tectonics of the western margin, Cretaceous Western Interior Seaway, Nations, J.D., and Eaton, J.G., eds., 47–64. *Geological Society of America Special Paper* 260.

———. 1995. Cenomanian and Turonian (Early Late Cretaceous) multituberculate mammals from southwestern Utah. *Journal of Vertebrate Paleontology* 15, no. 4:761–84.

Eaton, J.G., and Cifelli, R.L. 1988. Preliminary report of Late Cretaceous mammals of the Kaiparowits Plateau, southern Utah. *Contributions to Geology, University of Wyoming* 26, no. 2:45–55.

Estes, R. 1964. Fossil vertebrates from the Late Cretaceous Lance Formation, eastern Wyoming. *University of California Publications in Geological Sciences* 49.

Gregory, H.E. 1951. Geology and geography of the Paunsaugunt region. *U.S. Geological Survey Professional Paper* 226.

Gregory, H.E., and Moore, R.C. 1931. The Kaiparowits region: Geographic and geologic reconnaissance of parts of Utah and Arizona. *U.S. Geological Survey Professional Paper* 164.

Hopson, J.A. 1975. Evolution and cranial display structures in hadrosaurian dinosaurs. *Paleobiology* 1:21–43.

Hutchison, J.H. 1993. *Avisaurus*: A "dinosaur" grows wings. *Journal of Vertebrate Paleontology* 13, supplement to no. 3:43A.

Lohrengel, C.F. 1969. Palynology of the Kaiparowits Formation, Garfield County, Utah. *Brigham Young University Geology Studies* 16:61–180.

Lucas, S.G. 1993. Dinosaurs of New Mexico. *New Mexico Journal of Science* 32.

Nichols, D.J. 1995. Palynology in relation to sequence stratigraphy, Straight Cliffs Formation (Upper Cretaceous), Kaiparowits Plateau, Utah. *U.S. Geological Survey Bulletin* 2115-B: B1–B17.

Parrish, J.M. 1991. Diversity and evolution of dinosaurs in the Cretaceous of the Kaiparowits Plateau, Utah. *Journal of Vertebrate Paleontology* 11, supplement to no. 3:50A.

Peterson, F. 1969. *Cretaceous sedimentation and tectonism in the southeastern Kaiparowits region, Utah.* U.S. Geological Survey Open-File Report.

Peterson, F., and Waldrop, H.A. 1965. Jurassic and Cretaceous stratigraphy of south-central Kaiparowits Plateau, Utah. In *Geology and resources of south-central Utah*, Goode, H.D., and Robison, R.A., eds., *Utah Geological Society and Intermountain Association of Petroleum Geologists Guidebook to the Geology of Utah*, no. 19:47–69.

Russell, D.A. 1972. Ostrich dinosaurs from the Late Cretaceous of western Canada. *Canadian Journal of Earth Science* 9, no. 4:375–402.

Weishampel, D.B. 1981. Acoustic analysis of potential vocalization in lambeosaurine dinosaurs (Reptilia: Ornithischia). *Paleobiology* 7:252–61.

Weishampel, D.B., and Jensen, J.A. 1979. *Parasaurolophus* (Reptilia: Hadrosauridae) from Utah. *Journal of Paleontology* 53:1422–27.

NINE: THE CURTAIN FALLS: DINOSAURS OF THE NORTH HORN FORMATION

Late Cretaceous-Tertiary Mountain Building in Utah

DeCelles, P.G., and Mitra, G. 1995. History of the Sevier orogenic wedge in terms of critical taper models, northeast Utah and southwest Wyoming. *Geological Society of America Bulletin* 107, no. 4:454–62.

DeCelles, P.G., Lawton, T.F., and Mitra, G. 1995. Timing of Sevier thrusting, central Utah Sevier fold-thrust belt. *Geological Society of America Abstracts with Programs* 27, no. 4:8.

Dickinson, W.R., Klute, M.A., Hayes, M.J., Janecke, S.U., Lundin, E.R., McKittrick, M.A., and Olivares, M.D. 1988. Paleogeographic and paleotectonic setting of Laramide sedimentary basins in the central Rocky Mountain region. *Geological Society of America Bulletin* 100:1023–39.

Goldstrand, P.M., Trexler, J.H., Jr., Kowallis, B.J., and Eaton, J.G. 1993. Late Cretaceous to Early Tertiary tectonostratigraphy of southwestern Utah. In *Aspects of Mesozoic Geology and Paleontology of the Colorado Plateau*, Morales, M., ed., 181–88. *Museum of Northern Arizona Bulletin* 59.

Hintze, L.F. 1988. *Geologic history of Utah.* Brigham Young University Geology Studies Special Publication 7. Provo, UT: Brigham Young University.

Wiltschko. D.V., and Dorr, J.A. 1983. Timing of deformation in the Overthrust Belt and foreland of Idaho, Wyoming, and Utah. *American Association of Petroleum Geologists Bulletin* 67: 1304–22.

Depositional Environments, Paleogeography, and Non-dinosaur Paleontology of the North Horn Formation and Equivalent Strata

Anderson, T.H., and Schmidt, V.A. 1983. The evolution of middle America and the Gulf of Mexico-Caribbean Sea region during Mesozoic time. *Geological Society of America* 94:941–66.

Archibald, J.D., Rigby, J.K., Jr., and Robison, S.F. 1983. Systematic revision of *Oxyacodon* (Condylartha, Periptychidae) and a description of *O. ferronensis* n. sp. *Journal of Paleontology* 57, no. 1:53–72.

Bracken, B., and Picard, M.D. 1984. Trace fossils from Cretaceous/Tertiary North Horn Formation in central Utah. *Journal of Paleontology* 58, no. 2:477–87.

Fillmore, R.P. 1991. Tectonic influence on sedimentation in the southern Sevier foreland, Iron Springs Formation (Upper Cretaceous), southwestern Utah. In Stratigraphy, depositional environments, and sedimentary tectonics of the western margin, Cretaceous Western Interior Seaway, Nations, J.D., and Eaton, J.G., eds., 9-25. *Geological Society of America Special Paper* 260.

Fouch, T.D., Lawton, T.F., Nichols, D.J., Cashion, W.B., and Cobban, W.A. 1983. Patterns and timing of synorogenic sedimentation in Upper Cretaceous Rocks of central and northeast Utah. In *Mesozoic paleogeography of west-central United States, Rocky Mountain Section*, Reynolds, M.W., and Dolly. E.D., eds., 305–36. Denver: Society of Economic Paleontologists and Mineralogists (SEPM).

Franczyk, K.J., and Pitman, J.K. 1991. Latest Cretaceous nonmarine depositional systems in the Wasatch Plateau area: Reflections of foreland to intermontane basin transition. In *Geology of East-central Utah*, Chidsey, T.C., Jr., ed., 77–93. *Utah Geological Association Publication* 19.

Franczyk, K.J., Fouch, T.D., Johnson, R.C., Molenaar, C.M., and Cobban, W.A. 1992. Cretaceous and Tertiary paleogeographic reconstructions for the Uinta-Piceance Basin study area, Colorado and Utah. *U.S. Geological Survey Bulletin* 1787-Q:Q1–Q37.

Gazin, C.L. 1938. A Paleocene mammalian fauna from central Utah. *Journal of the Washington Academy of Science* 28, no. 6:271–77.

———. 1939. A further contribution to the Dragon Paleocene fauna of central Utah. *Journal of the Washington Academy of Science* 29, no. 7:273–86.

———. 1941. The mammalian faunas of the Paleocene of central Utah, with notes on the geology. *Proceedings of the U.S. National Museum* 91, no. 3121:1–53.

Gilmore, C.W. 1942a. Osteology of *Polyglyphanodon*, an Upper Cretaceous lizard from Utah. *Proceedings of the United States National Museum* 92, no. 3148:229–65.

———. 1942b. A new fossil reptile from the Upper Cretaceous of Utah. *Proceedings of the U.S. National Museum* 93, no. 3158:109–14.

———. 1943. Osteology of Upper Cretaceous lizards from Utah, with a description of a new species. *Proceedings of the United States National Museum* 93, no. 3163:209–14.

Lawton, T.F. 1986. Fluvial systems of the Upper Cretaceous Mesaverde Group and Paleocene North Horn Formation, central Utah: A record of transition from thin-skinned to thick-skinned deformation in the foreland region. In *Paleotectonics and sedimentation in the Rocky Mountain region, United States*, Peterson, J.A., ed., 423–42. *American Association of Petroleum Geologists Memoir* 41.

Lockley, M.G., and Hunt, A.P. 1995. Ceratopsid tracks and associated ichnofauna from the Laramie Formation (Upper Cretaceous: Maastrichtian) of Colorado. *Journal of Vertebrate Paleontology* 15, no. 3:592–614.

Mullens, T.E. 1971. Reconnaissance study of the Wasatch, Evanston, and Echo Canyon Formations in part of northern Utah. *U.S. Geological Survey Bulletin* 1311-D.

Olsen, T. 1995. Fluvial and fluvio-lacustrine facies and depositional environments of the Maastrichtian to Paleocene North Horn Formation, Price Canyon, Utah. *Mountain Geologist* 32, no. 2:27–44.

Robison, S.F. 1986. Paleocene (Puercan-Torrejonian) mammalian faunas of the North Horn Formation, central Utah. *Brigham Young University Geology Studies* 33. part 1:87–133.

Ryer, T.A. 1976. Cretaceous stratigraphy of the Coalville and Rockport areas, Utah. *Utah Geology* 3, no. 2:71–83.

Schmidt, J.G., Jones, D.A., and Goldstrand, P.M. 1991. Braided stream deposition and provenance of the Upper Cretaceous-Paleocene(?) Canaan Peak Formation, Sevier foreland basin, southwestern Utah. In Stratigraphy, depositional environments, and sedimentary tectonics of the western margin, Cretaceous Western Interior Seaway, Nations, J.D., and Eaton, J.G., eds., 27–45. *Geological Society of America Special Paper* 260.

Spieker, E.M. 1946. Late Mesozoic and early Cenozoic history of central Utah. *U.S. Geological Survey Professional Paper* 205-D.

———. 1960. The Cretaceous-Tertiary boundary in Utah. *21st International Geological Congress, Copenhagen*, part 5, 14–24.

Spieker, E.M., and Reeside, J.B., Jr. 1925. Cretaceous and Tertiary formations of the Wasatch Plateau, Utah. *Geological Society of America Bulletin* 36: 435–54.

Talling, P.J., Burbank, D.W., Hobbs, R.S., Lawton, T.L., and Lund, S.P. 1994. Magnetostratigraphic chronology of Cretaceous to Eocene thrust belt evolution, central Utah. *Journal of Geology* 102:181–96.

Talling, P.J., Lawton, T.F., Burbank, D.W., and Hobbs, R.S. 1995. Evolution of latest Cretaceous-Eocene nonmarine deposystems in the Axhandle piggyback basin of central Utah. *Geological Society of America Bulletin* 107, no. 3:297–315.

Tomida, Y., and Butler, R.F. 1980. Dragonian mammals and Paleocene magnetic polarity stratigraphy, North Horn Formation, central Utah. *American Journal of Science* 280:787–811.

Zawiskie, J.M. 1983. Sedimentology and trace fossils of the dinosaur beds of the North Horn Formation, central Utah. *Geological Society of America Abstracts with Programs* 16, no. 6:726.

Dinosaurs of the North Horn Formation and Equivalent Strata

Bonaparte, J.F. 1984. El intercambio faunistico de vertebrados continentales entre Americo del Sur y del Norte afines del Cretacico: *Memoirs, III Congreso Latinoamericano de Paleontologica*: 438–50.

Currie, P.J., and Dodson, P. 1984. Mass death of a herd of ceratopsian dinosaurs. In *Third Symposium on Mesozoic Terrestrial Ecosystems,* Atempto Verlag, Tubingen: 61–66.

Dodson, P., and Currie, P.J. 1990. Neoceratopsia. In *The Dinosauria*, Weishampel, D.B., Dodson, P., and Osmolska, H., eds., 593–618. Berkeley: University of California Press.

Forster, C.A. 1996. Species resolution in *Triceratops*: Cladistic and morphometric approaches. *Journal of Vertebrate Paleontology* 16, no. 2:259–70.

Gilmore, C.W. 1922. A new sauropod dinosaur from the Ojo Alamo formation of New Mexico. *Smithsonian Miscellaneous Collections* 72, no. 14.

———. 1938. Sauropod dinosaur remains in the Upper Cretaceous. *Science* 87, no. 2257:299.

———. 1946. Reptilian fauna of the North Horn Formation of central Utah. *U.S. Geological Survey Professional Paper* 210-C:29–53.

Jensen, J.A. 1966. Dinosaur eggs from the Upper Cretaceous North Horn Formation of central Utah. *Brigham Young University Geology Studies* 13: 55–67.

Johnson, R.E., and Ostrom, J.H. 1991. A refined model of *Torosaurus* forelimb posture and gait with implications for the ceratopsia. *Journal of Vertebrate Paleontology* 11, supplement to no. 3:39A.

Lawson, D.A. 1976. *Tyrannosaurus* and *Torosaurus*, Maestrichtian dinosaurs from Trans-Pecos, Texas. *Journal of Paleontology* 50: 158–64.

Lehman, T.M. 1987. Lata Maastrichtian paleoenvironments and dinosaur biogeography in the western interior of North America. *Palaeogeography, Palaeoclimatology, Palaeoecology* 60:189–217.

———. 1990. The ceratopsian subfamily Chasmosaurinae: Sexual dimorphism and systematics. In *Dinosaur systematics: Approaches and perspectives*, Carpenter, K., and Currie, P.J., eds., 211–29. Cambridge: Cambridge University Press.

Lozinsky, R.P., Hunt, A.P., Wolberg, D.L., and Lucas, S.G. 1984. Late Cretaceous (Lancian) dinosaurs from the McRae Formation, Sierra County, New Mexico. *New Mexico Geology* 6:72–77.

Lucas, S.G. 1981. Dinosaur communities of the San Juan Basin: A case for lateral variation in the composition of Late Cretaceous dinosaur communities. In *Advances in San Juan Basin paleontology*, Lucas, S.G., Rigby, J.K., Jr., and Kues, B.S., eds., 337–93. Albuquerque: University of New Mexico Press.

Lucas, S.G., and Hunt, A.P. 1989. *Alamosaurus* and the sauropod hiatus in the Cretaceous of the North American western interior. In Paleobiology of the dinosaurs, Farlow, J.O., ed., 75–85. *Geological Society of America Special Paper* 238.

McIntosh, J.S. 1990. Sauropoda. In *The Dinosauria*, Weishampel, D.B., Dodson, P., and Osmolska, H., eds., 345–401. Berkeley: University of California Press.

Ostrom, J.H., and Wellnhofer, P. 1990. *Triceratops*: An example of flawed systematics. In *Dinosaur systematics: Approaches and perspectives*, Carpenter, K., and Currie, P.J., eds., 245–54. Cambridge: Cambridge University Press.

Paul, G.S. 1991. Giant horned dinosaurs did have fully erect forelimbs. *Journal of Vertebrate Paleontology* 11, supplement to no. 3:50A.

Tyson, H. 1981. The structure and relationships of the horned dinosaur *Arrhinoceratops* Parks (Ornithischia: Ceratopsidae). *Canadian Journal of Earth Science* 18:1241–47.

Selected Recent and General References on the K-T Extinction

Allaby, M., and Lovelock, J. 1983. *The great extinction.* Garden City, NY: Doubleday and Company.

Alvarez, W., Alvarez, L.W., Asaro, F., and Michel, H.V. 1980. Extraterrestrial cause for the Cretaceous-Tertiary extinction. *Science* 208:1095–1108.

Archibald, J.D. 1989. The demise of the dinosaurs and the rise of the mammals. In *The age of dinosaurs*, Culver, S.J., ed., *Short Courses in Paleontology*, No. 2:162–74. Knoxville, TN: Paleontological Society.

———. 1991. Survivorship patterns of non-marine vertebrates across the Cretaceous-Tertiary (K-T) boundary in the western U.S. In *5th Symposium on Mesozoic Terrestrial Ecosystems, Extended Abstracts*, Kielan-Jaworowska, Z., Heintz, N., and Nakem, H.A., eds, 1-2. *Contributions from the Paleontological Museum, University of Oslo* 364.

———. 1996. *Dinosaur extinction and the end of an era.* New York: Columbia University Press.

Benton, M.J. 1989. Patterns of evolution and extinction in vertebrates. In *Evolution and the fossil record*, Allen, K.C., and Briggs, D.E.G., eds., 218–41. Washington, D.C.: Smithsonian Institution Press.

———. 1990. Scientific methodologies in collision: The history of the study of the extinction of the dinosaur. *Evolutionary Biology* 24:371–400.

Bohor, B.F., Foord, E.E., Modreski, P.J., and Triplehorn, D.M. 1984. Mineralogic evidence for an impact event at the Cretaceous-Tertiary boundary. *Science* 224:867–69.

Briggs, J.C. 1995. *Global biogeography: Developments in palaeontology and stratigraphy*, No. 14. Amsterdam: Elsevier Publishing.

Carpenter, K., and Breithaupt, B. 1986. Latest Cretaceous occurrence of nodosaurid ankylosaurs (Dinosauria: Ornithischia) in western North America and the gradual extinction of the dinosaurs. *Journal of Vertebrate Paleontology* 6, no. 3:251–57.

Dodson, P., and Tatarinov, L.P. 1990. Dinosaur extinction. In *The Dinosauria*, Weishampel, D.B., Dodson, P., and Osmolska, H., eds., 55–62. Berkeley: University of California Press.

Fouty, G., comp. 1987. *Death of the dinosaurs and other mass extinctions.* Phoenix: Oryx Science Bibliographies.

Glen, W. 1990. What killed the dinosaurs? *American Scientist* 78:354–70.

Hulbert, S.H., and Archibald, J.D. 1995. No statistical support for sudden (or gradual) extinction of dinosaurs. *Geology* 23:881–84.

Lucas, S.G. 1994. *Dinosaurs—The textbook.* Dubuque, IA: Wm. C. Brown Publishers.

Officer, C.B. 1994. Chicxulub structure: A volcanic sequence of Late Cretaceous age. In *Dino fest*, Rosenberg, G.D., and Wolberg, D.L., eds., 425–36. *Paleontological Society Special Publication* No.7. Knoxville, TN: Paleontological Society.

Prinn, R., and Fegley, B. 1987. Bolide impacts, acid rain, and biospheric traumas at the Cretaceous-Tertiary boundary. *Earth and Planetary Science Letters* 83:1–15.

Raup, D.M. 1986. *The nemesis affair.* New York: W.H. Norton and Company.

Rigby, J.K., Jr. 1987. The last of the North American dinosaurs: In *Dinosaurs past and present, vol. 2*, Czerkas, S.J., and Olsen, E.C., eds., 119–35. Los Angeles and Seattle: Natural History Museum of Los Angeles County and the University of Washington Press.

Russell, D.A., and Rice, G. 1982. Cretaceous-Tertiary extinctions and possible terrestrial and extraterrestrial causes. *Syllogeus* 34.

Sheehan, P.M., and Fastovsky, D.E. 1992. Major extinctions of land-dwelling vertebrates at the Cretaceous-Tertiary boundary, eastern Montana. *Geology* 20:556–60.

Sheehan, P.M., Fastovsky, D.E., Hoffman, R.G., Berghaus, C.B., and Gabriel, D.L. 1991. Sudden extinction of the dinosaurs: Latest Cretaceous, Upper Great Plains, U.S.A. *Science* 254, no. 5033:835–39.

Sloan, R.E., Rigby, J.K., Jr., Van Valen, L., and Gabriel, D.L. 1986. Gradual dinosaur extinction and simultaneous ungulate radiation in the Hell Creek Formation. *Science* 232:629–33.

Wolbach, W.S., Gilmour, I., Anders, E., Orth, C.J., and Brooks, R.R. 1988. Global fire at the Cretaceous-Tertiary boundary. *Nature* 334:665–69.

Page numbers printed in **boldface** type refer to figures or tables